POACHED

INSIDE THE DARK WORLD OF WILDLIFE TRAFFICKING

RACHEL LOVE NUWER

A Merloyd Lawrence Book
Da Capo Press

Da Capo Press
Hachette Book Group
1290 Avenue of the Americas, New York, NY 10104
www.dacapo.press
@DaCapoPress, @DaCapoPR

Printed in the United States of America

First Edition: September 2018

Published as a Merloyd Lawrence Book by Da Capo Press, an imprint of Perseus Books, LLC, a subsidiary of Hachette Book Group, Inc. The Merloyd Lawrence and Da Capo Press name and logo are a trademark of the Hachette Book Group.

The Hachette Speakers Bureau provides a wide range of authors for speaking events. To find out more, go to www.hachettespeakersbureau.com or call (866) 376-6591.

The publisher is not responsible for websites (or their content) that are not owned by the publisher.

Photo page 1 of civet in plastic bag © Tim Gerard Barker

Print book interior design by Amy Quinn.

Library of Congress Cataloging-in-Publication Data

Names: Nuwer, Rachel Love, author.
Title: Poached : inside the dark world of wildlife trafficking / Rachel Love Nuwer.
Description: Boston : Da Capo Press, [2018] I Includes bibliographical references and index.
Identifiers: LCCN 2018014926I ISBN 9780306825507 (hardcover) I ISBN 9780306825514 (e-book)
Subjects: LCSH: Wildlife crimes. I Wildlife smuggling. I Wild animal trade.
Classification: LCC HV6410 .N89 2018 I DDC 364.16/2859—dc23
LC record available at https://lccn.loc.gov/2018014926ISBNs: 978-0-306-82550-7 (paperback), 978-0-306-82551-4 (e-book)

LSC-C

10 9 8 7 6 5 4 3 2

To Mom, who taught me to love the animals

CONTENTS

INTRODUCTION

"Don't tell anyone, but we just got word that Vietnam's last Javan rhino was found dead with its horn hacked off."

I had little idea of what my colleague was talking about, but I had a sinking feeling—a sense that something much bigger and more sinister was at play. It was April 2010, and I was in Vietnam carrying out scientific research on how people living near two national parks use the forest, animals included. Rhinos, however, were well above my pay grade. My knowledge of illegal wildlife trade was confined to the interviews I conducted with a few local hunters and to the exotic meat that many rural people told me they loved.

As the details of the rhino's story unfolded, however, my fears—and morbid curiosity—grew. The rhino had lived for many years alone in Vietnam's Cát Tiên National Park. And by alone, I mean really alone. Surveys confirmed that, in all of mainland Asia, she was the only one left of her kind. Fate finally caught up with her, though, when a hunter took aim, shot her through the leg and hacked off her horn—most likely while she was still alive. As the culprit absconded with his prize, Vietnam's last rhino laid her head down in the mud and died.

Why did her killer go to such lengths to find her, and why hadn't she been better protected? What did people want with her horn, and what, if anything, was being done to prevent them from getting their hands on that forbidden material?

It was these and similar questions—not only for rhinos, but also for elephants, pangolins, bears, tigers, songbirds, tortoises, and more—that ultimately compelled me to pivot from a career in conservation ecology to one in journalism. I thought I could do more for these disappearing species by spreading the word about their plights than by conducting research on them. People can't care about something they do not know exists. But perhaps if they knew, for example, that there are just fifty or so Javan rhinos remaining in the world—and that the last one living in Vietnam died a sorry, sad death, driven purely by human greed—we could do more to save such species from extinction.

As my journalism career ramped up, I followed and contributed to the creeping coverage about the illegal wildlife trade. I knew that virtually every country in the world now played a role and that organized criminal groups were increasingly calling the shots. Animal trafficking had grown to become a $7- to $23-billion industry, to the point that it ranked just behind drugs, arms, and human trafficking as the most lucrative of contraband industries.

I also became familiar with the mind-numbing statistics about impending species extinctions. Just 30,000 rhinos are left globally, and more than 1,000 are killed for their horns each year. Likewise, in just seven short years, 30 percent of all savannah elephants have disappeared, mowed down with bullets so that poachers can collect their ivory. Meanwhile, fewer than 4,000 tigers are left in the wild, but there are far more in captivity—many of which are raised for their body parts and meat like cattle. And pangolins—those adorable, oddball scaly anteaters that have taken the Internet by storm—have become the world's most trafficked mammal, with a million slaughtered over the past decade.

But where was it all headed?

This question ultimately led me to *Poached*. There would be interviews with experts and rigorous coverage of the scientific findings, yes, but to find the answers I was looking for, I would absolutely have to go to the field, to the very places where the elephant and rhino killings are taking place, where pangolins are being butchered, and where the law is being flouted.

The end result is not exhaustive—I was constrained by the usual money, time, and logistics woes of any journalistic undertaking—but my investigation did encompass the major themes shaping the illegal wildlife trade today. It also drove me to four continents and twelve countries in just under a year, from Chad—where paranoid friends warned me I'd be kidnapped but where one of Africa's most unlikely elephant success stories is under way—to my original research site in Vietnam, where I joined a hunter in the forest as he stalked his endangered prey. Sometimes, I was forced to go undercover: in China, I secured an offer of a bag of illegal pangolin scales in a dark side alley, under the guise of helping my sister produce breast milk. But, more often than not, I found that even criminals were willing to speak with me—including the Thai man sentenced to forty years in a South African prison for plundering the nation's wildlife, who confessed to me, his voice shaking, that he's been abandoned by his boss and former collaborators. And the rhino horn user in Hanoi who brought some along to dinner—never mind that it's highly illegal—and told me that he doesn't care if all rhinos go extinct, just before offering me a shot of ground horn mixed with alcohol.

Going into this project, I thought I knew a thing or two about the illegal wildlife trade. I was shocked, though, by the amount I had to learn not only about trafficking itself but about the conservation world, which is full of interpersonal drama and decades-long infighting. At times, I found myself despairing that corruption, bureaucracy, petty jealousies, and simple apathy will prevent us from making headway before it's too late.

But then I'd meet yet another person who has given his or her life to this cause and who has made a difference in spite of what seem like insurmountable odds. There's Jill Robinson, who—following a life-changing encounter with a caged bear in a dark basement—rescued hundreds of animals and helped to end bear bile farming in Vietnam. And Nguyễn Văn Thái, a leading grassroots activist who gives otherwise doomed pangolins seized from trade a second shot at life. There are the rangers I met in the field who risk their lives nightly to protect their natural heritage from poachers and the journalists who continue to report the truth about the trade, despite frequent death threats and the occasional arrest.

All told, I was at times shocked by the depravity to which some people sank to get what they want—but I was also encouraged by the lengths that others go to protect what they love. Most of all, though, I was humbled to be a part of this story.

Poached is a book for anyone who enjoys a bit of adventure, who is curious about the world, and who has a fondness for animals—of both the two- and four-legged variety. It's a story for all those who think our planet would be a less wonderful place were elephants, rhinos, tigers, pangolins, and more to disappear. It's a dark story, but one full of hope.

PART I
DRIVERS OF DEMAND

I like to watch them. They fill me with joy. . . . I said to the Red Bull, "I must have that. I must have all of it, all there is, for my need is very great." So the Bull caught them, one by one.

—Peter S. Beagle, *The Last Unicorn*, 1968

A live civet for sale at a restaurant in Ho Chi Minh City. (Credit: Tim Gerard Barker)

A Himalayan griffon vulture captured by a hunter in Vietnam.

Rhino horn is ground into a powder at a restaurant in Hanoi.

Illegal ivory openly displayed for sale in Laos.

The remains of an elephant poached for its tusks in Malawi.

One

THE HUNTER

Lục Văn Hổ no longer dreams of the animals he kills. But, for a while, it was becoming a real problem. The dreams—nightmares, really—persistently played out in the same way. He'd catch an animal in the forest, and then, several days later, someone or something—a very old man, a pig, the animal itself—would visit him in his sleep. "Tám Hổ," it would say, calling him by his nickname. "You must pay."

Sometimes, those words would jolt him awake. Other times, he'd get up in the morning to find a sheen of sweat clinging to his body. Either way, the nocturnal visions left him feeling rattled. A superstitious man, Tám Hổ takes these things very seriously. Through trial and error, he found that the only way to banish the ghosts of the animals he hunted was to make a sacrifice, offering up another life—of a duck, pig, or chicken—as appeasement. "To be a hunter," he said, "you must believe in the spirit of the forest."

That spirit, however, has lately seemed less pleased with Tám Hổ. Several years ago, the dreams began to wane and so, too, did his luck. Rising each morning before sunrise to check traps concealed in thick brush and tangled canal beds, these days he inevitably finds them empty. Times have gotten so bad that he's had to start supplementing his income by growing rice and raising shrimp and crabs.

Twenty years ago, when Tám Hổ moved to this tough patch of waterlogged jungle at Vietnam's southern tip, animals were everywhere. He never returned home without something to show for his efforts. Gradually, though, the forest's furred, scaled, and feathered residents became scarcer, with some species

3

disappearing altogether. No longer able to make a living, poachers in these parts are becoming as rare as the creatures they hunt.

"Today, most hunters are changing their careers because the animals are so few, they cannot earn enough," Tám Hổ explained. But he's tenacious—and the best at his craft. He has no plans to retire.

Pride aside, the potential rewards make it worth Tám Hổ's effort to stick in the game. When he does get lucky, the money from the sale can support him and his family for six months. Last year, he trapped two pangolins—highly sought after in Vietnam as a delicacy and medicinal elixir—and sold them for around $450 each. "Pangolins will be extinct soon," he predicted. "But they carry a price like gold." In his neck of the woods, the average household earns just $1,000 per year, so a pangolin payday is truly a windfall.

FOR MANY AMERICANS, VIETNAM STILL CONJURES IMAGES OF HELICOPTERS, protests, and soldiers in the jungle. But to continue to associate Vietnam exclusively with the Vietnam War (or the American War, depending on whom you ask) is painfully outdated. Visitors today to Ho Chi Minh City (a.k.a. Saigon), Vietnam's economic center of 8.4 million residents, will discover rivers of motorbikes, sidewalks clogged with tourists wearing "Good Morning Vietnam!" T-shirts, shop windows displaying $5,000 local designer shoes, haute tasting menus, and international DJs spinning ambient tunes at exclusive clubs perched atop high-rises. Vietnam remains communist on paper, but a market economy is its beating heart.

The country's transformation began in earnest in 1986, when the government initiated a series of economic reforms known as Đổi Mới (Renovation) that paved the way for private for-profit enterprises. Entrepreneurialism flourished, as did Vietnam's bottom line: its economy grew at an annual rate of 7.5 percent from 1991 to 2000, while the poverty rate fell from 29 percent in 2002 to 11 percent in 2012. Vietnam, according to economists, was Asia's "rising dragon," a country whose markers of growth were right on the heels of China's, albeit on a smaller scale.

As is often the case, Vietnam's developmental gains came at a cost for the environment. Logging, agriculture, and aquaculture have reached even the remotest deltas, forests, mountains, and grasslands, to the point that few if any of Vietnam's natural places can be called truly pristine today. Wildlife has suffered accordingly. Researchers have warned of an impending epidemic of "empty forest syndrome"—habitats that look intact at first glance but that are in fact devoid of all but the most common animal residents. Illegal trade in particular has helped drive more than 130 native Southeast Asian animals onto the critically endangered list—a worrying tally that will likely only grow because there is no realistic deterrent to hunting the region's remaining animals out of existence. The same applies for the traffickers who move wildlife from forests to cities, the merchants who sell it, and the buyers who consume it. By some estimates, between 13 and 42 percent of Southeast Asian animals and plants—half of which are unique to the region—will be extinct by the end of the century if nothing changes.

"There needs to be a real threat of getting caught and punished, but right now that threat is minimal," said Chris Shepherd, executive director of Monitor, an organization working to reduce the impact of illegal and unsustainable wildlife trade, and the former Southeast Asia regional director for TRAFFIC, the trade-monitoring network of World Wildlife Fund (WWF) and the International Union for Conservation of Nature (IUCN). Although wildlife trade has a higher profile now than ever before, he continued, the increased talk in the media, at governmental meetings, and in international conference halls has yet to translate into significant changes on the ground. Why? "It's corruption, collusion, and an absolute lack of concern," Shepherd said. "Too many people just don't care."

Such callousness toward the survival of other species may strike Western readers as completely unacceptable, but animal welfare and conservation were incorporated into the North American and European psyche only in the past century or so. Interspecies empathy in the West was partly inspired by a greater appreciation of biodiversity and of animals' capacity for intelligence and feeling. But it was also enabled by an increasingly comfortable lifestyle that gave people the bandwidth to worry about animals, rather than focus solely on where their next meal was coming from.

As Asia has begun catching up economically, some citizens there, especially young people, have grown increasingly concerned about animal welfare and conservation. But an additional variable complicates things there: for thousands of years, many Asian cultures have viewed wild animals and plants as commodities that exist for the betterment of humans, not just as meat but also as medicine and status symbols (and, sometimes, all three at once). In China, for example, "little non-consumptive value, such as the pleasure of watching or photographing wild animals without killing or removing them from the wild, is attributed to wild animals or natural ecosystems," wrote Vanda Felbab-Brown in *The Extinction Market*. "Rather, nature and wild animals and plants are seen through the prism of their utilization as sources of income, food and prestige." Wildlife, in other words, is simply a resource to be exploited.

Throughout China and Southeast Asia, meat from wild animals—referred to as "wildmeat"—is often considered a tonic that can bestow that animal's particular energy and characteristics upon the person who eats it. A snake may be eaten to cure arthritis or a skin disease, because snakes are flexible and shed their skin, or a tiger may be consumed for strength and power. Such values and beliefs are widely held, even today. "In the 1980s, when I was small, eating wildlife wasn't really a big deal," said Lishu Li, manager of the wildlife trade program at the Wildlife Conservation Society's China branch. "We grew up with the knowledge that everything has a medical use or function, including consuming meat from wild animals." When Li's rural relatives were fortunate enough to capture a pangolin, the whole family would gather to eat it.

In addition to their perceived nutritional and medical value, certain rare animals are considered status symbols that only the rich and powerful can afford. In posh wildmeat restaurants wealthy businesspeople and officials show off or curry favor by ordering exotic dishes like pangolin or bear—the way Kobe beef or beluga caviar are served in the West. In the past, such excess was out of reach of most peoples' budgets, but now more and more individuals are earning enough to afford a piece of the wildlife pie. "People want something special," explained Madelon Willemsen, former country director for TRAFFIC Vietnam. If the species is going extinct, all the better, she said. It means you're influential enough to have gotten hold of one of the last.

The market has enthusiastically responded to this demand, starting with hunters and the way they do business. Subsistence hunting—trapping or shooting animals to feed one's family—has largely been replaced by hunting to satiate the appetites of the rich and upper-middle class. What was once a survival strategy has become a profit-driven enterprise—and a pillar of a global trade priced in the billions.

Tám Hổ is part of an immense underworld of players encompassing not only the wild and urban centers of Asia, but, increasingly, the savannas and jungles of Africa, the forests of South America and Russia, the museums of Europe (where more than seventy rhino horns were stolen in 2011 alone); and the antique shops and Chinatowns of North America. As in any global trafficking network, the men and women involved span all walks of life, from the small-time trader who smuggles wildlife from village to town and the corrupt customs agent who signs off on shipments of those animal parts, to the trade boss who considers himself untouchable, as well as the wealthy patrons who motivate all of their crimes.

This is all above Tám Hổ's pay grade, however. He's just a simple hunter, expendable, poor, and in ample supply. Without him, however, there would be no illegal wildlife trade.

I MET TÁM HỔ IN 2010, AT A VERY DIFFERENT TIME IN MY LIFE. AN ASPIRING CON-servation ecologist, first I needed to collect a few academic degrees. My master's research took me to U Minh, a boggy, mosquito-infested wilderness in Vietnam's deep south, where Tám Hổ lives. The place has a menacing reputation: it's still known for the tigers that once prowled its tangled paths and the crocodiles that formerly plied its dark waters. Legend has it that in 1952 five hundred French paratroopers dropped into the hostile morass, only to be swallowed up and never seen again.

Much of U Minh's wildness has since been tamed, however. Thousands of square miles of peat swamp forest were drained, chopped, and cultivated, leaving just 230 square miles remaining of the region's characteristic melaleuca woods and reed-lined channels. Yet the place's storied danger and difficulties live on in the tales people tell and in the spooky reverence with which they speak of it. Even the name itself conjures fear. U Minh: "a darkness like in hell," one Viet-namese friend explained. "It's not a normal darkness."

My ecology master's thesis addressed how people in U Minh use natural resources. To find out, I knocked on two hundred doors (figuratively speaking, that is, as many of the palm shacks did not have doors) and, with their permis-sion, quizzed the owners about everything from whether they harvest honey in the forest to what their favorite type of meat is. From these interviews, a picture emerged of life in U Minh and the hardships it entails.

Though located in Vietnam's deep south, many residents, I learned, are northern Vietnamese, including former Viet Cong soldiers. Decades ago, the gov-ernment encouraged them to move to U Minh as part of a resettlement program. There were promises of rich, fertile earth; of waters brimming with fish; and of instant, easy wealth. Today, many of those original pioneers feel duped: their youthful dreams have long since been broken by U Minh's harsh realities.

From the beginning of that venture, the land was against them. For one, the soil beneath U Minh's characteristic peat is exceptionally acidic. When disturbed by plow, shovel, or channel, it turns the water in a would-be fish pond, well, or rice paddy bright orange and undrinkable—"sour," as the locals say. This makes crops difficult to grow and aquaculture nearly impossible, depending on where your plot of land happens to fall. In the dry season, fire also poses a serious threat. The crisp brown peat can ignite with the flick of a match, and the resulting flames are voracious. In 2002 two large fires consumed more than twenty square miles of forest. As one interviewee described it to me, "There used to be a forest here before, but it caught fire and it burned, burned, burned." To prevent such a disaster from recurring, locals are now tasked with hours-long rotations perched atop tall, hand-built towers on the lookout for smoke.

Poverty is therefore nearly universal. One woman heartbreakingly told me that her biggest dream is to have electricity; a young man implored, "Please go back to your country and tell them about U Minh. Tell companies to please come make investments in U Minh, to help people here."

Of the two hundred residents I interviewed, more than 80 percent relied on nature to support some part of their lives: fish and animals to eat, wood to burn, honey to harvest and sell. Though most were subsistence hunters and fishers rather than professionals, quite a few recognized that they were caught up in a real-life tragedy of the commons, acknowledging that the animals are disappearing because of their collective activities. This is a common story not only in U Minh and Vietnam but throughout the world's tropical ecosystems: a 2017 analysis of 176 case studies found that mammals declined by 83 percent and birds declined by 58 percent in hunted compared with unhunted places.

On top of its challenging environment and declining resources, though, U Minh suffers one more major setback: lingering impacts from "ecocide" carried out by the United States against Vietnam. Seeking to decimate crops and destroy the Viet Cong's forest hideouts, from 1961 to 1971 US aircraft assaulted the landscape—including U Minh—with high-explosive munitions and 72 million liters of defoliants, including the infamous Agent Orange. Up to an estimated 4 million Vietnamese were and continue to be affected by dioxin poisoning. None ever received any compensation from the US government, and most received only minimal support at best from their own country.

Tám Hồ believes his six-year-old son counts among the victims of the American poisoning. A quiet boy who often hid behind his mother's legs when I met him, he was born with "brain illness," as Tám Hổ vaguely described it. He took up hunting—something he never had interest in, he said—to cover his newborn's hospital bills. The decision paid off. Tám Hổ proved to be a natural at his trade, and he more than quadrupled his family's annual income, from $1,000 per year to sometimes more than $4,000. He emphasized, though, that he doesn't enjoy the work: after spending all night outdoors, he returns home covered in mosquito bites, leeches, and bloody scratches. "Many times, when I step out of the forest, I don't want to go back ever again," he said. "But, because of my life, I have to go."

Putting the well-being of his family first is completely understandable, but some still cannot excuse his actions. "When people say hunting is a livelihood issue but it's illegal—like, 'Oh, the hunter is really poor and he has five children'—I can't get on board," Shepherd said. "If you're going to make an exception for hunting, then why not let them sell two of their kids, as well? Or deal in cocaine?" Hospital bills or not, Tám Hổ is still breaking the law and driving animals to extinction.

In reality, though, Tám Hổ doesn't have to worry much about the law. Everyone knows what he does. He is popular and well liked—not only by neighbors but also by the police. In 2010, when I asked people in Khánh Thuận hamlet, population one thousand, whether they knew anyone who hunted, they said, "Sure!" and pointed down the dirt road. In such a small community, few secrets stay secret for long—even breaking national laws. At one point when I was talking to Tám Hổ, the local police wandered in to check my government-issued documents granting permission to be there. Afterward, rather than head back to work, the officers took a seat next to me to watch a Vietnamese-dubbed Chinese soap opera on Tám Hổ's gritty television, paying no heed to the hunter as he rhapsodized about his illegal exploits between drags on a hand-rolled cigarette.

I can still remember the butterflies in my stomach that day as my translator, Uy, and I made our way to Tám Hổ's house for the first time. I was eager to finally meet a real, live professional hunter but nervous about blowing the interview. We soon arrived at our destination: an unexceptional U Minh home with roof and walls built of tightly woven palm leaves and melaleuca branches and a dirt floor smooth from years of use. Tám Hổ met us outside and welcomed us in. Lean and fit at forty, with a mop of wild black hair and a mischievous glint in his sharp eyes, his bombastic nature and natural charisma needed no translation.

He confirmed that he was indeed the famous pangolin hunter—an admission supported by the traps and nets balanced in corners and lining the ceiling of his home. "I'm willing to give you my knowledge and reveal my secrets, because you are a student and I like your research," he continued, gesturing for us to take a seat on his wooden bed—one of the only pieces of furniture in the room. "I believe science is very important."

He will catch anything he can get his snares and traps around, he began, including cobras, monitor lizards, pythons, turtles, otters, civets (small carnivores), fishing cats, and more. He's not a huge fan of monkeys—they creep him out with their humanoid little faces, he said—but he'll catch them, too. Above all else, though, he prides himself on his skill at trapping pangolins, one of the most elusive but lucrative creatures in the forest.

Now, unless you're an animal fanatic or nerd like me, at this point, you might be wondering, what on earth is a pangolin, anyway?

In the West, the world's eight species of pangolins have various names and nicknames—scaly anteaters, artichokes with legs, or walking pinecones—but in Vietnam, they're known simply as *tê tê*. They are the world's only mammal with true scales, but their second and more recent claim to fame is as the world's most highly trafficked mammal.

Yet, until recently, even some ecologists weren't aware of the pangolin's existence. The situation has since improved vastly: these days you'd be hard pressed to find a wildlife researcher who isn't familiar with the pangolins' plight, thanks to an increasing number of scientific papers and conference talks warning of their impending doom. A million are estimated to have been killed over the last decade.

The general public is also slowly getting to know the oddball animals. The last few years have seen a massive pangolin PR blitz, including the creation of a World Pangolin Day (the third Saturday in February, if you'd like to celebrate). Pangolin fans can show their love through pangolin T-shirts and totes, and read pangolin-themed picture books to their kids. Walt Disney's 2016 live action take on *The Jungle Book* included a pangolin cameo, and pangolins have appeared on the front page of the *New York Times'* science section. There's even an award-winning pangolin game you can download for your smartphone.

Pangolins may lack the widespread appeal of beautiful tigers, powerful rhinos, or majestic elephants, but they are becoming an underdog hero—precisely because they are none of those things. The more you learn about them, the more endearing and unbelievable they become. For starters, their sticky pink pipe-cleaner-like tongues can be longer than their bodies—perfect for lapping up their favorite treats of ants, termites, and larvae. Despite their insectivorous eating habits, though, they are more closely related to cats and dogs than to anteaters. Remarkable as contortionists, scared pangolins curl into roly-poly-like armored balls that lions sometimes bat around in playful frustration. To avoid such encounters, some species dig burrows while others prefer the high ground, taking to the trees where they hang by prehensile tails and glide about with a core strength and flexibility rivaling a teenage gymnast. Nocturnal, timid, and secretive, they are also total loners—the eccentric hermits of the animal kingdom.

"The interesting question for me is, why do pangolins resonate?" said Crawford Allan, senior director of TRAFFIC at the WWF. "Perhaps it's their intrigue and elusiveness, or the fact that they can roll up into a ball. Whatever the reason, thankfully for pangolins they have turned out to be quite appealing to many people."

Unfortunately, that appeal also extends to people with more exploitative interests. The animal's scales have become the focus of attention over the years, not because they have any medicinal value—they are made of keratin, the same material as fingernails—but because they are oddities. In India they're ground into a paste to cure armpit boils, while Sierra Leonians use them for treating everything from impotence to elephantiasis. Nigerians are more nose-to-tail in their use, believing that an entire pangolin can be prescribed for invisibility; the eyes, head, and tail for kleptomania; and the thorax for controlling the rains. A pangolin's tongue, according to some communities in Indonesia, protects against black magic.

The largest demand for pangolins these days centers on China and Vietnam. Consumers in those two countries alone are primarily to blame for the deaths of more than 100,000 pangolins each year. Pangolin flesh is considered a delicacy by some people there, while the scales factor into traditional remedies for treating a variety of maladies, including rheumatism to tuberculosis, for improving blood circulation, and for assisting in lactation. As pangolins have become rarer, prices have soared. A pangolin that a hunter like Tám Hô sells for forty to sixty dollars per pound will fetch hundreds per pound by the time it reaches a restaurant in a major city, where it's often the most expensive, and therefore most high-status, item on the menu.

No one knows how many pangolins remain in the wild or how long they have left before they disappear entirely. What we do know—through interviews like the ones I conducted in U Minh and through seizure data—is that, across their range, pangolin populations are in precipitous decline. Harvesting figures in China from the 1960s through the 1980s indicate that up to 180,000 pangolins were pulled from the wild each year, to the point that researchers extrapolated in 2003 that China's pangolin population has crashed by 94 percent.

China remains the most common destination for large-scale, multiton illegal pangolin shipments, even as harvest numbers in China and other places in Asia have dropped to a fraction of what they formerly were, likely because there are significantly fewer pangolins left. Over the past decade, more than a million pangolins have been killed.

Under this strain, it didn't take long for the supply of Asia's pangolins to begin to diminish, causing traders to look farther afield. Pangolins from India, Nepal, and Pakistan began turning up in eastern Asian markets, and trafficking networks ballooned out even farther around 2008, when pangolins appeared en route to China (and, to a lesser extent, Vietnam) from Africa. As Dan Challender, chair of the IUCN's Pangolin Specialist Group, put it, "China depleted its own population, then started to hoover up animals from other countries." At minimum, 19,000 pangolins have come out of Africa since the mid-2000s, to the effect that all four of Africa's species are now considered threatened. Asia's four species are in even more dire straits. They're endangered to critically endangered—statuses that Tám Hổ helped to achieve.

I RETURNED TO U MINH TO HOPING TO INTERVIEW TÁM HỔ ON THE RECORD AND experience a hunting trip firsthand. I had no idea if he would agree to this, but for starters I had to find him. I didn't have his phone number or address, but I did have the number of a guy living nearby, Hưng. An exceptionally friendly older man, when I met him he had jokingly put his Viet Cong military cap on me and insisted we take photos together. I hadn't been in touch with him for half a decade, but I hoped he'd help me find Tám Hổ. When a Vietnamese friend called him on my behalf, he told her, yes, he remembered me, but he had no idea who this Tám Hổ character was. Rather than give up, my tenacious friend printed out and mailed Hưng the single photo I had of Tám Hổ (e-mail hasn't really taken off in U Minh), and he sportingly agreed to circulate it in the community. A week or so later, Hưng called back with a phone number.

That was the easy part. Now came the critical question: Would Tám Hổ be willing to meet me again and even let me join him in the forest? And if so, whom could I rope into coming along to help? Slogging through leech-infested swamps isn't everyone's thing. I reached out to my old translator, Uy, and he agreed. Uy called up Tám Hổ, who remembered us well and said, no problem, he'd be happy to show us his hunting work. Everything seemed to be falling into place.

I met Uy at sunrise at the Rạch Giá airport, and—true to form to the quiet personality I remembered—after exchanging some niceties, the next hour and a half passed in near silence. About three-quarters of the way into the ride, though, Uy had no choice but to talk to me, when the road abruptly ended in an impass-able pit of construction. Uy persuaded some random guys at a roadside restaurant into letting us rent their motorbike. The taxi driver agreed to meet us back at that exact spot around noon the next day, and, with that, our problem was solved. It was a typical Vietnam experience: something unexpectedly goes wrong, but just as fast—and as long as you're willing to pay—the people around you come up with an ingenious solution.

We crossed a lazy, mud-brown river by rickety ferry, snacking on some fresh mangoes Uy had magically procured without my noticing, and proceeded on our way across steep concrete bridges and increasingly rural roads. Eventually the roads—trails, really—grew so narrow as to be wide enough to accommodate only a single motorbike. Veer even slightly off the trail, and we'd tumble into canals whose acrid water glowed a familiar shade of bright orange—the acidic ghost of U Minh's peat past.

A few wrong turns and stops for directions later, we pulled up at a palm and wood house. A small attached deck overlooked one of those stagnant U Minh ca-nals, this one not orange but the color of root beer. Bird cages hanging along the porch's edge held pigeons colored like green and pink Easter eggs and watercock that looked like the love children of a chicken and a crow. A group of men were sitting on benches around a picnic table, laughing.

Among them, I immediately recognized Tám Hổ. Save for a few extra sil-ver hairs, he appeared not a day older than when I met him as a student re-searcher in 2010. He wore baggy khaki pants under a tattered, stained orange shirt with "Safety" written on the back in English. A cigarette—his ever-present accessory—hung loosely from the corner of his mouth. His crew included his dad, who had a spindly Ho Chi Minh–style mustache and goatee; his brother; and a tall, skinny friend with a grin that came across as slightly maniacal.

Several women, including Lĩnh—Tám Hồ's slip of a wife—were bustling around in the kitchen, visible from the porch. Lĩnh wore a pajama-like outfit of matching green and white stripes with "Gucci" written on the front in white cursive embroidery.

Tám Hồ, sitting cross-legged at the table, grinned and waved us over without bothering to rise. I noticed that he was missing his two front right teeth—a new development, I thought, since I last saw him. Uy chatted with him in Vietnamese, and although he translated only the basics—"He says welcome, and that he's happy to talk to you"—I swear I heard Tám Hồ saying I looked the same but fatter. I huffed to myself as I took a seat.

I told him I was very happy to be back here, meeting with him.

"You're lucky because you're an American and free to travel," he replied, smoke curling from his cigarette. "If you were a Vietnamese girl, your husband wouldn't let you travel, especially with so many men around!" His brother, dad, and friend all cracked up.

I let that one slide and moved on to asking about his work. He shook his head. In the past, he explained, when I first met him, he went to the forest every day, but now his rice and aquaculture ponds take up half his time. "There's more and more people around these days, so the animals are becoming very rare," he said. He gestured at the lanky guy with the wild smile. "He used to be a hunter, but he stopped about six years ago to work construction, because there's no more animals." The guy nodded solemnly, confirming this assessment.

"Pangolins especially—they're going to be extinct soon," Tám Hồ said.

When Tám Hồ first started hunting, he caught up to ten pangolins a year and even ate pangolin himself ("They're very delicious"). Lately, though, he's been lucky to capture just one or two per year.

Tám Hồ and his father moved to U Minh from nearby Bạc Liêu Province in the early 1990s, when the government was giving out small parcels of land to encourage people to populate the area. To the twenty-two-year-old and his father, U Minh was a sort of paradise. Putting in just an hour's worth of work, they could catch up to fifteen pounds of fish, he claimed. His mother and several of his nine siblings soon followed (Tám Hồ is the eighth child, hence the *tám* in his nickname, meaning "eight").

As I touched on before, when Tám Hồ and Lĩnh had their first son, Tám Hồ was distraught to find that the boy suffered from the mysterious brain illness—something about "pressure being exerted on the nerves." He took his son to numerous hospitals, including one two hundred miles away in Ho Chi Minh City. But it was no use. The boy's condition did not improve. "We became despondent," he said. "We had no hope." Several years ago, however, the family's luck changed. A traditional doctor prescribed a medicine made from a local tree, and his son grew stronger. "He's much better now," Tám Hổ said, pride in his voice. "He can study normally."

As he described this story, I caught a glimpse of the boy, now ten years old, watching television alongside his little sister through the open door leading into the family's bedroom. Crayon drawings of princesses and dinosaurs hung on the walls, and a grungy orange and white kitten played at their feet. Outfitted in a yellow soccer jersey and paying the strange visitors no heed, he did indeed look like a healthy, normal kid.

I congratulated Tám Hổ on his son's recovery but reminded him that, in 2010, he had told me that he had taken up hunting to pay the family's medical bills. If the boy was fine now, then why was he still hunting? "Of course, I'm saving to invest in the highest level of education for my kids," he said matter-of-factly.

"Will you teach your son to hunt?" I asked.

"No, no!" He shook his head emphatically. "It's so hard. He should have a better education, a better life. The leeches and thorns, the malaria—it's very difficult work. But I don't want my kids to move to the city, either. The city makes me nervous. I'd prefer for them to stay here, where it's very easy. Unlike in the big city, where you have to worry about so many things, we have food and fish always available. We don't have to worry about life."

As if to prove his point, the took out a plastic tub tightly covered in green net. Inside were nine turtles, ranging from saucer to plate sized. He removed one and held it up for me to see. Dark grey with intricately patterned yellow stripes, the terrified reptile withdrew its head into its shell but continued to peer out at me with unblinking golden eyes.

"Do you ever feel sorry for the animals?" I asked, betraying my own feelings. He didn't hesitate: "No."

Uy—whose love of animals rivals my own—piped up, "When my mother kills a duck or chicken, they look very strange before they die—like they know what's coming—and I feel very sorry for them. Don't you ever have that feeling?"

"No," Tám Hổ repeated, shaking his head. He took another drag on his cigarette and plopped the turtle back into its container.

Lĩnh silently interrupted us to set out a small feast: a platter of boiled shrimp fresh from the family pond, homegrown rosy-hued tomatoes and bright green herbs, hand-harvested rice, and a glutinous sweet treat Uy told me was made out of some sort of local leaf. As Lĩnh arranged the plates, I asked her whether she ever worried about her husband. She smiled shyly, shrinking into herself in a way that reminded me of the turtle, and gave her head a slight shake. "Không," she said softly. *No.*

Tám Hổ dug in with grit-covered hands, and I asked him between bites whether he's reconsidered his retirement plans (or lack thereof) since I last saw him. "It depends on the animal populations, but, for now, I'll continue," he said. He added, though, that he's getting tired of the forest. "I prefer agriculture, but I'll keep hunting just because I need to make a living."

For example, he continued, the other morning he bagged a couple of eagles. He'd never seen anything like them. They were circling a rice field in the mist, looking very hungry, so he baited them with meat. When they swooped in and began to eat, he captured them with a net. "Now I'm keeping them in a hidden location nearby," he said.

"Can we see them?" I asked.

He thought for a moment. "Sure, why not!"

The birds were being kept at his brother's house down the road. Lĩnh came along, perching sidesaddle on the motorbike behind her husband and draping her arms around his waist. Uy and I followed as they led us past idyllic golden rice paddies full of farmers wearing their country's trademark conical hats and over creaky wooden bridges. A few minutes later we pulled up to a larger, slightly fancier house than the one Tám Hổ lived in. Rather than palm and wood, its walls were made of corrugated plastic, and the floors were tiled instead of dirt. Fat ducks quacked at us from a ditch outside, and a scabies-ridden dog guarded the door.

Tám Hổ led us in, through the living room into a back bedroom. There, each bound by one foot to a dresser, were two massive birds. These were no eagles, however. Clearly, they were vultures. Himalayan griffon vultures, to be precise, an ornithologist later confirmed for me—a species that has been recorded only once before in Vietnam, in the far Northwest. Their heads were downy off-white; their hooked beaks deep grey; and their feathers a dark, chocolatey brown with tan veins running through the centers. The vultures' heads drooped low—a sign the birds were not faring well—but as we entered the room they puffed up, recoiling and hissing at us.

Eager to demonstrate his dominance, Tám Hổ strode over to the smaller of the two turkey-sized birds. Using a broom, he deftly maneuvered its snapping head out of the way then grabbed it from behind. He wrestled with it for a moment before gaining the upper hand and opening its wings to show us an impressive span. Had the vulture been human, I'd have described the look in its eyes as murderous.

"I'm thinking about asking permission to raise them," he said, releasing his grip on the irate raptor and jumping away before it could exact its revenge. "Or selling them."

Uy, thinking fast, pointed out that these aren't eagles, they're vultures. Given their closeness to death and decay, no one in his right mind would want to buy them. In fact, vultures are about the only animal that people in Vietnam won't eat. "These birds are bad luck," Uy continued, homing in on Tám Hổ's superstitious weak spot.

Tám Hổ's face fell. The bird's true identity was apparently news to him. He'd had the vultures for several days now, and each day was costing him 3.5 pounds of meat to feed them—not a trivial expense for animals that wouldn't sell. Looking crestfallen, he mumbled something about maybe selling them to a zoo.

What happened to the vultures, I do not know. Uy later told me that he anonymously tipped off the local authorities, only to find they weren't committed enough to pursue the case.

THE SKY WAS A SHADE OF DEEP PURPLE-PINK WHEN WE SET OFF THE FOLLOWING morning to join Tám Hổ in the forest. The evening before had been delightful. Uy and I stayed at our old guest house—the same rooms, even. The friendly owners had insisted we join them for a homemade dinner of chicken heads, rice, and vegetables, and I returned their generosity by presenting them with overpriced chocolate from Brooklyn. Hưng, the veteran who helped me find Tám Hổ, came out to meet us over a drink, as did a kind, committed ranger we'd closely worked with in 2010. Although the pangolin hunter was the excuse I had used to return to U Minh, the opportunity to see these friendly faces one more time was very much part of the draw.

By the time we reached Tám Hổ's place, the sky had lightened to a hazy white, and the air was a chorus of cock-a-doodle-doos. Tám Hổ and Lĩnh were already out front, expecting us. A bit inexplicably, considering that our destination was the forest, Lĩnh was wearing a white bicycle helmet and white peep-toe wedges, revealing the chipped remnants of a long-ago pedicure. Tám Hổ was barefoot.

As soon as I saw our mode of transportation, however—a teensy aluminum boat—I realized those cute summer wedges and bare feet might be more appropriate than what I was wearing. I'd dragged my massive hiking boots, each the size and weight of a small boulder, all the way to Vietnam, assuming we'd be tramping through thick brush. Climbing into the boat, I wobbled to and fro like a drunken jack-in-the-box until, at last, I plopped down on a stool half the width of my butt. Uy climbed in next with the grace of a ballerina in comparison, and Lĩnh took her seat with ease, perching at the bow like a pirate ship's angelic figurehead. She and Tám Hổ, who was seated in the back, took up a paddle and pushed in unison against the embankment. Our little vessel slipped into the warm black water.

Guns have been illegal in Vietnam since the early 1990s, but hunters like Tám Hổ haven't let that logistical hiccup get in their way. They've responded with a diverse array of snares, mist nets, catapults, pitfall traps, poisons, and more. Each animal has strong and weak points, Tám Hổ explained, and to be a hunter is to understand these characteristics and exploit them with different traps tailored for different species. To catch a water monitor, for example, he sets a trap with dead frogs, the smell of which is irresistible for the carrion-loving lizards. Monkeys, on the contrary, are smart and will figure out how to open a normal trap. He gets around this by baiting them with bananas attached to a snare that wraps tightly around their wrist. For cobras he doesn't even bother setting a trap; he just catches them with his bare hands. "I've never been bitten," he said with pride.

A true artisan, he makes all his traps himself, using whatever raw materials he can find around the house. Civet traps are fashioned out of swamp wood and bicycle brake wire (he learned the hard way that larger animals can chew through string and nylon), while his pangolin nets are meticulously and sturdily handwoven. A few other men in U Minh still hunt pangolins, he told me, and one of them uses a dog to sniff out the animals. But Tám Hổ doesn't need that kind of fancy assistance. "Most of the other hunters know of my methods in general, but I haven't released the copyright," he said with a chuckle. Of the eighty or so traps he had scattered throughout the forest, today we'd be checking and resetting around fifteen.

We took a sharp turn off the main canal, entering a narrow side channel. The dark water surrounding us sat just an inch or so under the rim of our little boat, which seemed to be defying the laws of physics to keep afloat. The vegetation lining the canal's banks grew thicker, almost forming a tunnel. As we brushed underneath it, ants rained down on us like confetti, falling onto my arms, into my hair, and down the back of my shirt. Hungry, buzzing mosquitos trailed us. Tám Hổ and Lĩnh appeared utterly indifferent to the insect assault, and—trying to play it cool—I did my best to resist frantically slapping all over my body.

"You're lucky today, because there's good weather," Tám Hổ said. "If there was a little rain, there would be a lot more mosquitos. In the rainy season, I become black because of the surrounding mosquitoes. They're my most hated insect."

We stopped at what appeared to me to be a random spot on the side of the canal but that Tám Hổ said was clearly an animal trail. He slipped out of the boat, and Uy and I followed; Lĩnh stayed behind. We pushed into the thick of a bamboo forest where, unlike on the canal, no cool breeze stirred the heavy, humid air. Within seconds I began to sweat as though I was nearing the end of a particularly rigorous SoulCycle class, clothes sticking to my body and hair plastering my face and neck.

I was just beginning to wonder how much farther we were going when Tám Hổ stopped and pointed down. I saw nothing. He took a stick, poked at something, and—SNAP! In a flash, a previously invisible loop of metal wire coiled tightly around the stick. He'd tuned this trap, he said, to spring only if something heavier than about two pounds—something worth his time, in other words—tread on it. "A lot of mice come through here, but they won't trigger it," he said. We checked a few more invisible-to-me-but-not-to-him snares, all of them empty.

Back on the boat, we passed through more canals and acquired more ants. A slender black leech plopped onto Uy's neck, which he calmly removed. At our second stop I had a moment of gringa shame when I stood to get up but lost my balance, wildly rocking the boat and causing some water to slosh in. "Wooooaaahh!" everyone yelled. Somehow—thankfully—I managed to stabilize my flailing body before capsizing us into the seven-foot-deep water. "Sometimes I go swimming," Tám Hổ said in a kind attempt to make me feel better. "I've fallen out of the boat many times."

We'd stopped this time in a part of the forest used for growing bananas. Though he was only walking, Tám Hổ set a sprint-like pace, weaving through leafy obstacles and across the uneven ground like a figure skater. Soon, I lost sight of him altogether; hearing nothing, seeing nothing, the only sign that he existed at all was the ever-present, faint whiff of a cigarette. Uy and I finally caught up with him only because he stopped to wait. "I've seen rangers many times in the forest, but I very quickly hide so they can't discover me," he said. After seeing him move like that, I did not doubt it. "Usually they travel in big groups and make a lot of noise."

We checked a few more traps—again, all empty—and began heading back in the direction of the boat. Suddenly, Tám Hổ stopped. "Rái cá! Rái cá!" he shouted with excitement, pointing down. As usual, I saw nothing.

"What's *rái cá*?" I asked Uy.

He told me it means "otter." I looked closer at the brush, excitedly expecting to see an otter but instead seeing what Tám Hổ had identified as the *signs* of an otter: empty snail shells and a couple of fish bones.

There are two kinds of otters living in this region, he explained, one with small claws and the other without claws. (The latter is likely the hairy-nosed otter, one of the world's rarest otter species. In 2000, it was rediscovered living in U Minh—the first sighting in Vietnam in twenty-three years.) Otters are exceptionally smart and won't be fooled into a snare trap, Tám Hổ continued, so he uses a bear trap for catching them. For reasons that escape him, though, traders no longer want to buy otters. "I'll come set traps here next time I'm out," he concluded.

"Wait, if traders don't buy them anymore, why trap them?" I asked, wondering what I was missing.

"Meat," he replied simply.

He took the lead again, walking with his hands folded behind his back, carrying a rusted machete. Back at the boat, Tám Hổ announced that we were done now: all the traps were checked for the day, and we were heading home. I sighed with relief—not only because I wouldn't have to witness an animal meeting its doom but also because being out here really was highly unpleasant. Though the excursion had lasted only an hour, I was covered in bites and scratches, and was so drenched in sweat that it looked like I'd fallen into the canal after all. Tám Hổ wasn't lying when he said the forest was not a hospitable work environment.

Back at his house, I thanked him and—despite his insistence that he didn't want my money—paid him thirteen dollars for his time. Out of curiosity, I asked whether he'd stop hunting if someone employed him, for example, to be a forest guide for tourists. Smoke spirals framed his face as he gazed out at the canal, considering the question. At last, he nodded slowly. "Yes: eleven to thirteen dollars per trip, and I'd quit hunting."

Rather than encouraging me, though, this answer only disheartened me. Thousands of such hunters operate across Southeast Asia. Employing them as forest protectors or guides may sound like a promising solution, but there simply isn't enough work to go around. As Felbab-Brown pointed out in her book, "It is one thing to employ twenty hunters . . . and quite another to bring employment to several thousand people who may reside in or near an ecologically sensitive area." And research shows that some poachers, she added, won't give up hunting at all, even when their subsistence is assured through other means.

Uy and I had already said our goodbyes and were climbing onto the motorbike when Tám Hổ called out to us, "Wait!" He ran around to the back of the house and returned, moments later, with a small plastic bag. Inside was a live baby turtle, the size of a silver dollar. "For you," he said, presenting that small life to me with two hands.

Uy, as usual, didn't comment. But minutes after we had pulled away, he stopped the motorbike. "Give me the turtle," he said quietly. He eased himself down the canal embankment, reached into the bag and then placed his open palm on the ground. The turtle, sitting in the center of his hand, needed no more encouragement. It bolted for the water and disappeared within seconds. "Good luck!" Uy called out. Without another word, he fired up the motorbike and drove us away.

THE VAST MAJORITY OF CREATURES THAT END UP IN THE ILLEGAL WILDLIFE TRADE get no such second chance. Downer endings are the norm, and the animals in Tám Hổ's possession typify the story of how wildlife finds its way from forest to market. After trapping an animal, Tám Hổ immediately calls a trader in nearby Cà Mau City to come pick it up. He doesn't call the same trader all the time, though. The snake guy won't buy a monkey; the pangolin guy won't be interested in monitor lizards—the way someone in London or New York would have a different dealer for weed and cocaine. All the traders know each other, though, so if a hunter comes up with an animal they don't handle, they'll tap their network to hook him up with the right person. There are about ten such dealers working in the Cà Mau area alone, Tám Hổ said.

Tám Hổ could make more money if he'd drive the thirty miles to Cà Mau himself, but he's not into taking chances. If he's caught on the road with a pangolin, he could face steep fines and even jail time (or, alternatively, steep bribes). He's so cautious, in fact, that he doesn't even allow the traders to come to his home. Instead, they rendezvous at a discreet meeting point. "If I have a very rare animal, I even keep it a secret even from my family," he said.

What happens to the animals after the pickup is not something that Tám Hổ concerns himself with. When I asked him, he shrugged indifferently. "I don't know where they go. I guess they're sent to the big city, or to China. Maybe they're eaten or kept as pets—I have no idea." Those are all pretty good guesses. Animals are sent to big cities like Ho Chi Minh and Hanoi, and they're also shipped to China. And although U Minh species wouldn't commonly be kept as pets, they are most certainly eaten, despite the fact that wildmeat consumption in Vietnam is illegal. The country's laws clearly state that taking an animal from the wild is illegal and that all animals in commercial trade must be of legal origin.

"Technically, that means if a kid catches a frog in a rice paddy, then according to law it's not of legal origin because the kid took it from the wild," said Doug Hendrie, director of wildlife crime and investigations at the nonprofit organization Education for Nature–Vietnam. Some species, including pangolins, tigers, bears, and native primates are given higher priority than others, though, with trade of their meat or parts counting as a criminal violation carrying a maximum penalty of $90,000 or fifteen years in prison.

The laws, however, are primarily decorative. "In Ho Chi Minh City or Hanoi, it's not hard to track down places to eat endangered species like pangolin," said Challender, of the IUCN's Pangolin Specialist Group. "Just ask for the jungle menu and you'll find it on there." At one such restaurant, he witnessed a pangolin being killed at the table next to his. The men paid $700 for the animal, which weighed just over four pounds. "The restaurant staff took out a rolling pin, held the pangolin upside down by its tail, and clubbed it on the head until it was unconscious," Challender recalled. "Then they took out a pair of scissors and opened its throat and drained the blood."

China, however, isn't as freewheeling as Vietnam when it comes to pangolin and other banned wildmeat. When President Xi Jinping took office in 2013, he declared war on corruption, vowing to crack down on "tigers and flies," as he put it—or both high-level and low-level officials guilty of abusing their positions. The anti-corruption campaign (which extended to anti–opulence and extravagance), Felbab-Brown wrote, was motivated by equal parts a desire to increase the party's popular legitimacy and to consolidating Xi's power. In addition to weeding out people who accepted bribes, leaked state secrets, bought votes, and more, the campaign included a clampdown on restaurants serving illegal wild-meat, which often cater to a governmental clientele.

Yet pangolin—which has been illegal to eat in China since 1989—is still served there, although much less overtly than in Vietnam. "Now that the Chinese pangolin is almost extinct, the restaurants that are able to provide pangolin meat are very elusive and exclusive," according to Li at the Wildlife Conservation Society. "You have to get to know them and become a member or VIP. Only then are you able to get the meat."

If caught, Chinese pangolin-eating patrons face up to ten years in jail, but, for some, the risk isn't a deterrent. In February 2017, for example, a Shenzhen woman dubbed by media the "Pangolin Princess" was brought in for questioning after social media users brought attention to photos of "pangolin blood fried rice," "eight animal stew," and "caterpillar fungus and pangolin soup" that she had posted on Weibo, China's version of Twitter. She bragged that the dishes were so nourishing they made her nose bleed.

I wanted to see one of these notorious wildmeat restaurants for myself. Would the shady establishments be located down a back alley, requiring a secret knock to gain entry? Were they patronized by tables of beefy, knife-carrying gangster types? I didn't have the connections to infiltrate the wildmeat scene in China, but Challender and others made it sound like it would be fairly easy in Vietnam. So, after bidding U Minh *hẹn gặp lại* (see you later), I headed straight to Ho Chi Minh City.

Nguyễn Kim Thảo isn't a woman who is easily rattled. A former flight attendant, she's dealt with everything from severe turbulence to passengers who demand a fresh vodka tonic every four minutes—all the while wearing a picture-perfect "ten-tooth" smile, as her boss regularly commanded. As such, she was the first person I called for help infiltrating the city's illegal wildmeat scene.

Thảo and I had become acquainted a decade before, when she and her family invited me into their Cần Thơ home as a foreign exchange student. We quickly bonded over *áo dài* glamour shots, curry goat hot pots, and tales of college romance, and we'd remained friends—sisters, we say—ever since.

A helpful source had shared a list of ten places he'd found serving pangolin meat in Ho Chi Minh City, places whose names translated as Forest Scent,

Vietnam Streets, and Restaurant Tràm Chim (a reference to one of the country's national parks). Over beers at a live music joint, I asked Thảo whether she'd be up for calling a few of those restaurants to see what she could find out. If things sounded good, perhaps we could even go together.

The next afternoon, a barrage of Facebook chat messages lit up my phone, detailing what Thảo had learned. "Oh scary, Huong Rung sells whole pangolins—7 million VND per kg," she wrote, excitedly launching straight in without so much as a "hello." Pulling up a currency converter, I ran the number twice, just to make sure I hadn't made a mistake the first time. Seven million Vietnam dong per kilogram is nearly $150 per pound. Not that I had planned to order pangolin, but, damn, even if I wanted to, I couldn't afford it!

Messages from Thảo continued to pour in: "You can just call two hours before n they will bring a pangolin back to sell. You can come n see, they bring the whole pangolin, weigh it to calculate the price for ya, n cook it right away. They sell civet n snake also. But they seem very fierce! If you act like a normal customer and not a journalist they may be willing to say something, otherwise I don't dare to come n translate. Terrified me!" To emphasize her point, she ended with a series of frowny-face emojis. *If Thảo is unsettled by just a brief phone call, then this probably isn't something I should be getting into. . . .*

I needed to fully understand the situation, so I asked Thảo to fill me in on a few more details. She'd called two places, she said. A receptionist picked up at the first, and when Thảo asked her whether they sold pangolin, the woman hesitated, seemingly taken aback. "She spoke to me like this wasn't an open story she could freely tell," Thảo said. The receptionist passed the baton, putting Thảo on hold to get her supervisor. The pangolins, he explained in a gruff, stern voice, aren't kept on site. Instead, once an order is made, he'll call his go-to guy, who will bring the pangolin to the premises within a couple of hours. To reassure Thảo that she would in fact be getting what she paid for, she would be invited to visit the kitchen before the meal. There, she could become better acquainted with her pangolin—still very much alive—and watch as it is weighed. Once the weight is determined, she would need to pay a deposit to hold the animal. When she returned that evening, the staff would present the animal to her table and then slit its throat in front of her and her guests—once again reassuring her that she would indeed be dining on genuine pangolin flesh.

Thảo's curiosity on the phone, however, lacked any hint of commitment, and eventually the manager had had enough. "Why are you asking so many questions?" he spat. "If you want it, just come here and get it!" He hung up.

The call had left a strong impression on her. "These kinds of people that dare to do business that's banned by the government, they surely have their backup—if you know what I mean."

"So you think it's not safe?" I replied. "Maybe it's better if we don't go?"

"If we tell them you are a journalist, then no, it's not safe. But how about this: we just act normal and observe, and if you don't inform them that you're a journalist, I think then it's ok."

"I'm just not sure I can pretend to be someone I'm not . . . " I typed back hesitantly.

"If we tell them, though, I don't know what kind of bad intentions they might have!"

Thảo had a point. Was walking up to a crooked, pangolin-killing restaurant manager and asking him for an interview about his wrongdoings really such a good idea? What if he pulled a knife and led us into a back room or sent his wildlife-smuggling cronies after us when we departed? A swift club to the back of the head while riding a motorbike would not end well. I could already see the headlines: "American Journalist, Friends, Murdered by Vietnamese Crime Chef."

"Ok," I wrote back, returning to reality. "Let's try your plan. I won't say anything unless it feels right."

I headed upstairs to a room I was sharing with Ty Parker, my best friend and fellow New Yorker, whom I'd convinced to join me in Ho Chi Minh City. His love of travel and lust for status-earning miles make him susceptible to things like flying to Vietnam for a long weekend of undercover investigations mixed in with some *phở* and drag shows. But although he's accompanied me on past reporting trips—Mongolia, Nepal, and India, to name a few—this trip's theme struck a particularly significant chord. Ty is no writer, activist, or conservationist—he's a computer programmer on Wall Street—but animal welfare is one of his pet concerns; he's the type of vegetarian who readily shoots withering looks to anyone who orders chorizo or chicken in his presence. A week or so prior, I'd run the idea of visiting an illegal wildmeat restaurant by him and was relieved when he agreed: "Yeah, that would be cool. As long as I don't have to eat it."

Now, I was even more thankful he'd be joining us. Skinny and pale with balding ginger hair, Ty won't be winning many boxing matches—but I still felt that his masculine presence would make Thảo and me less vulnerable.

When I came back to the hotel room, I found Ty scrolling through his phone. "Well, the good news is we're going out tonight," I announced, shooting him a sarcastic grin. "The bad news is we might be killed by wildlife mafia bosses."

"The drinks in this country are too cheap not to risk it!" he replied with classic Ty humor.

It was almost time to meet Thảo, so we headed downstairs. We were staying at the Majestic, a grand but faded old establishment that will always be my favorite Ho Chi Minh base. Outside, the sinking sun had set the metropolitan smog and sky ablaze in an orange-pink glow, transforming the pollution-choked Saigon River into something romantic and timeless. I could image a teenage Marguerite Duras in the faceless twilight crowds, strolling by, arm-in-arm with her illicit Chinese lover, on her way to some long-forgotten, fabulous engagement.

My daydreaming was broken as two motorbikes veered out of the manic onslaught of whizzing scooters and beeping taxis, stopping just in front of us. It was Thảo and Dũng, a friend she'd recruited for the evening. Thảo, it turned out, was taking this mission very seriously: she had convincingly transformed into a wealthy businesswoman, donning kitten heels, a smart black silk blouse, and a Marc Jacobs watch with a matching handbag. My scuffed flats and sweat-stained travel dress no longer seemed to cut it.

"Uh, I think I should probably go change," I said.

"No problem, you look fine," Thảo said, handing me her spare helmet with a manicured hand. "You're a foreigner. Everyone automatically assumes you've got a lot of money no matter how you're dressed."

Trusting her, I hopped on the back of her canary-yellow motorbike, and off we went into the insanity of Saigon's traffic. My anxiety had been building all afternoon—ever since Thảo's uncharacteristic reaction to the phone calls—and, now that we were on our way to the restaurant, a pangolin-sized knot had formed in my stomach. I was beginning to feel like a fraud whose pretend play at investigative journalism was about to come back to bite her.

I didn't have time to dwell on my worries for long; within about fifteen minutes, we arrived at our destination, Thiên Vương Tửu, or Wine for the Heavenly King. It was tucked into a side street, just off a busy road in District 3 that was lined with high-rise banks and bushy mimosa trees. Airy, two-storied, and open to the street, the restaurant was decked out in gold, red, and yellow New Year decorations, and the glowing green of a massive Heineken sign out front complimented well-manicured pots of bamboo and bonsai-style trees. A valet took Thảo and Dũng's bikes, and a hostess wearing a neat white *áo dài* met us at the door.

I was taken aback. Where was the unmarked entryway? Where were the glowering henchmen and bouncers? The blood-spattered walls from so many animal executions? I wasn't the only one with this reaction. "This is not at all what I expected," Ty mumbled to me as we entered the brightly lit dining room. "I thought we would be going to, like, some dark alley."

We passed a stack of clean fish tanks brimming with giant shrimp and catfish, triggering a memory for Dũng: "Oh, I've been here before! My company took us here last year for a party. This is an expensive place, really fancy." Judging by its size, the restaurant could comfortably accommodate half a dozen such parties simultaneously.

The hostess sat us at a front street-facing table and handed over massive, leather-bound menus. Opening mine, I wanted to quickly paw through to see what kind of wildlife horrors might be advertised, but I forced myself to slowly survey the options like a normal customer. I smiled vacantly, glancing over all the usual suspects of chicken, pork, duck, and beef, along with various noodles and rice dishes. But then, with the turn of a page, I hit the motherlode.

In the very back, complete with photographs, were several pages advertising a menagerie of wild animals. Fried bats were pictured next to the bony legs and rat-like tail of a roasted civet on a platter adorned with greens; on the next page, a boiled pangolin lay splayed out on a plate in a morbid belly flop. Some photos, rather than depicting prepared dishes, took the even less subtle approach of displaying the actual animal in question: a porcupine, two grinning bears, a bright green lizard, a turtle, and more. Thảo translated a few of the offerings, including pangolin stewed with Chinese herbs, snake-meat sausage, fried tortoise viscera, and bear paw cooked with ginger (twenty-four hours' notice required).

I was dumbfounded. I hadn't known what to expect, but an illustrated menu of illegal products handed out to anyone who walks through the door was definitely not it. Staring at the pages, I began plotting a way to covertly sneak some photos. Maybe I could get Thảo to distract the staff. Or I could put the menu in my lap and take pictures without anyone noticing. Or hide it under my dress and take it to the bathroom with me. . . .

Not everyone at our table was on board with our nothing-to-see-here, we're-just-some-average-customers role-play, however. Holding up one of the animal pages as though it was his turn to share at show-and-tell, Dũng emphatically gestured at the pangolin. "Look, Rachel! Look! *Wildmeat!*" he exclaimed, his eyes wide.

"Yup, got it," I said between a tight smile, silently willing him to shut up and play cool. He was going to blow our cover! Yet the servers hovering nearby—attractive young women clad in tight black-and-gold minidresses—seemed utterly uninterested.

Food ordered, beers poured, it seemed my chance to bust out the camera would arrive momentarily. Yet our hostess seemed firmly planted in place, standing just a couple of steps from our table. Each time Ty or I would take a small sip of beer, she rushed over and diligently refilled our glasses. Thảo, ever perceptive, noticed my distress. She turned to the young woman and said something in Vietnamese that immediately sent her scurrying away.

"Did you just tell her to fuck off?" Ty asked with an impressed raise of his brows.

"I just told her we want to enjoy our dinner naturally."

I laughed, beginning to relax. "So basically, yes, you told her to fuck off."

Finally free from prying eyes, I quickly snapped a few photos of each menu page, even daring to whip out my conspicuous SLR camera. No one seemed to notice or care. The food soon arrived, and conversation turned to other things. At one point, Thảo and I took a break to visit the ladies' room, peeping into the kitchen as we made our way through the restaurant. But everything appeared to be completely normal: no animal cages, no protected species on the cutting board, no pile of severed bear parts or pangolin scales. The night, it seemed, would end without incident.

My courage was steadily growing, reinforced by the beer and the mundane uneventfulness of the visit. I decided to try my luck with an interview, and Thảo agreed that things seemed safe enough. By this time, the place had begun to fill up with couples, groups of men and even families with toddlers, so I figured we were probably safe from physical attack at least, given all the potential eyewitnesses. Minutes after Thảo asked to speak with the manager, a soft-faced young man with an eager smile appeared at our table. His name tag, pinned next to a yellow smiley face button, read Quốc Trung.

Through Thảo, I told Quốc that I was an American journalist researching exotic meat in Vietnam. "Oh yes, that is our specialty," he said, nodding. He either did not notice or did not mention that it was odd that our table had not sampled a single piece of said specialty. I had jotted down a list of questions to ask, but Quốc needed little prompting. Thảo could hardly keep up with the translation.

"Exotic meat is extremely popular," he began. "Civets and pangolins especially. Tortoises and snakes sell well, too. I think civet served with sticky rice is the most delicious."

When asked about the exorbitant price for pangolins, he explained that it stems from the fact that they cannot be raised in captivity. "Everyone wants them," he said. "But only high-class and special guests get to enjoy this animal."

"But why do people want pangolin—what makes it worth paying so much?" I prodded.

"People are willing to pay, not only because the pangolin's meat is tasty, but also because the pangolin's scales treat a lot of sicknesses," he confidently informed me. "The scales are good for the body. They can treat all sorts of things, like back or joint pains. Or if a woman is having trouble lactating, she can take them to help her produce milk."

Judging by his earnest tone, it did not seem like he was just making this stuff up to push his pangolin products. He believed it—and customers apparently did, too. Those who order a pangolin almost always want to keep their animal's scales, he told us. The fee patrons pay for their pangolin includes removing, drying, and packing the scales up in a doggie bag.

Dũng piped up with his own question, finally understanding this game. "So does the government allow this?"

"No," Quốc smiled slyly. "But we have our sources. We get no problems from the authorities because we have good connections with the police. Although everyone knows it's banned, we can still advertise it and put the pictures in the menu—we don't have to worry about anything. Anyway, the demand is so high for these things, we have to supply them."

Quốc didn't know the origin of the animals that found their way to his restaurant, but he conceded that they could very well hail from U Minh. "I've never been to U Minh forest myself, I've just seen it on TV," he said. "But there's a lot of people down there who sell exotic meat." Once the animals reach his kitchen, he added, they have already changed hands many times.

"Oh, look, that table has ordered a cobra!" Quốc interrupted himself, gesturing to a five-top composed of two white men, two Vietnamese women, and an older Vietnamese man. Overweight, middle aged, and wearing ill-fitting polo shirts and glasses, the two foreigners looked like they belonged in a sad suburban office park, not a posh restaurant catering to a wealthy Vietnamese clientele.

Speaking French to each other, they switched to Vietnamese when addressing their dates, who were trim, well dressed, and also middle aged.

Two servers clad in red uniforms with clown-like yellow buttons had just come out of the back, pushing a plastic trolley with a silver tray and white ceramic bowl on top of it. One carried a large yellow mesh bag. Inside, it appeared that something was moving. "You can take photos if you'd like," Quốc offered helpfully.

Unlike me, the Frenchmen did not wait for permission. Grinning and rising from their chairs, one of them whipped out an iPhone, the other an iPad. The women remained seated, but their dates crowded close to the cart. I jumped to my feet, too, dreading what I suspected was about to happen, yet knowing this was what I had come here to see. The servers untied the bag, reached in, and withdrew a writhing black cobra, its mouth tightly bound with green twine. The snake had to be at least five feet long. It thrashed and twisted, fighting for its life. Almost certainly plucked from a rice paddy or forest days or weeks before, I imagined the deadly predator was for the first time experiencing an uncomfortable new sensation: fear.

With their ear studs, tattoos, and swooped bangs, the young men holding the snake could very well be Vietnamese hipsters. But here at work, they were animal-killing professionals. They went about their duties with a practiced ease, as though they were preparing nothing more complicated than a venti latte. Swoop boy, the shorter of the two, grasped the snake's throat in his left hand, its tail in his right, and extended his arms, which were not quite long enough to hold the animal taut. Tattoo boy then felt along the snake's stomach with his thumb, forming a painful-looking indentation in its body as he worked his way up toward its head. At last, he found what he was looking for. Grabbing a pair of black-handled scissors, he inserted the tip into the snake's belly, and then wiggled it around until he was able to slip one of the blades under the skin. Then, he began to cut.

The snake's pupils dilated, and its purple tongue slipped out of its bound mouth as though it were panting. If snakes could scream, this one certainly would be. Vibrant red blood began to seep, and then pour, from the incision, now about five inches long. Meanwhile, the Frenchmen who had ordered this execution were scurrying to and fro, trying to find the best angle to film the spectacle.

The show, it turned out, was just getting started. Tattoo boy inserted three of his bare fingers into the moist slit, feeling around thoughtfully and then pulling.

Grasped delicately between his now blood-coated thumb and index finger was the cobra's beating heart. With one final snip, it was all over. Into a small dish went the heart, out went the cobra's life.

"Are you going to eat that?" I asked incredulously, turning to one of the Frenchman. Without breaking his gaze on the snake, he nodded sternly, his brows furrowed in concentration—or perhaps annoyance.

Swoop boy now angled the animal's body downward while tattoo boy worked the scaly corpse like a tube of toothpaste, squeezing the blood into the ceramic bowl. Its pristine whiteness made the shock of red all the more stark. Later, the blood would be mixed with alcohol, to be taken in shots in a show of masculine bravado. Although the snake's eyes were glassy, its body, as if still unable to accept the finality of its fate, continued to twist and spasm.

The shrimp paste and fried spicy tofu no longer seemed so settled in my stomach. The servers were still working the snake over, however, so I forced myself to continue looking, snapping photos every few seconds. Out came the animal's viscera, along with globs of bright yellowish fat. Finally, swoop boy took the snake's head, and with a couple of determined snips, tattoo boy decapitated it. I turned away, sensing the show was over.

Floating back to our table, I lowered my numb body into my chair, staring at my friends in blank shock. Just then, Quốc reemerged from the kitchen, bearing yet another yellow mesh bag. *Oh God—more??* I really did not feel up to seeing another animal being tortured to death. This bag contained a civet. It was about the size of a Yorkie but with a fur patterns reminiscent of a raccoon. Its snouted face was lowered in defeat; any fight it once had, it seemed, had long since been extinguished. It reached up, placing its small, cat-like paws against the sides of the bag, as if trying to brace itself for what was to come. It hardly moved from that position even as Quốc wildly spun the bag and tossed—nearly slammed—it carelessly to the ground.

My chest clinched in bitter, helpless frustration. I had experienced this sensation before. Memories flooded back: a day on the playground when a group of tyrannical third-grade boys began stomping on baby toads that had just emerged from spring puddles; a kitten that was brought into the veterinary clinic where I worked, caked in blood and comatose after the owner's boyfriend had kicked it across the room; a group of teenage visitors at a zoo in Vietnam who used a hose to water-cannon caged animals while the staff placidly looked on.

Quốc was saying something, but by this point—if Thảo was translating at all—it no longer registered. "I think we should go now," I said, abruptly rising from the table and now feeling less the urge to vomit than to cry. Ty, who looked like a deer in the headlights, nodded emphatically.

Fetching the motorbikes, we reconvened outside in stunned silence. Even Dũng seemed to be at a loss for words. Finally, Ty cleared his throat. "Obviously, that was absolutely horrifying. . . . But wow! That manager really just sang for you like a canary. Not that a canary would sing here for very long. . . . "

I laughed, grateful for the comic relief.

"My uncle trusts this kind of thinking, that you can eat exotic meat and blood and recover from illnesses," Thảo said. "Many old Vietnamese think this way. But those poor animals . . . why can't they just eat duck or chicken? They're perfectly delicious and fine!"

"Or vegetables," Ty added dryly. He admitted that he had averted his gaze throughout the entire snake spectacle. "I just couldn't do it," he said, looking down. "I couldn't watch that." In a way, I envied him.

As we pulled away, I could hear the women clapping and cheering shrilly as the Frenchmen took their first shots of the cobra's still-warm blood.

Two

HER SISTER'S PANGOLIN SCALE GUY

M EAT, as Quốc Trung indicated, isn't the only reason someone would want a pangolin. Traditional medicine—predominantly, traditional Chinese medicine, practiced in various forms throughout Asia—is another driver of the illegal wild-life trade. Pangolins are listed in its ancient pharmacopeia, alongside a host of other endangered species: tigers, rhinos, tortoises, and more. Very few have been shown to have any medical benefit at all, however—and yet some of the purported pharmaceutical ingredients derived from protected animals sell for hundreds or even thousands of dollars.

Why?

TRADITIONAL CHINESE MEDICINE APPEARED ON THE SCENE ABOUT 3,000 YEARS ago—the ancient culture's answer to the universal human desire to maintain health, conquer disease, and delay death. The practice evolved over the millennia, eventually encompassing a diverse array of medicines and treatments, including acupuncture, tai chi, and massage, used by hundreds of millions of people today. It also led to the discovery of many mainstream pharmaceuticals used today, including artemisinin, a leading malaria treatment, and ephedrine, prescribed to relieve shortness of breath in asthma patients. Other herbs originally identified in its pharmacopeia are the subjects of ongoing clinical trials and evidence-based drug development.

Even as traditional Chinese medicine expanded and matured over the years, however, its underlying philosophy remained for the most part unchanged, stemming from the belief that the body contains a vital energy called *qi* (literally, "air, breath"). According to traditional practitioners, *qi* is our life force, powering our organs and bodily functions by circulating through channels called meridians. Traditional Chinese medicine seeks to maintain, balance, and restore *qi*.

Things get a bit more complex from there. As first described in *The Yellow Emperor's Classic of Medicine* dating from the Han dynasty (206 BCE–220 CE), the body is composed of yin and yang—opposite yet interdependent, complementary principles that govern the world. Examples include earth/heaven; cold/hot; male/female; winter/summer; and night/day. To prevent disease and ill health, yin and yang must be harmonized, and *qi* must be regulated. As Richard Ellis, author of *Tiger Bone and Rhino Horn,* put it, "Weak organs are strengthened, congested channels are opened, excess is dispersed, tightness is loosened, agitation is calmed, heat is cooled, cold is warmed, dryness is moistened and dampness is drained."

Figuring out how to achieve those effects depends on understanding the relationship between the so-called five elements that traditional Chinese medicine uses to categorize all things in nature—parts of the body included—as well as other components thought to factor into health, including the five spiritual resources, the five climates, the five viscera, and the five flavors. The solution to a patient's problem could be a matter of exercise or diet change, or it could entail pharmaceuticals thought to possess the deficiency in question. Rhino horn, for example, is considered to have a cooling effect, so it would traditionally (and illegally, today) be prescribed for cooling the blood or reducing fever.

Although traditional Chinese medicine and Western medicine are often presented as at odds with each other, they weren't always so different. Born in 460 BCE, Hippocrates asserted that disease was the result of an imbalance of four bodily humors, and medicine was the antidote to restore that balance. As in traditional Chinese medicine, Hippocrates's humors each had their own characteristics and were associated with specific seasons, ages, elements, organs, and temperaments.

These ideas persisted for centuries in Europe, until modern science began to emerge. Advances—including Antonie van Leeuwenhoek's 1683 discovery of microbes and Louis Pasteur's nineteenth-century refutation of spontaneous generation—paved the way for the germ theory of disease. Sickness was no longer considered the result of imbalances within body but of an attack waged by invisible invaders.

Even as these views swept through the West and some parts of Asia in the nineteenth and early twentieth centuries, many traditional doctors in China paid them little heed (exceptions existed, however: nineteenth-century Chinese medicine thoroughly assimilated the smallpox vaccine, for example). Germ theory wasn't the only medical oversight, however. A centuries-old Confucian taboo against violating the human body also stymied development of detailed anatomical knowledge.

By the turn of the century, the average Chinese citizen lived just thirty years, compared to forty-seven in the United States. As the health of China's citizens continued to fall behind other countries, some came to view traditional medicine as the cause. In 1879, Yu Yue, a prominent Qing dynasty scholar, published the first known call for an end to the practice. Yu's beliefs gained traction in the coming decades, especially among younger people, many of whom were educated in Japan. Enthusiasm for Western medicine increased even more after the Sino-Japanese War of 1895 and the Russo-Japanese War of 1905. Having seen how Japan's modernized methods of combat and its Western-style military medicine enabled it to become an international power, China was eager to follow suit. The young Mao Zedong also grew up during these tumultuous years, and, as a young man, he, too, firmly supported relegating traditional Chinese medicine to the past.

These sentiments had reached a fever pitch by the time the Nationalist Party took control of China in 1928. The country's new officials quickly voted to abolish traditional Chinese medicine in favor of a Western medical system. Traditional practitioners fought back, however. The formerly ragtag group mobilized under the banner of the National Medicine Movement, with a goal of integrating their practices into the modern state. They organized protests and fought government suppression, which included statewide bans on teaching traditional medicine or advertising for its services.

The conflict between the two medical camps was still raging when the Second Sino-Japanese War broke out in 1937, followed by civil war in 1946. Amid those distractions, support for traditional medicine quietly grew, especially in the countryside. When the Communists finally emerged victorious in 1949 and Mao assumed control, he found that he was forced to endorse traditional Chinese medicine. He wanted to win the support of the rural population, and there simply weren't enough Western-trained doctors or Western hospitals to meet the needs

of China's 500 million–plus people. Li Zhisui, Mao's personal physician, later re-
counted the chairman saying, "Even though I believe we should promote Chinese
medicine, I personally do not believe in it."

China's health care wouldn't be based solely on traditional medicine, however. Mao aimed to unify Chinese and Western health care under the banner of
"One Medicine." Traditional physicians were taught basic Western-style treatments, science-friendly terms such as "holism" and "preventative care" entered
the traditional lexicon, and traditional medicine's oftentimes contradictory and
idiosyncratic knowledge was condensed into standardized textbooks. New laws
also prevented self-trained or apprenticeship-trained physicians from providing
care, a rule that disproportionately impacted traditional practitioners, and a mandatory exam based on Western medical knowledge excluded still more. As a result, many traditional doctors gave up their professions.

It wasn't that traditional doctors were being singled out, however; medical
reform was a two-way street. As one 1960 slogan read, "Chinese medicine must
become scientific, Western medicine must become Chinese." To fulfill the latter
order, Western medicine practitioners were forced to study Chinese medicine in
reeducation programs, and Chinese medicine was integrated into the curriculum
at Western-leaning medical universities. Many Western-trained doctors were dis-
gruntled about the new system, but the most successful of those who embraced it
advanced to high positions in the Ministry of Health.

Everything changed, however, when the Cultural Revolution kicked into gear
in 1966. China's "lost decade" saw the gross simplification of the medical system. Certain renowned physicians became "forces of evil" who were tortured and
sometimes killed (or else committed suicide), while many others were banished
to the countryside to tend to workers and peasants. Other doctors, conversely—
especially traditional ones—were praised for their commitment to the indigenous
genius of the Chinese working people.

Two years after Mao's 1976 death, the state acknowledged that the chairman's experiment had failed. The following years brought a wave of reforms that
resumed efforts under way prior to the Cultural Revolution. As Volker Scheid
and Sean Hsiang-Lin Lei put it in *Medical Transitions in Twentieth-Century
China,* "In the long run, the Cultural Revolution merely interrupted the process
of expansion and modernization that had been set in motion during the previous
decade." At the end of the 1970s China opened its doors to the outside world, and
within a decade it transformed from a poor, backwater nation that imported and

exported few goods to "the factory of the world," as Howard French wrote in *China's Second Continent*. It remains one of the world's fastest-growing economies.

Health care has also developed significantly over the past decades. Today, many Chinese opt for a dual-care model, with traditional medicine used to maintain health and treat chronic disease and Western chosen for more acute illnesses. The latter makes up the majority of health care, but traditional medicine is seen as an integral piece of cultural identity—the "pride and prize of the nation," according to Shu-Feng Zhou of the University of Melbourne's Division of Chinese Medicine. It's also important from a financial perspective. In 2005, traditional medicine generated more than $10 billion for China's economy, accounting for a quarter of overall medical production value. Hoping to further bolster those numbers, the government has ramped up its financial support of the industry. In 2017, the Law on Traditional Chinese Medicine also went into effect, putting traditional medicine on par with Western medicine in terms of training, research, standards, and access.

Despite the ongoing intermingling, Western and traditional Chinese medicine remain quite distinct. "These are really two very different systems," said Lixin Huang, executive director of the American College of Traditional Medicine at the California Institute of Integral Studies. "One is looking at health from a purely scientific base, while the other comes from the theory of yin and yang, from how people live and what affects their lives. In Chinese medicine, you're not just another of the one hundred people treated that week with flu or diabetes. Doctors are really looking at you as an individual to know what brought you to that point, and, from there, they prescribe a very individualized treatment. So even if you are diagnosed with a certain disease, your treatment will differ from other patients with that same diagnosis."

Such treatments tend to be more popular in the Chinese countryside because they're more affordable, but traditional medicine also appeals to certain city dwellers as well. Famous traditional doctors have recently authored best-selling books and make regular media appearances, and their clientele consists of urban elites—the sort of Gwyneth Paltrow types of China—who seek to better their minds and bodies with the trendiest natural remedies.

Although most ingredients used in traditional Chinese medicine are plant based, they also extend to endangered and protected species. Around 1,500 animals are included in the traditional Chinese medicine pharmacopeia, and of the 112 most commonly used species, 22 percent are endangered, and 51 percent are headed in that direction, according to Zhibin Meng of the Institute of Zoology at the Chinese Academy of Sciences.

Some products derived from imperiled wildlife, including tiger bone, rhino horn, and deer musk, are banned in China, while others, such as pangolin scales and bear bile, are supposedly strictly regulated. Evidence indicates that the rules are often broken, however. "A certain small number of consumers continue to use endangered species, either out of ignorance or because they place no value on the environment," Huang said. "Some are stuck in old ideas, while others want to show off by giving their bosses expensive gifts. And some—the sellers—promote these things only for commercial gain."

Echoing Yu Yue's 1879 call for a ban on traditional Chinese medicine, some prominent scholars today point out that one way to solve the endangered species problem would be to simply abolish the practice altogether. Such a proposal is just as inflammatory now—perhaps even more so. At the heart of the contemporary controversy is Zhang Gong-Yao, a recently retired professor of history and philosophy of science at Central South University in Changsha, who published a 2006 article titled "Farewell to Chinese Medicine." His thesis: traditional medicine is an irrational, nostalgic pseudoscience that needs to be purged from the official health-care system. Later referred to as "the 'farewell' incident," Zhang's paper kicked off a heated debate that continues today.

I met Zhang in a hotel lobby in Changsha, where he explained his ideas over green tea. He was a slight, well-dressed figure, quick to smile, with expressive black eyebrows that shot up and down as he talked. "Traditional Chinese medicine is all about belief—blind belief," he began, pulling no punches. "It is a lie that has been fabricated with no scientific proof." The root of the problem, he explained, is that traditional medicine originated from "witchcraft," yet the practice has never modernized fully. Most prescriptions have either never been scientifically evaluated or else have failed to show any efficacy in scientific trials, he said. Take ginseng, for example. Although it's popularly referred to by traditional practitioners as the "king of tonics," research has shown ginseng to be neither medically valuable nor especially nutritional. If paired with certain diseases or symptoms, moreover—including high blood pressure, insomnia, colds, and allergies—ginseng can be harmful. For other prescriptions, the problems are more obvious: some traditional remedies call for lead, mercury, venomous centipedes, dirt, or dog poop, Zhang pointed out.

Zhang is also concerned about the harm traditional Chinese medicine inflicts on animals. As he wrote in his paper, practitioners erroneously chase after "strange and rare things"—monkey brain, tiger penis, and rhino horn, to name a few—to achieve "miraculous effects." The rarer the wildlife, he said, the severer the devastation. "The public needs to understand why Chinese medicine harms society by ruining the environment and using up precious species," he said. "It's a waste of resources, while gaining nothing for medical treatment."

Many are outraged by Zhang's claims. "I've been told that I'm betraying the nation," he said. "Someone on the Internet even threatened to kill me." The years following his article's publication also saw a flurry of more than two hundred papers and reports, plus countless media stories, criticizing him. As two scholars from Nanjing University of Traditional Chinese Medicine wrote in 2009, "The overwhelming response to Zhang's assertions suggest that his opinions fail to accord with educators, researchers, practitioners, government funding authorities and, critically, the consumers of [traditional Chinese medicine]—the general public."

Zhang wasn't surprised by any of this. "The Chinese lack the ability to look at this issue in an objective and scientific way," he said. "Those who disagree with my ideas do so from an emotional point of view." Contrary to what his critics suggested, there were also quite a few prominent Chinese who agreed with him, both publicly and privately.

Although the government never reached out to Zhang directly, the state did make its views known by suppressing his work. An online petition Zhang launched calling for the abolishment of traditional medicine was shut down after ten days, and a follow-up article and a book that he wrote on the subject were barred from publication. Rather than give up, though, he signed on with a South Korean publisher that translated and distributed his works there. In China, however, "I'm no longer allowed to publish articles that object to traditional Chinese medicine," he said.

JUST HOW EASY IS IT TO FIND BANNED MEDICINAL WILDLIFE PRODUCTS IN CHINA today? Zhang, for one, had insisted that, despite protections, endangered species parts remain "rampant" in traditional markets. I wanted to verify this claim for myself. I headed to Guangzhou, a Cantonese port city of more than 13 million people, located near Hong Kong and the Vietnamese border. A thoroughly modern metropolis, Guangzhou sports an impressive skyline, an excellent subway system, and bustling, tree-shaded boulevards. It's also a hub for both trafficking and consumption of illegal wildlife. As Lishu Li, WCS's wildlife trade program manager in China, succinctly put it, "In Guangzhou, the trade volume is high, and traditions are heavy and rich."

This isn't surprising, considering the city's history. It is and has been for centuries one of China's greatest trade centers. Guangzhou's international airport and seaport are among the busiest in the country. In addition to its commerce, Guangzhou's other standout feature is its cuisine. In China, everyone knows about the Cantonese obsession with good food. Southern appetites also extend to rare and exotic dishes, which are often simultaneously viewed as delicacies and remedies. As a famous Chinese saying goes, "Medicine and food are homologous."

With my destination determined, I decided to focus my hunt on pangolins. Why? I like them, for one, but, more importantly, they play a prominent role in traditional Chinese medicine. Nearly five hundred prescriptions call for their scales, skin, meat, and blood, and many of those remedies date back centuries. In the 1597 classic *Compendium of Materia Medica,* for example, Li Shih-chen wrote that pangolin scales can be used for treating nervousness and nocturnal fretfulness in children, paralysis of the hands and feet, insect bites and malaria, and devil and ogre possession. Although reports of ogre possession have subsided over the years, pangolins remain in demand for other uses, including curing anorexia, healing sores, clearing up skin infections, and improving blood circulation. Some practitioners claim that the scales increase men's sexual potency, while women consume them for regulating their periods, combatting infertility, promoting lactation, and even treating breast cancer.

Despite all this, there's scant evidence that pangolin scales—which, again, are mainly composed of keratin, the same protein found in hair and fingernails— have any medical value at all. Some peer-reviewed Chinese papers claim they do, but the evidence is weak, based on small sample sizes and lacking bias-eliminating measures such as control groups and double-blind trial designs. Another red flag: some of those papers reported an unbelievable 90–100 percent efficacy for treating cancer-related pain, fallopian tube obstruction, fingernail infections, and poor lactation. (Note that these problems aren't unique to pangolin scales: since the 1990s, outside researchers have pointed out that clinical trials of various traditional Chinese medicine remedies tend to be of poor quality. Likewise, a 2017 survey found that 40 percent of biomedical research conducted in China is tainted by some form of misconduct, and a *Quartz* analysis of data published on the website Retraction Watch revealed that China-based researchers publish more papers that are retracted for fake peer reviews than all other countries combined.)

Nevertheless, many laypeople continue to buy into erroneous beliefs. A 2015 phone survey of more than 1,000 people in Hong Kong, for example, found that just 15 percent thought that pangolin scales have no medical use.

Pangolins have been on the protected species list in China since 1989, meaning consumption of their meat is forbidden. CITES (the Convention on International Trade in Endangered Species of Wild Fauna and Flora), the treaty that regulates international trade of species, also bans commercial pangolin trade across national borders. Perplexingly, though, not all domestic trade of pangolins in China is illegal: the government still allows some legal sale of the animals' scales. According to regulations issued in 2007, certain clinics and hospitals may sell scales supplied to them by licensed dealers. The list of approved sellers includes 716 locations all over the country—nearly every traditional medicine hospital in China—and scale quotas issued by the State Forestry Administration are staggering. From 2008 to 2015, they totaled 186 tons, the equivalent of about 55,000 pangolins killed per year. To add further confusion and opportunity for shady trade, the government regulates only raw scales—not ones that have been processed into powder or drugs. As a result, more than two hundred pharmaceutical companies in China legally manufacture sixty-six different products containing pangolin.

That's about the extent of what we know about the legal trade. The government will not say how many tons of scales the country has stockpiled, how it manages the stockpiles, or what's going to happen after existing stockpiles run out, because import from abroad is illegal and China's pangolins are strictly protected from hunting—not to mention almost gone. Authorities also do not make clear where existing stockpiles originate. At least some scales were acquired from legal auctions the government previously held for pangolins seized from the illegal trade, and an additional fifteen tons or so came from previously legal imports, at first largely from Malaysia and later mostly from Uganda and Congo. Smuggling and laundering likely account for much of the rest of the existing stockpiles.

Regardless of where the scales came from, that legal trade of pangolins exists at all is extremely questionable. As Li pointed out, because pangolin hunting and meat consumption are already illegal in China, there should be zero use of those animals—scales included. Trade continues, however, because the traditional Chinese medicine business is both strong and pigheaded, she said. "There are substitutes for pangolin scales, but the [dealers] still stupidly, selfishly, and shortsightedly think the genuine thing is the best," she said. "They still try to promote these endangered species products, even though there's no future for this industry because the scales are not going to last forever."

But until either the government steps up, stockpiles run out, or species go extinct, sales—both legal and illegal—carry on. A team of TRAFFIC investigators who visited several hundred traditional medicine shops in nineteen Chinese cities found that although the number of vendors offering illegal pangolin scales for sale has decreased from 80 percent in 2007 to 60 percent in 2016, they are still readily available. Additionally, the percent of wholesale merchants illegally selling scales actually increased over that period, from 12 to 35 percent. A quick look online, the researchers reported, also revealed advertisements for illegal pangolin scales, meat, or live animals on six of 39 surveyed ecommerce sites.

That's not to say that China hasn't been cracking down somewhat on its pangolin problem. Authorities there have even issued suspended death sentences and life sentences for pangolin smuggling. Yet, despite the risks for criminals, as the TRAFFIC report and others have shown, the situation on the ground is far from watertight. "While certified scales can be sold legally in China, they can still be found for sale illegally all over the place—and they shouldn't be," said Dan Challender, chair of the IUCN's Pangolin Specialist Group. "China's got some pretty strong legislation, but the regulations just aren't enforced adequately."

Paired with ongoing demand, it's precisely this lack of enforcement that has nearly driven China's own pangolins to extinction, said Shibao Wu, a zoologist at South China Normal University in Guangzhou. "The day is coming," he said, "when there will be no more pangolin scales available, either from stockpiles or from the wild."

MY CAB DRIVER KNEW EXACTLY WHERE I WANTED TO GO WHEN I OPENED MY reporter's notebook and showed him the characters for Qingping Market, Guangzhou's traditional medicine wholesale epicenter. Below the address I'd also gotten someone to write down the characters for "pangolin scales"—a flimsy attempt to try to offset the fact that I speak zero Chinese (I had originally hoped to bring along a local expert from the Wildlife Conservation Society, but a scheduling mix-up left me on my own for the afternoon). I had no idea what, if anything, I'd find.

I stepped out of the cab and was immediately hit by the unmistakable perfume of traditional Chinese medicine. Whiffs of fragrant wood, pungent dried sea creatures, earthy mushrooms, and spicy herbs blended into an olfactory orchestra. Visually, the scene was dominated by Qingping Market proper, whose five stories towered overhead and occupied most of the block. Like moths drawn to the light, clustered around that wholesale beacon were all manner of small-fry traditional medicine peddlers; some manned shops the size of a modest living room, others displayed their wares in a space no larger than a closet.

Some of the stalls sold live (or very recently live) animals. A man hunched over a writhing tub of pinky-sized scorpions, picking out dead ones with chopsticks. A woman next door used a pair of scissors to dismember a brown-gray turtle—its head thankfully already severed. Mostly, though, the plants and animals for sale here seemed to have been dead for quite some time. Almost all of those dried specimens subscribed to a 1970s color scheme of brown, beige, orange, and yellow: chocolate-colored ears of fungus as big as frisbees, sea cucumbers that looked like petrified pickles, fish swim bladders resembling giant used condoms, dehydrated frogs with legs bound like amphibian prisoners of war, dried abalone that looked unsettlingly vaginal, and caterpillars with a single stalk of black parasitic fungus erupting from their shriveled heads. The identity of most of the shops' contents completely escaped me, however. There were twigs, sticks, and roots of all sizes, chartreuse curlicues that looked like tiny spools of yarn, poofy balls that resembled old cream puffs, and much more.

I really had no idea what I was doing, so I decided to just pop into the nearest store and ask whether they had pangolin scales. Feeling a bit like a first-time drug user walking into a glass pipe shop and asking the cashier for crack, I strolled in with a smile. The owner, a younger woman, greeted me in English, which I took as a good sign. But when I handed the paper with "pangolin scales" written in big characters, her face fell. "No, no!" she said.

"Around here?" I asked.

"No—this is illegal!" she insisted, shaking her head. "We cannot sell anymore."

"But I heard there are special places where you can still buy this legally?"

"Not this area. There is no permits here." With a firm shake of her head, she ended the conversation.

A few doors down, an older woman saw me and held up some dried goji berries. She quickly realized it wasn't goji berries I was after, however, when I pointed at the characters in my notebook.

"Oh—no, no, no, no, no, no, no, no!" she cried, shaking her head and waving her arms back and forth emphatically. She paused for a breath, and then added another string of "No, no, no, no, no, no, no!" to clarify.

Given the reactions I'd gotten so far, I thought this wasn't going anywhere. Yet I reminded myself that I'd come all this way to see traditional Chinese medicine. I should at least pop into the main market before calling it quits.

Qingping's five floors were linked by creaky escalators (some of which did not work) and a grimy glass elevator situated in the center of the sprawling complex. Each floor was packed, wall to wall, with vendors displaying their goods in overflowing bags, heaping piles, and stuffed jars. Some shopkeepers sat at desks in the back, scrolling through their phones or eating lunch. Others were busy preparing and packaging their merchandise for shipment, while still others were occupied with meticulously picking imperfections off bits of wood or sorting caterpillars into little bundles of ten or so, held together by bits of twine tied around their parasital head stalks.

Most shops, I noticed, dealt in just one or two products, and like seemed to attract like, with similarly themed stalls grouped together on the same floor. The sheer scale was overwhelming. One floor, for example, was almost entirely dedicated to deer antlers. There were jars and buckets of antlers sliced into communion-like wafers; antler chandeliers hanging from the ceiling like a Texan's dream den; buckets of black deer hooves still attached to long yellow leg bones; and taxidermied Bambis with red bows tied around their dead little necks. The fungus section, likewise, seemed to take pride in elaborate, collage-like displays of their mushrooms and lichens, while shops on the birds' nest floor went in the opposite direction: they were shinier, fancier, and more sparsely filled, like expensive clothing stores that contain just a couple of racks.

I headed upstairs to the seahorse section, where the air smelled of salt and fishy demise. Seahorses gazed at me from dried, unseeing eye sockets, their snout-like mouths frozen in a macabre O! of surprise. These dainty fish are one of the most heavily traded marine animals in the world, with more than 5 million individuals caught in Southeast Asia alone to enter the legal international trade each year. Some of the most heavily fished species are classified as threatened with extinction, but the seahorse trade, like everything else I'd seen in this market, is legal. By now I had checked all five floors, keeping a careful lookout for images of pangolins, stuffed pangolins, the Chinese characters for pangolins or pangolin parts—anything to hint that a business might be engaged in the black market—but I hadn't seen so much as a single scale. I headed downstairs, congratulating China on a job well done.

As it turned out, though, I just hadn't been asking the right people: I had foolishly approached the medicine sellers, when in fact I should have asked the pearl dealers. The glowing beads, displayed at a single stand near Qingping's entrance, were unexpected and out of place here. A bit dazzled, I decided to stop and buy early Christmas presents for my sister and mom.

The shop was run by a couple of cutely outfitted young women, both wearing pearls, sweater dresses, and baby doll flats. The younger shopkeeper spoke a bit of English, and the two were tough negotiators. In the end, we settled on a price that was much more than I had hoped to pay—about $300 for three strings—but I figured, what the heck, I'll splurge. The only problem was I didn't have enough cash, and my credit cards weren't working on their machine. The younger woman offered to chaperone me upstairs, to the market's sole ATM.

In the awkward silence of the glacial elevator ride back down, I happened to remember the paper I had in my purse that said "pangolin scales." I figured it couldn't hurt to ask her about it. She looked at the paper, then back up at me, then back down at the paper.

"You want this?" she said at last, her words slow and uncertain.

"Yes."

"No . . . not here . . . " Her voice trailed off. It seemed like she wanted to say more, but she let it drop. I figured she was simply at a loss for the word "illegal."

When we returned to the pearl counter, however, she said something to the other woman, who shot me a dubious look, as though to say, *"Her?"* Then the older woman took out her phone and turned her back toward us, facing the wall. She made a call and began speaking in a hushed voice. Intuitively, I felt that they were talking about me, but I had no idea, so I just smiled inanely and counted out the money I owed them.

Transaction complete, the younger woman was packaging up the necklaces into individually wrapped velvet bags when the older one turned back around, lowered the phone, and said something to her coworker. The younger woman looked up at me with a pleased smile: "Yes, we have!"

"You have . . . ?" I wasn't entirely sure what she was talking about, though I had a suspicion.

"Have those things!" she said, pointing at the notebook sticking out of my purse. She handed me the pearls, then practically took my hand. "I bring you."

We left the market, and she told me in broken English that the other woman was her sister. We were going to see her sister's boyfriend, who sells pangolin scales. We took a right, and then another right, each turn taking us down increasingly narrow side streets. Although still dedicated entirely to traditional medicine, the shops here were less professional looking—more haphazardly arranged, more tatty. Finally, we stopped at a place in a covered alley. Someone was playing Chinese music nearby, and kids scampered around between stalls.

The shop we'd arrived at looked like any of the other dozens of shops, albeit weirdly empty, almost as if it were serving as a front for some other business. Its sparse display included some cobras in a jar with yellow liquid, large pieces of fungus, and a few boxes of tea. A man sat on the floor, sorting through some kind of wood or mushrooms. On the walk over, I had discreetly turned on a voice recorder app I have on my phone, and after I returned to New York, I had the conversation between my pearl-selling hostess and the shopkeeper translated.

"What can I help you with?" he asked in Cantonese.

"She wants pangolin," the pearl lady said.

"We don't have this kind of thing."

"Mr. Hua just said you have it. And that he went to get it."

"Oh, Mr. Hua said it!" My translator in New York noted that the man's voice sounded suspicious at first, but that he relaxed as soon as Hua's name was dropped.

I wasn't privy to any of this at the time, however. Taking a seat on a tiny stool, I asked the pearl lady whether the man on the floor was her sister's boyfriend. She shook her head and then took out her phone and opened a translator app, typing on it with turquoise-painted nails. A mechanical female voice on high volume announced the translation of her words out loud: "Wait a minute. Someone is going to get the goods."

I suppressed a grin at the absurd turn this afternoon had taken. We sat around for a while, making small talk with the translator app. I decided to throw my younger sister under the bus, telling the pearl lady that the pangolin scales were for her, because she couldn't produce milk. "My sister, she has problems!" I said, pointing at my own boobs.

"Ah!" My host turned back to her phone for help. "This is very precious medical material in our country. A lot of people use it," the robot voice explained. "But not in the US."

"Have you tried it?" I asked her.

"No, no!" she said in her own voice, giggling. "Too young!" As it turned out, she was just twenty-one.

"I'm thirty-one," I lamented. "So old!"

Fifteen minutes or so later, a young man appeared at the opposite end of the alley, clutching a black plastic bag in a self-conscious way that made me strongly suspect this was our guy. He looked to be in his early twenties, was chubby and wore jeans and a nondescript blue sweater.

"My sister's boyfriend," my hostess confirmed.

He came up to us and quickly opened and closed the bag for me to see, like a flasher on the subway. Inside were pangolin scales—a lot of them! They were shaped like little fans or seashells, and they had the muddled brown and beige coloration of a turtle shell. He put the bag on a scale to show me that it weighed five hundred grams, or just over one pound. He was asking $300 for the whole lot.

I did my best to conceal my surprise and nervousness. I wanted to ask a few questions, but not so many as to give myself away as a journalist spy. "How do you use it?" seemed like a good enough starting point.

"You need to stir fry it and then grind it into powder," the boyfriend answered confidently, speaking through the pearl lady. "It doesn't need to be refrigerated, but store it dry."

"This isn't powder, though," I pointed out, playing the part of the discerning customer. "How do you make it into powder?"

He said he had the equipment and he could process it himself. This was a full-service operation, apparently.

"How much do you want?" he asked.

Q&A time, it seemed, was over. Thinking fast, I brought up the sister thing again. I needed to find out how much my sister wanted, I explained, but in the United States, it was now the middle of the night. I'd have to wait and call her this evening—her morning—to confirm what she wanted. "In fact," I added, "it would be really helpful if I could take a photo to show her."

The young woman translated, and the man seemed perfectly satisfied with this explanation. "Okay, okay," he said, opening the bag, allowing me to snap a photo of its illicit contents with my phone. I asked for his business card, which he happily handed over, and I shook his limp hand goodbye. After we parted ways, I quickly caught a cab out of there. Though I had never sensed danger, I couldn't help but look back over my shoulder a few times.

I HAD FOUND SOMEONE WILLING TO SELL ILLEGAL TRADITIONAL MEDICINE PRODucts, but now I needed to explore the other side of that story: the people willing to buy and use them. I wanted to know why they believed it was worth breaking the law and what, if anything, might convince them to stop.

Finding such a person was easier said than done. I went about my search in a very unscientific way, by simply asking everyone I interviewed if they could introduce me to a medicinal wildlife user, either in China or Vietnam (Vietnam's rich traditional medicine culture was heavily borrowed from its northern neighbor, though with a stronger reliance on strictly local ingredients). Conservationists all declined my request, however, saying they were either too busy to help, didn't know anyone who fit the bill, or had to protect the privacy of the people they had interviewed for their studies. Journalists I reached out to who had quoted such sources in the past were equally unhelpful.

I'd all but given up when an acquaintance from Ho Chi Minh City texted me, saying his girlfriend's aunt in Hanoi was a longtime rhino horn, tiger bone, and bear bile user and that she would be happy to chat, so long as I did not publish her name. "Her aunt gave me bear bile last year to put on my foot when I injured a nerve in a motorbike accident and lost feeling in it for three months," he said. "This was her solution to the problem. Out of curiosity, I let her try it once, but I very much doubt that it had any effect." He added that, "interestingly," his girlfriend also just confessed to him that she had used rhino horn in high school to clear up her acne, of all things. With that, he sent me a phone number and a Google Maps link. His girlfriend's aunt—Ms. M, as I'll call her—would be expecting me on Saturday morning.

MOST VISITORS TO HANOI, VIETNAM'S HISTORY-FILLED YET VIBRANT CAPITAL OF 7.5 million, stick to the Old Quarter. With its faded yellow villas, unruly banyan trees, and conical-hat-wearing corner vendors hawking everything from baguettes to bananas to *bún,* it's no doubt the urban Vietnam of many tourists' imagination.

But Ms. M, like many residents, lived well outside that foreigner-friendly core, southwest about half an hour by car. Accompanied by my Hanoi-based translator, Mai Thị Hồng Tâm, our Uber wound through the smoggy capital's dense traffic of motorbikes, bicycles, and cars. We passed blocks and blocks of clothing shops, restaurants, and bars; crept over concrete canals of putrid black water; and zipped under the construction of a long-delayed elevated train system. Finally, we arrived at a small, grassy suburban park surrounded by gated homes. A slender young man standing in front of one them waved.

Mr. M, as I'll call him, introduced himself as Ms. M's son. A cute, clean-cut architect with earnest eyes, he wore Harry Potter glasses and a blue plaid shirt tucked into black jeans. Although thirty years old, he looked at least five years younger. He told us Ms. M wouldn't be able to meet me, after all. Despite the wildlife elixirs she uses, it seemed she wasn't feeling well.

I sighed, assuming the trip was for naught, but Mr. M quickly dispelled my disappointment. He uses all his mom's wildlife medicine, too, he said, and he'd be happy to chat. He led us inside and seated us at an ornately carved Chinese-style wooden table in the living room. Although not wildly posh, judging by the look of things, Mr. M's family appeared to be doing quite well. The space was decorated with a huge grandfather clock, a large mirror, walls full of art, and big ceramic vases stuffed with fresh flowers (tomorrow was Teacher's Day, a popular holiday in Vietnam, and Mr. M's father, a teacher, had received the bouquets from current and former students). A small black-and-white cat darted around the room, batting at the fresh blossoms.

Mr. M emerged from the back carrying a tray with a teapot and several small cups. I had wondered how I would get traditional medicine users to open up about their dabblings in illegal pharmaceuticals, but Mr. M seemed completely relaxed about discussing this with two complete strangers. The fact that I knew his cousin's boyfriend, it seemed, was enough to earn his trust. Or maybe he just didn't think it was a big deal.

We started with bear bile, a product that has been banned in Vietnam since 2005. "Yes, we use it, both me and my mom," Mr. M said. According to the family traditional medicine doctor, bear bile aids digestion, improves functioning of the liver and kidney, and is good for the heart. Mr. M takes it as needed—when he's feeling tired or run down, for example—by mixing a pinch of dried bile with water before bed. Mostly, the bile comes from Vietnamese bears, he said, and the price is broken into categories according to the bear's age and whether it was farmed or wild. Wild adult bears are the most expensive because they're the rarest, Mr. M said, but he usually has to settle for bile from farmed adult bears, which costs about fifty dollars a gram. "You have to make sure you get it from a place with a good reputation, because fake bear bile can cause side effects," he said. "We always get it from the same place because it's guaranteed to be safe and real."

Mr. M didn't have any bear bile on him—the family orders it only when they need it—but he did have something else he could show me. He went to the back again and came back with a clear plastic bag containing about half a cup of chunky stuff that looked like butterscotch. I tentatively took out a piece. It was sticky and smelled vaguely rotten, like the lingering stench left by a bag of overdue garbage just removed from the kitchen.

"This is solid *cao*," Mr. M said. "It comes from all rare animals: chimpanzees, tigers, bears, deer—many animals." Attesting to this, a little piece of paper in the bag read *Hổ* (Tiger).

Also called tiger bone paste or tiger glue, *cao* is made by boiling down tiger bones until they turn to putty. The maker may also throw in monkey parts, turtle shells, water buffalo horns, or pretty much any other random wildlife ingredients. As tigers have grown scarce, imported bones from South African lions killed in game hunts are becoming a popular substitute. From 2010 to 2014, South Africa reported legally exporting around 3,000 complete lion skeletons plus thousands of individual bones to Vietnam and Laos. The numbers are likely underestimates, however, considering that in 2013 alone Thailand, for example, reported importing 2,910 lion skeletons from South Africa, while South Africa claimed to have only exported 14 skeletons to Thailand.

Whether made from tiger or lion bones, the dark brown goop that results is sold like bars of chocolate in hotels and restaurants throughout Vietnam, marketed for around $1,000 per one hundred grams. The steep price tag stems from *cao*'s purported usefulness as a sort of magical cure-all for a range of ailments and as a general health booster. Mr. M, for example, said he and his family take it because it's good for the blood and brain. Men also use it as a contraband Viagra. (If Mr. M uses *cao* for sexual purposes, he preferred not to tell me.) A less shy user boasted to investigative journalist and filmmaker Karl Ammann, however, "I can make love forty to forty-five times per month without feeling exhausted." Another told Ammann that he gained "superpowers" in bed after taking *cao*.

I asked Mr. M whether all this stuff—the *cao*, the bear bile, the sea turtles he also mentioned to me—is legal. "Some if it is, some of it isn't," he shrugged.

"It's difficult to identify what is legal or not. We're not afraid of getting busted, though. By the time we get it, our doctor has taken care of everything." That smooth operator, he added, has been the family's go-to physician for twenty years. "He's the best," Mr. M said. "When he suggests that we should use something for our health, then we use it." Western medicine, he added, is the family's second choice—something they turn to only when traditional options are lacking.

Mr. M was clearly an educated guy, so I asked whether it bothered him at all to know that some of these animals he's consuming are disappearing. He smiled and looked down, perhaps a bit exasperated with me for bringing up something so silly. "If the animals go away, then actually we can use Vietnam's many traditional medicine plants instead," he said. Apparently, he had misunderstood my question to mean, "Will the inconvenience bother you?"

Rather than start lecturing him about the intrinsic value of biodiversity, though, I was more interested now to know then, why he doesn't just use those many traditional medicine plants, rather than pricey and exceedingly difficult to find wildlife?

"Based on the principles provided by our family doctor, you should always use things that are more effective," he explained. "Everything that is prescribed by our family doctor is the most effective."

"So you just do what your doctor tells you to do?" I asked.

"Yes."

"So if your doctor prescribed a herb instead of an animal, you'd use that?"

"Yes. There's lots of substitutes, so it's not necessary to use medicines from rare animals. But I trust my doctor. If herbal plants were more effective, then he would prescribe them."

There's often talk among conservationists about the younger generation coming to reject illegal wildlife use and moving on from the superstitions of their parents and grandparents. In Mr. M, however, I saw none of that. Meeting this well-educated young man—who later told me he enjoys yoga and reading in his spare time, and who considerately escorted me to catch a cab—made me feel all the more disheartened at the prospects of stemming demand for wildlife in a timely fashion. Though obviously intelligent, to Mr. M, his doctor's word was the law. He obeyed it without question.

Madelon Willemsen, former country director for TRAFFIC Vietnam, later explained this hierarchical, Confucian aspect of Vietnamese culture. "It's very much, if your elder tells you that you need to do something, you assume it's the best thing and you do it," she said. "If your mom says, 'I raised you on pangolin scales for lactation,' then you do it, too. Or if your doctor says, 'You really should take some tiger bone or rhino horn,' then you do that, too."

I brought up rhino horn with Mr. M as well. He said he has only tasted it, but others in his family use it for curing food poisoning or treating skin diseases. "There's five species of rhinos, and their horns are all different," he said. "The price is very high right now. If you buy a rhino horn, it's about $45,500 per pound."

"Wow, your family must be rich!" I said.

Mr. M smiled bashfully but did not deny it.

"Maybe, yes," Tâm, my translator, interjected, speaking for him. He nodded.

"We have to order rhino horn a year in advance if we want to buy it," he continued. "The supply is completely secret, and it's all coordinated by our doctor. He tests it to make sure it's real. A lot of it is fake buffalo horn, but he ensures what he gives us is genuine. Then he sends someone here to bring it to us."

"Do you have rhino horn now?" I asked.

"It's very protected," he said. "We have just one small, tea-cup-sized piece of solid horn. We have a machine to grind it, like rice. But it's all put away, so I can't show you."

"Maybe you're just trying to brag," I teased, trying to goad him into taking the rhino horn out. "How will I know you're telling the truth if you don't show me?"

Mr. M wasn't falling for it: "If you want to know what it looks like, you can just Google it."

As I soon learned, though, not everyone is as shy about showing off their horn.

Three

RHINO HORN IN THE COOKIE TIN

Multitudes of species are used in traditional medicine, but in terms of pharmaceutically caused crises, one group of animals stands above them all: rhinos. Their horns have been used as antidotes and health tonics for millennia, but, thanks to skyrocketing demand, extinction now looms for all five remaining rhino species. The demand for rhino horn has evolved well beyond traditional medicine, to the point that many experts consider these new threats to be the primary drivers of rhino poaching today.

In Vietnam, where the problem is so far most acute, rhino horn has morphed into a status symbol, hangover remedy, and miracle cancer cure, while China—whose market for rhino horn seems to be quickly growing to rival that of Vietnam—treats rhino horn carvings, jewelry, and whole specimens as smart investments. Whether in the form of medicinal powder or ornately carved goblets, though, prices can be exorbitant: on average, $15,000 per pound wholesale as of 2015, although on occasion reaching up to $45,450 per pound.

Escalating demand in Asia is reflected in poaching trends in Africa. After being hammered by bullets and machetes in the 1970s and 1980s, rhinos enjoyed a brief period of respite and population growth: in 2006, just 60 white and black rhinos were poached for their horns in Africa. But 2015 saw them plunge again into disaster mode: 1,342 were killed—a significant number considering there are only around 30,000 rhinos left globally. More than 1,000 rhinos have been killed in South Africa alone each year since then. There is also a human toll: hundreds of rangers and illegal hunters have been killed in Africa's "poaching wars," as some have taken to describing the situation there.

Before delving into those dire struggles on the ground, I wanted to first understand the people ultimately responsible for the killing: the consumers. Why do they think this substance—which, like pangolin scales, is little different from fingernails or hair—is worth five figures? Why are they so willing to break the law to get their hands on it? The epicenter of rhino horn demand, Vietnam, was the obvious destination for seeking out those answers.

RHINO HORN EVOLVED ALONGSIDE OTHER TRADITIONAL MEDICINES IN CHINA, YET it has always been seen as something extra special, something exotic and even semi-magical. Oddly enough, a millennia-old mix-up with unicorns, of all things, is likely to blame. These mythic creatures first turned up in Chinese texts in 2697 BCE, centuries before their Western debut in ancient Greek records. Scholars are uncertain whether the West inherited the unicorn myth from the East or whether both cultures developed the story independently, sparked by a common catalyst: fossils of *Elasmotherium* (a.k.a. the giant rhinoceros of Siberia). That twenty-foot-tall, four-ton behemoth ranged across Eurasia as recently as 29,000 years ago, and its remains are notable for the massive, unicorn-like horn that sprouted from the center of its forehead. As Jeannie Thomas Parker of the Royal Ontario Museum hypothesized in *The Mythic Chinese Unicorn,* unicorns may be the result of ancient folklore passed down through the ages about this beast. Or the stories could have originated when astounded discoverers sought to explain *Elasmotherium* fossils.

Rhinos look a bit like awkward, oversized unicorns, and, indeed, they have been conflated with those mythic creatures throughout the ages. With their upward-facing horns, the Chinese considered them sacred—providing direct access to heaven—while the horns themselves were believed to be imbued with healing powers. A fourth-century CE Chinese text describes rhino horn as useful for treating snakebites, hallucinations, typhoid fever, food poisoning, and more, while "unicorn horn" (likely also rhino horn) was said to detect the presence of poison. As such, emperors often received gorgeously carved rhino horn goblets— gifts that were meant to both impress and to defend against assassination by tainted beverages. (There could actually be something to this: some experts have postulated that alkaloids found in certain poisons may react with the keratin and gelatin in rhino horn to produce a bubbling effect. But scientific trials have not tested this.)

Given all these purported properties, rhino horn became one of the most precious and pricey materials in traditional Chinese medicine. The unicorn myth also eventually cast its spell on the West, including for its use to detect and counteract poisons. But like a round of the "telephone game" gone terribly awry, the Europeans added an additional layer of confusion: they mistook narwhal tusks for unicorn horns. Sometimes referred to as "the unicorns of the sea," these small whales possess a single helix-spiraling tooth that protrudes from their upper jaw like a long horn.

Europeans who managed to get their hands on these teeth used their imaginations to fill in the unicorn blank, dreaming up an elegant, lanky white animal to match the elegant, lanky white "horn" in their hands (commonly called an alicorn). Take a look at unicorn-themed Middle Age tapestries or paintings, and you'll recognize the narwhal tusk sitting atop the magical horse's head. Until the late eighteenth century, in addition to appearing in art, both narwhal tusks and rhino horns were used in Europe—including by the French royal court—to test for poison, treat fevers, heal dog bites and insect stings, and recover from strokes. Surprisingly, consumers in both the East and West accepted that these two very different objects came from the same animal.

Historically and today, people's lust for rhino horn has also extended beyond medicine. When carved, the previously dull, rough material becomes gorgeously dappled in various shades of jet black, chestnut brown, and muddled amber, and, when held to the light, it emits an otherworldly golden glow. Between 1849 and 1895, 170,000 rhinos were killed for their horns, and although some went to China for medicine, many wound up in Britain as kitschy carvings, cane handles, doorknobs, and other junk. As rhino experts Esmond Bradley Martin and Chryssee Martin wrote in *Run, Rhino, Run,* "A dandy with something made from rhino horn could almost certainly count on attracting the attention of his peers."

The various wars and depressions of the early and mid-twentieth century brought a lull in rhino horn trade, but, in the 1960s, the market reawakened. At first, the killings resumed primarily to satiate demand from traditional medicine practitioners in China and Hong Kong but later to fulfill desire for rhino horn in Yemen. People there believed that rhino horn neutralizes snake venom and other toxins, but, more importantly, they used it to make hilts for *jambiyas,* or traditional daggers. In the 1970s and 1980s, up to 90 percent of Yemeni men—in a not-so-subtle display of masculinity—wore a *jambiya* on their belts. Fine crafts-manship and superior materials were important markers of status, and rhino horn was considered unparalleled.

Prior to 1970, rhino horn was a luxury that most Yemeni men were too poor to afford. But when civil war ended in 1969, many Yemenis found work in the booming oil industry, which had just taken off thanks to the recently formed Organization of the Petroleum Exporting Countries. Although Yemen was not an OPEC member, its citizens found ample work at oil fields in Saudi Arabia and beyond, increasing the per capita income sevenfold. Suddenly, everyone and his brother wanted a high-class *jambiya,* and rhino horn increased in price by a factor of twenty. Poachers responded with shocking enthusiasm. In 1970, some 65,000 black rhinos—the Yemenis' preferred species—lived throughout Africa, but by 1987 just 3,800 were left, despite an international trade ban that went into effect in 1977.

As demand surged in Yemen, China and other Asian countries kept their hands in the game, accounting for about 60 percent of total rhino horn ex-ported from Africa. What the Yemenis didn't use for dagger handles—the loose bits that had been carved away and even the dust left over from sanding and polishing—also went East. As author Richard Ellis put it, "Nothing is wasted in this process—except, of course, the rhino." Martin and his research partner, Lucy Vigne, estimated that 60 percent of each horn turned into a *jambiya* ultimately wound up in Asia.

Although customarily prescribed as a cooling agent, one thing that rhino horn was never traditionally used for in China was sex. This runs counter to a colorful urban legend that has been propagated for decades by naive Westerners. Based on extensive research, Martin believes the myth got going around 1870, when white traders in Zanzibar came into contact with Gujarati merchants from India who, unlike the Chinese, actually *did* use rhino horn as an aphrodisiac, by mixing powdered horn with water and applying it to their penises before sex. The factually flaccid mix-up has been repeated ever since.

Myths aside, no compelling evidence supports even rhino horn's actual tradi-tional uses. Little research has been conducted on the material's efficacy, but two animal studies in the UK and South Africa found no pharmacological effects. The lackluster results aren't surprising, because rhino horn is basically equiva-lent to a big mass of hair. In contrast to the Western research, however, six out of seven studies conducted in China claimed that rhino horn did effectively reduce fever in lab animals. To arrive at these results, notably, one of the research teams had to administer rhino horn to rats at doses more than one hundred times greater than the scaled equivalent normally taken by people.

Among the peer-reviewed literature is just one human study, a 1993 double-blind trial conducted with 142 children in Taiwan. All had fevers and were treated with either rhino horn, buffalo horn, acetaminophen (generic for Tylenol), or a placebo. Although the rhino horn did cause a statistically significant reduction in the children's fevers after fifteen minutes, the improvements stopped short of a full degree Fahrenheit. The acetaminophen, by contrast, dropped their temperatures by nearly two degrees. "Since the rhino is going to extinction and antipyretic efficacy of rhino horn is less effective than acetaminophen, rhino horn is NOT recommended," the authors concluded.

Western science–based findings tend to do little to shake true believers' faith in traditional medicine, however. "Belief in traditional medicine is so ingrained in some parts of the world that it is almost religious in nature," wrote John Sellar in *The U.N.'s Lone Ranger.* To tell a rhino horn user otherwise would be like "telling an evangelist that there is no scientific evidence to demonstrate the existence of God."

Therefore, when rhino poaching came to a near halt in the 1990s, it wasn't due to science-based demand reduction but to strengthened laws in Asia and changing tides in Yemen. Taiwan—the world's largest rhino horn market at the time—banned the trade in 1992 after US president Bill Clinton threatened sanctions if they didn't clean up their act, and China followed suit a year later. Yemeni culture, meanwhile, had begun shifting toward Western fashion preferences (at least for men), and the country had also suffered plunging incomes due to civil strife and loss of work abroad. Even if some men were still interested in rhino horn *jambiyas,* many could no longer afford it.

As poaching subsided, rhino populations began to rebound, and conservationists breathed a sigh of relief. The threat, they assumed, had passed. But as Ronald Orenstein wrote in *Ivory, Horn and Blood,* "It was the eye of the storm."

No one knows exactly what triggered the new wave of killing. Most likely, it was a confluence of multiple factors. But what is clear is that rhinos are again in crisis mode, thanks to rising demand and escalating prices for their horns. About 1,300 of them—around 5 percent of Africa's total population—are killed every year. The preponderance of deaths occurs in South Africa, however, which houses around 70 percent of the world's remaining rhinos. "Three rhinos will be killed in South Africa today for their horn, simply because the trade has come into vogue in Vietnam," said Crawford Allan, senior director of TRAFFIC.

If poaching trends continue, losses will likely exceed births soon. Some impacts are already irreversible, however—or will probably be in the near future. In 2011, the western black rhino, a subspecies of the black rhino, was declared extinct, and only two northern white rhinos remain alive today. In Asia, the Javan and Sumatran rhinos are two of the most endangered species on earth, with respectively sixty and one hundred remaining individuals, thanks to both habitat loss and poaching.

The rising body counts correspond with a rhino horn renaissance—as status symbol, objet d'art, and consumable—currently taking place in the East. In China, the number of rhino horns and carvings sold at auctions from 2010 to 2011 alone increased by 90 percent and collectively totaled $179 million. Chinese bidders—sometimes working through proxies by phone—also began snatching up rhino horn from Western auction houses, with a single rhino horn libation cup selling to a Chinese buyer in the United States for $900,000 in 2010, for example. Although the auctions have since been shut down, demand hasn't dropped.

Vietnam, however, remains the number one destination for rhino horn. Rhino horn's popularity there coincided with some peculiar new trends that break from tradition, including its use as a treatment for cancer. This is not the first time that too-good-to-be-true medical claims have been made about the material. In 1986, rumors flew that rhino horn could treat AIDS, and in 2009 some purported that it cured SARS. Many believe that horn hawkers themselves spread such stories to increase sales—an example of "organized crime preying upon people when they were at their weakest, both physically and mentally, in the most cruel and exploitative manner," as Sellar wrote.

No one knows how the cancer rumor got started, as patient zero (or media story zero) behind it has never been identified. But, regardless of its origin, rhino-horn-as-cancer-cure is now firmly in place, especially for the desperate. Stories have circulated of rhino horn touts—including hospital staff—pushing their product in cancer wards and of unscrupulous specialists at the Ho Chi Minh City University of Technology who test users' horns to ensure they are legitimate. Even some physicians—including Vietnam's director of the National Hospital of Traditional Medicine—have fallen for the scam. In 2012, he told *National Geographic*'s Peter Gwin that he uses rhino horn to block the growth of cancer cells in his patients. More recently, researchers found that horn is also being procured by relatives of the terminally ill, as a purely symbolic gesture of consolation—a "final source of pleasure to demonstrate that their families have done everything to help them, according to Martin Nielsen, associate professor at the University of Copenhagen.

A much more common new use of rhino horn, however, is hangover prevention, especially among wealthy urban men. Given the material's historic role in detecting and removing poison, this sort of makes sense; at high levels, alcohol is, after all, just a fun poison. As a night of partying winds down, among some circles there's no better way to earn your friends and colleagues' respect than by breaking out your rhino horn and sharing it with everyone. It is, as one Vietnamese website put it, the "drink of millionaires." "Rhino horn is a great way to show off status and wealth without actually saying how wealthy you are," explained Madelon Willemsen, former country director for TRAFFIC Vietnam. "You take out the horn while you're out drinking and show your friends that you know it's real because here's a picture on your phone of the dead animal."

Rhino horn is also coveted by more common folk. Those with limited means are most likely purchasing much cheaper water buffalo horn, however, which makes up 70–90 percent of what is marketed as rhino horn in Vietnam (government officials, Vanda Felbab-Brown pointed out in *The Extinction Market,* tend to tout the higher estimate to deflect criticism about their country's role in the rhino poaching crisis). Tuan Bendixsen, Vietnam director of the nonprofit group Animals Asia, is acquainted with such individuals. His barber—who is not a wealthy man—knows what Bendixsen does, and one day, mid-trim, he asked his client what he thinks about rhino horn.

"It's nothing more than fingernails," Bendixsen replied.

"Oh, really?" the barber replied, clearly dubious. "When I go out drinking with my friends, I come home and grind a little horn, take it with water, and the next day, I'm good to go."

Despite all these newfangled uses, rhino horn remains a popular traditional remedy for everything from fever to measles to epilepsy. That it doesn't actually work well or at all for any of these things doesn't seem to matter; the placebo effect can be powerful. Bendixsen, for example, has met plenty of rhino horn users, including ones with college degrees, who swear by it. For example, when his father-in-law fell ill recently, he spent a lot of time at the hospital and often chatted with other visitors in the shared ward. One woman told him that her oldest son had once come down with a bad fever that Western medicine could not cure.

Hearing about her desperate situation, a friend gave her some rhino horn. Within half an hour, she said, her son's fever had broken. "I understand what you're saying about wildlife products and protection," she told Bendixsen. "But if my son or daughter gets a fever again, I will use rhino horn."

Overhearing them, another woman in the ward suddenly chimed in: "My uncle had stomach cancer, and the doctor sent him home to prepare for death. A friend gave him rhino horn, and a year later, he's still alive. Explain that!"

Bendixsen admitted that he could not.

"This is why we're losing," he told me, sighing. "I was sitting in a ward with six people—just normal people—and two of them have used rhino horn. If you say you used it and it worked, then that's a thousand times stronger than any study showing whatever non-effect."

IN NOVEMBER 2016, I HEADED TO BACK TO VIETNAM, HOPING TO MEET ONE OF THE country's new status-hungry rhino horn users and to learn more about what's being done on the ground to stop trafficking. I scheduled my trip to coincide with the Hanoi Conference on Illegal Wildlife Trade, the third annual meeting meant to bring world leaders together to tackle wildlife crime. Representatives from sixty-plus countries were due to attend, with the UK's Prince William—who has long campaigned against the illegal trade—billed as the star attraction. The conference's website confidently stated that the event "will result in an action plan that will call for reasoned, tangible and unified action against illegal wildlife trade."

From the beginning, though, there were signs that the organizers didn't quite have their act together. Rumors spread that Vietnam hadn't even wanted to host the conference, but that it had been pressured into doing so. I still wanted to go, though, and in my attendance application I included letters from my editor at *National Geographic* and my book agent, both attesting that I was a journalist writing a book about the illegal wildlife trade and that I'd be covering the conference. Apparently, this didn't cut it. The organizers replied to say that, unfortunately, my application had been turned down because my work on illegal wildlife trade was not deemed relevant to a conference about illegal wildlife trade. "We regret that [we] could not accept your registration and search for your understanding," they concluded.

They did not have my understanding. With a plane ticket already booked,

I was obviously going to do what I could to get in—even if it meant crawling through a window.

The creeping feeling that something was clearly off only continued after I arrived in the country. A day before the meeting began, Vietnam kicked off the festivities by holding its first ivory and rhino horn burn. As the media described it, the government destroyed "huge" amounts of illegal products in a powerful show of "cracking down on illegal trade." Vietnam's deputy agriculture minister echoed these sentiments, declaring the event "a clear indication of our government's political determination to fulfill our international duty in conventions to protect wildlife."

Those in the know, however, pointed out that the amount of material destroyed—2.2 tons of ivory and 150 pounds of rhino horn—represented a mere fraction of the country's total stockpile. In fact, Vietnam has seized 30 tons of ivory since 2010, and, at minimum, 1,200 pounds of rhino horn from 2010 to 2016. (The latter figure is based on seizure data compiled by the nonprofit group Education for Nature–Vietnam, but it's impossible to say for sure how much rhino horn the country has. Authorities won't let anyone see it, including South African and American officials who have been trying to access it for years for auditing and testing. As Willemsen at TRAFFIC said, "The horn is held at the Ministry of Finance, so it's being treated as an asset.")

I skipped the lackadaisical publicity stunt in favor of meeting up with some sources. Mai Thị Hồng Tâm, the translator who helped me interview Mr. M, again joined me. Tâm is outgoing and stylish, always arriving in heels, bright dresses, and matching jewelry. She lived and studied in the United States for a decade and is clearly proud of her time there: "Everything I'm wearing is from the US!" she once gushed. "This is from Macy's!" In interviews she comes across as both bubbly and insistent—attributes that were often quite handy for the work we were doing.

Our first meeting was with Đỗ Doãn Hoàng, one of Vietnam's leading investigative journalists. He writes about everything from deforestation to corporate corruption, but wildlife—including rhino horn—is one of his favorite topics. I met Hoàng on a lovely warm morning at a café overlooking one of Hanoi's many lakes. Although one of Vietnam's most hard-hitting journalists, Hoàng—with wire frame glasses, a plaid button-up shirt, and a tweed golf cap—appeared quite unassuming. After we sat down he ordered a fresh coconut, which was brought out bearing a comically long orange straw.

Hoàng's interest in rhino horn—just like my own—began in 2010, when Vietnam's last Javan rhino was killed for its horn. Upon hearing the news, "I felt shame," he recalled. He began investigating the trade, sometimes posing as a trader or buyer to gather information (he later showed me a small baggie of rhino horn that he had in his car, which he said he bought for $200 to maintain his cover). He even went to South Africa to better understand how Vietnam's demand affects people and animals a world away, and he wrote a book about his experiences and findings. "In Vietnam, a lot of people are so stupid, especially businessmen," he told me through a mix of English and Vietnamese. "They only want benefits for themselves. They don't care about the environment or about other people. I want to expose all of this."

Hoàng has received death threats, and in March 2016 he was physically attacked. It was the middle of the afternoon, he recalled, and he had just parked his car not far from where we were sitting now. When he stepped out, he was accosted by three young men on motorbikes. One deliberately struck Hoàng's right hand with a stick, breaking his fingers and sending a warning clearly meant to silence him. He suspects that the men had been following him for quite some time, waiting for an opportunity to strike, and that they had been hired by someone. But because he writes about all sorts of unsavory subjects, there's no way to know whether the attack was connected to rhino horn. Despite having images of the men from a security camera, the police never apprehended anyone.

Months later, Hoàng can still type only with three fingers on his right hand. But he hasn't allowed the attack to intimidate him. "I'm from the countryside, so I'm strong," he chuckled. His principles also prevent him from quitting. "When people tell me that my job is dangerous, I say, 'No problem,' because I want to do something for Vietnam," he told me. "I want to make things better for my country and for my daughter, sons, and parents. I'm doing this for society and for truth."

Taking a sip of coconut juice from his cartoonish swizzle straw, he added that he likes to help visiting journalists get the word out. "If you want," he said casually, "I can take you to a village where they trade rhino horn. And introduce you to a rhino horn user. It's not dangerous."

"Not dangerous!?" I interrupted, pointing to his hand.

"They cannot attack a beautiful girl."

"You should be protected, Rachel," Tâm interjected, looking worried. "You need to be careful."

Hoàng waved her off. "Wildlife trade is not really as dangerous as other things," he said. "They're just interested in money and profit, so if we pretend to be people who can bring them profit, it's no problem. You know how much it is for one rhino horn in Vietnam? $50,000! It's more expensive than my car."

Hoàng's kind offer was tempting, just the sort of insider help I needed if I wanted to do more than just talk to conservationists. Putting aside any lingering doubts, I told him yes, let's do it. Appearing delighted at this news, he confessed, giggling, "I'm helpful because you're beautiful."

Oh dear. I sensed that the meeting was taking a turn.

"Me—I'm not beautiful," he continued. "When I interview people, sometimes they don't want to talk to me, so I smile and say something funny. I have to be funny, because I'm not beautiful!" He then asked if we could take a photo together. Gazing down at the resulting image, he sighed melodramatically: "So beautiful!" While such behavior would immediately be labeled as inappropriate in the States, I'd long ago learned that in Vietnam, for better or worse, looks are readily commented on. And, because Hoàng's attentions struck me as harmless, I decided to just roll with it. Even Tâm agreed, later noting, "He's very flirtatious with you: you should use it to your advantage."

After wrenching away from Hoàng, Tâm and I headed to Hanoi's Old Quarter, where I'd been tipped off by Bendixsen that Prince William was visiting a local elementary school to talk about rhinos. Afterward, he'd be hosting a meeting with a handful of influential local personalities. Hoàng confirmed these details: in fact, he was the only journalist who had been invited to the meeting.

The Old Quarter's narrow streets are congested under normal circumstances, but with the prince nearby, traffic had come to a near standstill. Tâm and I jumped out of the car early and elbowed our way to the café where Hoàng said the meeting would take place. We snagged a seat out front, directly next to a table reserved for the VIPs. Pretty soon, television cameras began showing up, and a buzzing crowd gathered with iPhones ready. While the other journalists, film crews, and onlookers were confined to the street facing the café, we were on the inside.

The prince's handlers showed up next, looking harried. "Excuse me, who are you with?" one of them asked pointedly, spotting my notebook and SLR.

"*National Geographic,*" I replied impassively. There was no way I was going to give up this seat.

"Ok, look, we just want this to be natural," the handler insisted.

I glanced around at the dozens of cameras, security guards, and packed crowd surrounding us. *Very natural indeed.* I reassured her that I'd be cool.

A moment later, though, another handler showed up. "Are you here working? Can you just not be intrusive?" she barked. I stifled a grin—and the urge to offer these women a drink.

The talent began to arrive, including actors, musicians, and Hoàng. Spotting me, he put his hands to his heart, winked, and then waved. Singer Lê H`ông Nhung, wearing a pale pink velvet *áo dài* with her long hair sweetly styled in pigtail braids, took a seat across from Hoàng at the VIP table. Her American husband was banished to my side table, though, along with their twin girls. They looked to be about five years old and were dressed in adorable traditional silk robes. "Sit down properly, here comes the prince!" their father sternly instructed them.

Indeed, the prince was hard to miss: William's six-foot-three frame towered above the masses, which his guards shooed away like pigeons on a crowded sidewalk. Despite the frenzy of activity around him, he did appear quite natural. He took a seat at the table next to us and immediately began chatting with his guests. His expression was earnest and intent, but his words impossible to make out from where I sat.

As the minutes passed, the two little girls next to me grew restless. One of them spotted my camera and reached for it, and I obligingly showed her how use it. The girls began taking photos of each other making hilariously unattractive faces, and then they turned the camera toward their mom, sitting next to the prince. Click, click, click! Click, click!

Realizing with apparent horror what was happening, one of the prince's handlers gave me a scathing look. If she could have slapped me, I think she would have. Instead, she slowly shook her head back and forth and silently mouthed the word "NO"—a gesture not unlike the one my mom used to make when I was acting up in a Girl Scouts meeting. I just shrugged and smiled—kids will be kids! Did she really think that I'd recruited these little girls as my paparazzi moles? (Incidentally, they were quite good photographers—I got some great shots!)

Eventually, the spectacle came to an end. The prince was whisked away, and the crowd quickly dissipated. Hoàng came skipping over, giddy from the meeting, despite having understood only "about 50 percent" of what the prince had said. He was also happy to report that he had spoken with his rhino horn user contact, who had agreed to meet us for dinner tomorrow. Hoàng would come along, too, to make sure things went smoothly. I gave him a hug in thanks, and he asked whether we could take more photos together. "Trời ơi, anh!" I exclaimed—"Oh my God!"—but I happily obliged. As I stood there, grinning at the camera with Hoàng's head snuggled on my shoulder, I felt pleasantly surprised at how well everything seemed to be working out. *Now, if I could just get into that conference tomorrow . . .*

THE HANOI CONFERENCE ON ILLEGAL WILDLIFE TRADE TOOK PLACE ON THE SIXTH floor of the towering Lotte Hotel. On the opening morning of the conference I strode into the fancy high-rise with my head held high, trying to look casual and confident—but in fact very concerned about my chances of getting in. There was no avoiding the registration table, which stood right at the entrance. *Here we go,* I thought.

I gave the woman at the desk my name, and she flipped through the pages of attendees. "Hmm . . . you're not on the list," she frowned. "Did you register?"

"Yes."

"Ok, here's a badge." She handed me a pass and a swag bag without so much as asking for an ID. I was astounded: apparently, being vetted to get into a room with the Duke of Cambridge and other world leaders isn't the kind of detail that Vietnam worries about!

I passed through a corridor lined with booths staffed by various wildlife groups and then into a ballroom. As far as conference venues go, this one was quite swanky. White tablecloths matched the white-draped chairs, and the podium was decorated with a spray of fresh orchids. The seats in the front bore little flags, indicating where the delegates from various countries should sit. The speeches soon began, the first one delivered by Đặng Thị Ngọc Thịnh, vice president of Vietnam. She was speaking in Vietnamese, however, so I flagged down a worker to ask for an interpreter headset. "Sorry," she replied, "headsets are only for delegates."

"But I can't understand anything."

She shrugged and handed me a headset, which I triumphantly put on. I was beginning to understand this game!

"In order to effectively protect wild animals and plants," said the simultaneous translation, "I believe that the international community needs a comprehensive approach which focuses not only on individual activities such as harmonizing the legal system, enhancing new law enforcement effectiveness, eradicating the market for illegal wildlife trafficking, developing sustainable livelihoods for the local community living in the reserves, and strengthening international collaboration and coordination, but also to implement these measures in an exhaustive measure." Vice President Thịnh paused, taking a much-needed breath, and then thanked everyone for coming today.

Next up was Sonexay Siphandone, deputy prime minister of Laos. "At a regional level, Lao PDR has played an active part in implementation of relevant work, including strengthening law and enforcement to combat illegal trade in wildlife," he said—a claim that, were his name Pinocchio, might have caused his nose to grow. "It is my firm belief that this international conference will form a solid ground and chart a future direction for preservation of natural resources in all countries."

Finally, Prince William took the podium: despite progress on this issue, he said, a betting man would still put his money on extinction. "If we cannot tackle this, it is hard to see how we will overcome the other global challenges that we face," he continued, his voice deep, posh, and polished. "But we can win this battle, and in doing so, we can take a small, important step of reminding ourselves that we are capable of rising to the challenges of our age."

Although the prince's speech came across as honest, sincere, and inspiring, the rest of the conference was not. A few side events walked audiences through the same tired challenges, and themed breakout sessions were mostly confined to generalities. A document-finalizing meeting between conservationists and government officials was reportedly held up over such excruciatingly trivial concerns as comma placement. As a source I ran into summarized the overall sentiment: "I have no idea why I'm here. Will me being here make a difference? No."

WHILE ALL THIS WAS TAKING PLACE IN HANOI, 5,500 MILES AWAY IN THE NETHERlands, another group had also gathered to discuss the situation in Vietnam. The Wildlife Justice Commission, a nonprofit organization dedicated to disrupting transnational wildlife crime, had called a two-day public hearing to present evidence of massive, unabashed illegal trade in rhino horn, ivory, tiger parts, and other endangered species products taking place in a village thirty minutes south of Hanoi. Following a year-long investigation, for months the group had tried—and failed—to engage Vietnamese authorities, so the investigators decided to go public with their findings. The hope, they said, was to "activate justice."

Nhị Khê, the notorious town in question, is one of three quaint villages near Hanoi that traditionally specialized in woodwork. Recently, though, carvers have expanded to ivory and rhino horn, which they sell to a 90 percent Chinese clientele. Investigative journalist Karl Ammann first sounded the alarm about this troubling development back in 2012 and approached both Interpol and CITES. But nothing came of it. Ammann's Vietnamese operative even heard that a local Interpol team did visit Nhị Khê, but that they allegedly accepted a bribe in return for allowing residents to continue with business as usual.

Following Ammann's leads, the Wildlife Justice Commission decided to look into the place themselves. In Nhị Khê alone, it discovered illegal wildlife trade operating on an industrial scale, including rhino horn products from 579 animals worth $42 million, ivory from 907 elephants worth $6.8 million, and parts from 225 tigers worth $3.6 million. It also identified fifty-one key people at the heart of the contraband empire.

These findings were presented to an audience of more than three hundred at the hearing, and they were confirmed by a panel of independent experts. Vietnam turned down the invitation to join the event officially, however, and instead sent a single nonparticipating observer. Despite Vietnam's almost complete lack of engagement, Olivia Swaak-Goldman, the commission's executive director, said that she and her colleagues were committed to seeing this thing through. "We have repeatedly offered our support to the Vietnamese government and continue to do so even today," she said. She also implored those gathering at the Hanoi conference to push for shutting down Nhị Khê, "one of the world's worst wildlife trafficking hubs."

Her request, however, did not resonate in Hanoi. Instead, neither the commission's findings nor the hearing in the Netherlands was so much as mentioned at the conference. In a meeting hall full of elephant posters, Nhị Khê was the true elephant in the room.

Some local experts weren't surprised that Vietnam blackballed the commission and its investigation, explaining that, from the start, the nonprofit had gone about things in the wrong way. "I think that any government, when presented with these external you've-done-our-job-for-us reports, is not going to react so positively," said Jake Brunner, program coordinator for the IUCN Mekong region group. In Vietnam, he explained, things need to work their way through the system, which often takes time—and sometimes requires portraying officials as heroes rather than villains. "Frankly," he said, "if there's a press conference in

The Hague or wherever, where people are saying 'You've done a really bad job, Vietnam,' it's not going to make an impact. Not to say it isn't true—but it isn't enough."

WITH ITS REDOLENT MEETING HALL AND GRANDIOSE YET INSUBSTANTIAL SPEECHES, the Hanoi conference, in many ways, epitomized Vietnam's current take on the illegal wildlife trade. To put it colloquially, Vietnam fronts: it talks the wildlife talk, but it doesn't walk the wildlife walk. As Willemsen at TRAFFIC said, "I think what Vietnam is very good at is putting a little gloss on everything. They have this idea that if they seem to do something, it's good enough."

"Vietnam's policy," added another source, "seems to simply be deflect, deflect, deflect." Indeed, since 2013, the country has been implicated in twice the number of rhino horn seizures than it has undertaken itself, and arrests and prosecutions, especially of high-level wildlife traffickers, are sorely lacking. As Scott Roberton, director of counter–wildlife trafficking at the Wildlife Conservation Society's Asia Program, said, "The fact that there are only a handful of people in jail for rhino or elephant crimes in Vietnam is a real problem."

Yet progress has been made. When Roberton first arrived in the country in 2003, illegal wildlife trade wasn't even a topic of conversation. The Vietnamese did not acknowledge it, while Westerners dared not talk about it, he said, because it was perceived as being "a really sensitive traditional culture issue."

That the illegal wildlife trade is now being openly discussed is a major improvement, but denial and censorship remain challenges. When conservationists present officials with results they don't like, the response is often, "You must have done your research wrong." In 2012, for example, the government dismissed a comprehensive 180-page TRAFFIC report detailing Vietnam's role in the escalating rhino crisis in South Africa. Rather than engage with the findings, Vietnamese officials, Orenstein reported, deemed the report "not objective and evidence-based." All groups working in Vietnam must also run their findings by the government prior to publication, and reports are often delayed if officials do not like what they read (which is frequently the case). To break the rule and publish without permission, however, is to risk having privileges—or even visas—revoked.

Sometimes, though, conservationists try to push the publication envelope. In the Hanoi conference's exhibition hall, for example, one of the groups snuck in a report that hadn't been approved in advance. Vietnamese officials stalking from booth to booth spotted it, however, and said they'd have to confiscate the entire stack. But rather than admitting it was because the researchers hadn't run the publication by them in advance, they claimed that they were taking it because the authors had failed to include a group of obscure, contested islands in the South China Sea on a map accompanying the text.

The tendency toward evasiveness, denial, and window dressing also hampers progress on the ground, including in Nhị Khê. Following the Wildlife Justice Commission's hearing, one arrest was made, and some fines were given out, but nothing like the big takedown the commission had hoped for. Meanwhile, much of the trade went underground, open only to Chinese patrons. I still wanted to see the notorious place for myself, though, so I swung by late one afternoon with Hoàng and Tâm.

I was surprised by how completely innocuous it was. Passing through, you'd never guess that Nhị Khê is an international hub for wildlife trafficking. Surrounded by idyllic rice paddies, the town proper is composed of quaint pedestrian streets. Children played in a palm-tree-shaded park, and old ladies sat chitchatting on benches.

The mom-and-pop-style wood carving shops that peppered either side of the narrow main drag advertised in both Vietnamese and Chinese, I noticed, but many were already closed for the day by the time we arrived. Those that weren't all looked about the same: small rooms open to the street, with glass cases in front displaying all manner of wooden trinkets, including necklaces, bracelets, statues, cups, and bowls. Surrounded by fluffy mounds of shavings, some men and women were carving new products on the spot. Their work perfumed the air with a pleasant fragrance, like fresh shavings from a hamster's cage.

Choosing a shop at random to investigate, we were greeted by a young woman with a pragmatic, no-bullshit air about her. Hoàng said something in Vietnamese, and she reached into a drawer and took out some bracelets with alternating wooden and white beads, billed at twenty-two dollars a pop. "Oh, ivory!" Tâm exclaimed in English, pointing at the white beads. "Elephant ivory!"

Through Tâm, I asked the woman whether the ivory was real. She looked at me like I was an idiot. "Yes, it's real—100 percent!" she snapped back incredulously. "This is my shop and my home. If I tell lies, I will be out of business!"

Hoàng asked whether she had anything else she could show us. She reached down and pulled out a red plastic bag containing delicate ivory combs and pure ivory bracelets. As Hoàng took photos, a young girl with an ivory-bangled arm wandered in from the back of the shop, picking her nose. "You're rich!" Tâm complimented the girl. "I never had the chance to wear such kinds of jewelry." The girl grunted back disinterestedly.

Satisfied with the ivory findings, Hoàng broached the rhino horn subject. "I ask you, honestly," he implored, looking into the saleswoman's eyes, "my mom has cancer, and I want to buy some rhino horn powder for her. Can you help me?"

The woman looked uncomfortable. "I cannot. Only if people here know you for sure, then they will sell it to you."

"But my mom is very sick. I just want a pound. Are you sure you don't have it?"

"You must have a lot of money to afford a pound!" she noted. "But no, I don't have any. If I did, I would sell it to you immediately."

She added that she knew someone who had just been put in prison for selling rhino horn and several others who had been fined more than $250,000 (Roberton, however, later disputed that amount). It seemed that our luck with this lady had run out, so I purchased some wooden beads (Hoàng: "This is my girlfriend, please give her a good price!") and we left.

Standing outside, I noticed that an older woman with a baby balanced on her hip was intently watching us. She had an amused look on her face, as though she was in on a joke at our expense. She, too, wore a thick ivory bangle—as did the baby. *This town is really starting to feel conspiratorial,* I thought. *Someone should make a movie about it called* Children of the Horn. As we passed her by, the woman was still so blatantly staring that I felt compelled to smile and say hello in Vietnamese. That was all the encouragement she needed. Approaching Tâm, she whispered, "I can get you some ivory, if that's what you want. My niece sells it." She held up a fist, showing off her bracelet.

We agreed to go with her, though Hoàng—who was afraid to venture further for fear of being recognized as a "famous journalist"—said he'd wait for us in the car. The woman led us down the block, chatting all the while. "People here are just nervous because the police keep showing up and doing these crazy things," she explained. "We used to sell ivory bracelets for $220 each, but now we've had to decrease the price to just $130 because of the raids." Parroting the woman from the shop, she adamantly denied involvement with rhino horn, however.

She took us down a little lane, and suddenly we were standing in front of a real McMansion of a home, complete with faux columns, neatly pruned shrubs, and giant windows. It was fittingly painted a shade of white that could only be described as ivory, and the open door revealed a massive table holding an elaborate orchid centerpiece whose flowers were also ivory-white. A woman appeared just then, wearing a tight, midriff-exposing outfit. Her face was marked with harsh scowl lines. At the sight of us, they deepened.

"What are they doing here?" she demanded.

"Oh, it's fine!" the older woman assured her. "They're just looking for ivory."

Tâm began to "flirt" with them, as she likes to call it, complimenting them on their home and trying to flatter them into compliance. Meanwhile, I smiled dumbly, twirling my hair and smelling the blooms on a rose bush, trying my best to look harmless.

"Oh, they think I am an undercover policeman!" Tâm told me, breaking from the Vietnamese chatter. "I told them, 'How can I be an undercover police? I'm with this foreigner!'"

I laughed along. "You—a policeman!? That's hilarious!"

The younger woman seemed to be relaxing, but she wasn't going to budge on the ivory issue. "Look, this isn't my place," she told Tâm. "You'll have to wait until the owner comes back to see the ivory." We didn't have time to wait—Hoàng needed to get back to Hanoi for a birthday party—so we told them, thanks anyway. Notably, no one ever denied having the ivory. The sticking point was simply whether we were trustworthy enough to show it to.

Reunited with Hoàng, I asked him whether he thought people here are still engaged in illegal trade to the same extent that they were before the Wildlife Justice Commission exposure. "If you come here a few times and buy things and show that you have money, you can earn their trust and get access to whole rhino horns and tusks and tiger bones," he said. "They still have everything, they just won't show you immediately because you're a foreigner." Indeed, when I shared images of the two people I'd interacted with in Nhị Khê with the Wildlife Justice Commission, they confirmed both were involved in the trade. The grandmother plays a role in the local supply of ivory, they said, while the younger woman—the one who had so adamantly denied having rhino horn—appeared to be Thảo Toàn, a bigger fish. "She was posting large quantities of rhino horn and ivory on her WeChat, to the value of approximately $350,000," a commission spokesperson told me.

After my visit, I asked Roberton—who tends to be in the know about all things wildlife in Vietnam—why the authorities hadn't shut down the Nhị Khê traders. He replied that he is confident that action will be taken—but only after a long-delayed penal code update, drafted in 2015, is ratified in January 2018, increasing punishments for wildlife-related criminal violations to a maximum fine of $90,000 or fifteen years in prison. Were authorities to move in now, he said, the laws are too weak to land anyone in jail for a serious amount of time. So patience will (probably, hopefully) pay off. "Wait until the end of this year," he said. "A lot is resting on this new penal code, and right now, that's the excuse. But if we're sitting here next summer and still no one is in jail for rhino or elephant trafficking, well . . . " He trailed off, preferring not to dwell on that possibility. (As of May 2018, around ten people had been arrested for rhino horn and ivory-related crimes since the penal code went into effect in January. But none were major players, according to Roberton.)

Andrea Crosta, cofounder of the Wildlife Justice Commission, is also hedging on the new wildlife trafficking law. "We know from backchannels in Vietnam that the blow has been felt," he said. "Now we're just waiting. But in the meantime, many of the traffickers flagged in our investigation are still free and in business, which is a problem."

Despite the talk and revamped laws, though, it's not clear that Vietnam genuinely wants to end wildlife trade. "When we ask rhino horn users what they think would resolve the rhino horn problem, instead of taking responsibility for themselves, they say the government needs to deal with it," Willemsen said. "But then when you ask the government about it, they say, 'Yes, we need to do this—but by the way, rhino horn really works.'"

Indeed, Vietnamese government officials have long been one of the primary consumers of wildmeat and illegal animal products, and allegations abound of certain officials' direct involvement in trafficking. Ammann, the investigative journalist, has witness statements alleging, for example, that confiscated containers of ivory and rhino horn were rerouted to an official very high up in the Vietnamese government, who then returned them to a carver he knows. "When it comes to Vietnam, the corruption level goes to the very top," Ammann said. "But this is not up for discussion at any of these conservation meetings."

Even Vietnam's wildlife authorities—the people who are supposed to be regulating wildlife products that enter and leave the country—have an alleged history of involvement with rhino horn, both in terms of some selling confiscated horns and others using it. One high-ranking individual allegedly continues to insist on rhino horn's efficacy as a medical treatment.

I tried to reach Vietnam's CITES director, Hà Thị Tuyêt Nga, for a month, hoping to interview her in person while I was in Vietnam about these allegations and about her government and office's commitment to battling the illegal trade. Finally, I got a reply from her deputy director, Vương Tiến Mạnh, who told me that Nga and everyone else in the CITES office were too busy to meet with me. So I asked over e-mail whether anyone he works with uses or has used rhino horn, or believes in the efficacy of rhino horn. "I am not sure what you mean with your questions," Mạnh wrote back. He told me that no one there uses rhino horn, and no one believes that it works. "It is not just CITES officials, but most Vietnamese people do not believe in using rhinoceros horns and other wildlife products as traditional medicines," he wrote. "Scientific evidence has shown that rhino horn has no therapeutic effect, and that the chemical composition of horn is mainly keratin, similar to human hair."

I hoped this meant that Mạnh didn't know about his colleagues' alleged dalliances with rhino horn, that he didn't believe in its efficacy himself, and that the culture of Vietnam's various wildlife authority offices has changed. Or, on the other hand, it could simply be that everyone working there knows what to say to annoying Western journalists. As a source later told me, "We thought Mạnh was on the path to good, but he has hasn't shown any progress over the last two years. I don't think he's consuming rhino horn, but I am not sure where his alliance lies."

When I asked Roberton about these rumors and allegations, he paused, and then—without naming names, answered, "The use of wildlife is common in our government partners. I'm disappointed, but not surprised, that some are using it."

"If that is the case, though, is it a conflict of interest?" I asked.

"Is it a conflict of interest if government officials who are responsible for combatting and reducing the demand for rhino horn are using it?" He gave me a long look. "Absolutely. It's a major conflict."

I HAD TO PASS ON DINNER WITH THE CONSERVATIONISTS AFTER THE CONFERENCE: I had a hot date with Hoàng's rhino horn user, Hoài. I'd made a reservation at Chim Sáo (the Whistling Bird), a traditional yet hip little place tucked off a small side alley that a friend had highly recommended. I was the first to arrive, and the hostess led me upstairs, to an empty room whose wooden floors were lined with low tables and red tartan pillows for sitting on. French doors at the head of the room opened onto a balcony, letting in the warm night air.

Rather than invite his wife and children, Hoài—who arrived about half an hour late—brought along Nhung, his beautiful young mistress. A middle school gym teacher, she was tall, with thick, wavy hair that fell below her shoulders and a deep, attractive voice. She wore tight black jeans and a white linen shirt embroidered with colorful flowers. Despite her striking appearance, she seemed very shy—but it also could have been that she simply didn't have much to say. Hoài appeared to be her sugar daddy, and indeed, they half-jokingly referred to each other as "uncle" and "niece" throughout the meal. As Tâm later noted, "The girl likes him because he has a lot of money."

I presented Hoài with a bottle of nice French wine that I'd picked up earlier that day, and he, too, had something for me. Nhung reached into her bag and handed me a round cookie tin, of the sort you'd find in a grandmother's pantry. It was labeled "Milk's Favorite Cookie: Oreo Collection" and was decorated with cartoon images of Oreo cookies splashing into milk.

I wasn't super excited about eating a bunch of Oreos, but I smiled in thanks as I opened the tin. For a second, I was very confused. Rather than a bundle of calorific black-and-white cookies, inside was a shallow white ceramic dish with the image of a little rhino imprinted on its side, and a nubby, fibrous brown object about the size of a cigarette pack. I suddenly realized what I was looking at: Hoài had brought his rhino horn to the restaurant! (He keeps it in the cookie tin, he explained later, to prevent rodents or insects from getting at it.)

"This is the piece of rhino horn that you must be interested in," he began. "There are many groups coming from the US, Japan, Holland, and Germany that want to talk about rhino horn with me. They ask me to bring it out so they can take a picture."

"Is it real?" I asked.

"It is real—I know it," he said. The ceramic dish, he explained, is used to grind the horn so the powder can be mixed with water to drink. "It's similar to grinding fingernails, because the material the horn's made out of is actually like nails or hair."

I was taken aback that he not only knew this but that he readily admitted it. "So why do you eat or drink it, then, if it's just like fingernails?"

Before he could answer, the conversation was interrupted as Hoàng finally arrived, looking flustered and griping about the location. I was surprised to see that Hoàng had brought along his two sons, aged sixteen and nine. The younger one wore Spider Man–themed pants, and the older one had emo-style Weezer glasses. They casually said hello to me in English and took a seat, looking a bit puzzled as to why they were here as well. I sealed the horn up and placed it to the side. We'd get back to that later.

"Today, I express sincere thanks to you, Mr. Hoài!" Hoàng said, taking his seat.

"Okay. Can I get a bottle of water?" Hoài replied, practically ignoring Hoàng's gushing declaration.

Hoàng wasn't going to let this go, though: "Truly, Mr. Hoài, you are my friend—that's why you come here. So I really thank you!"

I cringed at this over-the-top, eager-to-please treatment of the rhino horn user, but figured, okay, maybe this is just how it's done in Vietnam. . . .

We ordered some beer, make-it-yourself spring rolls, fried catfish, and a hot pot. "Whenever you come to a country, you should try the food of that country, right?" Hoài said to me, through Tâm's translation. I agreed and asked him to tell me a bit about himself. What does he do?

"Managing and trade," he said vaguely (Hoàng told me he's the general director of a timber import company). I asked him how he knew Hoàng, and he replied that he's a friend of a friend. He didn't seem keen to continue this line of questioning, though, and instead switched back to what was quickly becoming a very tired subject, instructing Tâm, "Please tell her she's very beautiful again."

I waved Hoài off and took another sip of rice wine.

"The most important thing that Tâm should translate is that you *are* very beautiful," Hoàng repeated.

"Ok, let's not get crazy here," I protested. "We are all very beautiful at this table!"

"Of course, my friend here is very beautiful," Hoài agreed, nodding at Nhung. It went on like this, even as the appetizers arrived and Hoàng noted with approving astonishment that I knew how to use chopsticks. As we chatted, Hoàng's youngest son took up the Oreo tin and opened it, peering curiously at contents within. Although Hoài kept up his end of the conversation, I noticed him watching the kid out of the corner of his eye. Hoàng offered to wrap a spring roll for him, and Hoài grunted "no thanks."

"Actually, I want to talk to her," he said, directing his gaze at me. "When I go overseas, I want to receive help from people. When you come to Vietnam, I help you. So, when I go overseas, I want to meet people who are kind and helpful, like me."

"I'm looking forward to showing you New York," I said, even as I tried—and failed—to imagine taking a Vietnamese wildlife criminal around my fair trade–, animal welfare–, and sustainability-obsessed neighborhood in Brooklyn.

The room, I noticed, was filling up. A Dutch couple sat across from us, and a group of chain-smoking Vietnamese men had gathered at the table to our right. Nhung ordered some extra vegetables for the hot pot, and Tâm encouraged everyone to eat more. Another round of beers arrived.

"Hoài, do you still have your wine cup made from rhino horn?" Hoàng asked.

"I got rid of that a long time ago," Hoài replied, picking up the tin. "I only have this now."

Sensing the time had finally arrived, I lowered my voice. "Should we go somewhere else to talk? Is Hoài comfortable talking about this here?" We were completely surrounded by people, and I imagined Hoài might not want to discuss his illegal exploits in front of an audience.

"You can ask me anything," he said.

"You can even ask how many wives he has!" Hoàng chimed in, cracking up. "The only thing he cannot say is that you are very beautiful."

"He is very shy to say that you are very beautiful," Tâm agreed.

"Foreigners also like the beauty of this girl," Hoàng said, gesturing at Nhung.

"Not only foreigners, I also like her," Hoài corrected him. "The foreigner likes the beauty of nature. But Vietnamese men like elegant, white ladies who are like dolls."

Sensing the conversation was yet again derailing, I cleared my throat. "Could you tell me again what kind of job you do?"

"I'm in business," Hoài replied. His grandparents were very wealthy, he added, but his parents lost much of the family's money in the war. He and his siblings worked hard to regain it. Although he wouldn't say they're upper class, they are firmly middle class.

"So why do you use this stuff?" I asked.

"The history of Vietnam and China says that it's good, that it can treat diseases."

I was confused. "But earlier you said that it's made from the same material as hair and nails. So why should it work to treat diseases?"

"I recently learned about that in the news," Hoài explained. "In fact, there are no scientists who confirm that it works. There is no scientific research. But I still don't believe it's the same as hair or nails. It's like Catholics—they've never seen

God, but they still believe. The older generations said it works, and they passed it on to the next generation, and they to the next. We just have such beliefs."

He hiccupped. "I already drank a lot, so please ask me a lot. Otherwise, I'll run away."

"Where did you get this piece of horn?"

"A long time ago, my grandfather bought it. A priest came to my hometown to build a church, and he had some rhino horn. When children got a fever, he would grind it and give it to them." But now, he said, he uses it for a very different purpose. He often grinds a bit before heading out to drink wine with friends. He mixes the resulting powder with a bit of water and puts it into a bottle to bring with them to a bar or restaurant. Once they begin feeling tired, they start taking swigs.

Hoàng took this as a cue to perform a demonstration. Grabbing the ceramic dish, he began vigorously rubbing the rhino horn into the bottom of the bowl, moving his hand in a circular motion. The horn began to release a rank, almost fishy smell.

I glanced around the room: the Dutch couple seemed completely oblivious, and the Vietnamese men, if they noticed at all, paid us no heed. The waitress had repeatedly stopped by while the horn was out, but she, too, just ignored it. Somehow I doubted things would go as smoothly if someone did a line of cocaine or injected themselves with heroin at a restaurant in the States—and the same would probably be true in Vietnam. But, unlike narcotics, which are specifically forbidden to possess, the law in Vietnam does not state that it's illegal to have rhino horn. So long as Hoài just uses it at home (or, apparently, at a restaurant), if caught, he would get an administrative penalty at worst. It just isn't seen as that big of a deal, and Hoài is not concerned. As Hoài told me, "In Vietnam, there is no law."

I asked Hoài whether, in his experience, rhino horn works. "People talk with one another about that, and they keep such ideas in their mind," he said. "For example, when Tâm called me today, she told me, 'Tonight you will meet a very beautiful lady.' So she already put such ideas in my head, before I met you. We are motivated by that."

I supposed he was hinting at a placebo effect or at the influence of peer pressure, but not wishing to get into the beautiful lady thing again, I asked him to be more specific. "If my children get a fever, I still use it now for that. It's effective: their fever will be reduced." He paused to light a cigarette. "We also use it when we are drunk, because it can reduce the poison in the liver."

"Many Vietnamese people believe it's very good for sex, too. You could try it," Hoàng said, winking at me.

"I am not clear on whether it is good for that or not," Hoài corrected him. "I want to repeat that it's good for reducing fever, because many people use it for that. And also that my friends use it a lot more than me. Their living standards are very high, and they always have it. They buy several pounds of horn at once, and then they divide it out for many people. They don't give it for free, but the sell it for a very reasonable price."

"How much would a piece like yours cost?"

"About $5,000," he said. The price, he added, is around $23,000 per pound.

"Would it bother you if rhinos go extinct?" I asked.

"People will search for rhino horn until there's just one rhino left in the world," he said, taking a drag on his cigarette. "That's no problem for me. Even now, when the government propagandizes about it, it doesn't bother me. In Vietnam, we have a saying: God gives birth to the elephant, God gives birth to the grass. It means when God delivers one kind of plant or animal, there will be another that is contradictory to it, that will consume it. It's the same with people and rhinos. It's natural if humans kill rhinos."

"Mr. Hoài speaks very well!" Hoàng piped up ingratiatingly.

Hoài and I ignored him, and I asked Hoài whether he or his friends would consider using farmed horn, or synthetic horn made in a lab, as a substitute for that taken from wild animals. He shook his head: "Vietnamese prefer rhinos from nature. These horns are the best for medical treatment, because the food, water, and way of life of wild rhinos generate the best horns."

"If someone gifts a lab-made rhino horn to a Vietnamese, he will throw it away," Hoàng added.

"Would you buy the last horn, from the last rhino?" I asked Hoài.

"With the price of horn being what it is, and with the option of modern treatments, actually I don't think the value is very high. I personally don't have enough demand for it. It's the same for other wildlife products. I used to use them, but not now. I know people who work in the medical field, and they say that in bear bile, for example, there are many viruses that can cause disease."

That was encouraging, at least, but what about his friends—what would it take to get them to stop using rhino horn or other banned wildlife products?

"It all depends on how their knowledge, ideas, and opinions are affected by the law, by the media and by other people," he said. "In short, it depends on who you are and which position you take, when telling me to stop. Today, for example,

I meet you because I'm introduced by a friend. And we've talked together and had a good time. If you tell me you want me to stop due to the extinction of the rhino, it will have an impact on me."

"Do you think the same is true for your friends?"

"Some would stop, and some would not. Some are very conservative. Their families have used rhino horn for many generations—they haven't just suddenly decided it's good. Everything is in their mind, and changing their attitudes and perspectives takes time. I'm an educated man—I know of the harm to nature— but if one rich and unscientific man believes that rhino horn can treat his disease, then harm to nature is nothing."

WHAT SHOULD BE DONE ABOUT PEOPLE LIKE HOÀI? IT'S A QUESTION THAT BIT- terly divides conservationists, activists, and others who wish to ensure rhinos have a future. Opinions fall into two basic, opposing camps: (1) make it legal to sell Hoài some form of rhino horn or (2) try harder to make or convince him to stop.

People in camp number one argue that prohibition does not work, and they point out that we are losing the war on poaching in spite of the rhino horn ban. Instead of outlawing horn, they say, we should just give people what they want. This line of thinking tends to be most popular among a Southern African crowd, with South Africa leading the charge. I talk much more about this in Chapter 11, but, for now, know that most private South African rhino owners wish to sustain- ably harvest their animals' horns—which grow back—to sell directly to consum- ers in Vietnam and China. This would help them pay for better protection against poachers, they say, and undermine the illegal market. The international trade of rhino horn remains firmly forbidden, though, so such a scheme would be impos- sible without breaking the law or making major legislative changes.

Other pro-traders favor a different approach: synthetic rhino horn, which several companies are attempting to create in the lab. So far, however, their ef- forts have not resulted in a commercially viable product. Many conservationists vehemently believe that bioengineered rhino horn risks stimulating demand and confusing law enforcement efforts to crack down on the real deal.

For all the arguing over trade, however, little is actually known about the overall demand for rhino horn—or how that demand might change, should a le- gal supply be introduced. Only a few studies have been carried out. In a 2013 TRAFFIC survey of six hundred randomly selected people in Vietnam, 5 percent said they had bought or consumed rhino horn, and another 16 percent said they would consider buying it in the future. In 2017, researchers from the International Trade Center identified and interviewed 239 rhino horn users in Hanoi and Ho Chi Minh City. Users, they found, are predominantly middle-aged and older men who enjoy above-average incomes—men like Hoài, in other words—although some women and younger male consumers (guys like Mr. M from Chapter 2) also partake.

While urban men valued rhino horn as a status symbol, the researchers found that most others used it for medical conditions, including for cancer, hepatitis, rashes, strokes, infertility, cirrhosis, and general detoxification—oftentimes on the advice of their doctor. Supporting what conservationists have said for years, most preferred wild horns to farmed ones. Specifically, they believed wild animals produce horns that are stronger and more potent, because they have to fight to survive and because they eat "pure" food from nature. Those who consume rhino horn for status also like the fact that they are flouting the law by accessing poached animal parts. Going to the corner pharmacy and picking up what equates to a package of Tylenol just wouldn't deliver the same thrill, apparently. For these reasons, some interviewees said they would not be willing to pay as much for legally sourced horn, which means legal trade could reduce the price of rhino horn. At the same time, though, some also said they would consume *more* rhino horn, were it to become legal—increasing overall demand. It's impossible to know whether legal trade could satiate that demand or lower the price enough to slow or even stop poaching.

Willemsen and her colleagues at TRAFFIC have found similar results about who and what drives demand for rhino horn: urban males who use it for status, sick people who use it for medicine, and older women who keep it on hand in case a family member becomes ill. But she disagrees with the International Trade Center's conclusions that "the introduction of legal trade may help crowd out poaching." No matter what, some people will still prefer rhino horn from wild animals, she said.

For this reason, Willemsen believes that reducing demand and increasing law enforcement, rather than supplying the market, is the only way to go. Others, including the nonprofit group WildAid, agree. Its popular slogan—"When the buying stops, the killing can too"—has been delivered by the likes of Jackie Chan, Yao Ming, Prince Charles, David Beckham, and Leonardo DiCaprio on billboards, commercials, and ads from China to the United States.

Is that the right kind of message for deterring rhino horn users in Vietnam, though?

Most likely, no. For such a message to work, people have to first care about animals and, second, acknowledge their role in harming them. But most rhino horn consumers in Vietnam, according to the International Trade Center's findings, don't connect the dots between the horn in their cupboards and the dead animals on the ground in Africa. Likewise, TRAFFIC found that many people in Vietnam know that rhinos are killed for their horns, but they either don't grasp their role in the poaching crisis, or they do not care. So Western-style campaigns in which famous people chide users or try to pull on their heartstrings probably won't change many minds.

What, then, would? Willemsen and her TRAFFIC colleagues have been working on this question for several years. They decided to focus on Vietnam's most prolific set of users, urban males. To figure out how to be most effective, first they started with what they know about this group of people. They are government officials, businessmen, entrepreneurs, and men born into money. All earn more than $1,500 per month (plus untold amounts from bonuses, bribes, and side dealings), and many have a wife and children as well as a mistress. They're the kind of men who don't like being told what to do but who do enjoy telling others what to do. They also relish feeling that they're above the law. In terms of their priorities, climbing the social ladder and maintaining status are tantamount. Rhino horn matters to them for its ability to project a luxurious lifestyle—not for some intrinsic property of the horn itself.

Armed with this knowledge, in September 2014, TRAFFIC launched The Strength of Chi demand-reduction campaign. Importantly, its messaging contains no mention of rhinos or the plight of the planet. There's no TRAFFIC logo or other indication that the ads are put out by a wildlife organization. Instead, the campaign uses influential figures—actors, businessmen, a composer—to deliver a simple message: you don't need rhino horn, because your strength comes from within. One ad, for example, shows actor Trần Bảo Sơn dressed in an impeccable black suit and smiling confidently as he steps out of a black car, next to the caption: "I have overcome many obstacles to achieve success relying only on my strong will, not on a piece of horn."

So far, the campaign has reached more than 5 million people and engaged more than 2 million urban males. After its first year, 57 percent of the men TRAFFIC originally surveyed said they intended to decrease their consumption of rhino horn, and 64 percent said they planned to tell their peers and friends to do the same.

The Strength of Chi's message, however, is not likely to sway Vietnam's most hard-core group of rhino horn users, according to Lynn Johnson, founder of Breaking the Brand, a volunteer-based project set up to understand wildlife users' motivations and change their behaviors. In 2013, Johnson interviewed around twenty ultra-wealthy rhino horn users in Hanoi and Ho Chi Minh City. They told her that celebrities—the very messengers that the Chi campaign relies on—are for children and that celebrities can be paid to say anything. Willemsen is also aware of this hurdle: "We found that frequent users actually really like the campaign and the logo, but when asked if it's effective, they say no."

But the Chi campaign's main issue, Johnson said, is its tone: it's overwhelmingly positive. To illustrate what she means, she uses the example of a bully in the office. To encourage the bully to change his behavior, HR reps may at first try to use positive reinforcement: asking the bully to treat others as he would like to be treated, for example, or describing how his actions harm his victims. But, at some point, the carrot needs to be exchanged for a stick. The bully needs to be fired, sued, suspended, or suffer some other loss of business or professional opportunities.

"When someone isn't intrinsically motivated to change, you can't encourage them to change by using positive messaging," said Johnson, who has more than twenty years of behavior change experience. Rather than feel-good ads about inner strength, she believes that rhino horn demand-reduction campaigns should take inspiration from effective anti-fur, anti-tobacco and anti–drunk driving public service announcements—of the sort that feature chilling, disturbing, or fear-triggering messages. For example, fur is murder and you will be shunned if you wear it. Smoking is disgusting and causes cancer. Drunk driving risks killing a child and being sent to jail. Others agree. As Felbab-Brown wrote of demand reduction, "The most effective campaigns have often been ones in which people perceive a particular behavior as a direct threat to their personal interests, especially within a relatively short time, such as severe negative health effects or a reduction in sexual vigor." One particularly effective antidrug campaign aimed at teens in Montana, for example, emphasized that methamphetamine would ruin their looks and make them undateable.

Yet the conservation community, Johnson said, is not comfortable with such an approach.

Although Willemsen agrees that negativity could play an important role in messaging, she pointed out that incorporating it into campaigns is challenging for nonprofits because donors want positive messages. Clueless donors have called or e-mailed her, for example, asking why the Chi campaign doesn't include a cuddly picture of a rhino—so she can only imagine the feedback should TRAFFIC launch a fear-based, negative-reinforcement-style campaign. Thus, she acknowledges that the campaign is really targeting occasional rhino horn users, rather than frequent, die-hard ones.

So what would work for persuading the most stubborn men to put down the horn? According to Johnson's findings, only social status anxiety or health anxiety. The former could be triggered if influential people whom rhino horn users aspire to emulate—like Warren Buffett, Barack Obama, Bill Clinton, or Richard Branson—start speaking out against it. Johnson found that die-hard users are not interested in what women think (regardless of how successful women are), and they aren't strongly swayed by men from their region, either (especially not Chinese men). In other words, they will only listen if global-level male business and political leaders deliver the message that capable men don't need rhino horn.

As for health anxiety, that's a promising approach, because rhino horn is already known to cause negative side effects for some people. In 2011, for example, a twenty-one-year-old woman in Hanoi used rhino horn to treat a mouth rash. Two days later, she developed a high fever, and her face and arms turned bright red and broke out in pimples. As an article about the incident reported, doctors diagnosed her with "an allergic reaction due to poisoning as a result of using rhino horn."

This is not an uncommon story, according to Nguyễn Hữu Trường, an immunologist at Hanoi's Bạch Mai Hospital. He sees about one patient per month suffering from side effects caused by an illegal wildlife product. "Because of culture and perception, people think that traditional medicine is perfect and, unlike Western medicine, that it does no harm," he said. "In fact, traditional medicine can sometimes be more harmful, because the ingredients are more complicated and not exact." He added that the victims tend to be those who are most desperate. "End-stage patients will use whatever they can get, and they'll use a large amount without guidance," he said. "Because they take so much, if there's a problem, they'll die."

The cases he sees most often involve bear bile poisoning, which can be life threatening. With rhino horn (and buffalo horn passed off as rhino horn), negative side effects symptoms usually include a full-body rash, diarrhea, stomach pain, and fever. This reaction could be triggered by the horn itself or by preservatives such as arsenic that are often applied to prevent the horn from rotting or becoming infested with insects. The risks, Trường added, are not worth it: "In my opinion, very few of these things are actually useful. The benefit is much less than the potential harm."

The high rollers who use rhino horn as a way of showing off don't care whether it works medically. But if they knew that they might turn lobster red or have to spend a few days stuck on the toilet after using it, perhaps they would reconsider.

But even if Vietnam's hard-core users abstain, there remains an additional threat: China. Researchers increasingly worry about that massive population being something of a slumbering giant in terms of rhino horn demand. When Johnson first launched her campaign in 2013, for example, she interviewed members of the Chinese community who dealt in illicit wildlife products, many of whom told her that China's laws about rhino horn are quite tight, so they preferred to deal solely in illegal ivory. But as the price for rhino horn has gone up, their interest has been piqued. "It used to be, 'We'll stick to ivory and leave rhino horn to the Vietnamese,'" Johnson said. "But now evidence indicates that they are entering the rhino horn market, not for medicine, but for speculation purposes."

In 2017, Crosta and his colleagues at the Elephant Action League, another nonprofit he cofounded, confirmed this trend in an undercover operation dubbed Operation Red Cloud. In an investigation spanning southern China to Beijing, they readily found rhino horn for sale. Interviews with thirty-five rhino horn traders revealed that the bulk of horn travels into China from Vietnam, often smuggled by individuals, including children and "old Vietnamese women." Corrupt law enforcement officials on either side of the border aid in facilitating the trafficking.

"Personally, I think there are more collectors for rhino horn than ivory," one Chinese dealer in Xianyou told the investigators. Several others indicated that horns with dried blood on them—proof that they came from a recently killed animal—fetch the highest prices. Still others said that they were banking on extinction: they welcomed the news that rhinos are on their way out, because it means prices for stashed horns will only increase as the resource becomes scarcer. Should interest in rhino horn continue to trend upward in China, such speculations will likely pay off. Rhinos will be wiped out.

Four

THE HOLY GRAIL OF HERPETOLOGY

DEATH is the currency of much of the illegal wildlife trade, but it is not always a prerequisite. As blood soaked as the industry is, in some cases, it's precisely an animal's life that a buyer seeks to own. The exotic pet trade is a massive market fueled by a special sort of collector—one whose misplaced fondness for wildlife manifests as a desire to possess it. For many of these individuals, the rarer the animal is, the more sought after it becomes.

Although exotic pets are technically alive, in terms of conservation they might as well be dead. Many, in fact, do die: untold numbers perish during capture and transport, and in captivity before being sold. As Vanda Felbab-Brown wrote in *The Extinction Market,* "Traders can be shockingly frivolous in how many individual birds or animals they are willing to have killed to ensure the survival of a few that can bring high profits on the international market." Even for those that survive, the end result is the same as if they were killed outright. Removed from nature, they no longer play any meaningful role for their species or ecosystem.

Europe, the United States, and Japan remain the biggest markets for nontraditional pets, which range from chimpanzees and cheetahs to endangered parrots and tortoises. The trend is spreading, though: high-end exotics have recently begun gaining popularity in Southeast Asia and China as well. "I can't think of any animal, with the probable exception of a panda, that you couldn't buy here, right now, in Southeast Asia," said Chris Shepherd, executive director of Monitor. "You could get a snow leopard by tomorrow, if you knew the right place to look."

Most species caught up in the pet trade are a far cry from snow leopards. Instead, they skew toward the obscure—the legions of birds, reptiles, amphibians, and fish that aren't featured on conservation billboards or discussed in policy meetings about saving wildlife. Many are scarcely known among scientists, let alone donors and decision makers, so more often than not they slip through the cracks of protection. As Shepherd put it, "It's really frustrating that wildlife trade and crime are big issues in the global media, but, because these aren't popular, charismatic species, the attention and help does not reach them. Not that rhinos, elephants, and tigers are in the clear, but it's not only about them."

Many exotic pet owners genuinely have no idea that their beloved spotted serval or adorable "ticklish" slow loris was snatched from the wild. Out of laziness, negligence, or willful ignorance, they choose to operate under the assumption that their animals were bred in captivity. They are often wrong. This is thanks in part to a gross lack of regulations for many species. CITES, the international treaty that is meant to regulate trade of endangered animals, includes fewer than 10 percent of known reptiles and 8 percent of known birds in its appendixes.

As for regulations that do exist, they are frequently abused or simply ignored. Wild-caught animal export quotas are vastly and routinely exceeded by the likes of Indonesia, Togo, Tanzania, Benin, and other significant source countries, while millions of other illegally captured animals—from baby apes to chameleons—are laundered into legality with fraudulent permits that purport captive breeding. Much of this comes down to corruption or naiveté rather than a fault in the existing rules themselves. "Everyone says CITES sucks, but that's like blaming a hammer for failing to build a house, rather than blaming the builder," Shepherd said. "It's the people charged with making it work who are failing."

Sometimes, though, pet traders don't even bother trying to launder their animals through regulatory loopholes and corrupt officials. Instead, they opt to smuggle them in. There was the trafficking ring in China, for example, that regularly snuck hundreds of critically endangered radiated tortoises from Madagascar onto commercial flights, wrapping the animals in tin foil to throw off customs agents. Upon arrival at the Guangzhou airport, the traffickers would rendezvous in a public toilet with a crooked airport employee, who then took the tortoises to a safe house in the city—details that emerged after the criminals were busted in 2015.

Other operations are cruder. Creatures have been found taped inside hair curlers, strapped onto passengers' bodies, stuffed into prosthetic legs, and sealed in specially designed smuggling pockets sewn within vests and trousers. In some cases, hijacked victims themselves manage to draw attention to their abductor. In 2015, a German was caught at the Jakarta airport when eight baby lizards in his underwear began to squeal, inspiring a local paper to run the headline, "Squeaking Crotch Foils Smuggling Attempt." Likewise, in 2009, fourteen birds were discovered on a passenger flying into Los Angeles from Vietnam after an inspector spotted poop on his shoes and feathers peeking out from his trousers.

Illegal pets that do make it past authorities turn up for sale online, in pet shops, at expos, and at markets. In 2015, investigators from TRAFFIC surveyed three Jakarta markets over a three-day period, tallying more than 19,000 birds of 206 species (including critically endangered ones)—98 percent of which were being sold illegally. "It's ridiculous how close many of the animals caught up in the pet trade are to extinction, and how little is being done about it," Shepherd said.

Therefore, it's not surprising that the pet trade's scope is staggering. In 2016, Indonesia alone exported more than 4 million animals—primarily reptiles—all labeled as captive bred when, in fact, virtually all came from the wild. Shepherd has been to almost every so-called reptile farm in Indonesia, and next to none have commercial-scale breeding facilities; they simply serve as laundering operations for turning wild-caught animals into legally permitted pets. How is this allowed to persist? "It's corruption and, to a certain extent, a complete lack of capacity for authorities to regulate it all," Shepherd said. "Wildlife dealers are running circles around everyone, it's a joke."

This includes the United States, where many of Indonesia's and other country's "captive bred" reptiles ultimately wind up. Although some US Fish and Wildlife Service agents are privy to this scheme, they have to accept shipments that arrive with the necessary permits issued by Indonesian officials. Under US law, the burden of proof is with the authorities: rejecting the shipments would require US agents to prove that the animals were falsely labeled—a nearly impossible feat, considering the service's lack of resources and Indonesia's lack of interest in cooperating. "Traders take advantage of the fact that large-scale importing countries do not have the expertise or policies in place to prevent this form of large-scale fraud," Shepherd said. "Europe and North America are the drivers behind this ongoing demand, and therefore, the scam continues."

As with most facets of wildlife trafficking, the immensity of the pet trade can quickly become overwhelming. But homing in on one peculiar yet exemplary case study can help bring the subject into focus: that of the earless monitor lizard of Indonesia.

The story begins on May 30, 2008, when a research team armed with GPS units, notebooks, and binoculars set out into a dense patch of jungle in Indonesian Borneo. An oil palm company had commissioned them to survey the area for important environmental and cultural assets that might be impacted should the forest be converted into a plantation. They had no idea, however, that an "exceptional herpetofaunal discovery" awaited them that morning, they later wrote.

As midday approached, the sweating group decided to take a break from their uphill trek to have lunch next to a shallow, rocky stream bed. Glancing at the creek between bites, one of the local team members spotted something of note: a brownish-yellow reptile, about a foot long, that he referred to simply as *kadal*—the generic Indonesian word for "lizard." The partially submerged creature had the elongated, snakelike body of a Chinese dragon, the facial features of a cartoon dinosaur, and the pronounced scales of a mini-alligator.

For a few minutes, the strange visitor became the focus of attention as the group photographed it and gently passed it around. To their amazement, it hardly struggled and did not try to bite them. Lunch soon resumed priority, though, and they put the creature back into the stream, where it sat, unmoving, for the next hour. As the group prepared to leave, one of the team members glanced back for a final look, and noted that it had disappeared.

It wasn't until the researchers returned to their computers and reptile identification books that they realized the importance of what they had found: the mystery creature was, in fact, the elusive earless monitor lizard, *Lanthanotus borneensis* (literally, "hidden ear from Borneo," named for its lack of external ear openings). Until recently, scientists and collectors had captured fewer than one hundred specimens since the species' 1877 discovery. Among reptile enthusiasts, its rarity and mystique have earned it a grandiose nickname: "the Holy Grail of herpetology."

In 2012, a few members of the Indonesian survey team published a paper about their finding in the *Journal of Threatened Taxa*. They were careful to limit the amount of detail they included about the lizard's location, noting that, "due to the species' rareness and its high conservation value, it cannot be ruled out that pet reptile collectors and traders may misuse this . . . information." Although they omitted GPS coordinates, they did print a rough map and a description of the habitat.

Unfortunately, the authors had underestimated the tenacity and resourcefulness of the world's unscrupulous reptile collectors. The map and scant description provided ample detail for them to go on—as evidenced by the snowballing number of earless monitor lizards that quickly began turning up in collections and online ads. In June 2014, Vincent Nijman, a conservation ecologist at Oxford Brookes University, spotted a blog post offering pairs of earless monitor lizards for sale in the Czech Republic. By July, specimens had made their way to Europe's largest reptile fair, held in Germany, while photos posted on Facebook, online reptile forums, and dealers' websites began surfacing in countries from Japan to the UK.

Nijman was torn about what to do. On the one hand, he didn't want to bring even more attention to the lizard. On the other, raising awareness about its plight could alert customs agents to look out for it and help it gain important protection. Like so many other obscure species, it was not yet included in the CITES international trade appendixes. In the end, Nijman decided to sound the alarm.

A quick walker with a firm handshake, Nijman stands out for his endearing eccentricities: he styles his shoulder-length curly hair like Kenny G's, continues to use a Nokia brick phone from the mid-2000s, and loves singing Dutch-accented ABBA at karaoke. When I asked him about a dusty human skull that rests on the windowsill of his cluttered office, he picked it up, looked into its empty sockets for a moment, and then replied, "I have no idea who this is or where it came from."

He also happens to be one of the world's leading academic experts on wildlife trafficking. Although he's spent time aplenty conducting surveys in the field, one of his favorite investigative methods can be carried out right under the gaze of that office mystery skull: Internet sleuthing to uncover new trends in the illegal trade. As he likes to tell students and reporters alike, "You can monitor these kinds of things and do entire studies without even leaving the office."

In 2014, he did just that for the earless monitor lizard, publishing his findings along with coauthor Sarah Stoner. Over a seventeen-month period, they documented nearly one hundred earless monitor lizards for sale online, offered by thirty-five different people in eleven countries. Germany and other European nations came out on top, although a few American buyers were also involved (not surprising, given that the United States accounts for 56 percent of all live reptile imports). Some lizards were originally priced at as much as $15,500, but, as the market became saturated, their value fell to $3,300.

"The scale and pace of this trade is something that, twenty years ago, would not have been possible to do through letters and phone calls," Nijman said. "The Internet allows people to very quickly become a part of a small global network of specialized, niche hobbyists who can instantly share information and arrange deals."

The earless monitor lizards that Nijman found for sale on Facebook and reptile forums no doubt originated from the region where the research team worked in Indonesian Borneo. Collectors now regularly travel there, and local villagers now eagerly provide them with what they're after. Hotel staff reportedly tell foreign guests that they can get earless monitor lizards for them, and shopkeepers—in the style of knock-off handbag hawkers in New York City—furtively call out, "We have lizards here!" Some villagers have supposedly made enough off the reptiles to afford a new a motorbike or television.

This is not the first time a species' discovery or rediscovery has triggered a collecting frenzy. According to a 2017 *Science* paper, more than twenty newly described reptiles have been targeted after traders learned of their location in the scientific literature. In 2010, for example, researchers described a new species of psychedelic gecko on a small Vietnamese island; two years later, the geckos began regularly turning up for sale in Europe, priced at up to $3,300 per pair. Likewise, in 2010, when a snake no one had seen since the 1930s suddenly turned up in Vietnam—a so-called Lazarus species, back from the dead of presumed extinction—its rediscovery was quickly followed by online ads touting pairs of "farmed" specimens for $1,800.

Therefore, conservationists have learned the hard way that some discoveries are better left a carefully guarded secret. They either omit location data from papers entirely, or—in the case of some security-savvy journals—upload sensitive information to locked files that can be accessed only with permission. "There are things we keep seriously quiet about, including very, very high-profile species," Nijman said. "Because we know if the news comes out, it'll be the end of them."

For the earless monitor lizard, such a fate may already be set in motion. But because no field data exist for the species—including such basic information as population size or distribution—there's no way of determining if and when the trade will become an existential threat. In the meantime, traders continue to plunder the wild for the lizards, and collectors continue to buy them.

OF ALL THE REPTILE ENTHUSIASTS INVOLVED IN *LANTHANOTUS BORNEENSIS'* STORY, one name stands out above the rest: Tsuyoshi Shirawa. A former wildlife smuggler, he is now Japan's largest wholesale dealer in cold-blooded animals. Among his claims to fame is his standing as the first foreign collector to have gotten hold of the earless monitor lizard following its rediscovery. In 2013—a full year before the lizards began turning up for sale in Europe—he posted a YouTube video filmed at his facility in Japan showing one of the lizards eating an earthworm. This virtual announcement was followed by a 2014 Facebook post claiming that he had achieved the first successful captive breeding of the species, as evidenced by an accompanying live-streaming of the eggs hatching.

Shirawa could be considered a starting as well as ending point for the earless monitor lizard's story. He helped spread word about the species' rediscovery through his YouTube and Facebook posts, which garnered thousands of views. As one enthusiast gushed, "You are a herpetological Gagarin!"—comparing Shirawa to the first human to travel into space.

For some fanboys, watching videos of the lizards online was not enough—they needed to visit in person. As Nijman put it, "There's people who are willing to fly to the other side of the world just to see this lizard and have a photo taken with it." In one Facebook picture shot at Shirawa's facility, for example, Steve Sykes, owner of Geckos Etc. Herpetoculture in California, grins elatedly, mouth hanging open like a puppy, as he gazes down at an earless monitor lizard clutching his thumb. "Herpetologically speaking, this is one of the coolest animals I have ever held in my hands," he wrote in the photo's description. "It takes a lot to get me really excited, but this did it!"

Although Sykes told me that he was "not interested in participating" in a *Newsweek* story I wrote about the lizard in 2014, Shirawa was. After I reached out to him, he began phoning me late at night, enthusiastically professing his dedication to reptile conservation and his commitment to following Japan's wildlife laws. "It is not illegal traffic, and this is not for the commercial animal trade," he told me. "I want to keep the species in our zoo and cooperate with researchers and give everyone my data." In fact, he had already been visited by experts from universities in Japan and Europe, he said. "Conservation of this animal is very much needed, but if we don't know anything about it, we won't know how to keep it."

The *Newsweek* story wasn't exactly flattering for him, however. Although I did report his side of things, I also included TRAFFIC senior director Crawford

Allan's damning take on such reptile fanatics. Many of those involved in the pet trade possess "an almost pathological obsession with collecting the world's rarest animals," he said. "I've met many of these people myself, and some of them actually convince themselves that they're conservation heroes, that they're protecting the species from extinction. But oftentimes their captive bred animals cannot be reintroduced to the wild anyway, because they haven't been kept in strict quarantine conditions, and because they've been inbred. So, while collectors might feel they are doing a service, really, they're only doing a service for themselves—for their own collection and their back pocket." Given this scathing critique, I was a bit surprised that, three years later, Shirawa agreed to meet with me for an interview for this book. "Just please be positive," he implored.

Shirawa's public facility, iZoo (pronounced "ee-zoo"), is in Shizuoka Prefecture, a two-ish hour journey south of Tokyo. I caught the train down on an unusually warm November morning, stocking up on *onigiri* for the ride and putting Air's "Alone in Kyoto" on repeat on my iPod. Tokyo's frenetic hustle soon gave way to jumbled blocks of suburban homes painted in various shades of gray, which in turn softened into picturesque vistas of mist-covered rice fields and farms. Eventually, the landscape parted, revealing the gentle, swirling swells of the North Pacific.

When we pulled up at Kawazu, my destination, I found a sleepy *onsen* town sandwiched between forested green, brown, and orange hills and the glassy sea. A single cab driven by a white-gloved older gentleman was parked in front of the station.

"iZoo, *kudasai*," I said, climbing in.

"*Hai!*"

Before pulling out, the driver reached into the glove compartment and took out a bright brochure that he apparently kept stocked for just such occasions. Pictured on the front was the iZoo logo surrounded by a collage of various snakes, lizards, tortoises, and a grinning crocodile. "Look! Shake! Surprise!" it read in cartoonish, primary-colored Japanese characters.

Fifteen minutes later, we reached the facility. It would be hard to miss: a modern orange brick building with a sweeping shingle roof, iZoo decidedly contrasted with Kawazu's otherwise nondescript houses and drab apartment buildings. When Shirawa bought and renovated the building in 2012, it was a failing turtle aquarium, drawing just 20,000 visitors per year. Now, around 130,000 people stop by annually.

Next to two life-size brass Galapagos tortoises standing out front, the woman at the ticket counter told me that Shirawa wouldn't be here for an hour or so—which was perfect because I wanted to take a look around. I paid the $13.50 entrance fee and headed inside, where the air was at least ten degrees warmer, dense with humidity and the sweet smell of fruit and decay. An obnoxious kids' jingle played on a loop—a chorus of young voices screaming in Japanese "No lion, no giraffe! Only reptiles!" followed by a male voice shouting "iZoo! iZoo!"

It took only a couple of minutes to arrive at the earless monitor lizard exhibit, which Shirawa was clearly very proud of. The grating children's tune was abruptly replaced with an intense tribal drum beat, ushering visitors into a dark, cavern-like hallway lined with blown-up images of earless monitor lizards. At the end of the hall stood a casket-sized tank, illuminated with beams of light like Snow White's glass coffin. Hung up around, memorial-like were laminated newspaper clippings, a map pinpointing the species' origin, and a video display showing an earless monitor lizard eating worms. A placard—the only one in the facility that included an English translation—described the reptiles and bragged of iZoo's standing as the first facility to keep and breed them in captivity. "This must be one of the most rare reptiles in the world, and very few have ever been seen," it read.

Bemusement was my primary emotion as I gingerly approached the glass enclosure and peered down. There, smooshed up against the wall, I spotted my first earless monitor lizard. The motionless creature was curled into an S, its scales gleaming a deep brown, partially submerged in the shallow water. Like a game of Where's Waldo? my eyes began to dart around the tank, trying to identify any other scaled abnormalities. Sure enough, I spotted another lizard wrapped around a rock and a couple more hidden among the mess of stones and detritus.

I'd come all this way to see these animals, but after a few minutes loitering around the exhibit and trying (unsuccessfully) to get a good photo in the dim light, I realized that I was getting kind of bored. The lizards, after all, were just sitting there. I moved on.

After spending half an hour checking out ponds brimming with albino Mexican salamanders, an insect room containing millions of cockroaches behind an all-too-thin glass barrier, and an outdoor area with tortoises the size of toy Power Wheel trucks, right on time, Shirawa found me. We relocated to an empty café next to the gift shop. Professional and neat, he was soft in the face and belly, with strongly arched, thick eyebrows. We took a seat in the far corner, and a waitress brought over some coffee.

"People who don't meet me, they think I'm a gangster or in the mafia or something—that I'm scary," he began. "But I just love reptiles, and reptiles only—nothing else!" He let out a jovial, tinkling laugh. As we continued to chat, he came across, conflictingly, as both a sincere animal lover and a slick, smooth-talking operator.

Born in Shizuoka City, Shirawa's factory worker parents forbade him from keeping dogs or cats at home. But that was okay by him, because, by the time he was five or six years old, he had already developed a keen fondness for lizards, turtles, and snakes. The former two his parents allowed him to keep, the latter they refused. That didn't stop Shirawa, though: he took to smuggling snakes into the house and hiding them in his desk. As he got older, his love for all things scaled and cold blooded grew. "Some people like TV shows or music or cars, but for me, only reptiles," he said. "I don't know why I like them so much, but I've always wanted to be together with them. They're something strange and exotic, and some have mysterious lifestyles. I like for them to be close to me."

After high school, he began breeding and selling reptiles. When he had saved up a little money, he bought a plane ticket to Thailand, where he taught himself Thai and began connecting with reptile wheelers and dealers. Some were traffickers, and he soon followed their example, succumbing to the allure of smuggling. He'd fly into Japan with a suitcase full of animals, sell them in a day, and then fly straight back to Thailand to load up again. In 1989, when he was twenty years old, his luck ran out. He was stopped at the airport in Bangkok when customs officials discovered around fifty endangered turtles and lizards in his luggage, plus around 125 non-CITES-listed lizards. Shirawa was given a three-month suspended prison sentence and fined $100.

The light penalty was not enough to deter him. As he put it, "I was young and naughty."

The experience did, however, make him more wary. When a Japanese customer contacted him a couple of years later to ask whether he could obtain some shingleback lizards—an Australian species that looks like a cross between a pinecone and a very large grub—he instead recruited one of his buddies from Bangkok, a Swiss guy named Michael. Michael said he'd help with the sourcing but not the trafficking, so the buyer sent his wife to Australia to act as a lizard mule. Shirawa met the two there to facilitate, helping to collect eighty shingle-backs that they divided between two suitcases.

When it came time to leave, however, the buyer's wife begged Shirawa to take one of the bags himself. Sure enough, they were stopped at the airport (to this day, Shirawa thinks someone ratted on them). Michael wound up being deported after a month, while the wife served a ten-month prison sentence. Shirawa got it the worst: the jury deemed him the "big boss," so he was given twenty months behind bars. He considers his time in the Australian correctional center well spent, however. "I learned English!" he said, cracking up.

Youthful hiccups behind him, by the late 1990s, Shirawa was Japan's biggest reptile and exotic animal dealer, both wholesale for pet shops and for specialty items sought after by zoos. He became well known for his ability to source difficult-to-acquire species like elephants, orcas, rhinos, and polar bears, and business only grew as the Internet gained popularity, allowing him to connect with exporters and clients in sixty-five countries. "Facebook makes it easier to build relationships with people overseas," he said.

Yet, despite the undoubted success of Shirawa's business ventures, he still couldn't resist dabbling in illegalities. In 2004, a Japanese acquaintance asked him to help launder twenty-four protected radiated tortoises from Madagascar. Shirawa agreed and, colluding with a zoo, created fake permits for eleven of the animals. He kept the remaining thirteen as payment for the deal. The Tokyo police caught on, however, and in 2007 Shirawa and his accomplices were convicted of fraudulent reptile registration and fraudulent trading. "It was my mistake," he said. "I thought this was a very sweet deal. It was like sweet temptation! I'd get thirteen endangered animals for free, just to make papers." He sighed, shaking his head. "I was very stupid, because I thought, 'I'm a professional. I can write anything in my report and it will be accepted.' I was very, very, silly."

This time, he paid a fine of $15,330 and spent two years in prison. Again, though, he did not squander his time: he wrote a book called *The Price of Animals,* detailing his business experience and his adventures obtaining rare species for zoos. Its cover features a gaggle of exotic animals with bar codes on their sides.

Since his release, Shirawa has vowed to steer clear of illegal dealings and insists that he has thoroughly learned his lesson. "It is a fact that I have a shameful past," he said. "However, I am most repentant, and in my heart, I truly and deeply regret my sins. I need to do my utmost to reflect on the past and to erase it. I need to build a new life." So far, it's going well. He's managed not only to get his business back on track but also to get into the government's good graces. As the Japanese reptile market has grown, he's become a trusted source of information for officials, who turn to him for help with everything from managing illegally released former pet pythons to providing suggestions for animal cruelty laws and import quotas.

"Why the members of parliament cooperate with such a person, I do not know. It's crazy," said Masayuki Sakamoto, an environmental lawyer and secretary-general of the Japan Tiger and Elephant Fund, a nonprofit conservation organization. "I think it's because he's wealthy, and the real purpose is to protect commercial trade of reptiles and amphibians. Mr. Shirawa is also a very wise and clever person. He always has—how can I say it—two faces. He has his official face, and the face behind it."

Shirawa insists, however, that he is totally clean now. He's also bringing in fewer animals these days—"just interesting species I import for myself." Most interesting of all, of course, was the recent acquisition of the earless monitor lizard. His involvement began in 2013, when he bought two animals—a male and a female—from an unnamed Japanese dealer. "People think I go to Borneo and catch the lizards myself to bring them here, but no, never," he said. "It's not necessary to go there."

Instead, Shirawa prefers for others to take on the risk themselves, breaking local laws to smuggle the animals out of their native Malaysia, Brunei, and Indonesia where the lizards are strictly protected. Poachers can be fined up to $8,600 and imprisoned for up to five years for trafficking in the species. As Nijman spelled out, "You can't catch earless monitor lizards, you can't keep them, and you can't buy them. And you certainly can't take them with you out of the country."

Once smuggled out, however, the species is fair game for trade in the eyes of many nations. Over 90 percent of reptile have not been evaluated by CITES, and until 2016 this included the earless monitor lizard. The oversight is how Shirawa managed to obtain legal permission to slip specimens into Japan, which—unlike the United States—does not take other countries' domestic wildlife laws into account. Shirawa knows all of this: "In Indonesia, maybe the species is protected and maybe it's not—but it's a domestic law, it's just Indonesian law. In the US, you can't import things that go against domestic laws because of the Lacey Act, but here in Japan, we don't have that. Everyone says it's non-CITES listed, so trading is no problem."

Such weaseling does not sit well with conservationists. Shepherd, for example, points out that even if the lizards were technically legal to buy in Japan, they were ultimately poached and smuggled out of Indonesia illegally. Shirawa's role in the trade was only legalized by holes in Japan's legislation.

When I asked Shirawa whether it bothers him to know that his animals were originally acquired in violation of Indonesian law, he shrugged. "It's not myself who broke it. If I go there, then I have a problem. But I don't even know where exactly these lizards are from. People say Kalimantan in Indonesia, but I never ask because it's not my business to know." He added that Malaysian officials aren't even concerned with upholding their domestic laws pertaining to the earless monitor lizard, because they have actually issued export permits for specimens. "I myself have imported earless monitor lizards from a Malaysian exporter," he said. "We don't hide it, we just import it as commercial trade."

Shirawa's efforts paid off for his collection—and for further solidifying his esteem among fellow reptile enthusiasts. In 2015, he produced four successful hatchlings, while 2016 brought thirteen more. In the meantime, he picked up around thirty additional earless monitor lizards from sellers in Europe. Not a single one has died under his care, he said, and he has refrained from selling any, preferring to remain the only zoo in Japan that has them. "Many people are looking for that lizard," he said—but stressed that commercial gain isn't his motivation. "I want to save this animal for the future," he said. "I've made some mistakes, but now I've changed. Please understand my mind and situation: I just love reptiles."

IN THE YEARS SINCE THE BORNEO RESEARCHERS STOPPED FOR LUNCH AND UNWITtingly released the earless monitor lizard from its Pandora's box, Indonesia has begun cracking down somewhat. In October 2015, the country made its first *Lanthanotus borneensis*–related arrest: a German caught at the Jakarta airport with eight of the animals. He said that he had paid local traders just three dollars a pop. Months later, a second German was stopped with seventeen earless monitor lizards at the West Kalimantan airport.

Unfortunately, however, Indonesia's commitments to conservation only go so far. Although officials there are not okay with seeing the country lose its lizards to Germans, they do seem all right with the profit. Following the lizard's rediscovery, Nijman and other conservationists approached Indonesian authorities numerous times about addressing the growing crisis but were ignored. Likewise, in the months leading up to the 2016 CITES conference—a gathering at which countries submit and vote on species protection proposals—Indonesia ignored pleas to participate, even as Malaysia prepared a proposal requesting the highest level of protection for the earless monitor lizard. "Before the Conference of the Parties, the European Union, for instance, requested numerous times from Indonesia to indicate whether or not it intended to support Malaysia's proposal," Nijman said. "They simply did not answer."

At the conference, when Malaysia presented its case for the highest level of protection for the earless monitor lizard—the level that forbids international commercial trade—Nijman and others had their fingers crossed. But then, for the first time and at the very last minute, Indonesia piped up. Its officials proposed, instead, a lower protection listing with a zero-export quota tacked on. Although this may sound like a good compromise, it's not. The zero-export quota pertains only to wild-caught animals—not ones allegedly bred in captivity—which means earless monitor lizards caught in the wild, like so many other reptile species scooped up in Indonesia, can simply be laundered into legality.

Malaysia, to everyone's horror and surprise, agreed to Indonesia's proposal. Later, the truth came out: Malaysia and Indonesia were in cahoots. A few days before the meeting, the countries had decided to trade votes. Malaysia would support Indonesia's position on the earless monitor lizard and Banggai cardinal fish, and Indonesia, in return, would stand with Malaysia on saltwater crocodiles.

Indonesia's capacity to breed earless monitor lizards at a commercial scale, is extremely doubtful. Shirawa, Nijman said, remains the only one he knows of who has managed to pull it off—and it was no small feat. It required reptile staff tending to the animals 24/7 at a cutting-edge facility that neither aims to churn the lizards out on a commercial scale nor needs to make a profit off them. "If you're a little forestry department out in f-ing wherever, you can't set up a first-class facility and make breeding viable," Nijman said. "Instead, you capture the animals in the wild, keep them in a shed for a few hours, and then they become captive bred second-generation."

Indonesian representatives, however, waved off conservationists' concerns about laundering. To the ire of many, they also insisted that earless monitor lizards constituted a "livelihoods issue"—a favorite buzzword for justifying unscrupulous hunting and trade.

"Livelihoods, ha!" Shepherd said of this claim. "Livelihoods of who? A couple Germans and some illegal reptile dealers?"

Nijman was equally exasperated. "Everyone involved knew it was a lie, but Indonesia wants to make money," he said. "I love Indonesia—I lived there for years—but sometimes I feel so embarrassed by how they approach things. I knew this would happen, though, because that's how they are."

For him and others concerned with the earless monitor lizard's future, it was a big loss. Had the species been given the highest level of protection at CITES, then illegal trade would have persisted on some level, yes, but it would have been much easier to control. Any earless monitor lizards found in anyone's possession would have been illegal—period. Now, as Nijman put it, "it's an absolute mess."

Still, he does not place the entirety of the blame on Indonesia for choosing profit over preservation—nor even on the authors of the original paper that announced the lizard's discovery. Instead, he believes the people who did the most damage to the species' conservation are none other than himself and his coauthor. By going public with their findings about the escalating trade, they further raised the lizard's profile and spread the word that it's available. "I'm not sure if I'd do it again," he said. "I think I have a moral obligation to report it, but perhaps it's a case where good intentions went wrong."

If I'm being honest with myself, I have to admit that I, too, have likely played some role in those good intentions gone wrong, by writing a cover story for *Newsweek* about the earless monitor lizard, and with this chapter. As Nijman said, "Perhaps the worst thing that could have happened for the species's conservation was me and Sarah publishing the TRAFFIC report, and then talking to you, a journalist."

Indeed, Shirawa, in passing, confirmed these fears. Back at the zoo, he told me that my *Newsweek* story had brought him some positive attention. Grinning, he thanked me.

Five

WHITE GOLD

Wᴇʀᴇ the illegal wildlife trade to select a poster child, elephants would probably be it. No other species elicits such passion among the public—or controversy among conservationists, who have argued for decades about how best to go about saving the world's largest land animals. Much of the debate boils down to one deceptively simple question: Should we trade ivory or not?

Ivory, to be clear, is the hard, creamy-white dentine that makes up an elephant's tusks. Tusks are nothing more than two large teeth—the animal's upper incisors. Almost all African elephants, and most male Asian elephants, have them, and they use them for all sorts of things: digging for water, lifting objects, stripping bark from trees, protecting trunks, gathering food, and defense. Elephants' tusks are not the only material traded as ivory, though; the teeth of mammoths, walruses, hippopotamuses, warthogs, and narwhals sometimes fall under the ivory umbrella, too. But, of all the variations, the tusks from Africa's two species of elephants—particularly, forest elephants—are generally the most prized, for their size, color, density, and quality.

Ivory is beautiful when carved, and our lust for it is timeless. As far back as 25,000–35,000 years ago, people in Germany and Russia were creating ivory jewelry and tools. By 2750 BCE, ancient Egyptians in search of ivory may have extirpated elephants from their stretch of the Sahara, while the Romans ensured the rest of North Africa's and Asia Minor's herds went extinct by the seventh century CE. Arab traders and European colonialists soon took over emptying the continent of elephants, and after independence the killing continued.

From an estimated 26 million elephants in the 1500s, by 1900, the Arab and colonial ivory frenzy had reduced continent-wide elephant populations to an estimated 10 million—at which point the fever had also reached North America. The United States alone imported tusks from 600,000 elephants in the first two decades of the twentieth century, often turning them into piano keys. Recreational hunters also contributed to the killing. Around midcentury, though, interest shifted from colossal hunting safaris to hunting-free protected areas supported by tourism. The killings subsided, leaving the continent with around 1.3 million savanna and forest elephants. Iain Douglas-Hamilton wrote in *Battle for the Elephants,* "In the 1960s, no one in their wildest dreams imagined that one day armed men with automatic weapons would invade the parks and slaughter elephants and rhinos." Yet that is precisely what happened.

The 1970s and 1980s saw elephant killings reach such skyrocketing proportions as to threaten the continued existence of Africa's two species. By the mid-1970s, seven hundred tons of ivory on average—roughly equivalent to 70,000 dead elephants—were leaving Africa each year, much of it stopping in Hong Kong for carving before being sold in other countries. As sales abroad grew, the price a poacher in Africa could expect to fetch for ivory jumped from around $2.50 per pound in the 1969, to $34 per pound in 1978, to more than $90 per pound in 1989.

Although ivory was exported to the United States, Europe, China, and elsewhere, "the first elephant holocaust," as this period is sometimes called, was largely driven by growing demand in Japan. The country was in the midst of its "economic miracle" years, and personal incomes there soared. Meanwhile, newly developed mechanized carving techniques made ivory manufacturing faster than ever before. Japan quickly became the world's largest ivory consumer, with 40–50 percent of all tusks that left Africa ultimately winding up there. Much of that ivory was turned into *hankos*—personalized name stamps used for authorizing everything from bank account documents to marriage certificates. One *hanko* factory claimed to plow through a ton of ivory—the equivalent of at least a hundred elephants—every day.

Although a portion of the ivory traded at this time was done legally, an increasing amount was not. Many African nations had retained colonial-era laws pertaining to hunting and wildlife conservation, which included—at least on paper—strict controls of ivory exports. Oftentimes, though, authorities themselves—including presidents—were behind the breaking of those laws. In 1973, Douglas-Hamilton estimated that just 44 percent of ivory harvested in Kenya was of legal origin, while researchers at the Environmental Investigation Agency calculated that over 90 percent of ivory that left Tanzania around that time was illegal. Somalia, Sudan, South Africa, Uganda, and others regularly laundered tusks smuggled in from animals poached in neighboring nations. By 1988, ivory trade expert Esmond Bradley Martin estimated that up to 88 percent of ivory imported into China was illegal, while Masayuki Sakamoto, secretary general of the Japan Tiger and Elephant Fund, found that 70 percent of Japan's ivory imports from 1981 to 1990 were.

As the price of ivory rose, the political turmoil that engulfed several nations created ideal conditions and incentives for poaching. AK-47s—which had poured into the continent by the millions since the 1960s—were used to kill not only fellow human beings but also animals, whose valuable parts helped purchase even more guns. As Douglas-Hamilton wrote, "In the new wars unleashed in Africa, ivory was a currency of conflict." UNITA rebels in civil-war-plagued Angola, for example, exchanged poached rhino horns and tusks of as many as 100,000 elephants for weapons and ammunition provided by the South African Defense Force, which in turn sold the goods to Taiwan and Japan. Jonas Savimbi, the UNITA rebel leader, was so thankful for the trade that he gifted South African president P. W. Botha a life-size AK-47 sculpture carved out of ivory.

As the killings continued, aerial surveys began to reveal many more dead than live elephants. "If the bodies had been human," Douglas-Hamilton wrote, "what had happened would have been called genocide." Kenya's elephant population declined by 85 percent from the early 1970s to the late 1980s, while Sudan's 100,000 elephants fell to perhaps 10,000 over those years. Between 1969 and 1971 alone, Uganda—which was contending with political and civil chaos following a military coup—lost half of its 40,000 animals. Similar stories played out in Zambia, Cameroon, the Ivory Coast, and more.

Corruption went hand in hand with much of the killing. In Kenya, for example, official involvement went straight to the top. President Jomo Kenyatta's daughter, Margaret—who served as mayor of Nairobi and the Kenyan ambassador to the United Nations—and his fourth wife, Mama Ngina, were likely the country's largest traders in ivory and charcoal (made from Kenya's felled forests), according to a recently declassified 1978 CIA report. As the CIA authors write, "Although the export of these items is banned because depletion of Kenya's forests and wildlife threaten the underpinnings of the Kenyan economy, both women have been able to obtain special licenses and are rumored to be involved in smuggling." Evidence also indicates that President Kenyatta authorized additional ivory export permits in direct contravention of Kenya's laws and retroactively legalized illegal ivory in his daughter's possession. So, when the president pledged to stop poaching in 1978, some, understandably, were dubious.

Yet Kenya was actually on the lighter end of the corruption spectrum at the time. In the Central African Republic, by contrast, dictator Jean-Bédel Bokassa openly declared the entirety of the country's elephants and ivory his personal property and vowed to flog to death anyone caught trying to steal those assets. Thousands of elephants were killed under his watch, with the proceeds from their ivory—predominantly sold to France—use to fund Bokassa's disastrous decade-long reign.

In 1979, the world received a serious wake-up call about the gravity of the poaching threat when Douglas-Hamilton—following tireless aerial surveys in thirty-four countries—reported that elephant populations were declining in all but a few Southern African nations. The ivory trade, meanwhile, had proliferated since 1950, from about two hundred tons traded per year to about seven hundred. Clearly, there was a connection. Douglas-Hamilton and other like-minded conservationists increasingly believed that closing the international ivory trade was the only way to save African elephants from complete obliteration (CITES, the treaty tasked with regulating international trade of endangered species, had already banned trade in Asian elephant ivory in 1975). Even ivory dealers agreed. As one major trader in the Central African Republic sneeringly told Oria Douglas-Hamilton, Iain's wife and research partner, in 1985, "What your husband is doing is a waste of time. . . . To save elephants you must close the ivory trade—world wide."

It took years before that happened. Governments—mostly Southern African states—argued that closing the trade would hurt their economies, and certain conservationists astonishingly continued to insist that the ivory trade posed no threat to elephants. The increasing number of tusks being exported from Africa, they claimed, came from natural elephant mortalities, animals killed to protect crops, and carefully controlled culling operations meant to keep populations in check. Later, however, it was revealed that some of the fiercest opponents of closing the trade were accepting payments from the ivory industry.

In 1985, experts contracted by CITES tried to take a middle-of-the-road approach: rather than support calls to close the trade, they proposed an ivory quota system, meant to set sustainable, science-based limits on ivory exports. In fact, however, the system was riddled with laundering-friendly loopholes. For one, it enticed countries that were not yet members of CITES to join the treaty by offering them ivory amnesty—that is, they could legally sell their stockpiles of poached ivory, so long as they signed up for CITES. Hundreds of tons of formerly illegal ivory began flooding the market, to the effect that 78 percent of "legal" ivory traded in the years following the quota system originated from poached elephants. With CITES's blessing, Burundi, for example—a country with no surviving elephants of its own—legally auctioned off eighty-nine tons of poached ivory from its neighbors' elephants. To keep the laundering party going, traders and carvers simply hopped from place to place as they signed on to CITES—from Hong Kong to Singapore to the United Arab Emirates.

While conservationists wrung their hands over the quota system, ivory manufacturing bigwigs celebrated a major windfall. Especially in the West, people wanted to believe that they weren't purchasing products from murdered elephants, so legally certified ivory sold for twice as much as ivory lacking requisite paperwork. The new quota system legitimized poached ivory, ushering in millions in extra earnings for dealers. K. T. Wang, one of the most powerful ivory barons in Hong Kong, was so excited about this development that he donated $20,000 to CITES in thanks. He wasn't the only one. In 1989, evidence emerged that ivory traders in Japan and Hong Kong had contributed at least $200,000 of supposedly no-string-attached donations to CITES. As Allan Thornton, president of the Environmental Investigation Agency, wrote in *To Save an Elephant,* "In those circumstances, who could believe that CITES had ever had the elephant's best interests at heart?"

As all of this was going on, major conservation organizations—including WWF and its scientific partner, the IUCN—mostly buried their heads in the sand. They issued no recommendations against buying or selling ivory, let alone voice support for closing the ivory trade. "When we asked WWF why they don't support an ivory ban, the soundbite we kept hearing was because Africans don't want an ivory ban," Thornton said. "Or they'd just say it was impossible, and that was that."

The Western press, however, did not remain silent, and public opinion began to turn against the trade. In addition to that mounting pressure, several reports released prior to a major CITES meeting in 1989 provided damning evidence of the quota system's failings and the ongoing threat to elephants' survival. They were still being killed at a rate of around 200 per day. In just ten short years, over half of Africa's elephants had disappeared—from 1.3 million in 1979, to just 600,000 in 1989. Put another way, total losses over a two-decade period topped 80 percent.

Like dominoes, individual countries began to ban new ivory imports and exports—first Britain, followed by France, the United States, Canada, other European nations, and even Japan. WWF changed its tune in favor of a ban, joining dozens of other conservation organizations. Nonprofit groups and individual scientists had no direct say in whether a trade ban would be passed, however; that would require at least two-thirds of CITES countries present to vote in favor of protecting elephants.

Tempers were hot at the decisive 1989 meeting. "Entrenched positions were adopted and insults were hurled," as Keith Somerville described in *Ivory,* and for four days the debate raged on. A vote to put all African elephants on Appendix I—the highest level of protection allocated by CITES, which would ban all international commercial trade—was shot down. Another two proposals, ones that would ban trade with the exception of certain African nations, also failed to pass. As a final option, Somalia proposed a compromise that would put African elephants on Appendix I and thus ban ivory trade, but that would also allow for the possibility to resume the trade in the future should countries prove they have the necessary controls in place.

As expected, China, Burundi, South Africa, Congo, and Zimbabwe voted against Somalia's proposal. But many more nations—more than ninety—voted in favor. The proposal passed. In the meeting hall, applause suddenly broke out, and attendees began jumping to their feet, many with tears their eyes. As Douglas-Hamilton recalled, "It was as if an innocent man who was condemned to death had been reprieved."

Indeed, it was almost immediately apparent that the ban was a lifesaver for many of Africa's remaining 600,000 elephants. Across the continent, the value of poached tusks plummeted to less than $1.50 per pound, which translated into significantly fewer elephants killed—with some countries enjoying a 90 percent reduction in poaching. Customer bases also crumbled, causing the industry to dry up. A year after international trade ground to a halt, just 5 of 550 carvers retained their jobs at the Beijing Ivory Carving Factory, while 75 percent of Hong Kong's ivory craftsmen moved on to different work. As Thornton said, "People just stopped killing elephants because no one wanted to buy ivory."

That's not to say illegal trade came to a complete halt. Notably, Zimbabwe's army carried out mass poaching in the years following the ban, while South Africa acted as a major conduit for contraband tusks smuggled from Zambia, Mozambique, and elsewhere. The CITES decision to up-list elephants, which went into effect in 1990, also excluded both "pre-convention" and "pre-ban" ivory, so many countries, the United States included, continued to allow domestic trade of "antique" ivory. Unscrupulous dealers attempted to pass new ivory off as older material, sometimes staining it with tea to give it a weathered look.

But for the most part, live elephants were, once again, worth more than dead ones. As Dave Currey of the Environmental Investigation Agency wrote in 1991, "The shadow of extinction which had hung for so long over the African elephant had begun to lift."

FOR THE NEXT DECADE, THINGS CONTINUED TO LOOK UP. BUT, BY THE TURN OF THE century, signs of trouble—quietly at first, and then more insistently—began to emerge. Poaching was steadily growing, and experts warned that history was in danger of repeating itself.

Demand for ivory in the East had simultaneously begun to reignite—especially in China, where ivory carvings have served as a status symbol since the Ming dynasty (1368–1644 CE). Until the 2000s, however, ivory was the purview of only a privileged few with expendable income. Now that more people had joined that group, China suddenly sprung up as the single largest importer of illegal ivory, a determination based on seizure data. "In our 2002 analysis of this data, we were able to demonstrate that China had emerged as the world's driver in illicit trade of ivory," said Tom Milliken, TRAFFIC's elephant and rhino program leader, who also runs CITES's Elephant Trade Information System. When he and his colleagues announced this at a CITES meeting, however, the Chinese government, by some accounts, threw a tantrum; officails did not want to accept the findings. "They unsuccessfully challenged our presentation of these results—up to the highest levels of the CITES Secretariat," Milliken said.

As the years passed, China's central role in the illegal trade became impossible to deny. Poaching rose steadily throughout the 2000s, shot up exponentially between 2009 and 2011, and then plateaued. Experts found that rising household consumption in China—but not in any other nation—tracked closely with the number of elephants killed, "suggesting a direct link between Chinese buying power and African poaching," wrote Ronald Orenstein in *Ivory, Horn and Blood*.

Contemporary Chinese collect ivory for all sorts of reasons, from its aesthetic beauty and investment potential to its religious and cultural value. Because ivory jewelry gradually turns from white to yellow as it ages, some people believe it absorbs toxins from the body and thus wear it for health. Others think it brings good luck, because the Mandarin word for "ivory"—*xiang ya*—is similar to the word for "auspicious," *ji xiang*. "All of these values are interconnected, and sometimes people buy ivory for several different reasons," said Yufang Gao, an anthropology and conservation doctoral student at Yale University. "Distinguishing these motivations individually can help conservationists design more appropriate messaging for behavior change."

When Gao first began his research, most Western conservationists assumed that ivory trade in China was primarily, or even solely, driven by middle-class and newly wealthy consumers who buy the material to show off. Entrepreneurial businessmen will, for example, buy elaborate ivory carvings—sometimes for as much as $2 million per piece—to display in the lobby of their headquarters or their CEO's office as sign of their success. But although this group is part of the story of China's ivory consumers, it does not represent the full cast. With his research, Gao aims to clear up such misunderstandings and oversights among Chinese, Africans, and Westerners. "Each person is constrained by his or her own perspective, but I'm trying to combine and integrate everyone's perspectives," he said. By paving the way toward greater understanding, he hopes to enable different groups to better work toward the common goal of ending illegal wildlife trade.

Lishu Li, manager of the wildlife trade program at the Wildlife Conservation Society's China office, agrees that status is not the primary driver of ivory trade in her country. Instead, she pins much of the recent interest on a new type of consumer—the cultural collectors, as she describes them—who seek ivory as a means of tapping into old traditions. Cultural collectors fit within the broader context of China's root-searching movement (*xungen*), which began taking off in the 1990s, partly in response to the lingering wound left by the Cultural Revolution and other socialist policies that attempted to snuff out aspects of Chinese tradition. Now that wealth has made life easier and society has begun to loosen up somewhat, "we start to miss our identity—even if it may be a false identity," Li explained. "This is probably a stage that every society that's transitioning into modernity goes through. The old times become more beautiful in memory."

To cultural collectors, ivory carvings—along with traditional medicine, acupuncture, martial arts, Chinese antiques, rhino horn cups, and more—represent old times. Simultaneously, they may also view ivory as an investment that they can proudly bequeath to their children. In 2002, wholesale ivory was priced at just $55 per pound, but in 2014—a few years after China's state-run television network endorsed it as a wise purchase—prices soared to $955 per pound. Stores reportedly could not keep enough ivory—which marketers sometimes referred to as "white gold" or "organic gemstone"—on shelves.

"In China, there's not many channels for investing money besides real estate or the stock market, but people have more and more disposable income," Gao said. "After 2008, the real estate and stock market didn't perform as well as people expected, so they started to channel capital into art investment—traditional paintings, calligraphy, porcelain, rare books, furniture and more." Ivory and rhino horn also fall into that category, although they may hold an even greater appeal for some collectors-cum-investors, because they are made from disappearing wildlife. "Buyers think to themselves, 'There will be less and less of these things in the future, therefore, they will increase in value,'" Li said.

In other cases, though, ivory collection seems to be more innocent: people simply do not realize that their purchasing decisions hurt elephants. In 2007, the International Fund for Animal Welfare (IFAW) surveyed around 1,200 Chinese in six cities and found that 70 percent believed that ivory falls harmlessly out of elephants' mouths—like a person losing a tooth. Grace Ge Gabriel, IFAW's Asia regional director, was shocked to learn that two of her staff members even believed this. The confusion, she hypothesized, may stem from the Chinese word for "tusk," which literally translates as "elephant tooth." When the IFAW surveyors explained to people that ivory extraction kills elephants, however, they were pleased to find that over 80 percent said they would not buy ivory. "That was really telling," Gabriel said. "I used to think that Chinese are prejudiced against elephants, but this made me realize we're not. We just don't know."

It's also a misconception that everyone in China wants ivory. Buyers are only a tiny fraction of the Chinese population—less than 1 percent, according to Gao. The problem, however, is that China is such a large nation, even a small minority can cause significant impacts for elephants.

From 2010 to 2015, Mozambique lost half its elephants to poachers, while Tanzania's population declined by 60 percent. In Zambia, dead elephants counted in aerial surveys outnumbered living ones six to one, while Chad's herds were mowed down by Janjaweed raiders on horseback. "This killing is not a normal one," said Alfred Kikoti, a research scientist at Tanzania's World Elephant Center, in 2012. "In the past, poachers were selective. But now, no more. They kill whole elephant families and take even the tiniest ivory."

Continent-wide surveys confirmed that the new trade threatened the existence of Africa's two species of elephants. From 2002 to 2011, poachers contributed to a 62 percent decline of forest elephants—the diminutive and more enigmatic western cousin of East and Southern Africa's iconic savannah elephants. Savannah elephants are faring only slightly better, as revealed by an epic project dubbed the Great Elephant Census. With backing from philanthropist and Microsoft cofounder Paul Allen, Cessna-flying census researchers crisscrossed almost 290,000 miles in eighteen African countries counting every live and dead elephant they spotted.

The results were telling: from 2007 to 2014, 144,000 elephants died, equating to an overall population decline of 30 percent in just seven years. The deaths, the researchers found, were also accelerating, with the latest figures putting population losses at about 8 percent each year. Although poaching is not entirely to blame—elephants do succumb to old age, injury, and disease, and crop-raiding animals are often put down—illegal killing for ivory, the authors concluded, was the primary driver behind downward-spiraling numbers. Conservationists knew the situation on the ground was bad, but the census revealed that things are much worse than many imagined: only about 415,000 savanna elephants remain today.

Many believe that decisions made at CITES, once again, in fact helped drive this latest wave of death—this time by succumbing to pressure to allow two one-off auctions of many tons of stockpiled ivory. The sales were "directly responsible for the intensification of elephant poaching," said Bill Clark, an honorary warden and US liaison to the Kenya Wildlife Service. "The newly legalized ivory provided the perfect vehicle into which contraband could be laundered."

The first sale, which was agreed on in 1997 and took place in 1999, before the new crisis had heated up, was generally seen as a way to test the waters of a reopened trade. Following intense lobbying by Japan and Zimbabwe—including personal interventions made by President Robert Mugabe—CITES representatives agreed to let Zimbabwe, Botswana, and Namibia undertake an "experimental" sale of fifty tons of ivory to Japan, for $4.7 million total. A couple of years earlier, CITES had also granted Botswana, Namibia, and Zimbabwe the additional bonus of down-listing their elephant populations to Appendix II—a lesser level of CITES protection that typically permits trade—and in 2000 South Africa's elephant population was down-listed as well. But the transfers were accompanied by a stipulation that, for the time being, ivory would remain off limits, save for the one-off sale.

The 1999 sale piqued China's interest—and jealousy. "Private entrepreneurs in China saw this as an opportunity to revive the ivory industry," Gabriel said. Chinese officials soon joined the Japanese in badgering CITES for a second sale. By 2007, their efforts were clearly working. Gabriel still recalls in vivid detail a run-in she had with the head of China's CITES delegation around that time: "If you can hold off Japan, then we don't need the ivory," he told her. "But if you cannot, then you'd better back away."

Being from China, Gabriel immediately understood his meaning. "It's a matter of face," she said. "For Japan to be approved and China not—well, I also felt that this is not fair. On the other hand, I knew this was another disaster waiting to happen." Indeed, when Japan received quick approval for the second one-off sale, China shortly followed. "Literally, I have had a front row seat, watching this disaster play out, from as early as 2000," Gabriel said. She and her colleagues had repeatedly shown that neither China nor Japan had strong enough regulations in place to prevent illegal ivory from being laundered into their legal markets, but those findings were brushed aside. She wasn't alone. The Environmental Investigation Agency, likewise, released a report in 2007 showing that China lacked the capacity, legislation, and political will to control ivory trade—as exemplified by the fact that 110 tons of ivory had recently gone missing from a government-controlled stockpile. The findings fell on deaf ears. "There was no factual or evidentiary basis for supporting China's inclusion in the ivory sale, but WWF and TRAFFIC were saying things like 'Oh, this will flood the market with ivory and drive prices down,'" said Thornton. "We couldn't stop it, and as a result, everything we said would happen has happened—and worse."

The sale went forward. Botswana, Namibia, Zimbabwe, and South Africa were granted permission to auction 107 tons of ivory, which sold to China and Japan for more than $15 million—an amount far less than the ivory's estimated value, due to alleged price fixing by the buyers.

Opinions vary widely over whether this and the 1999 sale heightened demand for ivory and contributed to the upsurge in poaching. "Was the 2008 sale a mistake? I personally believe that, whether it had happened or not, we'd still be in the same situation," Milliken said. "Look at other aspects of the wildlife trade—pangolins, rhino horn, you name it. There's been no one-off sale for those things, and demand is soaring." Others, however, strongly believe that the sales—2008 especially—were a deadly misstep for elephants. Some ivory traders in West and Central Africa told researchers that they interpreted the auctions as signaling that the ivory ban would soon be lifted, while China claimed that the 1999 sale confused its citizens about the legality of ivory. Anecdotes and opinions aside, empirical evidence of the 2008 sale's repercussions is shown in a 2016 working paper published by Solomon Hsiang, the chancellor's associate professor of public policy at the University of California, Berkeley, and Nitin Sekar, a conservation scientist at Princeton University. Crucially, neither researcher had ever studied or involved himself in ivory trade issues before, and thus was free from the entrenched biases that have stewed over the last three-plus decades.

Hsiang and Sekar analyzed poaching trends based on the best available data of the number of elephants illegally killed before and after the sale, and the amount of ivory trafficked. Poaching was stable, they found, between 2003 and 2007, but in 2008—following the sale announcement—this abruptly changed, with both poaching and smuggling jumping significantly. Hsiang and Sekar wanted to be sure they weren't confusing correlation with causation, so they tested more than a dozen other possible factors that might account for the sudden upward shift, including changes in the Chinese economy, increasing numbers of Chinese workers in Africa, or the 2008 financial crisis. None explained the jump. They also looked at whether poaching of rhinos and tigers had also surged in 2008, but, again, nothing.

Hsiang was surprised by the results, but he trusted the data. "We can never be totally conclusive, but it looks as though a very large amount of the increase in poaching seen in the last few years can be traced back to the sale event in 2008," he said. He believes there are three explanations behind this finding: (1) people who previously did not purchase ivory because it was illegal now felt it was acceptable to buy; (2) the Chinese government actively marketed ivory as a good investment; and (3) the presence of fresh, legal ivory made fresh, illegal ivory easier to conceal.

Steven Levitt, a distinguished professor of economics at the University of Chicago and author of *Freakonomics,* who was not involved in the study, said Hsiang and Sekar's study was convincing and thoughtful and that he was persuaded by it. But others—some of whom have worked or continue to work for CITES, and a few who work for the World Bank—considered Hsiang and Sekar's work deeply flawed. Fiona Underwood, an independent statistical consultant and co-opted member of the CITES technical group that tracks illegal killings of elephants and trade in ivory, was one of the most vocal opponents. "We looked at Hsiang and Sekar's findings and found a number of difficulties with their approach," she told me in an e-mail cosigned by Bob Burn, another independent statistical consultant who has worked for CITES. She and Burn concluded that Hsiang and Sekar did not properly account for certain properties of the data. The logic behind their approach was also flawed, they said, because Hsiang and Sekar oversimplified the complex drivers behind the illegal ivory trade.

But Sekar countered that he and Hsiang *did* account for everything Underwood, Burn, and others accused them of overlooking—citing the lengthy, statistics-filled responses they published online. "We really have painstakingly responded to every serious contention they have made," he said. At this point, Underwood and others' concerns, he said, can stem only from their unfamiliarity with the methods that he and Hsiang used. Meanwhile when he and Hsiang examined a 2011 analysis that Underwood and Burn carried out, they discovered that the researchers had unintentionally smoothed out their data, obscuring the abrupt change that occurred in 2008. Hsiang now uses the 2011 paper in class as an example of "how statistical tools can hide patterns if you're not careful."

Underwood and Burn stand by both their critique and their findings. "We acknowledge that the presence of the domestic ivory trade in China is one potential driver of the illegal ivory trade, just not the 'only driver,' as Hsiang and Sekar apparently believe," they wrote. "Simply put, we believe illegal ivory trade is more complicated than that. Studies that provide evidence of the relative importance of different drivers of the trade are challenging and have yet to be done."

Sekar and Hsiang, however, are not arguing against the fact that illegal trade is fueled by more than one driver. "Obviously, there are a multitude of cultural, economic, and ecological factors that affect how ivory markets function," Sekar said. "But we couldn't find a sudden change in any such factors that would explain the sudden jump in poaching, beginning in 2008. Future work might find alternative explanations, but policy decisions have to be made with the information we have now."

Eventually—after publishing more than a hundred pages of text defending themselves—Hsiang and Sekar stopped engaging. As Hsiang said, the latest criticism "was such obvious cherry picking of data, it didn't seem to even merit a response." At the same time, the researchers publicly shared the code they used to arrive at their findings—which were successfully replicated by their detractors. "What all this shows is that we didn't make some fundamental mistake in processing or analyzing the data," Sekar explained. "Our analysis wasn't wrong, it was just different and—we would argue—better. We just showed the conservation community what the data say. If critics think we tampered with the data or used screwy analytical techniques, then let them point out where we did that in the code. They have everything they need to find evidence of wrongdoing."

As arguments over legal trade's role in triggering illegal trade continue, others are making a more radical proposal: to sustainably supply consumers with deliberately harvested ivory. Yet such ideas are based on erroneous assumptions. Elephant tusks do not grow back if removed—and they actually need them for all sorts of survival-related tasks. What's more, even if we deemed it acceptable to mutilate elephants for this purpose, there is no feasible way to harvest tusks: they are embedded in the animals' skulls and have a nerve running down their center. This means ivory would have to come from culled elephants and ones that die naturally. But according to a 2016 *Current Biology* study, over the long run, culling would not work, either, because elephants reproduce and grow too slowly to harvest enough ivory to satiate the market without decimating the species. Even if multiple elephant "farms" of managed herds were set up across Africa, it would still be impossible to meet the estimated two-hundred-plus tons of ivory—roughly 20,000 elephants killed each year—that the world currently demands.

Even if the numbers did line up, though, that scheme probably wouldn't stop poaching. Timothy Tear, executive director of the Wildlife Conservation Society's Africa program, explained why: "The problem is, you can't distinguish between legal and illegal tusks. Heroin or human trafficking—that's easy to distinguish, because it's all illegal. The situation with ivory, however, is more similar to arms trafficking, because some weapons are legal, others are illegal. But even arms have serial numbers. That's where ivory falls off. People wind up homogenizing all ivory as either legal or illegal, and, on top of that, there's corruption, making it even harder to navigate. Until we can sort that out, all we're doing with legal sales is supporting a really awful illegal industry. There should be a better way, but for now closing the market is one of the few things we can do."

Some global leaders agree. In September 2015, President Barack Obama and China's president Xi Jinping agreed to shut down much of the domestic trade within their nations' borders. Obama made good on his word the following June by enacting a near-total ban on US ivory trade, and in December Xi announced that China would do the same by the end of 2017. Conservationists were elated, calling Xi's decision "the single greatest measure" thus far in the fight to save elephants.

This represents quite a shift for China. Just a few years ago, officials denied that China's ivory consumption had anything to do with the slaughter of Africa's elephants. Reporters who inquired about such a link were labeled "unprofessional" and "misleading," while nonprofit groups were accused of disseminating inaccurate information.

The reality on the ground, told a very different story. By 2013, Chinese customs agents had made about nine hundred ivory seizures and doled out more than thirty life sentences to higher-level traffickers (experts estimate that seizures typically represent just 10–15 percent of total illegal trade). Awkwardly, even as China repeatedly claimed to have thoroughly secured the trade, evidence emerged that high-level officials were allegedly involved in ivory trafficking. According to a report published by the Environmental Investigation Agency (EIA), government officials accompanying President Xi on a state visit to Tanzania in 2013 reportedly bought up so much illegal ivory that local prices doubled. Thousands of pounds of ivory were allegedly smuggled back to China in diplomatic bags on the presidential plane—an accusation that officials in both China and Tanzania adamantly denied. After the report was published, the Chinese embassy in London invited the EIA investigators to a meeting, where they presented their findings and shared footage and visuals obtained in the investigation. But, rather than continue with an internal investigation of their own, "the only response from the embassy was a request to take down the report from our website, which we politely refused to do," said Shruti Suresh, a senior wildlife campaigner at the EIA.

President Xi's abrupt change of tune and decision to ban ivory are likely the result of several persuasive factors. Eliminating the trade dovetails nicely with his administration's goal of squashing corruption, and it also does away with the increasingly embarrassing international finger pointing about his nation's role in the demise of elephants. In a nation of 1.4 billion, the ivory trade is also just a minuscule economic speck, employing fewer than 3,000 people at thirty-four manufacturing outlets and 130 retail shops. By banning ivory, Beijing had nothing to lose and everything to gain.

Gabriel is optimistic. After the news dropped, she recalls asking a law enforcement officer in China what he thought about the development. "It's going to make our job so much easier," he replied. She believes that Chinese law enforcement is genuinely committed to enforcing the new rules and expects that the black market will soon be a faint shadow of its former self.

She might be right. Encouragingly, after China announced its impending ban, longtime ivory researchers Martin and Lucy Vigne found that the wholesale price of ivory in China dropped by nearly 50 percent, from $950 per pound in 2014 to $500 per pound in 2015. Those whom they spoke to in the industry about the future of their profession are, Martin said, "pessimistic, without exception."

IN EARLY 2017, JUST A COUPLE OF MONTHS AFTER THE IMPENDING BAN WAS AN-nounced, I visited one of China's 130 licensed ivory retail outlets. Nicola, a young program officer at TRAFFIC's China office, joined me (to maintain her cover, she asked that her Chinese name not be used). We met at McDonald's (not my choice) on Wangfujing Street, one of Beijing's most famous shopping cen-ters. Nicola's innocuous appearance also likely helps her avoid suspicion: it is not what you'd imagine a stereotypical investigator to look like. Her hair was styled in a cute bob, and she wore a multicolor checkered sweater beneath a stylish brown leather jacket. Her glasses were blinged out with rhinestones, and her cell phone case featured British guards in bright red uniforms—homage to her time spent in the UK completing a master's degree.

Each year, she told me, she and her colleagues survey Beijing for illegal wild-life products—ivory, of course, but also rhino horn, pangolin scales, sea turtle carvings, live birds, and more. Ivory, she said, is by far the most common. They share the results only with law enforcement, but she confirmed that—although the situation is much better than it was five or ten years ago—for now, the de-cline of illegal products on a year-to-year basis is only marginal. She and her colleagues are elated about the upcoming ivory ban, however, which they hope will make a significant dent.

After a brief chat, we headed next door, to the Arts and Crafts Market—one of Beijing's primary state-owned ivory retail outfits. Each floor of the multistory complex featured a different material, from soap-green jade and other colorful stones to bright red lacquerware and pastel-painted porcelain. Prices ranged from six-figure breathtaking decorative vases to cheap little animal carvings worth a few bucks.

The ivory was located several floors up, and Nicola steered us toward an immaculate, glass-walled shop. The cabinets and cases inside proudly displayed ivory of all shapes and sizes, gleaming creamy white under expert lighting. There were sculptures of spindly ladies in flowing silks, full tusks macabrely decorated with mini–elephant herds, scenes from Chinese folklore, and ivory cabbages with glass grasshoppers and katydids perched on their ghostly white leaves. There had to be at least fifty large carved pieces, but the store felt airy and uncluttered, like an art museum display. Some of the pieces were from the 1980s, but many came from the 2008 one-off sale, as indicated by the state-issued cards displayed beside each carving. Nicola told me that a few of the pieces were the works of famous artists, with prices upwards of $300,000. As I looked around, an employee hovered behind me, likely not to help with any questions I had but to ensure I didn't break the shop's no photo policy, further emphasized by numerous signs depicting a red *X* overlaid on the image of a camera.

All ivory sold in China is supposed to be of legal origin, either from the one-off sale in 2008 or from before the 1989 ban. To ensure this is the case, the government allows only certified shops to sell ivory, and it requires that all carvings weighing more than fifty grams be accompanied by an official ID card. The system was supposed to be airtight, but in fact it has been regularly abused, as shown by numerous field studies. In 2010, the Environmental Investigation Agency found that 90 percent of ivory for sale in Guangzhou was illegal, and in 2014, Martin and Lucy Vigne revealed that a quarter of the ivory for sale in Shanghai and Beijing was illegal. A 2011 IFAW survey reported that just 57 of 158 ivory carving and retail outlets that investigators visited were licensed, and, of the licensed facilities, nearly 60 percent still violated the system in some way.

Everything I saw at the state-owned store appeared to have the proper paperwork, however. Satisfied, I joined Nicola, who was chatting with one of the employees, a middle-aged woman wearing a smart black uniform. She stood behind a glass case full of ivory bracelets, pendants, and beads. A round fish bowl sat on top with a couple of plump orange goldfish lazily swimming circles inside.

"Could you ask the saleswoman why photos aren't allowed?" I asked Nicola. She looked a little uncomfortable but humored me, translating the question.

"They're not allowed," the woman replied.

"But why?"

"Because you might put them on the Internet, and that is forbidden."

That topic seemed to be closed, so I asked her what will happen to the unsold ivory at the end of the year. Looking increasingly bored with this conversation, she said she didn't know.

"What about your job?" I asked.

"I don't know. We'll sell something else."

She added that the shop won't be having a clearance sale or anything like that, because the state doesn't care whether its ivory sells. At the end of the year, the most lavish leftover pieces might go to museums. As for the small stuff, no one knows: maybe it will be destroyed, maybe it will just be stuck in a box somewhere to gather dust. "They don't care about it," Nicola shrugged, explaining all of this to me.

All of the "I don't knows" were pretty typical at the time of my visit. China had only just stated its intention to shut everything down by the end of the year—a month after my visit, the first wave of shops and factories was closed—but what will happen to the remaining stockpiles is unknown. It is also feared that China's ban will simply shift the hub for illegal ivory trade to locations outside the country that are frequented by Chinese buyers, including Laos, Vietnam, and Japan. Awareness also seems to be lacking: a 2017 TRAFFIC and WWF survey of more than 2,000 Chinese in fifteen major cities found that just 19 percent knew about the ban without being prompted, and fewer than half recalled hearing about it when asked directly. Yet, when told more about it, 86 percent said they'd support it.

For now, Nicola and her colleagues work in a sort of ivory purgatory, biding their time until the trade is phased out—after which they'll get to work on understanding how the market responds: "2017 is like a year in between," she said. "Basically, we're waiting."

How China moves forward with the ban will likely influence its success, Milliken said. He has identified several issues of key concern: the fate of the country's stockpiles (both legal and illegal); how authorities plan to catalogue, audit, and track ivory into the future; and what, if anything, they plan to do about Chinese ivory-trafficking syndicates operating in Africa. Without cracking down on all these things, ivory sales could simply continue underground. "In China, a particularly fertile avenue of trade right now is WeChat—their equivalent of WhatsApp—where you can create your own group and market ivory through that group," he said. "That poses a huge law enforcement problem, and if it continues to flourish, the stockpiles, if not strictly regulated, are likely to go into that avenue of illegal trade."

Mammoth ivory—dug up in Siberia, often using environmentally destructive methods—is another concern. Products made from tusks of those extinct animals will still be legal in China, and by August 2017 many ivory carvers had already

announced that they were transitioning to mammoth. To a novice like me—and
to many law enforcement agents—mammoth ivory looks exactly like elephant
ivory. Conservationists warn that a legal trade in mammoth ivory could serve
as a smokescreen for illegal trade in elephant ivory, and it may also help keep
demand alive. Elephant ivory is generally more expensive and typically preferred
over mammoth, and it is unlikely that people will simply stop wanting it overnight. Just as China's 1993 tiger bone and rhino horn ban did not end demand or
illegal trade of those materials, the domestic ivory ban could also fall short of its
goal—especially if enforcement is lacking.

Some groups are trying to get ahead of that problem by changing opinion
through public service announcements and awareness campaigns. Former bas-
ketball superstar Yao Ming, who works with the nonprofit group WildAid, is one
of the most vocal and well-known figureheads. "We would be outraged if people
were killing our pandas," he once told journalists. "We should be just as upset
with what's happening to rhinos and elephants in Africa."

Besides WildAid, one of the first groups to get involved in such campaigns
was the International Fund for Animal Welfare. In 2008, IFAW launched its
Mom, I Have Teeth campaign, meant to educate Chinese society about where
ivory actually comes from. The posters—which continue to reach 23 million people per day—depict an elephant mom and baby walking into the sunset. The baby
proudly tells his mom that he has teeth, asking, "Aren't you happy?" She does
not reply, so he repeats his question. Again, silence. "Babies having teeth should
bring joy to a mother," the poster goes on to explain. "But what does it mean for
elephant families? Because of people's unnecessary want of ivory, hundreds and
thousands of elephants are killed for the ivory trade."

"Instead of using blood and gore and killing—the kind of thing the government isn't going to allow us to put up in a subway anyway," Gabriel said, the ad's
message "is politically and culturally sensitive." Apparently, she and her colleagues hit the mark: attention the poster generated surprised even her. "I guess
Chinese people are not used to seeing ads urging them *not* to buy something!"
she said.

People began posting photos of the poster on social media and Weibo (China's Twitter), and the ad even turned up in a question on a college entrance exam
that subsequently reached millions of applicants. Others did more: one woman
was so horrified by the message—which she said reminded her of her son, whose
teeth had just started to come in—that she took her ivory bracelet off on the spot

and vowed never to wear it again. She then posted a lengthy explanation on an online forum for young mothers and urged them to do the same. Even an ivory carver was affected by the ad; he contacted Gabriel directly to say that he hadn't known that ivory came from dead elephants, but that, from now on, he would stick with the plenty of other carving materials that don't entail taking a life.

IFAW is not the only group running such campaigns. A subway station located just steps from the Beijing ivory market that I visited was plastered with attractive ads designed by WildAid, which pioneered animal-related public service announcements in China in the early 2000s. The posters I saw featured hip-hop singer Jay Chou looking soulful and brooding as he spoke out against shark fin soup and the ivory trade. Like all of WildAid's ads, these posters also displayed the organization's tagline: "When the Buying Stops, the Killing Can Too."

"Everyone in China knows this slogan," Nicola told me as we passed by. "Jackie Chan and Yao Ming say it, so we know it."

It's impossible to measure how effective such campaigns actually are, however. A 2013 IFAW survey of around seven hundred urban Chinese—half of whom had bought ivory in the past—concluded that the Mom, I Have Teeth ad did make a difference. Among people who had previously bought ivory, two-thirds of those who saw the ad said they would definitely not buy ivory again, compared to just one-third of those who hadn't seen the ad. Likewise, just 8 percent who saw the ad said they would still consider buying ivory in the future, versus 18 percent who hadn't seen the ad. The survey was not perfect—seven hundred people out of a population of over a billion is a speck of a sample size—but it does indicate that the campaign's message was persuasive for at least some individuals.

WildAid had originally focused on combatting the shark fin trade, but consumption of shark fin soup has decreased so dramatically over the past six or seven years—with prices dropping up to 70 percent and fin imports declining by 80 percent—that the group has now largely shifted its focus to elephants, rhinos, tigers, manta rays, and pangolins. (The shift may have been premature, however: while consumption has dropped, research conducted in 2016 revealed that 98 percent of Hong Kong restaurants still served shark fin soup during the Lunar New Year and that patrons were purchasing it). Whatever the degree of decline, did shark fin fall out of favor because of the WildAid ads—the most famous of which, produced in 2009, showed Yao Ming pushing away a bowl of soup—or because the government banned shark fin soup at official banquets in 2012? Steve Blake, chief representative of WildAid in China, believes it was a bit of both.

"Absolutely, I do not think the government ban would have happened without our campaigns," he said. "Yao Ming put the issue on the map and made it controversial. I don't have solid proof of that, but I think it's clear."

Others, however, are more skeptical. As one conservationist, who asked not to be quoted by name because he isn't an expert in behavior change, said, "These PR campaigns in China—what are they actually trying to change? Are they trying to reach consumers who are thinking of buying ivory, or those people's children? Or are they trying to contact the leadership who are making policy decisions—or somehow trying to create a general societal gestalt that ivory is bad? I find it frustrating when I ask them which of these groups they are trying to target, but I don't get a clear answer." Chris Shepherd, the executive director of Monitor, added that, in general, "I think a lot more thought has to go into these campaigns. In the wildlife trade world, this is a fairly new science. Everyone jumped on that bandwagon without any baseline data—but how can you show you reduced demand without baseline data?" Blake thinks that's missing the forest for the trees. "We know people see our ads, but it's hard to have a really scientific measurement of the effectiveness," he said. "We say it's more an art than a science."

Convinced they're onto something, WildAid plans to keep up its efforts until the killing does indeed virtually stop. Overall, Blake is optimistic for the future. "China definitely gets a bad rap—that they're allowed to eat everything, that they don't care, blah blah blah—but things are changing here really fast," he said. "People care a lot more about these issues and are talking about them a lot more. Even the state media frequently publishes photos and news pieces about the wildlife trade. WildAid's biggest supporter is Chinese state media. Everyone loves to bash the big, bad government, but they're really doing a lot more now. I think China should be given more credit in general."

Gao agreed that the younger generation is more actively engaged in things like conservation and animal welfare and that change is afoot. But he cautioned against assuming that consumption of ivory and other illegal wildlife goods will happen quickly and without prompting. "It takes time for a generation and society to change its culture," he said. "We can't wait until the old generation goes out and the new one comes in: we need to actively start to change the culture and move society in the direction we collectively think is better for all living beings on Earth—both animals and people. We need to take action right now."

PART II
INSIDE THE TRADE

"No matter where I looked I saw unsustainable use of natural resources. My sense was that before long, the richness of wildlife and forests . . . would be converted to a wasteland."

—Vladimir K. Arsenyev, *Across the Ussuri Kray,* 1921

Specially trained anti-poaching rangers demonstrate their work at Ol Pejeta Conservancy in Kenya.

A record 105 tons of ivory was burned in Kenya in 2016.

A private security guard at a South African rhino ranch shows off his "Anti-Poaching Unit" tattoo.

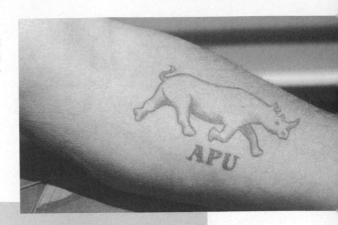

Zakouma National Park Ranger Issa Idriss holds a photo of his father, who was murdered by poachers in Chad.

Rangers at Lewa Wildlife Conservancy in Kenya celebrate World Rhino Day.

Six

THE $50,000,000 BONFIRE

Much of the demand fueling the illegal wildlife trade stems from Asia, but the trade itself reaches far beyond the continent, to many expat communities around the world. As Vanda Felbab-Brown wrote in *The Extinction Market,* "East and Southeast Asian diaspora communities often spread the taste for wildlife to new areas, expanding local habits of exploiting wildlife, whether as pets or for food or other uses." Globalization and increasing purchasing power have also intensified other preexisting markets in the Western and Southern Hemispheres, including the parrot trade in Brazil and production of reptile skin boots in Latin America.

In the United States, though—which ranks as the second-largest illegal wild-life market after China—trafficking is often linked to Asian communities. In 2004, for example, state and federal officials busted a crime ring of more than a hundred people involved in smuggling black bear parts and American ginseng roots to South Korea and domestic Asian markets. Likewise, Operation Crash, an ongoing US Fish and Wildlife Service investigation of ivory and rhino horn crooks, has resulted in thirty-plus convictions as of 2017, including prison sentences totaling more than thirty years and fines surpassing $2 million.

In other countries, however, enforcement has been less effective. Mexican fishermen illegally pursuing a Herculean, critically endangered species called totoaba (its laptop-sized swim bladders are highly sought in China) are driving the vaquita, the world's smallest porpoises, to extinction by drowning them as bycatch in their nets. Similar stories play out in other corners of the world, from India and Nepal—which continue to battle tiger poaching driven by demand from the East—to Bolivia, where authorities are pursuing a dozen cases against local Chinese residents caught smuggling hundreds of fangs from jaguars and other big cats, meant to be made into macho jewelry.

In terms of large well-known mammals, though, Africa is suffering the most. Going into this project, I was well aware of the statistics: I'd seen the headlines about elephant and rhino poaching, and I'd interviewed experts about these things myself. But I had never reported on wildlife trade from Africa, and I lacked in-depth knowledge of the situation on the ground.

As fate would have it an invitation to attend a conference and ivory burn in Kenya arrived in my inbox just days after I signed the contract to write this book. Kenya, then, would be my starting point—fittingly so, as I soon learned.

I HAD JUST A FEW WEEKS TO PREPARE FOR THE TRIP, AND IT SEEMED THAT EVERY-one I mentioned it to was keen to offer advice. Mostly it boiled down to warnings about Nairobi (a.k.a. "Nairobbery"). Take a cab, I was instructed, even if it's just for a few blocks—otherwise, I'd be robbed. Another colleague told me that her tour company barred her and her husband from leaving the hotel premises during their stay there, and yet another emphasized, "Nairobi's worse than Johannesburg for crime!"

So when I exited Jomo Kenyatta Airport on a cool April night in 2016, my guard was up. To avoid any funny business, I'd arranged for a pickup through my hotel. But scanning the mess of signs, I was dismayed to find that none listed my name. Ignoring a man in a rumpled security guard uniform who quietly whispered "taxi, taxi, taxi" to me as though he was pushing hashish, I instead beelined toward a large, smiling woman in a bright dress who introduced herself as Lucy. She charged such a fair price to the city that I didn't even try to bargain. Had I known in advance how smooth this transaction would be, I never would have bothered with the overpriced, overcautious hotel car.

"Nairobi is a mess and can take hours to cross" was another warning I'd received ad nauseam, so I sat back in preparation for a long slog into town. But the city yet again defied expectations: our way was clear. The dark outskirts slipped by in a jet-lag-induced haze, and any unease I still harbored was quickly replaced by the rose-tinted wonder that accompanies arrival in a new place. When under the influence of this fleeting yet potent swell of excitement, even the mundane becomes captivating.

Indeed, save for billboards, there was little to see on this dark stretch of highway. But even those commercial displays were interesting, as they revealed the central role that wildlife plays in Kenya. "Welcome to Kenya" read one sign decorated with giraffes. Another advertised Tuskys, a supermarket chain whose *T* was crossed with a cartoon elephant tusk. Still another touted the national beer, Tusker, whose bottle sported an elephant's silhouette.

The signs eventually gave way to scattered buildings that thickened like a forest, and the traffic grew weedier. Watery street lights illuminated the shadowy figures of pedestrians, some solo, others in raucous groups. Through the dimness occasionally shone the flash of a smile, the contours of sharp cheekbones or a pair of bright, laughing eyes—visions of strangers like "petals on a wet, black bough," as Ezra Pound once put it.

The cab took a sharp left, dispelling these dreamy apparitions and delivering me to my destination, the Sarova Stanley. Once the sleeping place of choice for visiting politicians, movie stars, and other high-society folk, the hotel's ambience still hearkens back to the days when Kenya served as a colonial hub—"the playground of the idle rich," as former US ambassador Richard T. McCormack called it. Today, though, the long-celebrated establishment seems more the Grizabella of five-star hotels: full of beautiful memories but no longer the socialite around which the city orbits.

Although a bit tired around the edges, the place still had its charms. I followed a friendly porter past the famous Thorn Tree Café, where a lively noticeboard once connected travelers in pre-Facebook days. A sweeping, dark wood staircase led to a handsomely gilded hallway decorated with wooden animal carvings, masks, and other curios. "Hemingway stayed at our hotel in 1934, and now you're staying here in 2016," the porter said, swinging open the door to a simple but comfortable room. After indulging in a cheeky pint at the hotel's Exchange Bar, I settled down for bed. Tomorrow, the events leading up to the great ivory burn would begin.

KENYA WAS SPARED NONE OF THE HORRORS OF THE FIRST ELEPHANT POACHING EPI-demic. Three-quarters of the country's ellies, as they're fondly called, were lost in those years, with populations falling from 85,000 in 1979 to just 22,000 in 1989. Some of the killings were carried out by corrupt rangers and wardens, whose habit of shooting animals from the comfort of their patrol vehicles earned elephant carcasses the nickname "roadsiders." In the late 1980s, Perez Olindo, head of the Kenyan wildlife department, identified sixty-seven corrupt wildlife officials but was able to fire only sixteen because the rest enjoyed political protection.

Other killings were the work of bandits—some of them desperate Somalis fleeing a civil war—who grew increasingly aggressive and ballsy. Many, however, think the Somali role was purposefully exaggerated. Journalist and author Keith Somerville, for example, wrote in *Ivory* that although some Somalis were undoubtedly involved in elephant poaching, they became "convenient whipping boys" for corrupt authorities. Tom Milliken, TRAFFIC's elephant and rhino program leader, agreed: "Kenya always says the Somalis came in and killed all their elephants, but I'm like, 'No, I think your own political elites did that.' They won't acknowledge their history."

An order from President Daniel arap Moi to shoot poachers on sight did little to stem the killings, as rangers—who lacked money, training, and gear—were woefully ill equipped to answer this or any other call to protect wildlife. In 1989, Kenya's last five rhinos were found shot in a supposedly heavily guarded park, and, a few weeks later, a gang of Somalis attacked and robbed a group of German tourists, killing one. For President Moi, these were the last straws. He fired Olindo and appointed Richard Leakey, the famed Kenyan paleoanthropologist, to fill the vacancy at what is now the Kenya Wildlife Service. It was a move that few saw coming—including Leakey. Learning of his appointment after a colleague heard about it on the radio, "I thought there must have been a mistake," he wrote in his memoir, *Wildlife Wars*.

Leakey quickly recovered from the whiplash of that surprise, though, and got to work reforming the service. He gutted the staff of bad apples and raised funds to train and equip the dedicated employees who remained. The effects were apparent almost immediately: poaching began to decline, arrests increased, and Leakey's reputation as a formidable force for elephants grew. He began receiving regular death threats from poachers—which he took as a good sign, because it meant he'd gotten under their skin. He even managed to recruit a few former elephant killers to join the Kenya Wildlife Service, some of whom were among his finest rangers.

As Leakey well knew, the ivory war could never be won so long as demand persisted. People needed to associate ivory with death and greed rather than beauty and luxury—but how to trigger such a shift? Pondering this question, he recalled Brigitte Bardot's 1970s campaign against the fashion industry's use of baby seal skin and wild cat furs. Bardot had taken to the streets of Paris and set fire to her coats—a dramatic gesture that helped to stigmatize the entire fur industry and led to a ban on certain exotic skins.

Could the same be done for ivory? Although Kenya had plenty to burn—government storehouses contained nearly thirteen tons of the stuff—Leakey was unsure of whether flames could actually destroy tusks. To his relief, a Hollywood special effects expert ensured him that fire, if aided by a generous helping of flammable liquid glue and gasoline, would most certainly reduce ivory to a pile of carbon and ash—just like human teeth in a crematorium. "It will be spectacular," he promised Leakey.

With one obstacle down, Leakey next needed to get President Moi on board. His dramatic proposal—"Let us try to smash the market! Let's burn the ivory!"—was initially met with incredulity.

"Burn the ivory?" President Moi replied in disbelief. "It is worth at least $3 million!" Kenyan citizens, he insisted, would be outraged by such a waste.

Leakey pushed, though, and emphasized that this was Kenya's chance to take the high road. Destroying the ivory would send a clear message that the country would not tolerate the trade—and the audacity of its delivery would force the world to pay attention. President Moi agreed. A date was set—July 18, 1989—and a location was selected at Nairobi National Park, a slice of protected savanna within viewing distance of the capital's skyscrapers, complete with giraffe, lions, and zebra. A breathtaking 850 million people tuned in to watch the event on television, which President Moi kicked off with a hard-hitting speech. "To stop the poacher, the trader must also be stopped. And to stop the trader, the final buyer must be convinced not to buy ivory," he declared. "I appeal to people all over the world to stop buying ivory."

Any lingering fears Leakey harbored about the ivory not burning properly were soon dispelled. President Moi touched torch to pyre, and the tower of tusks was consumed in shocking orange flames.

Amazingly, their stunt worked. Elephants became *the* story of the day, with leading newspapers, magazines, and television programs all condemning the trade. Images of women adorned in ivory jewelry were juxtaposed with photos of elephants with their faces hacked off, next to slogans such as "Dressed to Kill"

and "Accessories to Murder." Especially in the West, ivory turned into a stigma-
tized symbol of death, and, as described in Chapter 5, an international commercial ban soon followed. The burn, some said, had rallied the world.

Almost immediately, poaching subsided, and elephant populations began to
recover in Kenya: in 1990, the country lost just fifty-eight elephants compared to
several hundred in 1989. (Leakey's personal story, however, took a tragic twist:
In 1993, he lost both legs in a plane crash that he suspects was a retaliatory assassination attempt. The following year, facing false accusations of corruption
and mismanagement, he resigned his position as director of the Kenya Wildlife
Service.)

The better times for Kenya's elephants lasted nearly twenty years before
poaching resumed. In 2005, rangers found 67 poached elephants, but by 2008
that figure had doubled to 116. Things deteriorated from there, with 384 elephants killed for their tusks in 2013—a record high since the ban. Many of the
old-timers saw this coming for decades. "I was not at all surprised," said Joyce
Poole, codirector of the nonprofit group Elephant Voices, whose research on
poaching's impacts on elephant populations was used to strengthen arguments
for the 1989 vote to ban ivory trade. As was the case in the 1980s, she believes
"rampant corruption on all levels" is the primary driver of Kenya's present crisis.
"This current regime is so corrupt that I don't have much faith in the integrity of
most government officials, politicians or civil servants," she said. "But, that said,
Kenya also has some of the best, most dedicated conservationists on the continent and a thriving, growing, savvy middle class."

Although many of the individuals who fought for elephants in the 1970s and
1980s have since retired or passed on, some, like Poole, remain, and they have
been joined by a new wave of impassioned conservationists from the younger
generation. One of those heroes is Paula Kahumbu, CEO of WildlifeDirect, a
Nairobi-based nonprofit organization. A tireless elephant evangelizer, she can often be found discussing the poaching crisis on national television; holding meetings with everyone from Kristin Davis and Kristin Bauer (of *Sex and the City*
and *True Blood* fame, respectively) to President Barack Obama; and tweeting and
posting for her global awareness campaign, Hands off Our Elephants. As Leakey
said, "I'd list Paula amongst the very top players in Kenyan civil society. She's
popularized wildlife through social media and television, and her work demanding a better standard of justice has earned her a very special place in Kenya."

Paula is also an ace public speaker, as I knew from seeing her talk a few years earlier in Denver, at an ivory crush organized by the US Fish and Wildlife Service. Paula conveyed a sense of fierce urgency after all the dry, statistics- and policy-heavy speeches. "We've been here before," she said, her voice strong and clear. "As Africans and Kenyans, we take it for granted that we have elephants. But unless something is done to stop this, in ten years' time—by 2023—there will be no elephants. I cannot imagine Africa without elephants. This is about our heritage, our identity as Africans. But we cannot be despondent, and we cannot do this alone. Every person in Africa and around the world should say this is despicable and we will not tolerate it!" Applause broke out, and minutes later, as though powered by the force of Paula's will alone, the massive crushing machine rumbled to life, sending six tons of ivory to its end.

Paula, it must be pointed out, is Leakey's protégée. He no doubt played a fundamental role in shaping her life, especially her early years. Her childhood home was just opposite his, and she and her eight siblings could often be found running amok through the neighborhood's tangled, half-wild estates. Leakey's first interaction with Paula, however, was as backyard park warden, when he discovered her holding a catapult and conspiring with several seven- and eight-year-olds at the base of a tree.

"What are you doing with that catapult?" he demanded, approaching the suspicious huddle.

"We're looking at that hyrax," Paula innocently replied. She pointed to a round, furry animal that resembled a sort of grumpy guinea pig, clinging to a branch above.

"You sure you're not going to poach it?" Leakey shot back, narrowing his eyes. "You don't look at things with a catapult—you catapult them! I think you're young poachers, and you'd better shape up."

To hammer home his point, he issued a final, stern order: "I don't ever want to see you on this road again carrying catapults."

Decades after the incident, it still makes him chuckle. "They were very embarrassed," he recalled. Yet, from then on, the kids considered him an ally, bringing him snakes, frogs, insects, and other natural oddities for identification help before letting them go. As the years passed, though, one by one, the children moved on to different interests and stopped visiting. But not Paula: wildlife stuck with her, and she remained Leakey's devoted disciple. A future career in conservation, she said, was a no-brainer. "There was nothing else that interested me besides wildlife."

She was just a teenager when the 1989 ivory burn took place; she helped count the tusks and, of course, attended the history-making event. As with many others present that day, it left a strong impression. "The burn made me realize that it actually doesn't take that much to change things: just visionary leadership that creates something powerful that the public can align themselves with and believe in," she said. "At that time, the whole country was unified in one clear vision to stop elephant poaching. That experience influences very much how I operate today."

Leakey eventually got Paula a job at Kenya's National Museum, and then at the Kenya Wildlife Service and in wildlife policy. After completing a doctorate at Princeton University, she found her way to nonprofit work—and to her own voice. She remained close friends with Leakey throughout the years, a relationship that some say protects Paula, who—like her mentor—can get quite pushy with her activism. Her message and her reputation are further strengthened by the media, which generally adores her. As one journalist from the *Independent* gushingly wrote in 2014 of Paula, "Everyone from parliamentarians to senior criminal prosecutors [in Kenya] insisted I had to meet this life force behind Kenya's, indeed Africa's, conservation movement."

Obviously, I wanted to meet this life force, too—a task that wound up being a much bigger challenge than I imagined. She responded quickly and favorably to my request to feature her in this book, and we nailed down a date to meet in Kenya as well as a preliminary interview in New York, but the four days she was in town turned into a series of increasingly absurd false starts. E-mails and voice mails disappeared into the ether, and meeting after meeting fell through for various reasons, from "racing to buy some clothes" to getting caught up at an impromptu dance party under a bridge that raged on until midnight. Meanwhile, I carried my laptop wherever I went—dinner, drinks, a talk at NYU—on the off chance that Paula would suddenly come through.

For three days, however, she did not. I'd all but given up when she proposed a 7:30 a.m. meeting on her final day in town, at her hotel in the Upper West Side. I glumly slogged up to Columbus Circle the next morning in the cold dark. Her hotel's lobby was coincidentally decked out in a zebra stripe and leopard spot motif, and Paula was already downstairs when I arrived, sitting on a crushed velvet couch scrolling through her phone. Her outfit—an animal print blouse and a silver elephant charm—matched the decor, and her short, curly hair formed a soft halo around her face.

She immediately proposed coffee—a welcome suggestion—so we went to a Starbucks around the corner. "I'm heading to DC this afternoon to see my son," she told me, slipping a dollar into the barista's tip jar. "I haven't seen him in three years! It's not like I haven't been to the US—I've been here a bunch—it's just my priorities haven't been straight. This job takes up all of my time. . . . " she trailed off. Clearly, I realized, I should not take her busyness personally.

Our coffees arrived, and Paula requested we sit outside ("I don't like crowded places"). She handed me her cup to carry as she checked her phone, perhaps scanning the latest tweets about the upcoming burn.

"People in other countries feel so despondent," she said as we walked. "They think, 'Those damn Africans killing all these animals, shame on them.' There's this portrayal that Africa is irresponsible and there's nothing people living in places like the US can do about it." I couldn't help but agree, unfortunately. I often feel powerless myself to do anything about the poaching and illegal trade.

"Actually, there's a lot people in the West can do—they just don't realize it," Paula continued, as though reading my mind. "Corporations can get on board, as the airlines and even some cruise lines have done recently, by ensuring passengers don't carry ivory onboard. Etsy, eBay, and other Internet sales companies have also done something very meaningful, by banning ivory on their sites. Individuals can call their senators or talk about this stuff on social media and to their friends. It could literally be a note on Facebook—it could be as simple as that."

We sat down on a bench just next to Central Park, under a bright blue morning sky. Paula may be one of the world's most challenging women to pin down, but, now that I had her in front of me, she quickly brought me up to speed on Kenya's situation.

In 2012, Paula found herself getting nowhere with government officials. They took her statistics and warnings about escalating elephant poaching as personal attacks and assumed that her aim was defamation rather than conservation. "Like all governments in Africa, I think they were just afraid to admit they had such a big problem," she said.

The following year, things changed when Uhuru Kenyatta—son of Jomo Kenyatta, Kenya's first president—won the election. Paula sensed an opportunity and connected with the new president's wife, Margaret, who was also interested in reforming certain aspects of the country. At first, though, Paula was a bit over-eager in her approach. "Oh my God, you can be so powerful!" she told the first lady. "I want you to come get photographed next to a dead elephant!" Margaret looked at her like she was completely mad and said she'd pass. But she did agree to become patron of the Hands off Our Elephants campaign. With that, saving wildlife was, once again, a national priority.

Paula and others ultimately traced ongoing poaching back to the Kenya Wildlife Service—to a "gradual losing of the plot over the last six years," as a government-appointed task force described in 2014. Paula put it more harshly: "The leadership was completely broken." Leakey agreed that things needed to change: "I'd wager when I left KWS many years ago, it was largely free of corruption, because I took a personal interest in that. I think it returned quite significantly in the past twenty years." (The Kenya Wildlife Service did not respond to interview requests, neither for this book nor for a piece I wrote for *National Geographic* about the ivory burn.)

In 2015 and 2016, though, things began to improve. A number of rangers and more senior personnel were dismissed or transferred, some over allegations of corruption. Leakey was also reinstated as chair of the board of trustees. The service's 4,200 rangers received advanced training to bring them up to par for tackling the crisis, and their salaries were increased. Some also joined a newly formed, elite anti-poaching unit. "The integrity of the service has greatly improved," Leakey said. "Sadly, good guys can also fall prey to corruption, but the board has tried to stay ahead."

The efforts paid off. Poaching began to decline precipitously, from 302 elephants lost in 2013, the year Kenyatta took office, to just 96 killed in 2015 and around 70 in 2016. Rhino poaching likewise declined, from 59 poached in 2013 to just 11 in 2015. Trafficking, however—which is generally outside the Kenya Wildlife Service's jurisdiction—remains a significant problem. Since 2009, more ivory has been shipped out of Mombasa than any other place in Africa. "Kenya continues to this day to be moving more ivory than anyone, but it's getting all the credit for being the best African country for elephants," Milliken said.

Tim Wittig, a conservation scientist and illicit trade expert at the University of Groningen, expanded on this: "Kenya is doing a good job on counter-poaching but a horrible job on counter-trafficking. It's really like a rogue state when it comes to trafficking. A lot of people who allegedly deal in heroin are also dealing in ivory, including apparently senior government officials or their close relatives. A whole criminal ecosystem operates in Mombasa and along the coast, and does so quite freely: smuggled sugar, fuel, ivory, and heroin all move along the same routes. There's extensive corruption, all well documented and only barely underground. Kenya's message to the world seems to be, 'We'll protect our own elephants, but we're open for business to traffic the ivory from everywhere else.'"

This is despite the fact that Kenya has a thriving conservation community, Wittig continued, one that includes "very famous and very well known" organizations, most of which are spearheaded by white descendants of the ex-colonial English. "My big complaint is that—with a very small number of exceptions— these groups and individuals are not doing anything about Mombasa. There is a quote about the ex-colonial English in Kenya: 'Never has there been written so much about a group of people so inconsequential.' That is the problem: these famous white conservationists are very good about raising awareness and money, but they are also all wealthy people who own a lot of land—staying in their lodges can cost thousands of dollars a night—but, for whatever reason, they're not taking meaningful stands on things that matter, like cleaning up Mombasa. If the so-called leaders of conservation are not willing or able to stick their necks out and use their influence where it's most needed, they should get out of the way so others can. Right now, they are sucking away resources from people who could do something."

That Kenya has a problem with trafficking was reflected in the country's ivory stockpile, which had long been a not-so-secret piggy bank for corrupt officials, according to Paula. "The government kept saying, 'We don't know what Kahumbu's going on about! We have our ivory databases,'" she said. "But I knew for a fact that people would be handed a tusk in one part of the country, and by the time it gets to Nairobi, it would be smaller. The number of tusks was also an issue: you'd walk into an exhibit room one day and it would be full of ivory, and the next there would be just a few pieces left."

Paula and others didn't trust the government estimates of how much ivory the country held, so in 2015 they collaborated with the Kenya Wildlife Service to undertake a meticulous audit. They found that the government had about 15 tons *more* ivory than it thought, meaning the records—although certainly not up to scratch—actually had the opposite problem than the auditors initially expected. In total, the country had 137 tons of ivory, a cache worth some $150 million.

The next step, the government decided, was to destroy it.

President Kenyatta soon warmed to the plan: Kenya would once again torch its stock of ivory, he decided. But this time, rather than 12 tons, it would burn

105 tons—a record-breaking amount. (Some of the remaining 30 tons was still tied up in court cases, and the rest would be retained for training and educational purposes).

As in 1989, public awareness and behavior change were the primary goals. "We need a symbol that people will pay attention to," Leakey said. "It's not a stunt or a PR show, but a deliberate action to draw attention to the crisis—to demonstrate that it's shameful and a disgrace to buy and wear ivory."

"THE ROADS ARE ALL BLOCKED OFF BECAUSE OF THE PRESIDENTS," THE DRIVER said. We were snaking our way toward Wilson Airport, whose single-room terminal coordinates a fleet of tiny Cessnas that service small airports dotting the country. I would be taking one of those planes to Nanyuki, a town about a hundred miles north of Nairobi. Nanyuki lies "in the shadow of Mt. Kenya," as tourism outfits like to say, and it's the jumping-off point for some of the country's most deluxe private conservancies. I'd be spending the next two days with more than 170 "key influencers"—scientists, activists, philanthropically inclined businesspeople, and even a few presidents—at an event called the Giants Club Summit, where discussions would center on how to save elephants. On Saturday morning we'd all fly back to Nairobi to attend the burn.

When I finally made it to Wilson Airport, the lady at the counter didn't look at my passport or give me a ticket. Instead, she checked my name off a list, took my bag, and told me to have a seat. Behind her, courtesy of Paula's Hands off Our Elephants campaign, was a big sign reading "NO IVORY ON BOARD." I got a coffee and watched as the room slowly filled with executive directors of various conservation organizations. There was Mary Rice of the London-based Environmental Investigation Agency, and Timothy Tear from the Wildlife Conservation Society's Africa program, who looked like Matthew Fox on safari. I felt as though I'd missed a dress code memo: virtually every white person in the airport was wearing khakis and sturdy, Timberland-style boots. The most extreme examples, I noted, were two fully made-up women with matching bleached-blonde hair, skin-tight green shirts and tailored khaki trousers, army boots, and wide-brimmed hats. *Barbie goes on safari,* I thought snarkily.

The people-watching came to an end as we were herded onto the runway and up a few steps to board a hobbit-sized Cessna 2088. Eager to get the reporting going, I snagged the space next to Tim, who launched into a story about a wild morning zipping around town to find a suit jacket, which, in haste, he had forgotten to pack. (He'd found out just the day before that he had secured a spot at the conference.) It had all worked out: he'd managed to borrow one from a colleague.

"It's a couple sizes too big, but it'll have to do," he said, shrugging.

The plane lifted off, and Nairobi's gray sprawl gave way to shamrock-green farms, plains, and hills. Tim has been coming to Africa since 1980 and spent some of those years living in Kenya and South Sudan, so although these sweeping vistas were completely new to me, they were like a second home to him. He and his wife had recently moved to Tanzania, in fact, when the Wildlife Conservation Society contacted him with an opportunity he couldn't refuse. "I moved from the Serengeti to New York City," he said wistfully. "Let me put it this way: it's been quite a transition."

It took a conscious effort to wrench my attention from the scenery unfolding below, but I wanted to take advantage of this font of information sitting beside me. "So, do you think we actually have a chance at stopping the poaching?" I asked, jumping straight to the million-dollar question.

Tim paused for a beat and then launched into an answer that he has obviously pondered for much of his working life. "We get a lot of criticism because we haven't 'stopped' the poaching crisis, but it's not easy to get your arms around it, because we need to stop the killing, the trafficking, and the demand," he began. "Stopping one doesn't stop the others, and if you don't address them all, it turns into a 'War on Drugs'–type situation. The US spent millions and millions trying to take out cocaine farms without ever really stopping the demand back home, and right now, similarly, there's a lot of investment in anti-poaching. And although there is a correlation between increased investment and reduced poaching, it's a cat-and-mouse game—an arms race between rangers and poachers. For example, Kruger National Park in South Africa has invested more in anti-poaching than any other place on the planet, yet poaching there is still a huge problem because the demand driving it is so outrageous. That's why you also have to get rid of demand and the lucrative business of trafficking."

"So what's stopping us from doing that?"

"Well, one of the reasons is that we've chronically underestimated and undervalued the investment needed, in general, if we want to preserve our natural resources. We need to value conservation more in relation to other investments. Add up all the annual budgets of the big international NGOs—the BINGOs, as we say—and see what number you get. It's probably somewhere around 3 billion, plus or minus. Then go to the list of Fortune 500 companies, and see where the total conservation number would fall as a corporation. It's possible it might not even make the list—or at best, it'll be at the bottom. There is a fundamental mismatch: society needs to value our natural assets way more than we do now."

This all sounded painfully true, but it was also, I feared, a dead end. Unless fundamental shifts occur in society or human nature, I'd wager that personal profits will always trump planetary protection. That was a weedy discussion for another time, though; for the moment, I was more interested in exploring how those dynamics affect the here and now of the illegal wildlife trade.

"Given all that, what do we do about people who say the cost of protecting animals from poachers is unsustainable?" I asked. "That reserves can't keep spending a million dollars a year or whatever on their rhinos?"

"It really doesn't help to label these practices as 'unsustainable,'" Tim corrected me. "It's rather that we need to label them as insufficient in the face of the challenge. In terms of conservation, rhinos are way out there on the end of the challenge gradient—three standard deviations away from the average. Rhinos— and now elephants and weird stuff like pangolins and ploughshare tortoises, too—have bridged the divide and wandered into the illicit trade market, just behind drugs, arms, and human trafficking. Therefore, they need massive investment in anti-poaching, because now it's like they're walking around with crack or heroin or gold sitting on their noses. Considering the absurd levels that wildlife criminals will go—and the fact that there are millions of unemployed young men in Africa with few or no opportunities to earn money—this is a situation that's way out of balance with what could in any way be considered a norm for conservation. But it has become the norm for a small subset of increasingly rare and highly valued species. Despite all this, though, there are some success stories."

A few successful outliers or not, the situation struck me as pretty darn hopeless: the despondency that Paula had warned against was creeping in. "I take it, though, that the places that *are* protecting rhinos or these other species are the exception to the norm?" I asked. "I mean, is it at all feasible or even possible to implement what I assume are high-cost solutions across Africa, without addressing all these other forces driving poaching? Can pockets of success save rhinos from extinction if we don't do something about the larger problem?"

Somehow, Tim was still undeterred: "Those are metaphysical questions, but my quick answer is purposeful optimism. It's my answer to all questions like this:

yes, it is possible, because it has to be. We don't have all the answers, but pockets of success demonstrate that we *can* figure out how to have successes."

"But why haven't we been able to replicate that on a broader scale yet?"

"Think of rocket science," Tim said, with infinite patience. "We use rocket science as a term to describe really complicated stuff, when in fact, conservation science is way more complicated than rocket science. Why? Because rockets are essentially about moving an object from point A to B, mostly in the vacuum of space. Conservation has to factor in environmental variables as well as human behavior—some of the most difficult stuff in the world to predict. If we could predict human behavior, we would really be on to something, but we can't, at least not with any level of precision. Hence, it is really, really hard to solve some of our problems, because we combine human behavior and all the natural sciences into one big ball, and then we have to figure out how to get it to bounce in the direction we want it to go. Sending rockets to the moon and back has been easier."

Oh God, I thought. *The animals are all gonna die.*

"The truth is that we have limited ability to predict who will actually win and lose," Tim continued, his tone still somehow light and upbeat. "So, you end up with purposeful optimism: choosing to find the successes and building on them, as opposed to becoming overwhelmed by despair."

I really admired this approach and hoped he was right, even as I wondered whether this optimism was some sort of self-protective mechanism developed by wildlife professionals to enable them to continue functioning. Yet, if people like Tim—those working in conservation day in and day out—can maintain an optimistic outlook, then there must be something to their hope . . . mustn't there?

Nanyuki Airport, it turned out, was little more than a small café and some landscaped bushes. The pilots taxied right up to the edge of an unpaved parking lot, then hopped out and unloaded our luggage themselves. A man in a bright red traditional Maasai *shuka,* bedazzled with beads and silver disks shining in the overcast afternoon light, had come to collect the two safari Barbies in a large SUV.

The rest of us were all conference-goers. But confusion immediately ensued. Half of the group—including me—thought we were headed to a nearby reserve for preconference talks about elephants, while the others knew nothing about this. People began to argue.

Faced with the uncompromising reality of just one bus to serve two destinations in opposite directions, Tim took the lead and chipperly proposed we all just go check out the talks. The group acquiesced. Around eight of us piled in, leaving the driver to face the Tetris-like challenge of fitting all our luggage into the back. "It's like watching an Irishman trying to screw in a lightbulb," I heard someone with an English accent mutter sarcastically.

We made our way through Nanyuki, a grim tangle of dust, congestion, and shabby businesses. "Beware, Repent and be Holy! Jesus is Coming" read a hand-painted sign opposite a disco called Club Oxygen. Cows and goats grazed on the side of the road, and kids waved. Jet lag was catching up to me, and I settled back into my chair, half-listening to the lively conversations all around, about everything from rhinos in Chad to Microsoft cofounder Paul Allen's investments in African conservation.

The surroundings grew increasingly rural, and at last we came to a stop at gate adorned with two metal rhinos: the entrance to Ol Pejeta Conservancy. Like many of the conservancies in the area, Ol Pejeta was founded in colonial days as a cattle ranch. By the 1980s, however, problems had begun to chip away at profits. In 2004, a couple of conservation organizations purchased the land for a tidy $17.5 million and converted it into a wildlife reserve. Today, it houses East Africa's largest population of black rhinos and supports locals through jobs and an innovative integrated livestock grazing system.

A guard waved us in, and suddenly Nanyuki's clutter was gone, replaced by grassland all around. "There's a giraffe over there," the driver said within thirty seconds of our entry into the conservancy. It was the first time he had spoken since the trip commenced. The bus slowly rumbled deeper into the park, and the animal sightings increased. Impala with corkscrew Dr. Seuss horns scattered around us, cow-like cape buffalo looked up disinterestedly, and gaudily striped zebra stood out against sage-colored grass. A sign indicated a turnoff to the equator.

As we crested a small hill, Tim pointed: "Look, Rachel."

There, outlined against the horizon, were four massive silhouettes. There was no mistaking them: elephants! Though tiredly familiar in photographs and films, to see the world's largest land mammal in its natural habitat, I suddenly realized, was something entirely different. I giddily told Tim that this was my first time seeing them in the wild.

"There you go! That was worth the trip, then." He was a good sport.

Sensing we were nearing the end of our journey, my fellow passengers and I began to gather up our things. An impromptu parking lot had been set up in a stretch of grass near a collection of cute, hand-built latrines, and a large white tent filled with white banquet tables gave the place the look of a countryside wedding. As we piled out under an ominous sky, a young woman in a black Space for Giants polo shirt beamed at us from a nearby check-in table.

After gently informing us that we were late, she passed out gold stickers adorned with a large letter *D*. "You are all in group D," she said earnestly. "Please put these stickers on. We want everyone to feel included! And here's a waiver you need to sign, just because of the rhinos. . . . "

A meeting with one of those rhinos, it turned out, was first on the agenda. We found the animal in question a short walk away, placidly munching on some hay and seemingly unaware of the cameras, humans, and general buzz around him. His chillaxed demeanor made the waivers seem a tad overkill ("There exists an element of danger. . . . "), even if his head was larger than my torso.

The rhino's name, we were told by a keeper, was Sudan, and he happened to be the last male northern white rhino in the world. (Sudan passed away in March 2018.)

Last—huh? I assumed I must have heard this wrong. But no, I realized as the keeper continued his speech, I had not misunderstood.

"There's only three northern white rhinos remaining, and they all live here," the keeper said. "They are a subspecies of white rhinos, one of Africa's two rhino species. Some people think that northern white rhinos and southern white rhinos should be separate species, but for now, they're a subspecies. After thirty years in captivity at a zoo in the Czech Republic, they weren't breeding, so people brought them here to see if they could get them to do something. But Sudan is forty-three years old, and the two females can't have babies. There's a plan to collect ova and do in vitro fertilization with stored sperm, then implant the embryo into a southern white rhino surrogate. This might save the northern white rhino from extinction."

My head spun trying to make sense of all these details as I waited my turn to approach Sudan for a photo. *To be the very last of your kind, well, what a weight,* I thought. Munching away, though, Sudan seemed blissfully unaware of this burden.

I placed a tentative hand on his craggy back while Zac Mutai, his longtime keeper, stood nearby and softly cooed, "Sudaaaaaaan, Sudaaaaaaan," over and over again. Beneath Sudan's bark-like skin, I could feel the slow heaves of his breath. I turned and smiled awkwardly at Tim, who had volunteered to be my photographer, unsure of whether I should look somber or happy. It was hard not to think of finality of extinction in the presence of this deceptively placid animal, who stood so very close to the black hole of oblivion.

"Bye, Sudan," I quietly said instead. "Thanks."[1]

LIKE A SCHOOL FIELD TRIP, WE'D SPENT THE MORNING AT OL PEJETA CIRCULATING through various stations, learning about human-elephant conflict (raiding elephants can destroy a field of crops in minutes), rhino poaching (Kenya lost 105 black and white rhinos from 2013 to 2015), and forensics. The forensics talk was headed by Rod Potter, a plump South African wildlife investigator whose bountiful grey beard earned him the nickname Dumbledore among the journalists present. He walked us through a staged crime scene, pointing out evidence—cartridge cases, litter, boot prints, blood spatter—and instructing us how to document and collect it. "You can't put a crime scene in front of a magistrate, so you have to paint a picture in the court's eye," he said.

No matter how much evidence is meticulously gathered or how strong a case is built, however, it does not guarantee a speedy delivery of justice. In Kenya, just 40 percent of cases conclude within a year. Along with the endless delays, dismissals are frequent and defendants often disappear—problems that are common throughout Africa. A 2009 assessment conducted by TRAFFIC in Zimbabwe, for example, found that only 18 court cases resulted from 123 poaching incidents, which ultimately led to just 6 convictions. Likewise, of the 928 poaching cases finalized in South Africa's Kruger National Park in 2015, just 29 produced convictions by the end of the year. More than 400 were still listed as "under investigation," while 405 more were shelved because of insufficient evidence or disappearing suspects. "In one case, a gunshot was heard, and the guys were literally arrested in an hour," Potter said. "That was seven years ago, and still nothing. These things just don't go to bed in a hurry."

At the criminal justice tent next door, we learned that defendants who do

---

1. For a bonus chapter about Sudan, please visit rachelnuwer.com/poached/.

make it to court have the advantage of some of the best lawyers Kenya has to offer, almost certainly paid for by their syndicate bosses. Prosecutors, on the contrary, are woefully overworked, juggling as many as thirty cases at a time. "They're handed a file by an investigator and are expected to assess the evidence without having had time to properly prepare or read it," said Shamini Jayanathan, a former London criminal barrister who now serves as director of legal strategy at Space for Giants. "When cases start like that, no matter how strong they are, you're at a huge disadvantage. You simply cannot digest the facts, deliver quality witness care, or make crucial decisions on the file."

Jayanathan is a fast talker exuding confidence and competence. In the demo tent, she was joined by several colleagues to act out how wildlife cases in Kenya typically go. They opened their mock trial with the prosecutor and a police officer whispering frantically and pawing through a file before sloppily tossing a piece of paper at the judge, played by Jayanathan. She exasperatedly pointed out that it was missing the date. Apologizing profusely, the obviously flustered prosecutor corrected the error after more paper-rifling. Finally, the charges were read—possession of forty-four pounds of ivory—and the defendant pleaded not guilty. Though the evidence against the defendant was strong, the prosecutor continued to make mistake after mistake: she stumbled when asked how many witnesses she would call, she botched her answer when the judge asked for grounds opposing bail, and at one point she suddenly realized that she forgot to include possession of a firearm on her charge sheet.

The defense lawyer, however—a man dressed in a smart suit with head held confidently high—eagerly pointed out that the accused had no previous convictions and was a highly esteemed member of the community, serving as an official in the local county office. The charges against his client were lies, he emphasized.

Bail was granted.

Switching out of character, Jayanathan described the work she and her colleagues have undertaken to counter such scenarios. One of those colleagues is Paula, who first alerted Jayanathan to the problems plaguing wildlife justice in Kenya. Although the country had recently strengthened its punishments for poaching and trafficking from a fine of just $400 maximum to $200,000, life in prison, or both, in 2013, Paula, aided by Jayanathan, discovered a disconnect between the law in writing and the law in reality.

From 2008 to 2013, rangers arrested nearly 750 people, but 70 percent of the arrest records were missing—meaning they'd either been purposefully destroyed or incompetently lost. It also meant that those cases were likely dismissed. Paula further found that, of those who did go to court, just 4 percent received jail sentences. The rest got off with no punishment at all or else something "ridiculous," she said, "like a day of community service cutting the grass at the chief's office—for killing elephants." She immediately organized a press conference to announce the findings. "The government was so mad," she recalled.

Jayanathan, meanwhile, decided to resign from her job at the Foreign Office to work on conservation issues full time. "I care about wildlife, but I'm not an environmentalist and I don't know a lot about elephants and the science side of things," she said. "What I do have to offer, though, is a wealth of experience on the criminal justice side, which is something that the NGO community didn't know much about."

Her instincts proved spot-on. In late 2013, following intense lobbying by conservationists, Kenya passed the Wildlife Conservation and Management Act, which, among other improvements, raised the penalties for wildlife crime. Jayanathan and others got to work with the less-than-thrilling task of "a lot of training—endless training." Kenya Wildlife Service officers learned how to preserve the chain of custody, and prosecutors and investigators were versed in the "menu of wildlife offenses, and the ingredients you need for each offense," Jayanathan said. Jim Karani, a lawyer at WildlifeDirect, became the first African to hold a master's in animal law, and Strathmore University in Nairobi began offering the country's first specialized course in wildlife criminal justice.

Conservationists even began to poach defense attorneys. John Otieno Abwuor, a charismatic, highly successful lawyer, formerly worked for accused wildlife criminals but is now on retainer for Space for Giants as a legal advisor and trainer. "This came about because they noted the competency of the wildlife cases I was handling," he said, chuckling. "I was winning all of them." These days, his duty lies with the prosecution, including training lawyers, investigators, and officers; conducting pretrial briefings with witnesses; and providing feedback on cases.

Jayanathan and her colleagues' small but significant interventions have begun to make a difference. In 2015, just 6 percent of cases had missing files, and convictions resulting in a jail sentences—while still low—have more than doubled, to 6 percent. Kenya still has a ways to go, however. As Felbab-Brown pointed out, for law enforcement to have a pronounced deterrent effect on reducing homicides, for example, prosecution rates need to reach at least 40 percent.

Some of the convictions have been quite significant, though. In 2016, following a dogged campaign headed by Paula and WildlifeDirect, and a hard-fought prosecution led by an invigorated public prosecution office, Faisal Mohamed Ali, a well-connected businessman found in possession of $440,000 worth of ivory, was fined nearly $200,000 and sentenced to twenty years in jail. "We were able to propose a number of criminal justice solutions, but all of this has worked because it's very much owned by the Kenyans," Jayanathan said.

THE DAY AT OL PEJETA HAD STARTED STRONG WITH POTTER'S, JAYANATHAN'S, AND others' talks, but in the afternoon things began to unravel. The increasingly ominous clouds had finally begun to deliver on their threat, and group D—along with other summit attendees who belonged to different letters of the alphabet—huddled under the wedding tent, unsure of what came next. Lunch had long since concluded.

Glancing outside, I saw a six-month-old baby rhino named Ringo dart by, adorably wearing a raincoat like a spoiled Upper East Side thoroughbred. I noticed a few group D members piling into a van farther across the field, so I abandoned my shelterd spot just in time to snag a seat next to a South African couple, Rian and Lorna Labuschagne. Lorna had an easygoing lightness about her and was adorned head to toe in silver jewelry—mementos collected across the continent that were, however, "a nightmare for airport security," as Rian noted. Next to his breezy wife, Rian's lean features and furrowed brow seemed all the more stern. They had traveled to the Giants Club Summit from Chad, Lorna said, where they were running a park called Zakouma.

"We have a much bigger problem in there than they do here," she said. "Guys come in from Sudan, and they fear nothing. When they shoot, they shoot to kill."

After the park had lost 4,000 elephants to raiders in the span of just a few years, she and Rian had come in and managed to get the poaching situation under control. The killings have almost completely ceased, and for the first time in a decade, elephant numbers are growing. "Our rangers go out on horseback with rocket launchers and machine guns, just to try to stop these armed gangs," Rian said. The conversation ended as we pulled up at another tent, but I made a mental note to look into their intriguing story in a future adventure—described in Chapter 10.

Waiting for us inside were five tall men in camouflage, green berets, and black boots, standing at attention while a brown dog on a leash rested at their feet. They were members of the Kenya Police Reserve, we were told, and served in Ol Pejeta's Rapid Response Unit. When a poaching incident occurs, the police-cum-rangers are picked up by helicopter and dropped into the field. While the commander talked, a photographer pointed his lens directly down the barrel of one of the men's assault rifles and asked—a bit belatedly—whether it was loaded. The commander replied that it was not.

The men treated us to a demo, climbing into a blue helicopter, dog and all, and then leaping out as it came back in for a landing. As soon as their boots touched earth, the men fanned out, their movements coordinated and controlled as dancers. They crouched in unison, disappearing into the bush, and then raised their weapons, their expressions blank as they gazed through the sights. Zooming in on one of them with my telescopic lens, my heart fluttered. His gun was pointed directly at our tent.

The impressive show concluded, and the attendees hastened back to the buses, which quickly began pulling away like so many life rafts from a sinking ship. Though no announcements were made, there was an unspoken understanding that the field trip was over. With great relief, I managed to locate group D's bus before it sped away, although not everyone was so lucky: as the door slammed shut behind me, I caught sight of the young woman who had welcomed us earlier that day with the stickers. She was standing in the mud, hair plastered to her distraught face and her Space for Giants shirt soaked. "I think I've been left!" she said to no one in particular. "They left me!"

THE PANDEMONIUM CONTINUED THE FOLLOWING DAY AT THE SUMMIT PROPER, where President Kenyatta, along with the presidents of Gabon and Uganda, were scheduled to speak at the Fairmont Mount Kenya Safari Club—a gorgeous, sprawling colonial-style building that is Nanyuki's most exclusive hotel.

The hotel was unable, however, to accommodate even some of the most prestigious summit attendees, thanks to some last-minute changes. President Kenyatta, who was strictly allotted nine guests, showed up with an entourage of some twenty people. There was no arguing with him, so others had to be displaced from their rooms—including leading elephant expert (and senior citizen) Iain Douglas-Hamilton, who was put outside in a tent that nevertheless cost four figures. Kenyatta wasn't the only one making unreasonable demands, however; one wealthy attendee reportedly insisted that her helicopter pilot be given a room. "When you're dealing with this caliber of people, well, they're all very special," one of the organizers later griped. "They just think they can do whatever they want, whenever they want." This wasn't lost on the more humble attendees present, a few of whom cheekily took to referring to the Space for Giants event as "Space for Giant Egos."

None of the room kerfuffles really pertained to the media. We were told from the beginning that we'd be staying off-site. On the morning of the summit, however, the shuttle that was supposed to collect me from the modest hotel I'd booked, located some twenty minutes away, arrived half an hour late. I fretted and fidgeted on the ride over, and by the time we pulled up we were forty-five minutes late. I ran inside—only to be told by a guy I'd met the day before that the talks hadn't even begun.

"One of the presidents isn't here yet," he said casually. "It's Africa—everything is late."

After a quick bag check—I've experienced more thorough searches at nightclubs—I entered the main conference room. It was filled with media camera crews, uniformed guards holding large guns, and an eclectic crowd. Men in suits with animal-themed ties mixed with Maasai elders in red *shukas*. I spotted Paula, who was working the crowd near the entrance, beaming and posing for photos in front of a Hands off Our Elephants poster.

After more sitting around, someone announced that—rather than wait for the presidents to arrive—the program was flipped, beginning with talks that were scheduled for the afternoon. Although my agenda indicated that "media would be removed" from these "private" panels, no one seemed to care that the room remained chock-full of cameras. We began with a session called "Lessons from the Frontline."

Tom Okello, chief park warden of Uganda, took the floor. "We're arresting the people who are nearer to the national park and who collaborate with the poachers, not the real people who are motivating the poaching," he began solemnly. "We may be tackling the problem, but not the root cause."

"Okay—wow! Tragic!" the moderator commented, sounding like a game show host.

"We need to fight corruption in the system and conflicts of interests within communities on the front line, and we need to have the capability to react to information," Okello continued. "The most important thing, though, is stability in the range states. Without stability or security, our dream of securing the future of the African elephant will be a waste of time."

"Tom, you have areas along your border in Uganda that are a little bit unfriendly," the moderator delicately pointed out.

"We have coordinated patrols—"

Okello was suddenly cut off by a blare of trumpets and crash of symbols.

"Their excellencies will be joining us momentarily!" announced the emcee, jostling onto the stage. Everyone sat up, necks craning expectantly toward the back of the room. A minute passed. And then another. The emcee wrung his hands. "And while we're in this awkward moment . . . please get to know your neighbor!" he said, obviously trying to make lemonade. "And if it takes longer . . . get to know the neighbor behind you!"

Twenty minutes later, still nothing. But then, in a flash, the emcee was back on the stage, motioning for everyone to stand. The brass band started up again, accompanied by a flurry of whispers and shouts.

"They're coming!"

"We need this clear!"

"It's okay, it's okay!"

"Shit!"

"Here they come!"

In walked the presidents of Kenya, Gabon, and Uganda, surrounded by a posse of suits. It was 11:35, I noted with a frown, for a meeting that was supposed to have begun at 9:00.

Following a few speeches by eminent conservationists, the presidents took the stage. Ugandan president Yoweri Museveni wore an oversized safari hat that clashed comically with his proper black suit, but his message was anything but humorous. "We're very strict with the poachers in Uganda: we send them to heaven prematurely," he said, smiling slyly. "So they're not so much of a problem. My problem, though, are my voters, who want to go into the national parks because they want more land. That's a stronger problem for wildlife than those Asians who want some reinforcement for their—" he gestured emphatically toward his groin and laughed.

"There are some things that only the elders can say!" President Kenyatta boisterously interjected.

"The challenge is getting the African population to shift from low-tech agriculture to industry and service," President Museveni continued. "Even if you stop the market for ivory, until you deal with demography, we're going to have a problem."

President Ali Bongo Ondimba of Gabon—who looked like the Danny DeVito of African leaders and whose voice was velvety and sincere—delivered a similar message. "Poaching has turned elephants into refugees fleeing toward villages, where they find safety but eat and trample crops," he said. "They are a cause of hunger and misery to many people in rural areas. My voters are already suggesting that for the forthcoming election, I should ask elephants to vote for me."

With that, the emcee announced that it was time for lunch.

I TOOK A BREAK FROM THE TALKS TO WORK ON A STORY I WAS WRITING FOR *National Geographic* about the ivory burn. While I was gone, wealthy individuals and countries made various pledges to help save elephants, totaling some $5 million in donations and support. The news that stole the headlines, though, was an announcement that Kenya, along with other nations, would propose uplisting all African elephant populations to the highest level of protection afforded by CITES at a meeting taking place in Johannesburg in the fall.

When I briefly saw Paula—who was looking a bit tired and quickly waved me off so she could go find a cup of tea—she pooh-poohed that plan, however. "In terms of uplisting, good luck, but I don't think it'll work," she said. "The science isn't there. What we need is for the domestic markets to be shut down in China, Japan, Africa, and Southeast Asia."

I CLUTCHED MY SEAT THROUGH THE BUMPY FLIGHT THROUGH THICK RAIN CLOUDS back to Nairobi, where a quick ride from Wilson Airport brought us to the Kenya Wildlife Service headquarters, located on the edge of Nairobi National Park. The ivory burn was supposed to be capped at a thousand attendees, but the traffic situation in the headquarters' tight roads and overflowing parking lots indicated that limit had been far exceeded. A group of baboons ran across the road, holding up traffic; cars parked perpendicularly to others, creating impassable obstacle courses; and bewildered attendees on foot gingerly navigated pond-sized puddles. "I love watching complete chaos," the guy sitting next to me flatly commented, unprompted.

"As long as you have nowhere to be," I replied.

Where we needed to be, it turned out, was a big white tent set up in a field of mud. Behind the tent stood eleven ivory pyramids representing some 10,000 elephants, plus 1.35 tons of rhino horn. It was a sobering sight. Twenty-seven years earlier, Kenya had held the world's first ivory burn on this spot—an event that ultimately led to the global ban on ivory. Now, the nation was once again hoping to change the course of history.

Kenya, however, is no longer the only country that has elected to destroy some or all of its ivory. Since the inaugural 1989 burn, more than twenty nations have followed suit, holding around thirty crushes and burns that have permanently removed more than 260 tons of ivory from the market. (No one knows how much ivory is kept in dusty government storehouses and lockers throughout the world. Some countries do not have the resources to inventory their ivory adequately, while others simply ignore requests to submit their data. In 2016, CITES roughly estimated that 1,000 tons are stockpiled in total.)

Like Kenya, nations that opt to destroy some or all of their ivory usually do so primarily to sway public opinion, educate people about the elephant crisis, and demonstrate the government's commitment to stopping illegal trade. Another powerful reason, though, is simply to get rid of it. The constant threat of theft, especially by corrupt officials, makes ivory and rhino horn burdensome and expensive to protect. Tons have disappeared from supposedly well-guarded government storehouses spanning Africa to Asia. Some of the thefts have involved quite ridiculous twists. In 2006, for example, the Philippines' Wildlife Department sued customs officers for "losing" several tons of ivory—only to later discover that its own stockpile had also been raided (some tusks had even been replaced with exact plastic replicas, according to journalist Bryan Christy). In 2010, Vietnamese officials explained that ivory that had disappeared from their storehouse had been "eaten by rats," while at least 5.5 tons from Mozambique's stockpile vanished from 2014 to 2016 when the twenty-four-hour security cameras conveniently "failed."

Not everyone agrees that burning is the solution. Some think it's simply a waste. Rather than destroy its ivory, Botswana, for example, installed a life-sized elephant sculpture made out of 2.5 tons of tusks in its international airport.

Mostly, though, countries that oppose ivory burns and crushes do so not because they want to make art but because they wish to sell their stash in the future. In 1989, Zimbabwean officials mocked Kenya's burn and called Leakey a "bunny hugger"—a stance they maintain today. For Zimbabwe and other Southern African countries, burning ivory is tantamount to setting money on fire, while trading it is seen as a sovereign right.

Much of this comes down to cultural differences, Leakey said. "The stereotypic profile of Southern African game rangers and professional hunters are tough guys with hairy legs and big chests who decry and insult those who think you can actually be emotional about animals," he said. "If an elephant isn't bringing in enough money by being photographed, then the attitude is, 'Why shouldn't we kill these beasts!'"

This attitude was exemplified in a fiery editorial published in *African Hunting Gazette* shortly after the burn (the text was interspersed with ads for riflescopes and "the finest dangerous-game, bolt-action rifle in the world"). The author, John Ledger of the University of Johannesburg, did not mince words. The belief that ivory bans and burns will save elephants, he wrote, "is such a naïve and child-like perspective that it belongs in the nursery with the tales of Dumbo, the Disney World flying elephant, and Babar, the little elephant whose mother was killed by a cruel hunter and he was then taken in by a nice lady who dressed him in nice clothes so he could live in Paris." Elephants (or, rather, their ivory) are a valuable natural resource, he continued. To destroy that resource is a "travesty" perpetuated by the "animal rightists of the elephant-free First World" who bully, blackmail, and victimize hapless African leaders like President Kenyatta into carrying out their "neocolonialist" agendas. As Ronald Orenstein, a conservationist and lawyer, later noted of this argument, "Funny how these (usually white) guys are happy to assume that black African leaders are colonialist dupes who couldn't possibly care about their own animals. Leakey has rightly called this attitude insulting, but I would use a stronger word."

No matter how passionately either side argues for or against destroying ivory, though, we really do not know what effect, if any, burns and crushes have on poaching and trade today. Do they help sway public opinion in Asia in favor of conservation, as the 1989 burn did for Western audiences? A 2018 study hints that the answer may be no, finding that the majority of media coverage about the Kenya's record-making burn was published in the United States and Kenya— hardly the current sources of demand. Some argue that burns may even hurt rather than help, by making ivory so many tons rarer and triggering a surge in poaching and purchasing. Scientists have yet to carefully study these questions, so, for now, answers are lacking.

Those questions, though, were far from people's minds in Nairobi, where the mood was jubilant. A marching band played beneath overcast skies, and children in costume performed preshow dances in front of the stage. As usual, there was no one checking badges (which I'd never been given) or IDs, so I decided to skip the quarantined media section some distance away, across what appeared to be a mud wrestling pit, and instead sit near the front with the other summit attendees. In fact, the entire area was a bog. Red felt carpeting had been laid down toward the front of the stage, and huge green tarps were placed farther back, but, rather than block the water, large coffee-with-a-splash-of-milk puddles had formed all over, like a war-ravaged field pock-marked with so many craters. The pudding-like muck beneath the carpeting squashily gave way beneath each step, ushering in a stream of dirty, displaced water.

The speeches soon began. Ségolène Royal, France's energy minister, said that her government planned to implement a domestic ban and to urge other European leaders to do the same. US deputy secretary of state Heather Higginbottom, speaking on behalf of President Obama, delivered a few oft-repeated declarations, including that the only value ivory has is on an elephant.

Leakey, who was once described to me as "a very eloquent voice, one of the great orators of our time," was up next. Although he looked a bit worse for wear at seventy-one, his energy apparently had not subsided, and he delivered a powerful speech. "There are some countries on this continent who suggested they will put their stocks out of economic reach for now, but will not destroy them," he said. "They are speculators in an evil, illegal commodity, and they should be shamed out of their position once and for all." He half-jokingly concluded with a suggestion that CITES be replaced by a new treaty called KITES: Kill all International Trade in Endangered Species. (Notably, none of the pro-trade Southern African countries attended the burn, including Botswana, whose senior officials had been getting down on the conference gala dance floor just the night before. Their absence was a "snub to the Kenyan government," according to Paula.)

President Ali Bongo from Gabon—wearing an amazingly patterned Hawaii-meets-Africa shirt—stressed that his nation had already burned its entire stockpile of ivory. "One last message," he said, pointing at the audience. "To all the poachers, to all the buyers, to all the traders: Your days are numbered.

We are going to put you out of business, so the best thing you can do is go into retirement now."

"I hope the Chinese are listening!" said a woman behind me in an aggressive whisper.

Finally, President Kenyatta took the stage. Speaking in a lightly British accent, he vowed to continue to fight on behalf of Kenya and Africa's animals. "Before you, ladies and gentlemen, is the largest haul of ivory and horn ever to be destroyed," he said. "And our message is crystal clear: no one, and I mean no one, has any business trading in ivory, for this trade means death of our elephants and our natural heritage." He added that he was confident that future generations would appreciate Kenya's decision to destroy its ivory and rhino horns.

"Now, without further ado, and before Richard's legs get stuck," he said, giving Leakey a teasing grin, "I think we need to get out there and do what we've come here to do."

Following on the heels of the presidents and VIPs, the crowd hurriedly sloshed to where the ivory pyramids awaited. One huge pile stood in the middle, surrounded by two symmetric satellite groups of five smaller piles each. In front, rhino horns filled a metal crate the size of a giant's shopping basket.

Male and female Kenya Wildlife Service rangers sternly faced the crowd contained behind metal barriers. President Kenyatta, surrounded by his usual clique of suits, made his way to what looked like a small bird fountain that held a gently burning pile of wood. He dipped a torch into the tray, then touched its glowing tip to the pile of lighter-fluid-soaked ivory. He and the other leaders made their way around the lot, giving each pyre the same treatment.

For a few minutes, nothing much happened. But then, wisps of gray-brown smoke rose from each pile. These soon grew into a billowing cloud. The thickening plumes began to swirl hypnotically and soar upward, blocking out the sun that had momentarily peaked out from behind the clouds. The rhino horn, meanwhile, began issuing crackling-pop noises as the hairlike material caught fire. Kids on their dads' shoulders pointed, people shouted, and a thousand cameras clicked.

I could feel the heat on my face and arms now, and at last the brilliant orange flames began peeking out—and then erupting—from the towers. The fire climbed to ever-greater heights, reaching skyward as though trying to escape its own consuming force. The surrounding air bubbled and blurred, and small patches of nearby grass caught fire and were then extinguished by firefighters.

People all around me were taking selfies, some with serious or sad faces, others smiling widely.

As the spectacle continued and evening fell, kids turned their attention back to the mud, the music stopped, and the crowd began to thin. I was about ready to head out myself, exhausted. Before I left, though, I noticed Paula across the field. She had her arms thrown around colleagues in celebration: her excitement and energy clearly had not even begun to wane.

I recalled that she had originally hoped for each fire to be dedicated and lit by a different group of people—the presidents, the children, the rangers, the communities, and so on—to give everyone a sense of ownership. Although that did not come to pass, the ivory burn no doubt left a strong impression on all who were present, not to mention the millions more around the world who witnessed it on the news or social media. It was, as Paula had hoped, "the wildfire spectacle of this decade."

Seven

THE CITES CIRCUS

WILDLIFE protection is rarely as dramatic as an ivory bonfire. Instead, much takes place in the soulless conference rooms of CITES, the Convention on International Trade in Endangered Species of Wild Fauna and Flora. This binding treaty among governments was created "for the protection of certain species of wild fauna and flora against over-exploitation through international trade." The message sounds pretty straightforward, but dig a bit deeper and CITES quickly becomes confusing. What are the different levels of protection? Who exactly sets species listings and policy recommendations—and how? And what, if anything, happens if countries drop the ball on their commitments?

CITES dates back to 1963, when attendees at an International Union for Conservation of Nature meeting realized that unregulated trade directly threatened certain species—yet the world had no way to control it. The idea of creating a multi-government agreement to regulate the trade seems obvious now, but at the time it appeared utopian. Nevertheless, a treaty was drafted and signed, and two years after that, in 1975, CITES went into force. The convention now includes 183 governments, and its listings have grown to some 35,000 species. Countries register around a million transactions per year, which range from a single specimen to hundreds or thousands.

To ensure those trades are sustainable, CITES categorizes species under appendixes. Appendix I is reserved for plants and animals threatened with extinction. For instance, in 1989, CITES representatives voted to move all African elephants to Appendix I, banning those animals and their parts—including ivory—from commercial trade. Appendix I species can't be traded for primarily commercial purposes, save for a few exemptions, such as captive-bred specimens from approved facilities. Trade for noncommercial reasons—loans or exchanges of scientific specimens, donations from one country to another—is sometimes permitted but requires both an export and an import permit, issued by the CITES scientific authorities in the respective countries. The people holding those positions are supposed to be experts, and they should issue a permit only after making an evidence-based determination that the trade in question will not harm the species.

Appendix II species are those that are not deemed threatened with extinction, but—should they be freely traded—may enter the danger zone (in the threatened-with-extinction sense, not the Kenny Loggins one). Unlike Appendix I species, they require only an export permit and can be traded internationally for commercial purposes. Years after the parties voted to move African elephants to Appendix I, another vote approved the transfer of Botswana, Namibia, Zimbabwe, and South Africa's elephant populations to Appendix II. But CITES stipulated in an annotation that—in this exceptional case—commercial trade of ivory would still not be permitted, save for two one-off sales described in Chapter 5.

Decisions to "uplist" or "downlist" species to and from various appendix listings, or to add a new species or remove an existing one, are made at the CITES Meetings of the Conference of the Parties. Proposals require a two-thirds majority vote to pass and are supposed to be science based, taking into account evidence such as how many of the animals are left in the wild; how urgent the threats are to their survival; and how many, if any, can be removed sustainably.

The process is far from perfect. For many species, experts lack even the most basic data, including population estimates, making it impossible to know what levels of trade are in fact sustainable. "It is funny in a sick kind of way that we, on the one hand, agree to regulate the trade in these vulnerable species, but then we accept that for the majority of them, we have no clue what sustainable levels of offtake are," said Vincent Nijman, a conservation ecologist at Oxford Brookes University. "A logical next step would be to agree, then, that if we have no idea what we can take, we should minimize international trade. But instead we continue with a business-as-usual scenario, trading until we can clearly see that we have gone too far."

The scale of the trade is staggering: from 2006 to 2015, 1.3 million live animals and plants, 1.5 million skins, and 2,000 tons of meat were legally exported from Africa to Asia alone, according to a 2018 TRAFFIC study. Yet that example pertains only to CITES-listed species. In fact, a minority of plants and animals are so lucky as even to be included under the treaty. The volume of international trade in animals not categorized by CITES is about ten times greater than the trade in listed ones, Nijman said, while the domestic trade is ten times greater than that. To make these figures a bit more tangible, take frogs. About 20 million CITES-listed frogs and 200 million non-CITES-listed frogs are exported each year from Asia, mostly Indonesia. But traders there send out only about 12 percent of the total number of frogs their collectors catch—those whose tasty legs weigh eighty grams or more. The punier frogs—about 2 billion animals annually—are sold at home to Indonesian buyers. "And remember, this is all above board, and hence, 'legal,'" Nijman said.

Look a bit closer at legal trade, however, and it begins to appear more and more illegal. For starters, legally binding rules are broken with impunity, including ones that govern harvesting quotas and capture methods, dictate who can sell what where, regulate transport, and stipulate required licenses. Not surprisingly, very few people pay their taxes on wildlife goods trafficked through the system, so many are also guilty of tax evasion. "Once you have broken those rules and regulations, it makes it difficult to continue without bribing your way through the system," Nijman said. "Taking this view, then the majority of the wildlife trade in Asia, and probably elsewhere, is illegal."

For now, though, the legal-just-kidding-not-legal side of the trade remains widely accepted. Like jaywalking in New York City or driving five to ten miles over the speed limit, shady wildlife businesses have operated openly in this manner for such a long time that they've become normalized. "This kind of trade carries no stigma, and no one is prosecuted for it," Nijman said. "It's become legal, even if technically it isn't."

Amending the system is challenging, not the least because scientists and nongovernmental organizations can neither submit CITES proposals nor vote. The best they can do is lobby government representatives to do so. Government reps, however, also hear from those with commercial or personal interests, and they lobby each other to go along with particular agendas. Some countries unscrupulously trade votes in a "you scratch my back, I'll scratch yours" manner, while others in effect buy votes. Japan, for example, once hosted a less-than-subtle "dinner for countries receiving financial aid from Japan" the night before the bluefin tuna vote. The effect, as Ronald Orenstein noted in *Ivory, Horn and Blood,* is that species listings becomes an ad hoc and highly political process.

Various individuals and organizations have complained for decades about this, with many alleging that some CITES employees and government representatives prioritize personal gain over species conservation. "Watch what is going on outside the conference halls, with people having private meetings and doing deals on the side," said Annie Olivecrona, a Kenya-based conservationist. "It happens all the time, and you can be sure it is not beneficial for wildlife. It's like having the UN Refugee Agency without a focus on refugees, or UNICEF without caring about children. I think it's high time to do a proper external audit of the Secretariat and see what they have actually achieved over the last forty years." What started as a conservation treaty regulating trade, agreed conservationist and author Judith Mills in 2015, is "on the verge of becoming a *trade* treaty regulating conservation."

Chris Shepherd, executive director of Monitor, emphasized, though, that CITES has a people problem—not a treaty problem. "There's really not a lot that we need to do to improve CITES," he said. "It just needs to be enforced." CITES's power lies in the fact that it is binding international law. Even so, noncompliance is rampant. For starters, countries regularly fail to turn in data on the number of seizures or trades they undertake per year. In 2010, for example, China reported importing 130 ivory "carvings," forty elephant feet, ninety-nine pounds of tusks, and zero trophies from Zimbabwe, all under the supposed label of legal "personal" items. Zimbabwe's records of exports to China over the same period, however, told a completely different story: 2,512 ivory carvings, eight elephant feet, four trophies, and forty-one tusks. When trade data are even entered into the database at all, such glaring inconsistencies are often the norm. "Monitoring trade using data which is more or less gobbledegook is next to impossible," wrote John Sellar, the now-retired former chief of enforcement at the CITES Secretariat.

Reporting issues, moreover, are the least of CITES's worries. Some CITES representatives are negligent or abusive of the import-export system: they issue permits when they shouldn't, sell permits, or allow permits to be "stolen" from their offices. "Some countries will sell you a CITES permit for pretty much anything you want," said Tim Steele, the UN Office on Drugs and Crime's global anti-corruption advisor, at a panel on corruption.

Other longtime member countries lack even proper legislation to carry out their duties to CITES. "Everyone's freaking out about tigers going extinct, but of course they're going extinct if parties involved in the trade don't even have laws to stop it," Shepherd said. "Why not freak out instead about the CITES

Secretariat not holding those countries accountable?" Orenstein shares Shepherd's frustration, but he also emphasized that some countries genuinely want and try to do better but lack the resources. In other cases, honest wildlife officers are impeded by officials. "CITES can of course do a lot better," he said. "But to imply that it is entirely venal is an overstatement in the other direction."

Holding countries accountable is tricky, as CITES has few real teeth to bite with. Sanctions, however, are one powerful tool it does possess. If a party to the convention is found guilty of enough violations, CITES can issue sanctions that— if respected by other nations—prevent that country from trading in CITES-listed species. Those species may include timber, orchids, seafood, pets, reptile skins, or anything else included in the convention. For many nations, the economic repercussions of such sanctions would be significant.

When sanctions—or even a threat of sanctions—are issued, the results tend to be mixed. In 2013, CITES used the s-word to encourage Thailand to clean up its illegal ivory market—a move that did have the desired effect. "Everyone knew that Thailand was the world's largest unregulated illegal ivory market, but nothing was changing," said Leigh Henry, a senior policy advisor at WWF. "It wasn't until 'sanction' was put on a piece of paper that we started to see real progress." Indeed, the amount of ivory in Bangkok's markets dropped by 96 percent between 2014 and 2016, leading TRAFFIC to describe Thailand as "an outstanding example" of CITES propelling positive change.

Thailand, however, was an exception to the rule. Laos, in contrast, was briefly subjected to a trade ban after it failed to submit reports on its progress to combat illegal ivory trade. After the country scraped together an official National Ivory Action Plan to appease CITES, the ban was lifted—never mind the fact that illegal ivory is still openly sold there, alongside a Peterson Field Guide's worth of other protected species. In this case, the sanction did not have a meaningful effect—but at least it was issued.

In reality, sanctions are hardly ever passed, and they almost always gloss over bigger players in the illegal trade. As one source noted, it's up to the CITES parties—not the Secretariat—to decide who should be sanctioned, and too many countries are too influenced by powerful nations such as China to ever consider issuing sanctions against them. Country representatives also tend to be highly political when it comes to enforcement: avoiding embarrassment for colleagues sometimes takes priority over enforcing the treaty. Or, as Orenstein noted, it may simply be that they'd rather not have the same finger pointed at them.

Because of such failings, some consider CITES impotent, not only in its ability to combat illegal trade but also in its basic role of regulating sustainable legal trade. "The actual tool is excellent and could really make a difference," Shepherd said. "But parties need to hold each other accountable if the convention is going to function." The reality, though, is that "CITES seldom bites," he continued. "And if CITES never bites, then what's the point?" Crawford Allan, senior director of TRAFFIC, agreed that the system can be frustrating but pointed out, "CITES, for all its flaws, is the best we've got."

IT'S ONE THING TO REPORT ABOUT CITES FROM AFAR BUT QUITE ANOTHER TO PERsonally witness the regulatory behemoth in action, as I did in 2016 at the Seventeenth Meeting of the Conference of the Parties, or CoP17, in Johannesburg.

Johannesburg is an interesting place. When Leakey first visited shortly after the 1990 ivory ban, he wrote that the metropolis was different than any other he'd experienced in Africa: "Built by and for Europeans—only the vast sprawling slums, and so-called townships, were African." Apartheid's institutionalized racial segregation was abolished in 1991, and Joburg's 4.4 million citizens are now 75 percent black African. The rest are primarily white South African, Indian, Asian, or of mixed heritage. Although some diss Johannesburg as dirty and dangerous, I loved it. It's African but undeniably international. Pocket-sized galleries, home-grown boutiques, unique restaurants, cutting-edge street fashion, and striking public art all served to reinforce the global vibes. The residents, easygoing and effortlessly cool, are always open for a chat, even with a stranger like me.

Sadly, though, I didn't get to know Johannesburg and its gritty charm as much as I would have liked. Most of my time was spent in fluorescent-lit meeting halls watched over by intense though largely invisible security. The CITES CoP also had the disadvantage of being held in Sandton, one of Joburg's most affluent and expensive suburbs—and thus one of its most vanilla. Its broad roads were crowded with expensive hotels, office buildings, and international franchises, while the most decent bar around was a place called Riffs that served jalapeño poppers and mojitos.

The CITES CoP took place at the Sandton Convention Center, a towering block of glass and concrete on a side street decorated with animal-themed banners. A third-floor catwalk connected the convention center to a multistory, maze-like mall across the street, full of designer clothing shops and overpriced restaurants mostly serving Italian food. Entering the convention center to register required going through the mall entrance (only badge-holders could get through the main door). I passed through airport-level security and was directed to a hallway full of private booths. A man in a uniform managed the waiting area and ensured a smooth flow as booths became available. Passports—not just photo IDs—were required, no exceptions. The polite woman working my booth typed into her computer, took my photo, and printed out my laminated, bar-coded badge, which was brightly color-coded in red to indicate I was media. The level of detail and organization, I must admit, caught me off guard. Clearly, I wasn't in Kenya anymore. Or Vietnam, for that matter.

Badge finally in hand, it was time to explore. The venue was a lot to take in: five floors of side events, information booths, printouts, and NGO-headed PR rooms. Coffee shops, outdoor benches, and bar tables were crowded with more than 3,500 potential sources. Some sat in chatty groups; others hunched together in corners, talking in conspiratorial whispers; while others still worked on laptops, brows furrowed and fingers slamming away. The crowd was international, to say the least: there were saris; elaborate, brightly colored head wraps; smart black suits; djellabas; and khaki shorts. Above all, though, wildlife-themed outfits—zebra ties and lion ties, orchid dresses and fish skirts, animal print of all sorts—ruled the day.

The conference's main events took place in two huge halls, each about half the size of a football field. Members of the CITES Secretariat sat on an elevated stage at the head of the room, overlooking blocks of long, white tables that were reserved for official party representatives. Farther back were additional tables designated for observers—NGOs, international bodies, representatives of non-party states and more—all of whom had their own labeled, reserved spaces. Finally, in the very back, were areas reserved for journalists and other riffraff.

I wandered into the Committee II meeting hall just as the program was kicking off and grabbed a headset, which provided live translations. Two big screens on stage projected close-ups of the speaker—at the moment, Jonathan Barzdo, chair of this session. "There's been an escalating trend from 2010 to 2015 of large illegal shipments of ivory that should be of great concern to parties," Barzdo was saying, referring to the latest data from CITES's Elephant Trade Information System (ETIS), a monitoring tool for recording levels and trends in the illegal ivory trade. Although some individual countries may be making headway,

Barzdo continued, evidence indicated no change in the overall ivory problem. According to the data, it is primarily driven by a few key players: China and Vietnam as destinations; Hong Kong, Malaysia, and Singapore as transit hubs; and Kenya, Tanzania, Uganda, Togo, and Malawi as entrepôts and exporters. Together, those ten nations have been implicated in 94 percent of large-scale ivory seizures since 2009, Barzdo said.

Said countries' representatives were none too pleased about their inclusion on the ivory shit list. As soon as Barzdo stopped talking, one of China's representatives requested the floor. "The ETIS report is too academic and complicated for many people to read, and the role each country plays in the illegal trade in ivory is not expressed directly, but in the number and quantity of seizures," he complained. "We're concerned that ETIS accepts all data without efforts to validate the authenticity of those data. If ETIS is having difficulty in arranging manpower, China is willing to send experts to assess this work."

Uganda's rep jumped on the defensive bandwagon next: "The media has used such groupings to distort information and portray parties classified as such as 'bad boys.' They previously branded us as the 'Gang of Eight'!"

Singapore was equally miffed. "We're very disappointed," its representative said icily. "These findings came as a surprise to our delegation."

Having stoically listened to the criticism, Tom Milliken, TRAFFIC's elephant and rhino program leader, and manager of ETIS, finally took the floor. "In the history of human discourse, the bearer of good news is universally hailed, but the bearer of bad news is often shot," he dramatically began. "I recognize the ETIS messenger may fall into the latter category." However, he continued, there's no arguing with facts: the countries involved with the greatest quantities of illegal ivory are likewise those of the greatest concern. Yes, the analytical methods are complex, but they're readily available for all to assess.

"It's not ETIS that's placing any countries into these trade chains," Milliken concluded. "It's the criminal syndicates that chose those pathways because they believe it will get the ivory where they want it to go." The topic was closed.

THE MEETING CONTINUED IN THIS FASHION FOR MORE THAN A WEEK, WITH THE hours in between ranging from painfully dull to the stuff of Hollywood dramas. Ted Reilly, a feisty game ranger of fifty-seven years whom *National Geographic* once described as a "father of conservation" in Swaziland, delivered one of the meeting's most impassioned—and, as he well knew, futile—speeches. After South Africa opted not to submit a rhino horn trade proposal, Swaziland had thrown together a hastily written bid of its own. For nearly half an hour, Reilly implored the parties to grant his tiny nation permission to sell its stockpiled 730 pounds of rhino horn on the international market and to harvest and legally sell rhino horn from its animals in the future. The funds, he promised, would be reinvested in conservation and rhino protection.

> Swaziland has an exemplary record of defending its own rhino resources, at the cost of the blood of six rangers who paid the ultimate price in defense of the kingdom's natural heritage—a heritage restored and protected *without* the help of CITES. . . . Rhinos and rangers continue to die under the CITES ban. These fallen heroes were fathers of children, husbands of wives, friends of friends, and breadwinners of families and they were all overworked and underpaid and committed. They paid the ultimate price for protecting the most valuable natural resource on earth, made valueless by CITES. We *cannot* allow their deaths to be in vain.

By this point, Reilly was visibly crying, his voice trembling. "Member states, rhinos are in your hands. It's up to you if the criminals continue to take all the rewards, or if the communities that live with wildlife can start reaping the benefit of their sovereign resources. It's as simple as that." As applause broke out, Reilly, gripping his hands as though in prayer, sat back in his seat, his expression already defeated. Indeed, with just twenty-six votes in favor, Swaziland's proposal did not pass.

The elephant talks were also noteworthy—although for all the pre-meeting hoopla and debate, the outcomes were rather anticlimactic. Namibia and Zimbabwe's bids to allow their nations to internationally trade in ivory were quickly shot down, although they were supported, paradoxically, by China—which had just voiced its approval for domestic ivory bans days before.

The Kenya-led hope of getting all elephant populations back onto Appendix I likewise failed to pass. The proposal received sixty-two votes—including, surprisingly, from traditionally pro-trade Botswana—but that was still well below the two-thirds majority it needed to clear. Namibia may be partly to blame for that: in a jerky move, the Southern African country made it "unequivocally clear" that if its elephants were voted back onto Appendix I, it would—in CITES parlance—invoke its right to submit a "reservation." Reservations permit countries to excuse themselves from a particular listing change they don't like. In real-world talk, this means Namibia would essentially go rogue with its trade, flouting the moratorium and selling its tusks to any other nation that wished to go rogue as well.

Namibia's antagonistic threat aside, countries and NGOs that opposed uplisting elephants generally did so on the basis of science. As Paula had warned me back in Kenya, the elephant populations in question simply are not threatened enough to meet the criteria for inclusion in Appendix I. Although poaching is present in Southern Africa, it occurs at significantly lower levels than in Central, West, and East Africa. Disregarding the data and switching Southern Africa's elephants onto Appendix I would have undermined the credibility of the convention, according to Allan at TRAFFIC: "No matter how cute they are, they just do not meet the biological description for an Appendix I species."

Bill Clark, one of Israel's representatives at CoP17, however, argued that Allan and others' supposedly science-based conclusion is "fatally flawed" because it unnaturally splits elephant populations into arbitrary units determined by national borders. Instead, we should view the species as a whole. As things stand now, he told *National Geographic,* elephants may experience "different levels of international protection, depending on where a particular animal has wandered over the course of a day or a week or a month." That, he said, is the true bad science.

Such arguments will no doubt be revived at the next CITES CoP in 2019, but for now Africa's elephants remain just as they were before: divided between Appendix I and II. Importantly, though, international commercial ivory trade remains prohibited, as it has been since 1990.

All told, CoP17 produced new trade requirements for more than five hundred species of plants and animals, from rosewood and devil rays to tomato frogs and baobabs. Other decisions were made on corruption (it needs to be acknowledged and stopped), domestic ivory trade (CITES recommends that countries that play a role in the illegal trade close their internal markets), synthetic rhino horn (at some future date, CITES should consider potentially regulating it), and more.

It was pangolins, though, who really stole the CoP17 show. At the time of the meeting, Asia's four pangolin species were listed in Appendix II but with a zero-export quota for wild-caught animals traded for commercial purposes—a rule put in place in 2000. As you may recall from Chapter 1, despite these protections, illegal trade in the world's most trafficked mammal is rampant and appears to be increasing. Bodies, parts, and scales of nearly 230,000 Asian pangolins were seized from 2000 to 2013, and law enforcement confiscated a minimum of 120 tons of whole pangolin, parts, and scales passing through sixty-seven different countries and territories from 2010 to 2015. That likely represents only 10 percent or so of the animals actually killed.

Africa's four pangolin species, on the other hand, were listed under Appendix II at the time of the meeting but were still allowed to be commercially exported. Many countries have domestic laws protecting pangolins and prohibiting their trade, however, so most African pangolins in the trade are illegal. This includes nearly 20 tons of African scales recovered in just five seizures in Hong Kong, China, and Malaysia in 2016; two seizures in May 2017 in Malaysia of more than 1,500 pounds of scales from a flight originating from Ghana and the Democratic Republic of Congo; and 7 tons of scales from Nigeria, discovered in a shipment to Hong Kong just three weeks after the Malaysia bust.

The mere possibility of legal trade in African pangolins creates a smokescreen for laundering of both African and Asian species, however, as they're difficult to differentiate. Hoping to close such loopholes and standardize trade controls, several countries submitted proposals to CoP17 to uplist all eight pangolin species to Appendix I. This would also elevate pangolins as a priority for conservation, as some nations treat Appendix II animals as lesser law enforcement priorities. And there would be one additional benefit to putting them on Appendix I, as well: farming would be much more difficult to get away with. Pangolin farms sound odd, but conservationists have come to see them as a potential nail in the coffin, for the tremendous laundering opportunity they would open up.

I was first made aware of this threat when I received a panicked e-mail from Nguyễn Văn Thái, executive director of the nonprofit organization Save Vietnam's Wildlife, a couple of days before the pangolin vote: "At CoP17, a few parties do not want to move pangolins from Appendix II to Appendix I, because they are concerned that if they farm pangolins, they will not be able to export to China." He added that he and others had just sent a sort of cease-and-desist letter, signed by more than fifty conservation groups and zoos, to the Uganda Wildlife Authority, after learning that a Chinese businessman planned to invest $1 million in a five-year experimental pangolin breeding facility there. The investor's proposal included capturing 450 pangolins from the wild and using "highly technological scientific methods" to "undertake extensive breeding."

Among other issues, there's a fundamental problem with such investors' plans: pangolins do not breed in captivity. In fact, they usually don't even survive in captivity; most are dead by the six-month mark. "I tell you, farming pangolins is impossible," said Shibao Wu, a zoologist at South China Normal University in Guangzhou. "The current technology isn't mature enough to maintain them in captivity." This conclusion is drawn from more than a century of failures. Although more than one hundred zoos and wildlife facilities have attempted to breed pangolins, only a handful of animals have ever been born behind bars to captive parents. "Some institutions can maintain pangolins in captivity, but actually breeding them on a commercial scale is preposterous," said Dan Challender, chair of the IUCN's Pangolin Specialist Group. "It's a nonstarter."

Nevertheless, at least ten Chinese companies keep wild-caught pangolins for the purported purpose of breeding and selling them. That such facilities exist is about all that conservationists know. "We really don't know the situation at those farms because they're so secret," said Lishu Li, manager of the wildlife trade program at the Wildlife Conservation Society China's branch. Undoubtedly, though, the farms are simply laundering operations. As Wu said, "Chinese companies that say they farm pangolins actually just smuggle pangolins from the wild under that cover."

Conservationists fear that more and more copycat "farms" will begin popping up, creating a massive industry of legalized pangolin laundering—as is already the case for bears in China and reptiles and birds in Indonesia. Indonesia, in fact, seems to have already caught on to the pangolin farming possibilities, as Thái soon revealed to me. After receiving his e-mail about Uganda, he asked me to meet him on a secluded outdoor balcony at the convention center, where he whispered in near panic that he'd just learned that a Chinese businessman had allegedly bankrolled the Indonesian CITES delegation's attendance to the meeting, in exchange for them making a fuss about the pangolin uplisting. Later that day, a trustworthy conservation organization also confirmed this disturbing twist. In addition, Thái had heard that Japan agreed on China's behalf not to support the pangolin uplisting, in return for votes on some fisheries issues it cared about. He looked as though he were about to have a nervous breakdown.

Hearing all of this increased my skepticism about the entire CITES process. Could one of the most significant measures for saving pangolins really be blocked by the greedy whims of a few individuals? Tomorrow, we'd all find out.

The following morning was sunny, warm, and beautiful, but I hardly noticed as I hustled back to the meeting hall. I was feeling jittery for Thái and for the pangolins. Arriving at the convention center, there was no mistaking that pangolins were first on the agenda: their fans had really pulled out all the stops in terms of PR and lobbying. A person in a six-foot-tall pangolin costume was running around the hallway, taking photos with grinning delegates and giving people the thumbs-up as they entered the meeting room. Others were carrying around pangolin stuffed animals—the plush toys' arms extended as though asking for a hug—that another NGO was handing out. There was a wire pangolin sculpture, pangolin stickers, and pangolin shirts. Suddenly, something banged into my foot—a life-sized robo-pangolin! The remote-controlled pango-bot was zipping around on four wheels, with one clawed paw carrying a small trio of flags that read "I ♥ Pangolins" in Spanish, English, and Chinese. Unlike some of the elephant campaigners, whose approach leaned toward blood and gore, the pangolin folks seemed to rely not on hysteria and guilt but on their poster species' natural quirk and charm.

It was time for the meeting to begin. Karen Gaynor of Ireland was leading this session, and she called first on India to take the floor. "The intelligence gathered in India suggests that tiger hunters are shifting toward pangolin poaching because of the increasing market price," India's representative said. "India has tried captive breeding with no success, so it's not considered a way to help conservation. The present state of trade could drag the species to extinction. India proposes and strongly supports uplisting all pangolin species, including the Indian pangolin."

Nepal was up next: "The crime situation concerning this species is very serious. At the same time, this species is in rural areas, and many local communities do not understand its importance. That's why we support uplisting it."

The United States quickly echoed these sentiments, as did Mali.

"I'm just overwhelmed by the number of speakers requesting the floor," Gaynor said from the stage, with some surprise. Rather than go through the Asian pangolin proposals individually, she decided instead to introduce them all at once—"Otherwise, I'm going to have an unmanageable speakers' list."

The Philippines and Vietnam delivered uplisting proposals for their respective species, followed by more praise and support, including from Peru, Bolivia, Israel, Laos, Brazil, Pakistan, and the European Union.

But then it was Indonesia's turn.

Indonesia gets it, explained representative Wita Wardani, petite and wearing a *jilbab* head scarf. Pangolins have been on Indonesia's protected species list since 1999, she said, and Indonesia has confiscated pangolin products galore. "However," she continued in a tight voice, "in our view, listing the species in Appendix I will not much benefit *Manis javanica*'s survival. We believe in engaging people around this species with activities that will favor survival. These people might turn their eyes from illegal poaching to such activities. We are worried inclusion into Appendix I will discourage such alternatives and increase the appeal of the species in the black market. As long as there has been no significant change in domestic rules in some countries, then domestic demand for pangolins will continue to be high, and therefore uplisting will never be effective." She left it at that, stopping just short of explicitly saying that Indonesia wishes to farm its native Sunda pangolins.

China, seemingly emboldened by Wardani's remarks, took the floor. The Chinese delegate's message was garbled and unclear, however—something about "different consumption of pangolins in different cultures in different areas affect differently the use of trading pangolins."

"I note some concern from China, but did not hear opposition," Gaynor said hesitantly, trying to make sense of China's statement. "But I did hear opposition from Indonesia on proposal 11."

She asked Indonesia, as the sole vocal opponent to the Chinese and Sunda pangolin uplisting proposal, whether it was in the position to block the consensus or would be willing to concede and go along with the group.

"Our position is in line with the international community and other countries," insisted another Indonesian representative, this time a man in a suit. "We agree that *Manis javanica* is in an endangered position. But we don't agree that Appendix I will help. We regretfully say that we are not in favor of uplisting *Manis javanica* to Appendix I."

My chest tightened. Indonesia's awkward and seemingly illogical opposition strongly suggested that its delegates were indeed holding out for the right to farm pangolins. It also meant the parties would have to vote—opening up the Sunda and Chinese pangolin uplisting proposal to potential failure.

The room was tense and silent as countries took the next half minute to weigh in by electronic vote: yes for uplisting the species, no for keeping them on Appendix II. The seconds seemingly stretched on for minutes, until, suddenly, the results were projected onto the screens.

Yes: 114

No: 1 (Indonesia)

Abstain: 5 (Madagascar, Namibia, Oman, and—tellingly—China and Japan)

Wild applause and cheers broke the silence. People were high-fiving, hugging, and taking selfies. It was a home run for pangolins—and a humiliating moment for Indonesia and others who would wish to see the species farmed. All of Asia's pangolins would be given the highest level of protection afforded by CITES. I texted Thái, "Congrats!!!"

Africa's four species were up next, and the news was just as good. Senegal, speaking on behalf of all African range states, urged support for their proposal. Many others concurred. Mali lamented that, although it used to be a range state, its pangolins had already been hunted out of existence, while Gabon's Aurélie Flore Koumba Pambo added that ivory poachers in her country are increasingly caught also carrying pangolin scales. "If we continue to postpone strengthening of pangolin protection, we will find ourselves in a position where all African pangolin species disappear from our ecosystems forever," she said.

Even Swaziland's ever-prickly Reilly spoke up in favor of the uplisting: "The Kingdom of Swaziland is not persuaded about the value of Appendix I ratings to save species. However, pangolins are harmless, defenseless creatures which do not cause human-animal conflict. Therefore, Swaziland has no reservations of supporting proposals to Appendix I—notwithstanding its skepticism that the listing will make any difference for saving pangolins. Thank you, Mr. Chairman—er, Madame Chair."

"Good save, Swaziland," Gaynor said flatly. Having heard nothing but support for the African pangolin proposal, she declared the continent's four species uplisted, without the need for a vote. Once again, applause broke out.

"Now, it's black and white," a beaming Shepherd told me later that day. "Any pangolin parts found in international trade are illegal."

AS THE WEEK WORE ON, THE CONVENTION CENTER BEGAN TO FEEL A BIT LONELY. The hallways and benches cleared out, and NGOs began packing up their booths. Empty seats appeared in the previously crammed meeting halls, even as the Secretariat finalized decisions. The CoP was coming to a close.

On one of those days, perhaps the last, I met an old colleague, Daniel Willcox, for lunch. I hadn't seen him in six years—not since we'd spent a few days

together in a park in Vietnam where he was working, outlining a plan for my research down in U Minh. With his suit, full beard, and impressive job in London,
he was no longer the slightly emaciated, slightly wild forest man I remembered.
We chatted enthusiastically, catching up on each other's lives. But when I asked
him his thoughts on the pangolin victories, his smile faded.

"Decisions are made here at CITES, and the NGOs go away cheering and
saying 'Job well done, pangolins are saved,'" he said, looking at his plate. "But
it's then up to countries to actually follow through, which is something entirely
different. Most of these countries already *had* national laws in place to protect
pangolins. Many people just don't seem to realize how impotent CITES is for
actually getting things done." He paused, then picked his fork back up. "But as
you can see, I'm a very jaded conservationist. Sometimes I wish I could just go
back to doing field work."

Indeed, if the CITES experience taught me anything, it's that legislation
alone is not enough—but it's a start.

Eight

OF PROSTITUTES, POACHERS, AND POLITICIANS

Even as CITES delegates were discussing sustainable trade, species salvation, and methods of tackling wildlife crime, all around them—in Johannesburg and beyond—poaching and trafficking continued. As of 2017, more than fifty elephants are killed per day for their ivory, while nearly three rhinos die for their horns.

But who is behind these killings, and how do they manage to smuggle their bloody trophies halfway around the world, from rural Africa to the bustling streets of Hanoi or Hong Kong? No exhaustive central database exists that gives a holistic, global picture of the illegal wildlife trade. That's not for lack of trying—CITES, Interpol, the World Customs Organization, and the UN Office on Drugs and Crime have all attempted to collect and compile such data. But their efforts tend to be crippled by countries that, for whatever reason, cannot be bothered to submit their numbers. Until such a resource is created, the unknowns surrounding the trade include basic information like how much wildlife crime is taking place each year, the players facilitating it, and the total dollars involved. Meanwhile, what we do know comes from a scattershot compilation of media stories, NGO investigations, governmental reports, and the limited information that countries submit to CITES.

South Africa bears the brunt of the world's rhino poaching, with officials often describing themselves as being "at war" with poachers and wildlife trade syndicates. Given that I was already there for the CITES meeting, I decided it would be a good place to learn more about how poaching and illegal trade work, based on people's experiences on the ground. That search for understanding led me across the country, from one of the world's largest national parks to a notorious South African prison.

THE STORY BEGINS IN 2003, WHEN A PECULIAR TREND BEGAN TO EMERGE IN SOUTH Africa. Enterprising criminals realized that a loophole in the country's trophy hunting laws could be exploited to move rhino horns legally across international borders. Normally, North American and European hunters account for the bulk of South Africa's rhino hunting permits, but that year ten Vietnamese hunters quietly applied as well. Each of the approved hunters returned home with the mounted horns, heads, or even whole body of the animals they had shot. Word spread. Though Vietnam and other Asian countries have no history of big-game sport hunting, South Africa was soon inundated with such applicants, who sometime paid $85,000 or more to shoot a single white rhino.

If you're not South African or versed in the nation's laws or in big-game hunting culture, at this point, you may, justifiably, be very confused. As a New York friend recently texted to me: "I just heard there is legal rhino hunting??? How is that possible, given the numbers???"

CITES in fact does allow trade in legally obtained trophies from white rhinos and, as of 2008, up to five critically endangered black rhinos shot in South Africa and Namibia—provided that all permitting rules are complied with. Domestic laws also come into play. In South Africa, the person whose name appears on a government-issued rhino hunting permit must fire the first shot, for example, and he or she is also the only one allowed to export the resulting trophy.

In the aughts, however, no one was really bothering to ensure these rules were followed, and as a result up sprung a vibrant illicit industry referred to as pseudo-hunting. From 2009 to 2012, Vietnamese individuals represented nearly half of all foreigners who hunted for rhinos in South Africa. No one knows just how many rhino horns were actually sent back to Asia as purported trophies, however, because the South Africa CITES export permits do not match up with the Vietnamese import permits. South Africa has records for more than 650 rhino trophies leaving the country for Vietnam from 2003 to 2010—goods worth some $200 to

$300 million on the black market (compared to about $22 million spent on trophy hunting fees). Vietnam, however, has corresponding paperwork for only 170 trophies, including some export permits that appear to have been illegally recycled for reuse. Likewise, of the 20 trophies exported by Chinese hunters that South Africa has records of from 2007 to 2011, just 3 imports were recorded in China.

In 2009, the Professional Hunters' Association of South Africa, finally catching on to this con game, advised its members not to accept clients from Vietnam or other "Far Eastern" countries. But the suggestion was not enforceable, and many ranch owners remained happy to accommodate Vietnamese and other Asian hunters. As Dawie Groenewald, a safari operator who now faces hundreds of rhino-related criminal charges, stated in 2011, "I make very good money out of the [Vietnamese] hunts. . . . What does it matter who shoots a rhino, an American or a Vietnamese? You go with whoever can pay the most money. That's the way it works. It's not my problem what they do with the horn over there."

By 2012, South African investigators had identified at least five separate Vietnamese-run criminal syndicates exploiting the pseudo-hunting loophole. Of all those gangs, though, Chumlong Lemtongthai, a Thai national, and his band of gun-toting prostitutes is surely the most remarkable.

No one knows more about Chumlong's case than South African journalist-turned–wildlife crime investigator Julian Rademeyer. Julian once dreamed of becoming a game ranger, but he has also always had a morbid obsession with organized crime. He became a freelancer right out of high school, and, considering the times—1993 and 1994—the political beat was a natural draw. He spent nearly two decades reporting on crime, corruption, and conflict in South Africa and more far-flung destinations, including Somalia, Belarus, Equatorial Guinea, and Lebanon.

In 2009, Julian stumbled across a strange story that piqued his interest, involving arson, gun smuggling, and an Afrikaner outlaw turning wildlife tricks in Zimbabwe. The more he dug, the more convoluted a picture emerged. He began tumbling down a rhino-themed rabbit hole that ultimately led to his book about the horn trade, *Killing for Profit*—and to his new job as project leader at TRAFFIC's East and Southern Africa office, headquartered in Pretoria.

Julian has become something of a go-to for journalists, editors, filmmakers, and others seeking pro bono help with this or that rhino-related project. Even five years after his book came out, he continues to receive, on average, one such request per week. Yet, despite the time suck, he still patiently answered my ob-noxiously long list of follow-up questions about his book and even agreed to meet me while I was in town.

We linked up one morning before the CITES circus got going, meeting at an art deco coffee shop in Nelson Mandela Square. Julian's dark, handsome features were set in his typical serious expression. We both ordered coffee with a splash of milk, and as we chatted I had the feeling he was scoping me out a bit, trying to determine whether I was legit. I must have passed the test, though, as he was a generous font of information. "I was drawn to how bizarre and weird the wild-life crime side of things are," he began. "The characters involved are so strange. Like Chumlong: he came up with such a simple scheme, but it was the kind of thing that makes you wonder, who thinks of this stuff? His story showed me the lengths that people will go to get their hands on rhino horn."

Chumlong was the Thai leader of what is likely South Africa's most noto-rious pseudo-hunting ring, but he wasn't a top boss. He answered to Vixay Ke-osavang, a Lao man sometimes referred to as the "Pablo Escobar" or "Mr. Big" of wildlife trafficking. Keosavang enjoyed Lao government protection and, for a brief time, was likely the world's biggest rhino horn trader.

The details of how Chumlong first came to be involved with Keosavang are fuzzy. As one version of the story goes, he was a former fruit seller in Bangkok who happened to befriend a trafficker nicknamed Fatty, who introduced him to Southeast Asian bigwigs, including Keosavang. Or, according to another, more sinister take, he formerly supplied arms to criminals in Vietnam and Cambo-dia but had to move on to wildlife trade because the authorities were on to him. Whatever the circumstances, Chumlong found his way to Keosavang, who made him a deputy and sent him to South Africa.

Chumlong's initial mission focused on lion bones, which are permitted for international commercial trade by CITES. Once in Asia, they can be passed off as tiger bones for making tiger bone wine and "bone paste," considered a health remedy and aphrodisiac by some people in China and Vietnam (remember Mr. M from Chapter 2?). Business was good. In just a couple of years, Chumlong allegedly commissioned the deaths of hundreds of lions, reportedly netting him $350,000 in personal profits. But he was an aspirational guy, and an idea was beginning to grow in his mind—one inspired by the countless advertisements touting hunting operations in his newly adopted home. Rhino horn, he realized, was where the real profits were, and there was an easy way to get it.

Key to that scheme was a man named Johnny Olivier, an Afrikaans fixer and interpreter with a sort of Willy Wonka–meets–Hulk Hogan look. Johnny—to whom Julian introduced me one afternoon—traveled to Thailand on and off throughout his adult life. It was on one of those trips that he met Chumlong, through a Thai Air airport manager they both knew. For Chumlong, Johnny was quite the unicorn: a man who could speak Afrikaans, English, and a bit of Thai and who, crucially, was open to a bit of light wheeling and dealing.

Johnny was very good at his job, which entailed ensuring that all the pieces were in order for the Thais. He helped with logistics—renting the guys a house, filling out their paperwork, taking them shopping—but also with important business-related tasks, including sourcing lion bones and, later, finding a land owner who was happy to buy up rhinos and then sell them to Chumlong for pseudo-hunts. Marnus Steyl, the land owner he recruited, was a lion breeder who normally made his money through "canned hunts," in which an animal, oftentimes a lion, is raised in a cage its entire life and then briefly released into the wild before a paying customer shoots it. Because of his connections in the area, Steyl easily found provincial officials willing to sign off on the rhino hunting permits and to certify that the hunting sessions were all carried out legally.

Johnny claimed that, in the beginning at least, he thought it was all legal. "The permits were there, and the people from the parks board were there," he said. "Everything was in place." But things soon started to get weird. South African law allows for only one rhino hunt per year per individual, so Chumlong needed to find a surplus of foreign applicants to file for hunting permits. Although some syndicates flew people in for this task—frequently poor, ill-educated Vietnamese who had only the vaguest understanding of their role as horn mules—Chumlong and his Thai associates had another idea. In addition to flying in hunters, they began scouring the brothels and strip clubs of Pretoria and Johannesburg, recruiting Southeast Asian hookers and exotic dancers as "hunters." Most if not all of the women, of course, had never even held a gun before, let alone been on a hunt, but no matter. According to Johnny, Steyl and another professional hunter named Harry Claassens would be the ones to take down the rhinos—even though the regulations say that only the person named on the hunting permit is allowed to shoot first. (Steyl, however, later denied any wrongdoing.)

"They started getting too greedy," Johnny said of this new twist. "They started getting Thai prostitutes, and even though the girls never even shot, they used them to get a so-called trophy." Over the next eight months, more than two dozen women eagerly agreed to what no doubt seemed like a sweet deal. They received around $550 just to hand over a copy of their passport and take a brief "holiday" with Chumlong and his guys. Some even thought they were going on safari in another country—hence the passports—when in fact they were headed to a game farm near the Botswana border. There, according to Johnny, after Steyl and Claassens killed the rhino, the ladies would stand next to it (or, in some cases, climb on top of it) for a photo.

Johnny was paid well and enjoyed some of the perks of hanging out with Chumlong. He rode along in his boss's paid-for-in-cash silver Hummer ("Oh, Chai loved that thing," he noted, using Chumlong's nickname), and he often dropped the boys off at a Johannesburg casino complex, Emperor's Palace, where Chumlong would frequently burn through thousands in a single evening. While Chumlong warmed up on the game floor, his associates would empty the ATMs out front with their boss's debit card, stuffing the money from withdrawal after withdrawal into their pants or cramming it into Chumlong's Bad Boy rucksack. When they returned with sufficient cash, he'd give them a generous wad of their own to lavish on restaurants, booze, women, and gambling. "Chumlong Lemtongthai never worried about money," Johnny said. "That man could spend."

Johnny, however, didn't drink and wasn't much of a party guy. Instead, his favorite memories from that time were of Chumlong's birthdays, when he'd withdraw heaps of bills and command Johnny to take him "where there's poor people on the road." Then, in accordance with a Thai belief in the importance of giving, he'd hand out money to everyone he saw. He was equally generous on Johnny's birthday, gifting him a $3,500 watch. As Johnny said, "He wasn't selfish. He gave me plenty."

In the back of Johnny's mind, though, something was beginning to nag at his conscience. He could no longer deny that the hunts he helped to arrange were not entirely aboveboard, and he was becoming concerned about the high number of rhinos being shot.

It didn't help, either, that tensions had begun to build with one of Chumlong's lackeys, a Thai guy nicknamed Peter. Chumlong's Hummer was in Johnny's name, but Peter—who drove like a maniac—was usually the one behind the wheel. Johnny was receiving a constant stream of speeding tickets in the mail, to the point that his license might be suspended. He'd also increasingly had to deal with complaints from his Thai colleagues' landlady, who understandably did not appreciate their habit of partying all night with up to a dozen prostitutes, karaoke blasting from the massive television and speaker system (another Chumlong extravagance). When Johnny tried to bring these grievances up with Peter, however, Peter—made aggressive by drink—came at him. Johnny easily put Peter in his place, but the relationship was permanently soured.

Shortly after the altercation with Peter, Chumlong told Johnny that he planned to order another fifty rhinos to be killed. "This is not trophies or whatever," Johnny recalled thinking. "This is now getting into slaughtering, purely for money. These rhinos are my nation's inheritance. I don't want to see fifty die." Although Johnny didn't have any personal problems with Chumlong, he decided that this was it—he could no longer participate. Chumlong and his men likely would have gotten away with the scheme had Johnny not reached his breaking point. He ratted about Chumlong's dealings to a private investigator, who began digging. The investigator eventually presented 222 pages of evidence to the South African Revenue Services, the police, and the Endangered Wildlife Trust. They took the findings very seriously.

In June 2011, as Chumlong was passing through customs at O. R. Tambo International Airport, officers descended on him. They seized his laptop, cell phone, and camera, on which Johnny had told them Chumlong kept meticulous photos and records of all his shady dealings. Indeed, his computer proved to be a treasure trove: for investigators and conservationists it offered damning evidence of millions of dollars' worth of illegal goods to Southeast Asia and, for the first time, a shockingly detailed window into the inner workings of a major wildlife crime syndicate. Chumlong was arrested the following month, and Steyl, Claassens, and several of the Thai men were soon either picked up or turned themselves in.

When the case went to court in November 2012, the prosecution described Chumlong as the mastermind behind "one of the biggest swindles in environmental crime history." After changing his plea a couple of times on the advice of his lawyer and speaking through an interpreter, Chumlong pleaded guilty to fifty-two counts of contravening South Africa's customs and environmental laws. In true gangster style, he also insisted that he was the sole responsible party, protecting his men: "In short, they did not know that the hunts were a front for our decision to export rhino horn for trade and not for trophies," Chumlong said in his statement. "I humbly apologize to the court and to the people of South Africa for my role in this matter. I appreciate that the emotions of all animal lovers in South Africa are running very high and that I was part of the problem."

The court did not accept his apology. The regional court magistrate interpreted Chumlong's guilty plea as a strategic move, "not as a demonstration of genuine remorse." To Chumlong and others' shock, he was sentenced to forty years in prison. It was a punishment unheard of in its severity, especially in a country with notoriously low rates of conviction for alleged wildlife criminals. Of 317 rhino-related arrests in 2015, for example, just 15 percent resulted in guilty verdicts. (In 2014, Chumlong's sentence was reduced to thirteen years in prison—six months for each of the rhinos he had killed—plus a fine of about $78,000.)

Charges against Chumlong's other cronies, meanwhile, were dropped. After the trial, however, video evidence emerged from a GoPro camera that Steyl had strapped to his head during one of the hunts. The footage clearly showed him shooting a screaming rhino while a Thai "hunter" stood nearby, unarmed. Charges were reinstated against him, but he successfully argued in court for a permanent stay of prosecution by insisting that the rhinos he shot were "surplus" animals. He's now a rich, free man and still involved in lion and game breeding today.

Despite how it all turned out, Johnny doesn't regret his decision to expose Chumlong's scheme. "I must admit, a lot of people read Julian's book and said to me that I did the right thing, and I still believe that I did," he said. "I do miss Chai, though. He was a hell of a nice guy, and actually a very good man. I think he was misled somewhere along the line, and thought he was doing things on board. He's still not entirely innocent, but he's a good man."

Chumlong is not a wildlife trade kingpin, but, as someone who played a significant role in the trade for a time, I wanted to interview him. I knew, too, that my chances of tracking down a boss higher up on the hierarchy were slim to none (Vixay Keosavang didn't accept my Facebook friend request ☹). I was also curious about meeting this character who was so often painted by the media as a two-dimensional rhino-murdering mastermind but who seemed—from Johnny's telling, at least—to be a bit more nuanced than that.

I managed to reach Chumlong's lawyer though LinkedIn. He shared his client's prisoner ID number and told me I could find him at Pretoria Central Correction Center. I was in luck: by train, it was less than an hour from Johannesburg. And unlike prisons in the United States, which typically do all they can to bar journalists from visiting, South Africa didn't seem to have the same limitations.

As Julian told me, "You show up and put your name on the list. If the prisoner agrees to meet you, you're in."

A friendly guy—his voice barely discernible over a ruckus of shouts, clatters and bangs—picked up when I called the prison and told me the visiting hours. "Just drop by," he said casually, as though inviting me to a backyard barbecue.

Chumlong's lawyer had also warned me that I'd need a Thai-English interpreter. I tried for months to find such a person, reaching out to language schools and businesses, putting ads on South Africa's version of Craigslist, and even e-mailing Thai restaurants. No luck. I'm not the only one who has faced this problem: some court cases there have been thrown out because of delays in finding Vietnamese and Thai interpreters, and, in other instances, authorities have discovered that interpreters were in cahoots with the very syndicates being investigated. Julian told me Chumlong does speak some basic English, though, and I figured he might have gotten some practice over the last five years behind bars. I crossed my fingers and tried not to worry.

I caught the train to Pretoria on a sunny Sunday morning. In a last-second moment of inspiration, on my way out the door I had grabbed two Ferrero Rocher chocolates that my Airbnb host had left for me. It wouldn't hurt to try to sweeten Chumlong up with a small offering, I thought.

At the Pretoria Gautrain station, my Uber driver gave me a dubious look when he saw the destination I'd entered. We drove in silence, passing an outdoor food market, and then turning onto the R101 regional road. A quick right brought us to a squat brick building crowned with rolls of barbed wire. Signs outside indicated this was a no cell phone, no smoking, and no firearm zone, and a notice to visitors listed rules in English, Afrikaans, and Zulu: "No hand bags, suitcases, steel trunks, cellular phones, firearms, traditional weapons are allowed in visiting area. Shopping bags and parcels will be searched. No flowers, bouquets or pot plants will be received on behalf of a prisoner."

My driver appeared clearly unhappy now, eager for me to get out of his car. "I do not like this place," he said, tapping his phone to end my ride. "I'm South African, and I've never been in there."

I thanked him, took a deep breath, and stepped out.

The inside of the building resembled one of the bleaker DMVs I've had the displeasure of visiting: dirty tile floors, rows of wooden benches, and glaring fluorescent lighting. Xeroxed black-and-white copies of a few people's passports were taped to the wall, accompanied by handwritten notes such as "Don't let this man in, he smuggles illegal goods" and "Report this woman if seen—she's a drug trafficker." Although more signs inside indicated that cell phones were prohibited, at least half of the people sitting around had their devices out. The crowd was diverse: young and old, male and female, black and white. Many families seemed to have come directly from church or had at least donned their Sunday best: they wore suits, bright floral print dresses, and fun, Kentucky Derby–style hats.

I waited in line for my turn to speak with two women in uniform who sat at a folding table with a stack of papers. Handing them my passport, I told them my address and phone number and gave them Chumlong's name and prisoner number. "What's your relationship with this inmate?" one of the guards asked.

"Um . . . he's a friend."

She nodded and wrote "Friend" in the blank next to "Relationship."

Next, I was required to check in my purse, but I held onto a reporter's notebook, pen, recorder, and the two chocolates. My name was called minutes later, and I passed through a black turnstile that led into a small room. Immediately, one of the women pointed to the recorder. "What is that?" she demanded.

When I answered that I was here to conduct an interview, she stiffened: "Come with me." She took me to a door opposite the one that all the other visitors—those who had been approved—were being ushered through.

Dammit, I thought, *I am an idiot. Now I've blown it. . . .*

The woman led me into a cluttered office full of dusty folders, where she consulted another colleague. "Did you clear this visit with Mr. Qebengu?" she finally asked, turning back to me.

"Uh . . . yes," I lied.

She picked up the phone to call him—just to double check. *Double dammit,* I thought, preparing for the humiliation and perhaps trouble I was about to get into for lying to an officer. I did my best to look nonchalant as she chatted away in Zulu.

"Okay," she said, turning back to me. "He confirms that he spoke with you before. But he'll need to meet with you now to talk more about this."

"Oh, great!" I tried to conceal my surprise. I had no idea what was happening—I hadn't spoken with anyone in advance about interviewing Chumlong—but I'd take it.

I boarded a bus with a handful of other visitors. Although there were ample free seats, a little old lady in in a lace-knit sweater and pink scarf sat next to me and, without a word, nestled her body against mine. A couple of minutes later the bus stopped at the Kgosi Mampura II Management Area, our destination. The building had a distinctly Medieval Times look about it. A huge, thick wooden door stood between two stone drum towers crowned with battlements. I half expected to see Jaime Lannister gazing down at us, sword in hand, with Ned Stark's head impaled on a spike next to him. (It wasn't such a stretch: I later learned that, in the apartheid years, the gallows here—infamously reached by climbing fifty-two steps—hung up to seven people at a time.)

The guards at the entrance were expecting me. A smaller cutout in the fifteen-foot-tall wooden door swung open, leading me to a truly dungeon-like interior. The gloomily dark room had sweeping stone ceilings and bars all around—even overhead—that formed a defensive cage. The only natural light came from cracks in a small, shuttered peephole cut into the door—of the sort that someone might peer out of and demand, "Who goes there!?"

A few guards in brown uniforms were standing around, all overweight and all looking exceptionally bored. One guy chatted with me about New York City but soon sat back down to flip through a *Men's Health* magazine, while two female guards laughed and spoke in Zulu. There were more photocopied passports on the wall—"This woman, Vivian, is suspended from visits for 6 months for being in possession of traditional medicine hidden under her private parts"; "Watch out for this lady, she is a bag snatcher"; "This man is part of a drug ring"—along with other notices. One specified that no wet or dirty clothes are allowed inside, making me wonder what sort of interesting incident provoked this rule.

Other visitors filed in and were efficiently searched and taken through the barred door, but I was instructed to wait for Qebengu. From my seat, which was missing an arm and whose orange upholstery was riddled with holes, I watched them come and go. I waited, and waited. And waited more. *I should have brought a book to go along with my stupid recorder,* I sighed, wishing the guard would put down his *Men's Health* so I could borrow it.

Finally, perhaps forty-five minutes later, Qebengu arrived. He, too, was wearing one of the brown uniforms, but he exuded an unmistakable air of authority. When I rose to shake his hand, I had to look up to meet his stern eyes, towering over me.

"I hear you are a journalist, and you want to visit one of our prisoners," he stated in a booming voice. I confirmed these details and briefly explained the premise of my book and what I hoped to achieve here.

"I see," he nodded. "Well, normally this has to be cleared through our office, and you need to fill out the appropriate paperwork. We can't just have journalists coming in here, writing all about the prison."

I asked him whether I could fill out the paperwork now, but he informed me that the paperwork office was closed today. "You should come back next week."

My heart sank. I was so close, and yet this mission seemed doomed to fail. There was no way I could come back next week: I was leaving in a couple of days.

With nothing to lose, I began to practically plead. "I promise—I give you my word—that I will not write anything political about your prison! I only want to speak with this man about rhinos. Please . . . I've come so far! I can send you the signed paper work by mail or e-mail!"

He scowled down at me, mumbled something about waiting here, and then left.

Another ten minutes or so passed. I expected Qebengu to return any moment now to tell me to get lost. But then one of the guards motioned for me. I underwent a quick body search and the *Men's Health* guy opened the barred door leading into the prison proper. We entered what looked like a management-only hallway, and the door swung open to a spartan office. Inside was a big desk, a couple of chairs and . . . Chumlong Lemtongthai! A wave of gratitude toward Qebengu swept over me.

Chumlong was seated on a bench near the wall, wearing an orange jump-suit with "Corrections" written in circular patterns all over it. Wire-rim glasses framed his dark eyes, and his formerly dyed-black hair, shaved short, was now gray-white, matching the stubble around his chin and upper lip. His expression was one of absolute bewilderment.

Qebengu, standing, gestured for me to take a seat next to Chumlong on the bench. I felt like we were two naughty kids in the principal's office, about to receive a scolding. Unsure of what was expected of me, I turned to Chumlong and introduced myself.

"My English not good, don't understand!" he immediately blurted, shaking his head.

I slowed down, enunciating my words. "I am a writer from New York. I am writing a book about wildlife trade. I would like to hear your story."

Chumlong's expression softened somewhat, and suddenly his understanding of the English language miraculously improved.

"You not come from CITES? You not come from magazine?" he asked, raising his voice. "Me was in article for BBC and other magazine. But writer never talk to me! I look at magazine, magazine say 'Chumlong's a kingpin, he's big mafia'—but he never even talk to me!"

I repeated that I was neither a CITES employee nor writing for a magazine. I was writing a book. "I just want to hear your side of the story," I assured him.

Qebengu was getting bored. "Okay, okay! Are you okay to talk to this lady?" he demanded of Chumlong.

"Yes."

That was all Qebengu needed to hear. He left the room—leaving me alone with Chumlong—but shortly returned with a young guard.

"Is there somewhere we could get lunch?" I asked, imagining a nice prison café where we could sit and chat over a warm cup of tea. Both Chumlong and Qebengu looked at me as though I were mad. I had to settle for Qebengu's desk, with Chumlong seated in front like a job applicant. Qebengu departed, leaving Chumlong and me supervised only by the young guard. Bird tweets filtered in from a window directly behind me, but besides that the room was silent. Chumlong stared at me, his eyes uncertain.

I cleared my throat, turned on the recorder, and opened my notebook. "Can you tell me about your involvement with rhino hunting?"

He seemed only to half-understand the question. That or he wasn't ready to get personal. "Now rhino horn, I think one kilo is 100,000 rand [$7,640]," he began. "This is why people do poaching. People come from overseas to poach rhino."

"Why is it so expensive?" I asked.

As Chumlong spoke, he waved his hands emphatically to emphasize his points. "Government stops farms from selling horn, and rhino poaching goes up and up. Price goes up. If government gives permit for farm to sell, you make price come down. Never poaching again. If government stops selling, then too much poaching in one year. You understand? Rhino poaching goes up. You know how many rhino die? Maybe, 1,000 rhino in year! Maybe up to 2,000 rhino soon! After fifty years, I think, no wild rhino."

"But the question is—" the young guard interjected, clearly intrigued by this conversation, "*Why* is the rhino horn so expensive? *Why* do people want it?"

"They're making the medicine—medicine for thing like Alzheimer's. You know? When you forget, as old man."

"Do you believe that rhino horn is medicine?" I asked.

"No!" Chumlong said indignantly. "I think it's not true! If horn is medicine, we'd never be old. In China, in Vietnam, him think rhino horn is good for business. People come for shooting rhino every year, same name, come to kill one. Next year, same name, come to kill another one. Big one, big one! It's legal. He gets a permit and everything. He takes back to Vietnam, to China. Some people keep horn, some people make medicine from horn, some people show off horn."

"What about you?" I asked.

"Me, I get tourists to shoot. Me working three countries: South Africa, Vietnam, Laos. I get commission. I'm never poaching. I get tourists to shoot rhino, I go legal way. Me get form, me get everything, make legal—not illegal. Not fair for me. White rhino, it CITES Appendix II. Black rhino, it CITES Appendix I. Black and white rhino—not the same thing. I only go white rhino—legal, CITES II. I get permit! You understand? What you think—legal or illegal?"

I decided to avoid issuing any judgment and instead asked him whether he was still in touch with his former colleagues, the ones who helped him with the hunts.

"Me? Never."

"What about Johnny Olivier?"

"Ahhhhh—you know Johnny Olivier! Why you know?"

"I read about him. I don't know him personally."

"Johnny Olivier, he makes statement. He is working for me and for farm. Me help him out. I'm never fighting him. He need money, I give him money. I give him commission for contact with farm. But then Johnny gets angry and makes a statement. He runs away. But why he fear me? Why he make it like that? If he has problem, talk to me. If he say, 'I need money for this,' me work with him. But he makes statement, it makes big news, I'm suddenly 'Chumlong, the kingpin,' I control the farm, and I shoot everything. I'm on TV every day. But for what? Not wild rhino poaching, and never black rhino shooting!"

"Are you angry at Johnny?"

"Me, I'm not angry. Him make big problem for me. He know everything. His job make permit. Me not know English. Farm gives permit. I say, 'It okay? I can shoot?' Police station: check, say okay. Animal doctor from government: check, it okay. CITES: check. Airport office: check. Me pay taxes and pay permit. All good, all check. No problem. But then police arrest me for permit! They say, illegal permit! Illegal permit? It business for government! Why they say legal, if illegal? They say, 'Chumlong guilty.' They charge me, they say, 'You make paper fraud.'"

Chumlong was practically shaking now, his eyes wide, his voice high.

"My lawyer say, 'You pay big fine, you get to go home Thailand.' I say 'Okay, I pay. I sign guilty paper. I need to go home.' Next day I come back to court: forty year in jail! *What!?* He said lie to me, my lawyer! Rhino farmer go home, me go to jail forty years! Me phone to farm—no answer. He changes number! All numbers changed! Six people, all go home. Only me go to jail. My heart goes down."

The way he told it, it did indeed sound like Chumlong had been had—a scapegoat for other, savvier criminals who took advantage of his ignorance. But was this actually the case? I'd heard that, in fact, he had been paid handsomely by Vixay to keep his mouth shut and that a big payday was awaiting him when he finally returned to Thailand. I decided to broach this subject.

"Do you still talk to Vixay Keosavang?"

"Vixay? He run away! He never talk to me again!"

"*Really?*" This was not the answer I expected.

"Serious!"

"He just said 'bye?'"

"Bye-bye, me! Me guilty, me go to jail! Vixay, never talk. Only me, 'kingpin.' But me no understand—need to go home!"

"What about the Bach brothers?" I asked, referring to a couple of notorious Vietnamese traders allegedly at the heart of some of the illegal wildlife trade in Laos and tangled up in business with Vixay.

"Ah, they run away, too."

"They don't talk to you, either?"

"Never talk again."

"Let me get this straight: you got no reward, no help, no bonus?"

"They never talk to me. None. You know what? Me go to jail. Me in South Africa jail for five year. I never see my daughter. I never see my family. Five year. No family."

"Are you angry?"

He shook his head. "No. I Buddhist."

Clearly, though, he was distressed about all of this.

"Fifty-two cases, only for me," he continued, almost talking to himself at this point. "Not my paper, though. Not my gun. Lawyer, he make me sign guilty. What you think? Me and you, I talk to you with open heart. If I go out, I send to you all the information, and permit from the government. Maybe my daughter send you my case. My daughter in Thailand, twenty-six years old."

Assuming he was telling the truth—which my gut said was the case— Chumlong seemed to have been nothing more than Vixay's and the other higher-ups' puppet. Despite his faithfulness, his boss simply cast him aside the moment things went awry.

"Do you regret your actions?" I asked him.

"Huh?"

"Do you wish you never came to South Africa? Do you wish you never shot rhino?"

"If I free, I never come back. My money gone, my Hummer gone. My furniture, my home—everyone take. Me lose my money—and me lose my life in jail. Now empty, nothing."

He looked down at the table, appearing close to tears.

In spite of myself, I was definitely feeling sorry for him now. "Is there anything else you'd like to tell me?" I quietly asked.

"Me never bad boy, never bad man. Me working in business."

"When you get out of jail, what do you look forward to most?"

"Ah. . . . I go to Thailand again. I see my kids, two daughter, one boy. All in Thailand. My family don't know nothing."

I asked if he'd spoken to them recently.

"Been long time. I never get to talk. My name become dark. My feeling is no good. Farm never talk to me. Company, friend, family—never talk to me."

"Do you ever get visitors?"

"My family give money to someone to come visit to me. But only visit once. My heart become dark. Thank you come visit to me. Long time, no people visit. Four year, maybe."

There was a pause. I sensed that Chumlong had said all he wanted to say, and I was out of questions.

"I think we're finished here, thank you," I told the guard.

I turned back to Chumlong and handed him the chocolates, suddenly feeling a bit foolish for bringing such a trivial little gift along. But he seemed to appreciate it. He nodded and stood, and I noticed that he was markedly shorter than me, not the least because of his defeated posture.

The three of us headed out together, and another guard took over Chumlong's custody.

"Sabaidee, khob khun kha," I said. *Be well, thank you.*

"Sabaidee," he replied, and shuffled off to the right with the guard, not looking back. I watched him go and then turned to the left—to freedom.

I didn't see Qebengu to thank him, but, on my way out, the *Men's Health* guard did look up from his magazine. "Are you fine now?" he asked. "Remember me in New York. When I come to there, you must invite me out, okay? Thank you very much."

I told him, absolutely, I would.

SOUTH AFRICA TIGHTENED ITS SPORT HUNTING RULES THE YEAR AFTER CHUMLONG was arrested. Applicants now had to prove they were legitimate sport hunters, by showing, for example, previous experience hunting in Africa or membership to a bona fide hunting association. The government also decided to suspend permits for Vietnamese citizens until Vietnamese authorities confirmed that all rhino horn trophies exported there since 2010 were still in the possession of their original owners and regulations on their end were tightened.

Vietnam's compliance with this request, however, was half-assed at best. After discovering that nearly 90 percent of trophies had not been declared upon entry into the country, officials there whined that their CITES-implementing laws did not pertain to products that had already passed through customs, and therefore they had no legal authority to investigate. Never mind that other laws related to, for example, tax avoidance, conspiracy, or money laundering could have been applied as legitimate reasons to pursue the cases. Of the forty trophies the Vietnamese did wind up investigating, only seven were still with the original owners. The rest were "lost," "given away," or had already been processed into bowls and cups.

But, even without Vietnam's support, South Africa's actions quickly made an impact on the ground (although belatedly, considering that it had taken them nearly a decade after the first pseudo-hunts to respond). After the new rules came into place in 2012, just 66 people—8 of them Vietnamese nationals—applied to hunt white rhinos, compared to 226 in 2011. But, like a mutating pathogen, rather than go away, the problem began to manifest in different forms. "There's a constant struggle between government bureaucracies that move really slowly and criminal networks that are leaps and bounds ahead of them," Julian said. "Even before South Africa started cracking down on the Vietnamese, they'd already taken one stop forward. In a sick way, you have to admire them for this constant inventiveness."

Pseudo-hunts were soon partly replaced by "proxy hunts," in which Asian criminals hired real hunters—many from the Czech Republic, where more than 80,000 Vietnamese expats live—to conduct an all-expenses-paid legal hunt in South Africa. All they had to do was bring the trophy back with them to give to their Vietnamese benefactor. From 2008 to 2014, at least sixty Czech citizens applied for rhino hunting permits, and a subsequent investigation revealed that 73 percent of them were "white horses," as the Czechs say—those involved in the illegal trade. Once investigators began digging, they also found links between some of the Vietnamese leading the scheme and major syndicates that dealt in methamphetamine and counterfeit goods.

South Africa has refused Czech rhino hunting applications since 2014, causing the ever-flexible trafficking to shift for a time to Slovakian and Polish hunters. There has also been an increase of applications from the United States and China, and it seems likely that at least some are illegitimate. Indeed, in 2015 an ivory trafficking boss in Beijing told undercover Elephant Action League investigators that he had partners in South Africa and Namibia who helped his people undertake pseudo-hunts for importing ivory and rhino horns into Hong Kong and China.

Such tricks seem to have mostly fallen out of vogue, though. In the overall story of the illegal wildlife trade, pseudo- and proxy hunting have proven a "temporary sideshow," as Ronald Orenstein wrote in *Ivory, Horn and Blood*. Straight-up poaching and trafficking now dominate the plot. Yet many of the players are still the same. Again and again, Chumlong and Keosavang's associates from the mid-aughts have turned up in wildlife cases, including, most recently, Boonchai Bach, a notorious alleged wildlife trade "kingpin" who was arrested by Thai police in 2018. "There's a lot of suspects from Chumlong's crowd and time period who are probably still involved today," Julian said.

The impacts of their continued involvement are acutely felt in South Africa's Kruger National Park, often referred to as the epicenter of the rhino poaching crisis. South Africa is home to nearly three-quarters of the world's 30,000 remaining rhinos and over 80 percent of Africa's rhinos. Around 9,000 of them—the largest single population on the planet—live in Kruger. It's not an overstatement to say that those animals are under siege: Kruger's population bore approximately 60 percent of all African rhino poaching incidents from 2009 to 2016.

During a weekend break from the CITES conference, I joined a few dozen tourists on a small plane bound for Skukuza, Kruger's administrative headquarters and main camp. From above, Kruger was a sweeping marbled tract of orange sand and scruffy, grey-green bush—the parched palette of an extended drought.

The Skukuza airport seemed to have changed little since Richard Leakey visited in the early 1990s and observed that it is "rather like a Hollywood movie set." Sharply angled modern architecture melded with traditional touches like thatched roofs and carvings of wildlife. As was also the case then, many of the tourists who arrived on my flight were met by "young, bronzed-faced men in khaki shorts and shirts unbuttoned to show their chest hair," as Leakey wrote. Luggage collected, clients and guides piled into topless Land Rovers "and roared off into the bush."

I had made no such arrangements. Instead, my plans included a meeting with Ken Maggs, the park's head ranger, who has been working in Kruger for thirty years. He'd told me by e-mail that his office was situated directly next to the airport, and, sure enough, I spotted what appeared to be an official building just beyond the parking lot. I wheeled my suitcase down the baking road, passing busloads of tourists and a security guard who didn't so much as glance at me. After finally getting the intercom to work (my cellphone had conveniently run out of minutes on the tarmac), the electronic gate swung open. One of Maggs's colleagues took me to his boss's office, behind a door marked "Head Ranger." The walls were decorated with large African masks and art depicting elephants, rhinos, and giraffe. Photos of Maggs's family sat on a big blond wood desk alongside neat stacks of paper.

Maggs was tall and slim, with gray-white hair cropped short. Rather than a ranger uniform, he wore a striped shirt with the national parks logo on it, long khaki pants, and sturdy boots. I'd expected his demeanor to be that of a hardened, hypermasculine soldier type, but he struck me as thoughtful and deliberate. I quickly came to appreciate that he neither tried to sugar-coat the poaching situation nor exaggerate the successes.

In the six months prior to my visit, he told me, Kruger had seen an increase in poaching incursions of about 28 percent yet a simultaneous decrease in rhino losses of about 18 percent—signs that defensive tactics were likely having a positive effect (the drought, however, was a potential confounding variable). The good news wasn't universal, however. Poaching in KwaZulu-Natal, the province to the south, and in some of the private reserves bordering Kruger had shot up— likely an indication that poachers were shifting their targets in response to the heightened security in the park. Even with the drop in deaths in Kruger, Maggs continued, the 469 poached rhinos that the park staff had so far detected that year were still too many. "You cannot sustain levels of poaching like that, where you're losing more than one rhino per day," he said. "We're sitting on that brink where numbers of animals coming in is almost equal to mortalities, both natural and unnatural."

Established in 1898 as a safe haven for elephants, Kruger is roughly the size of Wales or Israel. That majestic sprawl is a boon for nature, but it also means that it's virtually impossible to keep uninvited humans out. "A lot of people don't understand Kruger," Maggs said. "It's a beast. It's not your friend."

These days, most rhinos—and thus poachers and rangers—cluster in a southern block dubbed the Intensive Protection Zone. Maggs and his colleagues have developed an almost fortresslike approach to defense there, pulling out all the stops in terms of technology, as well as detection and reaction capabilities. "Persistent and unpredictable"—that's how they describe Kruger's anti-poaching tactics. Yet, unless the same amount of effort is pumped into taking out all the other levels of wildlife trade—the traffickers, the bosses and their syndicates, the consumers—then Maggs and others working on the ground might as well be pissing into the wind.

As in other places in Africa, he explained, wildlife crime in South Africa is loosely organized into a pyramid-shaped hierarchy. Poachers form the base, followed by local, national and international couriers, buyers and exporters. At the very top are the final consumers. Kruger rangers typically deal only with the poachers, usually poor men from local communities. In an analysis of fifty-five intruders caught there, authorities found that 96 percent were black, all were male, and nearly half were from Mozambique, one of the poorest countries in the world. Mozambique lost the last of its rhinos in 2013, but it shares a 220-mile border with Kruger.

Given their lowly position in the wildlife criminal pecking order, poachers get paid the least. A Maasai man caught with tusks in Tanzania in 2016, for example, told investigators he received $250 for his goods, or about $3 a pound—an abysmal payout compared to their $500 per pound wholesale value in China. Rhino horn is worth much more, earning poachers operating in South Africa up to $20,000 for a full horn (on the Asian black market, horns sell for around $10,900 per pound, and they typically weigh three to nine pounds). Whether it's $250 or $20,000, though, for many of the individuals carrying out the killing, the earnings are significant. When one apprehended poacher was asked by a Kruger official why he came into the park to kill rhino, for example, he replied that his family didn't have food to eat. When told to clarify exactly what he meant by that, he replied, "We're eating grass."

This stark anecdote brought to mind a conversation I'd had with my seatmate—a bespectacled dad type who runs a technology security company—on the flight from London to Johannesburg. "What people in the West don't understand is the desperation of Africa," he told me. "People in Africa are earning in a year what someone overseas earns in a day. What are they going to do? Of course they're going to kill wildlife to feed their families."

Indeed, in Mozambique, the average annual income per person is just $250. But if a Mozambican gets hired to carry water for the rhino poaching team on the hunt—the least lucrative job of the up to five-person group—he may still earn up to $2,000. Through the lens of such profits, rhinos are rendered nothing more than walking fortunes. Any trace of respect or humane treatment is forgotten, as the killings themselves reveal. Poachers have sliced open pregnant rhinos to extract their unborn fetuses and hack off their tiny horn stumps, and in other instances, rather than waste bullets, the killers have used machetes to sever baby rhinos' spines. Whether juvenile or adult, they often chop off rhinos' faces while they are still alive.

Guns are most wildlife killers' weapon of choice, but some have thought up more inventive means of delivering death. In Zimbabwe, elephant poachers have left out buckets of cyanide-laced salt and poisoned water holes with cyanide or Temik. The latter toxin is known locally as "two-step" because—like the *Kill Bill* five-point palm exploding heart technique, but deadlier—after swallowing it, an animal or person takes two steps and dies. Both cyanide and Temik kill not only hundreds of their target species but also any other animal that comes along to drink, plus the dozens of vultures that feed on those tainted carcasses. Criminals in other countries have also taken inspiration from these base strategies: in Malawi, they've rolled out poisoned pumpkins; in Kenya, poisoned arrows; in Zimbabwe, poisoned cabbages.

Although many poachers are desperately poor, money is not the only motivating factor. Long-standing inequalities also come into play. "National parks were originally designed to keep black people out, because they were seen as a threat—as poachers," Julian said. "Conservation was a tool used very effectively by the apartheid state, from the 1960s to the 1980s. With the stroke of a pen, the bulk of the population was excluded from protected areas." Skukuza, in fact, comes from the Zulu word *khukhuza*—"to scrape clean"—and was the nickname of Kruger's first warden, who was infamous for clearing the area of black settlements. Decades ago, poaching had already come to be a form of rebellion against colonial rule, wrote Vanda Felbab-Brown in *The Extinction Market*.

Resentment lingers today, and such feelings can fuel and justify poachers' actions. A few wildlife criminals even position themselves as economic liberation fighters—the equivalent of modern-day, African Robin Hoods. As one local poaching boss in Mozambique told Annette Hübschle-Finch, a postdoctoral researcher at the University of Cape Town's Center for Criminology, "We are using rhino horn to free ourselves." He and others have utilized proceeds from successful rhino hunts to throw village-wide parties and to construct wells, shops, pubs, and motels. "Communities are the most important ingredient to conservation, but they've been systematically excluded during previous regimes," Hübschle-Finch said. "Now there's half-hearted attempts, at best, to involve them. It's very, very important, though, that we start talking to and including rural people."

Maggs is aware of this problem, but with millions of residents in Kruger's vicinity, solutions do not come easily. Those communities "need to become our biggest allies," he said. "But I don't believe we've done enough in terms of community ownership. We need to do a lot more." In the meantime, though, Hübschle-Finch found that the situation seems to be getting worse rather than better: the increasing militarization of anti-poaching measures is further alienating local people and impacting their well-being. "In interviews I've done, there certainly remains a sense that the life of a rhino is valued higher than a black rural life," she said.

There's justification for those feelings, as poachers are frequently killed. Jonas Mongwe, a well-connected Mozambican businessman from a town near Kruger, explained the realities to Julian: "Once you kill a rhino, you get rich quick. But, at the same time, you die early. . . . The bosses come from Maputo and they recruit here in the villages, especially among the youth. They say: 'We have the money, we have the weapons.' And the youth have a hunger to get rich. The line is endless. They won't stop. . . . People are dying, but daily, people are going in."

On Julian's visits to Mozambican villages, he discovered a "massive amount of anger" directed at the park. The first words from a father whose son was killed there, for example, were, "What made this animal's life more valuable than my son's?" In addition to the pain of losing loved ones, there is also the monetary loss. "Entire local economies have sprung up on the back of poaching, and the people bringing money into those communities are the people being killed," Julian said. "The rangers will say, 'His son had a choice, he didn't have to come into Kruger.' But it's that kind of disconnect that turns community members into poachers."

South African authorities avoid publicizing the number of poachers shot down by rangers and police. As Maggs said, "It's a figure we don't like to broadcast, because none of us really want or enjoy it." He added, though, that Kruger saw forty-odd poachers killed in 2015 and about twenty in 2016, as of my September visit. What information has leaked out on a national level indicates that, as of 2016, at least two hundred poachers have been killed across South Africa since 2011. In 2015, however, Mozambique's former president, Joaquim Chissano, claimed that at least five hundred poachers—most of them his citizens—have been killed in Kruger Park alone since 2010. "Each of these Mozambicans dead means more poverty for his family, because they can no longer count of him to fight for better living conditions," Chissano told Reuters. Even then, South African authorities did not release their figures. "Allegedly, we're a democratic country, and allegedly, all deaths here are a matter of public record," Julian said. "The silence is a problem."

Whatever the number lost, there is a practically limitless supply of desperate young men ready to be exploited by syndicates to do their dirty work. Yet some armchair critics continue to advocate shooting these men as a solution to the poaching problem. When Julian recently tweeted about three suspected poachers gunned down in South Africa, for example, he received disturbing responses along the lines of, "That's fantastic, let's kill more of the fuckers!" Most of those cheering on the deaths of poor black Africans, Julian pointed out, are well-to-do white citizens. Such cluelessly privileged individuals, he said, "just don't get it."

Moral issues and human rights aside, those who actually work in anti-poaching know that firing at intruders on sight is not a solution. "The threat of death is not necessarily a deterrent," Maggs confirmed. "Otherwise, we would have seen a marked reduction in poaching." Case studies also attest to this. In the 1980s and 1990s, Zimbabwe unleashed a shoot-to-kill policy that "did absolutely nothing for their wildlife," Julian said. Botswana, on the other hand, claims that its current shoot-to-kill policy works, but the country's elephants still face tremendous pressure, and the practice has caused tensions with neighboring Namibia, Zimbabwe, and Zambia, whose citizens—not all of whom were even poachers—have been killed by Botswana's rangers and police. In other places, including Tanzania, a now-discontinued shoot-to-kill policy led to widespread allegations of extrajudicial killings (plus rapes, torture, and extortion) of innocent people. "Policies of indiscriminate force beyond what is strictly necessary for self-protection easily turn law-enforcement units into gangs of brutal thugs," Felbab-Brown wrote. Not only is shoot-to-kill "morally reprehensible," she continued, but it is also ineffective.

In Kruger, as in many African parks, rangers are armed but they are allowed to fire only in self-defense. Poaching has been reduced there somewhat, but the number of incursions is still staggering. At least 7,500 intruders are estimated to have entered the park in 2015—43 percent more than the year before. Maggs estimates that, at any given time, five to fifteen such groups—composed of an average of three men—are present within the park.

To get their prize, rhino poachers tend to sneak in under cover of darkness, especially during the full moon—the "poacher's moon," as it's often called. Once in the park, they usually wait until first light to make the kill. After the deed is done, they may benefit from well-organized pickups, or they may bury the horn for later retrieval; others simply run home as quickly as they can. Lately, some bold individuals have also taken to posing as tourists, driving into the park with guns hidden in the engine block. They have shot rhinos in the middle of the afternoon, just a hundred meters from a main road.

These gentle giants, unfortunately, don't put up much of a protest. "A rhino is, really, a stupid animal," Maggs said. "They don't have good eyesight, and almost anyone could sneak up to one, day or night, and shoot it. Cutting off the horn takes just ten minutes, and you can easily conceal it."

As Maggs was explaining this, just then, a massive frame appeared in the doorway of his office. It was Colonel Otch Otto, Kruger's former mission area operations manager of ranger services. Otto had a gray pilot-style mustache, a button nose, and eyes the color of his olive-green khakis. My meeting with Maggs had run long, but Otto—ever the tracking expert—had still managed to find me.

As Otto joined us at the table, Maggs resumed telling me that the four-hundred-odd Kruger rangers tasked with defending against the poaching threat works out to be about one man per twenty square miles. Hardly sufficient, but that is the reality on the ground. "Twenty-four/seven, it continues," he said. "We have to work at it every single day, day and night."

"These are rangers, not soldiers," Otto interjected in a charmingly thick Afrikaans accent. "But they have become formidable—the best in the world. A soldier can't do this work; they're not trained to do it, and they're not successful at it. You need ten years of tracking experience. There are some guys here with thirty years of tracking experience! If you bring a soldier in, they can't track an elephant through a mud puddle. To be a ranger, you must be agile; you must be able to work in extreme temperatures; you cannot be scared of animals and you must understand how to deal with them; you need to be able to go long distances with little water and to know every noise you hear. You must be branded to the bush, and you must love it! This is something that is absolutely specialist."

Add poachers to that mix, though, and the demands of the job begin to take a serious toll. Posttraumatic stress disorder is a growing issue among rangers, some of whom have been involved in twenty or more firefights. As these issues became more serious, Kruger officials reached out to Susanna "Rethea" Myburg-Fincham, a clinical psychologist who specializes in trauma, for help. "At first, it was very difficult because of the stigma of getting counseling, but we've broken through that," Maggs said. Now, rangers are obligated to seek counseling following any life-threatening incident.

Myburg-Fincham, the first therapist ever known to study and treat the mental health issues of rangers, has seen around 120 rangers and their families since 2011, both at Kruger and at Sabi Sand Game Reserve, a collection of privately owned properties bordering the park. Some of what she found has been highly worrying. "As the poaching has escalated, these rangers are now having to face situations which they've never had to face before," she told me shortly after my visit. "They were trained to conserve, and previously the anti-poaching activities they took part in basically comprised removing snares, while firearm use was limited to controlling trouble animals. Now, they're expected to aim their firearms at other human beings. They're having to deal with very structured, very organized, and very well-equipped poaching cartels. It's a case of guerrilla warfare."

Rangers may also find that their job involves targeting their own neighbors, and they often feel isolated and ostracized in their communities. As Otto said, "Let me put it this way: you do not want to be a ranger at a party here at one of the nightclubs." Arresting neighbors isn't even to worst of it, though. Some rangers have had to apprehend family members, and one was even forced to "neutralize" a former colleague–turned-poacher, who fired on him in the field.

It was getting late in the afternoon, and the conversation in Maggs's office was winding down. I was staying at the Skukuza Rest Camp that evening, but in the craziness of the CITES meeting, I hadn't really thought about how I'd get there. When Maggs asked, I told him I figured I'd just walk. It was only a few miles. He and Otto stared at me and then exchanged a look, as though not comprehending what I just said.

At last, Otto—visibly trying to conceal his amusement at the absurdity of my plan—broke the silence: "Have you got a rifle?" he demanded.

My mouth dropped open slightly, and I felt my cheeks go red. Clearly, I hadn't considered the possibility of getting eaten by a lion.

"You cannot walk," Maggs emphasized, shaking his head. "It would be impossible. No one here walks."

Maggs, pointing out that he is a gentleman, offered to drive me. I felt like a dummy but eagerly accepted. Otto, meanwhile, said he'd meet me the following morning to finish up our interview and afterward would ferry me back to the airport. I was relieved to have found such accommodating babysitters.

The drive to camp, admittedly, was pretty far. There was also no shortage of four-legged residents on the road. Every time Maggs spotted an animal—a buffalo, an elephant—he'd slow or even stop the car to watch it intently for a few moments. So long as he wasn't in a hurry, he told me, he always did this—foreign guest in tow or not.

As we drove, I asked him whether his work frequently stressed him.

"Do I look stressed?" he calmly replied.

I had to admit, he did not.

"One of the things in my favor is that I love the work I do," he explained. "It makes a big difference—really loving your work—because if you're dedicated and committed, you can probably take a lot more punches. The days are long, yes, but they're rewarding. You get a good feeling when you win a battle, even if you understand you're not yet winning the war. Will we eventually win that war? Absolutely. Because we just have so much to lose if we don't. And the first people I'd have to look in the eye and tell that to are my children."

We arrived minutes later at the Skukuza Rest Camp, which turned out to be quite elaborate—the size of a small village. Maggs accompanied me to the check-in desk (I think he was worried, considering my apparent helplessness) and then drove me to my room another half mile down the winding camp roads, all the while smiling politely.

My accommodation was a circular, thatch-roof bungalow modeled on originals built after the park was opened to tourists in 1927. It was one of nearly 180. With the additional space reserved for tents and RVs, the camp could accommodate up to one thousand visitors. They share the space with various animals; lions, I was told, are often spotted on the road leading to Skukuza, while fruit bats hang from the open rafters of some of the facilities, which include a café, library, and gift shop. The latter was a sprawling affair, selling everything from beef jerky, eggs, and ice cream to safari hats, zebra-skin rugs, and dining sets.

Down a steep embankment, the Sabi River wound around the camp, marking its boundary with the bush. The river's shallow waters provide a constant source of entertainment: elephants saunter down for a drink, crocodiles drift by like logs, and birds zip overhead. It was a lovely spot to spend an evening with a beer and a book, though I found myself feeling a bit lonely as the sun set. All around me, families and groups of friends were out on their porches, playing music, drinking, and grilling. As I wistfully watched them, I realized that most didn't appear to be wildlife types. There were small kids galore, older folks with canes, ladies in shoes more appropriate for the runway than the range, and men who looked like they'd struggle to walk half a mile on flat ground. Yet everyone appeared to be having a fabulous time, and it heartened me to think that some may leave Kruger with a greater appreciation for nature.

Otto met me the next morning at the Cattle Baron, Skukuza's token sit-down restaurant. He arrived with a posse of four beefy guys, all speaking Afrikaans and all wearing shorts. They were also all very big, but Otto was still the biggest. Otto declared that everyone should partake in the less-than-inspirational breakfast buffet. "Yes, give him a plate—that fat guy," he instructed a waiter, pointing at one of his friends.

Otto loaded up on baked beans, sausage, grits, eggs, and savory beef mash, all of which he doused in a dark sauce, and joined me at a table outside. He sent his friends to a spot across the porch, for which I was thankful. It was early, but they had all ordered a round of beers, and their laughter had reached bellowing proportions even before the first sip. Not that I didn't like a good party, but it was 10 a.m., and I needed to extract all the knowledge I could from Otto.

"I'm a little bit concerned about what you're going to ask me, but because I don't have an affiliation here anymore, I will tell you the truth," he began provocatively, biting into a sausage. "Is the truth what you want? That is very dangerous."

Otto spent fifteen years in South Africa's Special Forces before pivoting into a career with the United Nations as a security chief in the Middle East. There, he collaborated with the US Army Corps of Engineers on a project clearing the main battle axis from Basra to Baghdad—one of fourteen wars he's been involved in. Before Iraq, there was Libya, Afghanistan, Syria, Mozambique, Angola, and, of course, South Africa.

For the past twenty-five years, he continued, he's been in and out of conservation, including three years spent at Kruger (he was hired as part of a $23.7 million grant that the US-based Howard G. Buffett Foundation made to South African national parks for a three-year initiative to combat rhino poaching). "They needed military and conservation skills, and I have both," Otto said. "I'm conversant with ranger work, environmental asset protection, and with counterinsurgency bush warfare—and I'm not a normal military asshole. I'm highly intelligent."

Even before he transferred to the conservation sector, he continued, he was a regular at Kruger, where he was stationed while tensions were high in Mozambique. In 1989, Johan Kloppers, chief of nature conservation at the time, gave him a prescient warning: "Otch, you have to prepare for the rhino war."

Kloppers and others, Otto said, saw the disaster coming two decades before it happened. Now that it has arrived, for better or for worse, it has generated an entire new industry, which he believes is overpopulated with underqualified individuals. "The rhino war is a popular armchair war," he said. "Everyone knows too much and claims to have the answer. There are specific principles that can win us this war, but they are not applied because so many people have egocentric opinions. So many are jockeying for the glory—for the campaign medal." His own motivation, he claimed, is different: "I like nature, I like the environment," he said. "And the animals in this park are much nicer than many people I know."

When Otto came on board in mid-2013, he employed an old-school tactic called the castle doctrine, which he summarizes as "don't wait for the burglar to come into the house." He adopted a proactive approach, often deploying men on very little information rather than waiting for further intelligence to confirm a hunch. He used some of the Buffett funds to purchase two helicopters on top of two Kruger already had and engaged them in up to fourteen air combat support missions daily. On an almost daily basis, the rangers apprehended two to three suspects, finished fifteen infiltration reports, and collected DNA and ballistics from at least one rhino carcass. Meanwhile, intelligence agencies combed through a few of the hundreds of mobile phones confiscated from suspects and looked into the fishy license plate numbers.

The job was demanding, to say the least—Otto spent just two days at home in 2015—but it was under his watch that Kruger's poaching rates began to decline. One of the keys, he said, was "not to be snowed under by intelligence. You take the top ten leads and follow those, and save the others for when you have time."

We were interrupted momentarily by the arrival of a chocolate milkshake Otto had ordered. Served in a 1960s-style glass and decked out with syrup and whipped cream, the cartoonish dessert looked all the more comical grasped between Otto's brawny, bear-paw-like hands. He took a delighted sip.

"I've heard from some people that the majority of poaching that goes on in Kruger is an inside job," I said. "Do you think that's true?"

He frowned. "You want a beer?" He waved the server back over. "Get this girl a beer. She wants the big one, not the small one."

Now that we were on the same page (Otto already had a beer and a gin and tonic to go with his milkshake), he cleared his throat and pressed on. "Yes, corruption has become huge. A hell of a lot of poaching here must have an agent. Corruption is the biggest challenge we have now, because we can't control it from the field. If guys run from us, we can get fitter, or we can get faster vehicles or dogs. If they send more people at night, we can put more night vision equipment out. That's straightforward combat. But if I brief a ranger to go look for poachers, and then he calls the poachers and says, 'I'm here, go somewhere else,' I can't control that."

That's not to say Kruger isn't trying to stop corruption. Every park employee, from junior rangers to the CEO, is subject to extensive deception testing, including polygraphs. Despite these measures, though, a handful of rangers and other staff continue to be implicated in poaching each year—including seven so far in 2016, when I visited. One of them, Rodney Landela, was an award-winning senior ranger—a man Maggs thought he knew well and had not suspected in the least. Landela and a Kruger veterinary technician were arrested after bloody shoes were found in their vehicle just after a rhino poaching incident (as of the beginning of 2018, Landela was free on bail and the trial was still under way). But while Maggs suffered from the sting of betrayal, he was not necessarily surprised. Rhino horn syndicates regularly target individuals working in the wildlife industry, and, for some, the cash criminals offer is too tempting to turn down.

"You can't help but question yourself: 'Where did it go wrong? Couldn't I have seen it?'" Maggs had told me the day before. "But I've been in this game long enough to understand that doesn't help. I understand that these things are possible. Today an individual can be squeaky clean, and in a week's time something goes wrong in his life or with his family, and he becomes desperate. When they do turn, it's very difficult to detect, because they understand exactly how we work."

Otto agreed: "The rangers and the poachers are exactly the same people. The only difference is integrity."

Rangers, police, and other personnel going to the dark side is not a Kruger-specific problem; it's everywhere, and it can infect both rich and poor, black and white. Especially in South Africa, rhino criminals have also hailed from relatively wealthy wildlife ranching communities, predominantly comprised of white Afrikaans individuals. Sometimes referred to as the "Boeremafia" or "khaki-collar criminals," such individuals seem to be motivated by "pure greed," according to a 2012 TRAFFIC report. Unlike conventional poachers, they often take rhinos down with a single shot issued by an expensive high-caliber gun, although a few prefer to kill using pharmaceuticals administered by corrupt wildlife veterinarians (drugged rhinos are usually left to bleed to death). Some ranch owners have even portrayed themselves as victims of their own poaching.

Given the impact that bad apples can have, "the biggest inroad you could make into this conflict is to fund an anti-corruption campaign," Otto said. "If we could take out the top fifty people who work on the inside—not only in Kruger, but all over the country—that would make a difference."

ONCE A HORN, TUSK, BAG OF BONES, OR BOX OF SCALES IS SMUGGLED OUT OF A park like Kruger, what happens next?

Usually, the goods are transferred along a chain of "runners" who take them to larger and larger cities. At some point, though, Africa-based Asian businessmen who act as bosses on the national level are almost guaranteed to get involved—generally Vietnamese for rhino horn, Chinese for ivory and abalone.

"Africa has never seen as many Asians on this continent as there are today, especially Chinese," said Tom Milliken, who runs TRAFFIC's elephant and rhino programs. "My wife is Japanese, and every shop she goes into these days in Zimbabwe, she's greeted in Chinese." China ranks as the largest foreign commerce partner of many African nations, including South Africa. Its involvement traces back to the Cold War, when Western nations stopped investing there and China stepped up to fill the gap. Since then, the country's provision of contracts, loans, and infrastructure development across the continent—oftentimes in exchange for raw materials—has only grown, hitting an estimated $200 billion in 2012. At least a million Chinese have moved to Africa over the past twenty-odd years in pursuit of jobs, opportunity, and freedom from the state. Some play a role in robbing their adopted home of its wildlife. In 2011, for example, more than 150 Chinese citizens were arrested in Africa for trafficking ivory, while Kenya alone reports that 95 percent of people caught smuggling ivory out of the Nairobi airport fit that demographic. Yet in 2013, Shifan Wu, a spokesperson for the Chinese embassy in Nairobi, claimed, "The number of Chinese nationals involved in ivory smuggling and illegal trade are very few."

In addition to denying or downplaying the problem, diplomats themselves sometimes become involved. Julian has found evidence of around thirty embassy employees in Africa trafficking in rhino horn or ivory. Almost all of them were Vietnamese, Chinese, or North Korean, and none of the cases have resulted in jail time. "The police don't always feel they have the political support to take action when diplomats are caught," Julian said. "So, invariably, nothing happens."

The Vietnamese embassy in Pretoria has a particularly shameful history of abuse. In 2006, for example, Vietnam's economic attaché to South Africa was arrested for possession of two rhino horns, while, in 2010, another senior diplomat was filmed conducting a rhino horn transaction out of the trunk of her car, parked directly in front of the embassy. Following the latter incident—which aired on national television—the diplomat insisted that she was "helping the dealer with his paper work." In both cases, the alleged culprits were recalled to Vietnam, but the problems have continued. For example, Vietnamese embassy officials—including an ambassador to South Africa—regularly visited and hunted on a game farm owned by a convicted Vietnamese rhino horn smuggler and business tycoon, according to Julian's published investigations. The Vietnamese embassy, Julian said, ignored his request for comment.

Others also emphasize Vietnam's role in the upsurge in rhino poaching— both in South Africa and beyond. "The early pioneering of rhino horn trade in Vietnam was spearheaded by the Vietnamese diplomatic community based in

South Africa," Milliken said. "You've had government complicity in the trade, both as users and illegal traffickers, since the beginning. The legacy of that has been disastrous."

There are some signs that, at least among Chinese diplomats, attitudes are evolving. When Grace Ge Gabriel, the International Fund for Animal Welfare's Asia regional director, spoke with the Chinese ambassador to Kenya in 2016, he told her that he was deeply concerned about ivory trafficking. "He felt that the issue was damaging China's reputation and hurting its development goals in Africa," she said. China's ambassador to Tanzania, Liu Xinsheng, expressed similar sentiments to the press in 2014, when he denounced Chinese citizens' "bad habits" in Africa. "Every time Tanzania says it will arrest someone for smuggling ivory, we immediately get nervous," he added.

Should China, Vietnam, and North Korea address their citizens' and diplomats' roles in perpetuating the rhino and elephant crises in Africa, they could make a significant difference. For now, though, they're a large part of the problem. "You've got unscrupulous nationals of China—the end use market—right at the source of the ivory," Milliken said. "They're the conduits for putting African supply together for Asian consumption. We've never seen that before. In the 1980s, for example, Japanese operatives were not on the African continent."

China's involvement, he added, introduces an additional conundrum: he has seen case after case in which Chinese are busted for ivory, but their cell phones and computers are in Chinese, which local investigators can't read. "All of that intelligence is then completely lost," Milliken said. When such information has been accessed, though, investigators found that Africa-based syndicate leaders use mules or couriers to transfer goods overseas. Rhino horns are usually hidden in luggage on commercial flights, while ivory is often packed in shipping containers, nestled beneath lower-value items such as fish, tobacco, tea, chilies, or plastic waste. The methods of concealment can be quite sophisticated: Hong Kong customs officials once spotted odd shapes in an X-ray of a container of timber from Cameroon, but when they emptied it, they found only wood. Yet the X-ray still revealed the same odd shapes. Eventually, they discovered an expertly crafted false wall welded in place. Once they wrenched it off, they found 3.9 tons of ivory. Back in Cameroon, the suspects had already absconded, but investigators found an identical false-walled container on their premises.

In addition to such tricks, the trafficking process is heavily greased by local corruption and bribes. African customs agents may work directly for criminals, or they may simply be opportunistic, viewing any wildlife violations they happen across as a chance to extract a quick personal bonus. Once wildlife contraband begins its trafficking journey, the route it takes oftentimes isn't direct. A China-bound ivory shipment may be sent first to Spain from Togo, or a passenger carrying rhino horn may fly to Dubai before heading on to Kuala Lumpur and then on to Hong Kong. This obscures the true origin and destination, and often reflects the placement of key compromised agents who ensure a smooth journey. "People who operate in the legal field—in government or in the transportation or wildlife industry—play a vital role in ensuring that rhino horn or any other wildlife contraband passes along the supply chain," Hübschle-Finch said. "They are the gatekeepers and intermediaries. They provide the link between the bush and the market."

Trafficking bosses themselves are often also involved in legitimate and even well-known local businesses. "Unlike in the West, where organized criminals live in a somewhat parallel society, here the big criminals are typically also big businesspeople," said Tim Wittig, a conservation scientist and illicit trade expert at the University of Groningen. "Usually, they're involved in logistics-type businesses—trading or shipping companies, for example—or in commodity-based ones, which is why it's easy for them to move things around." For example, Faisal Ali Mohammed, a convicted Kenyan ivory boss, also had a car dealership; Abdurahman Mohammed Sheikh, arrested in Mombasa for alleged ivory trafficking and now awaiting trial, ran an import-export company; and Yang Fenglan, Tanzania's so-called queen of ivory, also awaiting trial, owned supermarkets and a large Chinese restaurant.

Such individuals are sometimes referred to as kingpins, a term experts say is overused. One of the most important characteristics of poaching and smuggling networks, according to Felbab-Brown, is their diversity: while some are highly organized, others are completely dispersed, making generalizations impossible. "It becomes quite messy," Julian said. "In some ways, chasing after a 'Mr. Big' behind it all is a bit of a myth." Indeed, Wittig pointed out that, among them, Mohammed, Sheikh, and Fenglan are charged with exporting a meager 10.9 tons of ivory over the past decade—the equivalent of 1,500 elephants. It's safe to assume that they were responsible for trafficking more ivory than they were charged with, so Wittig multiplied the figure by a generous factor of ten. But this brings the toll only to 15,000 elephants—compared to the 100,000 elephants killed in Central Africa alone from 2011 to 2014. Together, the charges against

Mohammed, Sheikh, and Fenglan account for just 1–10 percent of total smuggled African ivory. Nor has poaching declined since those arrests were made. Therefore, Wittig concluded, "arresting a few alleged wildlife-trafficking 'kingpins' may be a useful symbolic tool for promoting the importance and feasibility of strong enforcement to the general public, [but] it is not likely to be effective in actually saving protected wildlife, especially if done in isolation."

Although disheartening, Wittig's insights are not so surprising. Virtually every detailed study of wildlife trafficking networks indicates that the trade is mostly composed of smaller organized crime networks and individuals who play specialized roles in a horizontal rather than vertical supply chain. A dealer smuggling ivory out of an African port may not know the local boss overseeing poaching or the trader who eventually sells the contraband in Asia.

Of the "Mr. Bigs" of wildlife crime in operation today, some are known, but probably a lot more are not, said John Sellar, formerly chief of enforcement at the CITES Secretariat. For a while, Vixay Keosavang—Chumlong's Laos-based boss—was described as one such player. In 2013, the US State Department offered a $1 million reward for information leading to the dismantling of Keosavang's syndicate (known as the Xaysavang Network, after his import-export company, Xaysavang Trading). Keosavang told the *New York Times* that he was being slandered and framed and that Lao officials knew all about his shipments of South African rhino horn.

Indeed, despite the reward and being labeled an internationally wanted criminal, Keosavang was never investigated by the Lao authorities. They claimed that the evidence against him—including Chumlong's testimony in South African court; numerous photos, receipts, and shipping notifications; a crate addressed to Keosavang containing more than 600 pounds of ivory seized in Kenya in 2009; and illegal wildlife goods worth millions, also addressed to him, seized in Bangkok in 2010 and 2011—was not sufficient to warrant a search or arrest. As an official in the Lao forestry department told the *New York Times* in 2013, "It's about influence. Trafficking syndicates have links to influential people—this is the main problem."

The international furor over Keosavang's case took a toll, however. Although he was never brought to justice, Keosavang's offices are now overgrown, and his Lao car showroom—previously used as a laundering front—is closed. "The government was basically authorizing Keosavang to do his trade, so there was no way he was ever going to be convicted, but he became quite an embarrassment to officials," a source in Laos told me. "He's lying really low these days, and there's no indication he's even in the country anymore." As of 2017, rumor had it he had taken his family to Vietnam or possibly China—and that he'd switched his focus to smuggling cars into Vietnam.

Other criminals operating in Laos have quickly filled Keosavang's vacuum—a development that is in no way surprising. As Felbab-Brown pointed out, removing kingpins never succeeds in dismantling an illegal economy—wildlife, drugs or otherwise—because leadership can be replenished. In Laos, according to a *Guardian* story, two companies, Vinasakhone and Vannaseng, are now at the forefront of animal trafficking. The companies pay officials a 2 percent tax on sales of tiger parts, rhino horns, elephant ivory, and more. In exchange, authorities grant them permission to trade in those forbidden products, including 100 tons of ivory, 4 tons of rhino horn, 20 tons of tiger products, and more than 1,400 tons of pangolins and reptiles in 2014 alone. Sales that year reportedly netted the companies $45 million.

Sellar has argued that the "wildlife" in wildlife crime should be dropped, and that we should instead just think of it simply as crime. "For far too long, wildlife crime has been seen as something on the sidelines of general criminality," he wrote in *The UN's Lone Ranger*. To give it a special label "risks reinforcing the impression that natural resource crimes are somehow different from other crimes" and thus not worthy of the same level of investigative and judicial support.

It's an appropriate suggestion, not the least because wildlife syndicates often include players who also have a hand in trafficking drugs, diamonds, humans, or other contraband. In South Africa, methamphetamine is shipped along with poached abalone, while in East Africa, heroin, cocaine, undocumented migrants, and ivory all share the same routes. Armed robbers, car hijackers, ATM bombers, and other conventional criminals have increasingly added wildlife to their résumés.

In certain places, evidence even indicates that poachers may be members of terrorist or murderous rebel groups, especially the Lord's Resistance Army in the Democratic Republic of Congo. Mostly, though, the threat posed by organized wildlife crime is more insidious than tusks funding terrorism, according to Wittig. As he wrote in 2016, the greatest threat posed by local, national, and transnational criminal networks is their ability to quietly penetrate and subvert national institutions through bribery and corruption, ultimately threatening the cohesion of states.

That such groups tend to include multinational players further complicates investigations, as governments are often bad at information sharing and collaboration. After decades of work, for example, Samuel Wasser, endowed chair of the Center for Conservation Biology at the University of Washington in Seattle, developed a game-changing forensic method that allows him to reliably determine geographic origins of seized tusks and thus to map poaching hot spots in Africa.[1] If provided with samples from major ivory seizures, Wasser could produce a map showing officials and law enforcement exactly where they need to go to shut down the ivory trade in its current form. Yet most countries don't get around to sending him their samples for a year or more after a seizure, and some refuse to share any samples at all. "That's the hardest part for me: seeing how powerful a tool we have, and yet countries are so reluctant to let us use it," Wasser said.

Even within-country organizations may not cooperate. "People don't trust each other," Maggs said. "The intelligence environment is like spy versus spy." Police, for instance, don't talk to customs. Customs don't talk to rangers. Rangers don't have access to policy makers. Policy makers don't consult conservation NGOs. And NGOs may view each other as competition.

Many agree that this is a serious—if not the most serious—obstacle to stopping the trade. As Sellar wrote, "If the genie in the bottle were to grant me just one wish to combat international wildlife crime, I would ask that everyone work more collaboratively. I remain convinced, utterly convinced, that we would make major inroads into combating international wildlife crime if we could only get our act together."

Although some of the disconnect is due to a simple lack of organization or to petty jealousies and rivalries, an unsettling portion also stems from officials who do not want the wildlife trade to end, because they're milking it for personal gains. "Among officials tasked with supervising the legal wildlife trade, corruption can be massive," Felbab-Brown wrote, adding, "the best way to be an ivory trafficker is to be minister for the environment or the head of the primary wildlife law-enforcement agency." This unfortunate truth applies to officials in both Africa and Asia. In 2015, California Republican representative Ed Royce told the

---

1. For a bonus chapter on Wasser's work, visit rachelnuwer.com/poached/

New York Times, for example, that Lao government authorities continuously cite the country's lack of resources as an excuse for not undertaking a single significant illegal wildlife seizure or arrest, when in fact "it's quite clear that officials are profiting from wildlife trafficking."

Whistle-blowers may put themselves in danger, while the rich and powerful typically escape justice for their corruption. When Zimbabwe's *Sunday Mail* published a 2015 article alleging the involvement of rangers and high-ranking police officers in the poisoning of twenty-two elephants, the government arrested the two journalists behind the story on charges of "publishing falsehoods." Likewise, journalist Gerald Tenywa received death threats after he reported in 2015 that officers from the Uganda Wildlife Authority, army, and police were smuggling rhino horn. Perhaps most disturbing of all was the 2017 murder of Wayne Lotter, a South African conservationist whose nonprofit group, the Protected Area Management Solutions (PAMS) Foundation, had almost single-handedly turned the poaching crisis around in Tanzania. The investigation into his assassination is ongoing. Just before this book went to press, Esmond Bradley Martin—who served as a frequent source—was also found murdered in his home in Nairobi. (As of May 2018, however, authorities suspected that his murder was motivated by a land grab, rather than his work on the illegal trade.)

NOT ALL NEWS RELATED TO ILLEGAL WILDLIFE TRADE IS BAD. IN SOME CASES, there has been pushback and positive developments. In 2013, for example, the Obama administration issued an executive order to tackle the "international crisis" of illegal wildlife trade, which the US Congress unanimously codified into law in 2016. There have also been notable successes in tackling crime: Interpol's 2012 Operation Worthy resulted in 214 arrests in Africa and the confiscation of tons of ivory, rhino horn, and weapons, while the US Fish and Wildlife Service's ongoing Operation Crash has resulted in more than thirty convictions as of 2017.

But a critical obstacle stands in the way of more success: most of those tasked with fighting wildlife crime are conservationists, rangers, and wildlife managers, when this should be a job assigned to police, detectives, money laundering experts, and the courts. As some have put it, it is like asking botanists to stop the cocaine trade or pharmacists to solve the opioid epidemic.

Sellar, one of the few CITES Secretariat employees who had an operational police background, pointed out that at conferences on illegal wildlife trade, "it is extremely rare to see senior police, customs officials or a minister of justice or finance in attendance." Basic policing and investigations are conspicuously missing from the millions invested in efforts to combat the illegal wildlife trade, he continued, and, even when training in those fields is provided, it's often not put into practice. In 2011, for example, Sellar arranged for some fifty enforcement agents from eighteen African and Asian countries to be taught a technique called controlled deliveries, in which detected contraband is allowed to continue its journey under close surveillance, laying bare trafficking chains along the way. Yet, a year after the course, none of the countries had used the technique on an international scale, and only South Africa had tried it out domestically.

It was such defeats, among other stressors, that contributed to Sellar's decision to retire. "I got fed up of the hypocrisy of country representatives coming to meetings and saying, 'Yes, we'll do this,' and then going home and basically doing bugger all," he said. "This is not rocket science—otherwise I wouldn't have ended up with the title of chief—but after fourteen years of knocking my head against the wall, eventually it became really painful."

Nine

THE FRONT LINE

SEPTEMBER 2, 2010, was supposed to be a normal day for Esnart Paundi, a park ranger in Zambia. She woke up early and made breakfast for her five children, dressed them, and sent them to school with a kiss. Then, as usual, she put on her uniform of camouflage fatigues and headed to work. Esnart was the only woman among her nineteen colleagues, but she was proud to be a pioneer and enjoyed the challenges of the job.

Esnart was guarding a wildlife checkpoint later that afternoon when an approaching pickup truck suddenly did a U-turn and sped into the bush. She and two other rangers chased it and eventually found it, parked and empty. They discovered two men crouched over a pile of dead animals nearby; although they had no handcuffs, they still managed to apprehend the poachers. One of the rangers then went to find transportation, leaving Esnart and another colleague to guard the men. Unbeknownst to them, however, a third poacher was hiding in the bushes. He leapt out and slammed the base of his machete into the male ranger's head. Esnart, who was unarmed, ran. The men followed. When they caught her, they chopped at her body and head with their machetes, over and over until she was dead. "I cried. It was a gruesome sight," William Soko, a senior ranger who collected Esnart's remains, told the *Guardian*. "I think about Esnart very much. She died a very sad death. She didn't deserve this type of death." Her killers, he added, were never caught.

In the wake of her death, Esnart's family faced not only the grief of her loss but also the stress of not knowing how they would survive. Esnart, who was twice widowed, was the sole breadwinner not only for her five children but also for her five siblings (Zambia's unemployment rate hovers around 13 percent). But despite the fact that Esnart died protecting her country's resources, it quickly became apparent that the government would not be offering any assistance. "No, they didn't support us," said Anna Phiri, Esnart's oldest child, who was fifteen when her mother was killed. "They didn't even say anything to us."

Anna and her siblings' experience was sadly typical. A 2016 WWF survey of rangers in forty countries found that about 50 percent of those in Africa and Asia did not have life insurance. Many also lacked health insurance or long-term disability, meaning they would receive no support should they be seriously injured on the job. Yet anti-poaching is one of the most dangerous enforcement roles, as it typically occurs in remote areas far from reinforcements and criminals are usually armed.

Around the world, more than a thousand rangers have been killed in the line of duty over the past decade. Few families—especially those in developing countries—receive adequate support following a parent's or spouse's death. Widows often lose their home and children must be pulled out of school. "Imagine how demotivating it is for a ranger to see a mate killed in the field and then, as a thank you for the work he did, his family is removed from their house because they have no wage," said Sean Willmore, president of the International Ranger Federation. "Seeing that, how would you even go to work the next day?"

Africa's 20,000–25,000 rangers are also often woefully underresourced—which only contributes to the danger of the job. A second 2016 WWF survey in twelve African countries revealed that 82 percent of 570 rangers had faced life-threatening circumstances and that 59 percent lacked basic supplies such as boots, tents, or GPS. Another 42 percent had not received adequate training. Indeed, Esnart did not have a gun, and neither she nor her colleagues had handcuffs. Had they been in possession of those basic supplies, or had they received more effective training in securing suspects and crime scenes, she might still be alive today. As Anna said, "Protecting wildlife is good, but my mom didn't have enough protection herself."

Rangers are on the front line, Willmore said, yet, despite the critical role they play, they remain something of an afterthought for mainstream conservation. Some prominent NGOs say they support rangers, he continued, but their contributions tend to be a minimal percentage of total donations, and whether the funds in fact reach rangers and make a difference in their lives is often in question. "There's all this high-level talk about combatting poaching, but there's very much a disconnect with what's happening on the ground," Willmore said.

"Large nongovernmental groups spend huge amounts, yet there are rangers calling me for socks," agreed Peter Newland, director of training at 51 Degrees, a private Kenya-based security company, and cofounder of For Rangers, one of the few nonprofits whose primary aim is to support men and women in the field. "Donors outside of Africa want sexy, high-tech solutions like drones and ground sensors. They don't want to hear about the need for warm clothing, boots, and better food for rangers."[1]

The Thin Green Line Foundation, a nonprofit Willmore founded and directs, is another charity solely dedicated to rangers. From 2014 to 2016, it provided $1.2 million in equipment and training and helped more than 150 families of men and women killed on the job—including Esnart's. "Thankfully, after my mom died, Sean found us," Anna said. "He started supporting us and gave us money for schooling."

Anna now lives with her father's sister in Lusaka; three of her siblings live with Esnart's sister, and the fourth is with her father's brother. Their houses are far apart, and the children seldom see each other. But their lives are secure, and the Thin Green Line agreed to fund each of them until they finish school. Anna recently earned a diploma from the International Air Transportation Association and began training in customer service with a Zambian airline. "It hasn't been easy for me and my siblings to be apart, but I'm just very grateful for the support we've received," she said. "I don't know what would have happened to us without it."

The charity, however, cannot provide for all of those in need. "We don't have enough money to even cover all the widows each year," Willmore said. "We need to be doing ten times more." That many rangers and their families lack such basic support is not only grossly unjust, he continued, but also counterproductive for protecting wildlife. When those working the front line know that management has their backs—and that their families will be taken care of should anything happen to them—morale is higher, and they perform better. As such, there is a "100 percent correlation" between how well rangers are looked after and how successful they are at combatting poaching, Willmore said. "All throughout

---

1. For a bonus chapter on anti-poaching drones, visit rachelnuwer.com/poached/

Africa, where rangers are well trained and resourced—and especially when they come from the local community—they reduce poaching."

I WAS EAGER TO MEET A FEW SUPERSTAR RANGERS WHO ARE EFFECTIVELY COMBAT-ting poaching. One place immediately came to mind: the Lewa Wildlife Conservancy in Kenya. That privately owned protected area is known as a stronghold of conservation today—but its success did not come without struggle.

Lewa did not lose a single rhino to poachers from the 1980s to 2009. But, like so many places in Africa, things took a turn in 2010. The next three years saw seventeen rhinos killed—6 percent of the conservancy's total population.

Lewa's management realized that, unless drastic measures were taken, their rhinos would quickly be gone. They responded aggressively with a major operational overhaul that included bringing in a helicopter, revamping their communications system, hiring new expert personnel, and strengthening community partnerships. Recently, Lewa also became one of the first testing sites for a cutting-edge conservation program called the Domain Awareness System. Created by Microsoft cofounder Paul Allen's company, Vulcan, the program's web application and ioS tracking app neatly visualize real-time monitoring of fifty radio-collared elephants along with other relevant data such as ranger, vehicle, and aircraft positions; gunshot detection; arrest and crime-scene records; weather; and more. If the system detects something aberrant, rangers receive real-time alerts, allowing them to respond immediately.

The investments paid off: Lewa has not lost a rhino since November 2013.

Technology gave Lewa an exceptional edge in combatting poaching. But an even more integral factor for success was the special attention paid to supporting and training rangers. "At Lewa, the rangers are a really hard-core, Western-trained, serious force. They could be fighting in Somalia," said Paula Kahumbu, CEO of the nonprofit WildlifeDirect. "Each ranger there is like the equivalent of forty regular rangers. They're damned good."

I wanted to hear directly from some of these men, so the morning after Kenya's ivory burn, I hopped a flight bound for Lewa. The conservancy is located near Mount Kenya, in a land of gently rolling hills known for its private reserves and farms. The region's history, however, is not as idyllic. Many of those properties are owned by the white descendants of former cattle ranchers who settled there when inequalities were rife and Kenya was still billed as "Britain's most attractive colony." Over those years, the country grew famous as a big game hunting destination for celebrities, politicians, royalty, and wealthy businessmen. Theodore Roosevelt shot more than five hundred animals with his son while on safari there in 1909, and although he and others like him were hailed for their masculine prowess, native Kenyans who hunted were labeled poachers.

Sport hunting continued even after Kenya gained independence in 1963, but the tradition soon came to an end when the government issued a complete ban on hunting in 1977. Some believed the move was motivated by long-standing resentment against white elites, but others viewed it as an ethical decision. "To the greatest extent possible, the Kenyans wanted to let nature determine who's to live and who's to die," said Bill Clark, an honorary warden and the US liaison for the Kenya Wildlife Service. "They wanted to let natural ecological dynamics determine what fitness is."

At the same time, many white-owned ranches, including Lewa, began shifting their focus from cattle to conservation, propped up by the country's booming safari industry, which has continued to flourish. Tourism today accounts for 12 percent of Kenya's GDP, 70 percent of which comes directly from wildlife. Lewa, however, isn't a busloads-of-tourists kind of place; it opts for quality over quantity. In fact, I never saw a single other guest during my time there.

The plane glided in for a smooth landing on Lewa's private dirt runway. No one was in sight, but a minute later a friendly driver pulled up to collect me. Passing through a thicket of woods, the driver sportingly slowed the car so I could take photos of loitering zebra. Minutes later, I reached home for the next two nights. Lewa is known for its lavish accommodations, but I was staying in a modest yet comfortable tented camp near the headquarters. Felista, the smiling cook and housekeeper, warned me to keep the green netting of my door zipped tight at all times; otherwise, monkeys would get in.

Unsure of what the day's plans entailed, I sat outside the tent to take in the view over a cup of tea. The bucolic scene was soon interrupted by an army-green, mud-splattered Toyota Land Cruiser that pulled up in front of my tent. Out stepped John Pameri, Lewa's head of security. He wore matching green camouflage and a dark green beret. He'd been sent to show me around the property and tell me a bit more about the place, he said. "I've been to Syracuse, which was really freezing," he told me as we bumped down a dirt road, passing two young men in camouflage, carrying large guns. "And I've been to San Diego—it was on a beach. And to New York City. Nice city."

We drove around a cluster of buildings—Lewa's security headquarters—and then headed into an open area punctuated with skinny trees and twiggy bushes. The sky was broody, and the road was soupy with puddles and mud-filled ruts. Guinea hens ran around us like fat little feathered dinosaurs, and a pair of crowned cranes glided gracefully by overhead. Pameri slowed the vehicle to let a young herder and his two dozen skinny cows and sheep saunter by.

Pameri told me a bit about himself as we continued into the conservancy: "When I was a teenager, my family didn't have money for more education, so I had to stop school. The Maasai didn't value education in those days." With his schooling abruptly ended, though, he lacked direction and was unsure of what to do with his life. "My dad wouldn't sell any cows to pay for me to go to school, but he didn't want me to just sit around, either," he recalled.

A zebra appeared on our right, watching us uncertainly. It was a Grévy's zebra, Pameri informed me, recognizable by its smaller stripes and bigger ears compared to the more common plains zebra. There are only about 2,600 of them left, and 11 percent of the remaining animals—the largest single population in the world—lives at Lewa.

I snapped a couple of photos, and Pameri resumed his story. His father knew one of the security officials at Lewa, so, lacking any other options, he decided to give it a shot. Without calling ahead, he left his house at 5 a.m. and walked more than 60 miles in one day to reach the conservancy. "I was walking, running, walking, running," he said. "I didn't really know where I was going."

When he stumbled in around sunset, he was taken to meet Lewa's owner, Ian Craig. Craig is one of the primary driving forces behind Lewa's conservation agenda: he first convinced his family to set aside some of their property as a rhino sanctuary in the 1980s, and he oversaw the ranch's complete conversion in 1995. He told Pameri that although he didn't have any openings at the moment, he was welcome to fill out an application.

A month later, Pameri was invited back as a volunteer. He learned to use the radio equipment and to operate in the field. He liked the work, and, with Craig's encouragement, he decided to try out formally to join the team. Competition, however, was stiff. More than a hundred men showed up at the recruitment event, vying for just twenty-four positions. One of the tests included a twelve-mile run. Pameri came in sixth, and he excelled at all the other tasks, too. He made the cut and has been working his way up the ranks ever since, including earning a pilot's license. "Someday, I'm going to write a book about my life," he said. "It will be called *To Walk to Fly*."

We were deep in the conservancy now, passing postcard-perfect green vistas crowded with giraffe, buffalo, and zebra. Elegant herds of impala scattered around the car, and eland with corkscrew horns and dangling dewlaps nibbled at swaying, knee-high grass. Lewa seemed endless, but, in fact, it's just larger than Seattle—relatively small as far as African protected areas go. That makes management an easier task compared to a place like Kruger, which is nearly as big as New Jersey.

Pameri stopped next to a group of six or seven elephants, all of whom appeared unfazed by our presence. They picked at the grass, stuffing their mouths with trunkfuls of green. A baby the size of a small pony trailed after its mother, mimicking her actions as grasshoppers fluttered around them like fairies. Elephants are incredibly intelligent, able to, for example, differentiate among human languages most often spoken by poachers and protectors, to sniff out and avoid land mines, and to shift to a nocturnal lifestyle when threatened by hunters during the day. The animals here were exceptionally relaxed because they knew that they were safe: Lewa sends rangers out on daily elephant patrols, which management plots out based on readings sent from the radio collars that some of the matriarchs wear.

"In Kenya, this is our gold, this wildlife," Pameri said, gesturing at the elephants. "People should remember the rangers out there in the field, sleeping under the trees, sweating and dealing with snakes all night to make sure the wildlife will live forever. Without their support, these animals won't be alive."

We continued on our way. As we crested a hill, two human figures in solid green uniforms, floppy safari hats, and black boots came into sight. They introduced themselves as Lewa rangers Francis Kobia Chokera and Jeremiah Thiaine. They were out in search of some of the 130 black and white rhinos that live on the property.

Lewa divides its land into nine security blocks, each of which is constantly patrolled by three rangers, referred to as rhino monitors. Unlike the elephant patrols that are informed by GPS readings from collars, the rhino guys rely solely on their wits to determine where to find their targets. As soon as they spot one, they identify the individual rhino and radio in the sighting. Their digital radios have built-in GPS units so management can track their movements, which show up as multicolor zigzags from a rainbow etch-a-sketch on the digital map back at headquarters. All calls and texts from the radios travel over a secure connection, and, as an extra layer of protection, everything is recorded and encrypted.

Today was a pretty typical day for Chokera and Thiaine. They had gotten up at 5 a.m., made a cup of tea and nibbled on some bread, and then set out on their patrol, leaving their third colleague behind to keep an eye on the camp. By 7 a.m., they'd already spotted four white rhinos. "When you wake up early, you can easily see rhino," Chokera said. "And you can also more easily see signs of unusual things, like poachers."

He and Thiaine had covered six miles, but they had a bit farther to go still. "We'll continue to the east," Chokera said, pointing at the horizon. "There will be black rhinos there. We also count all the ungulates we see—the giraffe, elephant, buffalo, and zebra—so we know the population, we know what we have."

Unlike the specialized anti-poaching team, Chokera, Thiaine, and Lewa's other ninety general security rangers do not carry firearms. Instead, they travel with a long, thin stick—a sort of club that they use to keep snakes at bay or to whack an aggressive buffalo. "That gives you the chance to escape up a tree," Chokera noted. In two decades of field patrols, he's only had to take to the branches five times. Snakes, however, he has met "many times—but they're very shy."

Chokera started working at Lewa in 1995, the same year as Pameri did. "Me, I was born where there's lots of animals, and I've always loved them," he said. "By good luck, my brother was working here, and I was given a chance to work here, too. I passed the interview. I've been here twenty-two years now."

I asked Thiaine, who was from one of the surrounding communities, what made him decide to join. He smiled shyly when Chokera translated my question into Swahili. "I've seen the animals profit our nation and community and families," he said simply. His job provides him with insurance and a pension, and he makes around $3,600 a year—more than twice the average in Kenya.

We needed to let Chokera and Thiaine get back to work, but, before Pameri and I left, I asked whether there was anything else they wanted to tell me. "There was a time when rhinos were poached here so much, and we got scared," Chokera said. "It's very sad when animals have been killed. They have a right to live and be free; they were here before human beings. So we tried our best, and we stopped the poaching. We had security before, but not like we do now. The security of wildlife is very tight, and it's been years without a rhino death."

CREDIT FOR THAT SUCCESS IS PARTLY DUE TO LEWA'S FAMED ANTI-POACHING UNIT, headed by Edward Ndiritu. I met Ndiritu in the afternoon in an office at headquarters, where the walls were decorated with confiscated spears and snare traps removed from the field. Tall and thin, his baby face, offset by a light mustache, made him appear younger than his years.

Ndiritu grew up on the slopes of Mount Kenya, an hour's drive from Lewa. A lifelong animal lover, joining the conservancy was an obvious choice. "When I was very young, I could see elephants and rhinos around my home, but now they're no longer there," he said. "If we don't protect our wildlife, we will not see them anymore. We might have to go to a zoo only." Ndiritu started out as a Lewa ranger in 1996, then became a rhino monitor, and later a member and eventually head of the anti-poaching unit. In 2015, he became the first recipient of the Tusk Wildlife Ranger Award, in recognition of his bravery and commitment. It was presented to him at a ceremony in London by Prince William. Ndiritu's most vivid memory of the UK was not being congratulated by the prince, however, but the freezing weather. "Even with gloves, a hat, a scarf and a big jacket, in England, I was just cold," he said, shaking his head. "I would go into a pub and they'd be like, 'Start a fire! There's an African in here!'"

The trips and awards all came after Lewa's incredible turnaround, which was made possible through hard work, heavy investments, and drastic changes. Ndiritu and his men in the anti-poaching unit received six months of training from the Kenya Wildlife Service and one month of training from the national police. After that, Newland at 51 Degrees—whose first career was as a senior noncommissioned officer in the British army—gave them additional specialized training, including instruction on how to deploy properly in relation to intelligence, how to use aircraft and vehicles, how to communicate effectively, and even how to use the moon to their advantage.

Every three months, the men undertake a ten-day refresher course, followed by tests in field techniques, first aid, and physical fitness. The latter includes performing forty pushups in less than a minute and sixty sit-ups in less than a minute. Then, they must run a mile in boots and full uniform in under ten minutes. "If you can't do that within the time limit, then you fail," Ndiritu said. "It means you're not fit enough, and you have to go do something else."

Ndiritu and his forty men are recognized by the Kenyan government as police reservists; they are allowed to carry automatic weapons and have the power to make arrests. As Ndiritu said simply: "We are police." Six of them are constantly on standby, waiting to respond to calls about robberies, attacks, or poaching events. "No one knows what will happen," Ndiritu said. "We could be deployed at any time, to anywhere."

Most rhino poachers, they have found, do not come from the communities surrounding the conservancy. Some are ex-military, and all are connected to well-organized cartels. But even the most adept criminal groups struggle to poach without local intelligence. Rhinos are simply too well guarded. "We say that 100 percent of rhino poaching must have an internal connection, that there must be someone leaking information from within the sanctuary," Ndiritu said. "With 150 people, you must have rotten eggs."

That rotten eggs were multiplying became especially apparent in one devastating stretch in December 2012, when the conservancy lost six rhinos in just two weeks. "I spent a lot of time talking to the guys, trying to build up their courage and telling them that we will be able to do it," Ndiritu recalled. "It was very difficult for me, but I had no other option because I had a passion for what we were doing for conservation. Every day, I wake up with a sense of purpose. When I see elephants and rhinos, I feel deep emotion and pride."

From 2010 to 2014, Lewa management either fired or arrested ten of their own who had been compromised. Poachers, they learned, sometimes paid rangers half a year's salary or more, just for information. "They don't even want you to come with them, because you might be setting them up," Ndiritu said. "They just want you to tell them the areas with high rhino populations, and when rangers are around and when they're not." Ndiritu and the other managers now try to keep the number of people who fully understand Lewa's operations to an absolute minimum.

Weeding out corruption was the first step to stop the killings, and getting the communities surrounding Lewa to commit fully to conservation was the second. That included not only educational campaigns but also ensuring that people received tangible benefits from the conservancy, including heightened security. Ndiritu and his men spend most of their time responding to problems that locals call in rather than pursuing poachers. "We don't ask our neighbors to pay anything, we just do it for free," he said. "In turn, we get intelligence from them. With intelligence, we know what will happen and we take action before it happens."

"For us, the priority is not about having guns on the ground, it's how to deliver awareness of the benefit of wildlife, so people stay happy," Pameri added.

"If communities can give us information, then our job is done: no poacher can make it through without us knowing. If everyone agrees that we will protect these animals, then we can see that the future is good."

Indeed, 70 percent of Kenyan wildlife lives outside of protected areas, so community buy-in is crucial for ensuring that wildlife persists. Recognizing this, in 1995, Craig helped one of Lewa's surrounding villages establish the first community-owned and managed conservancy in northern Kenya. Ten years later, an umbrella organization called the Northern Rangeland Trust (NRT) was formed to support the growing number of community conservancies across northern Kenya and beyond. The ownership—and thus the benefits—belongs to the half a million residents who live in the NRT's thirty-three communities and counting. "This is not just a few scraps thrown at them now and then—they own the process," said Mike Watson, Lewa's CEO. "One community may make $200,000 in a year from wildlife. That's a significant amount of money here."

In addition to direct monetary gains, Lewa and the NRT provide a variety of services, from building wells and giving out microloans to women to establishing health-care clinics and hosting school field trips. Formal education, though, is especially emphasized. In 2015, Lewa employed seventy-five teachers and supported 7,500 students, some of them rangers' children. They doled out more than four hundred scholarships to older pupils and saw sixteen local students graduate from college. Nontraditional students were also provided for: after a lifetime of illiteracy, a seventy-five-year-old grandmother recently graduated from one of the conservancy's adult learning programs, ecstatic that she could now help her grandson with his homework.

As Craig told me, "Lewa and the NRT have surpassed my expectations in the beginning by about a billion."

Although Lewa is among the most successful examples of wildlife protection in Africa, the conservancy does not provide a universal solution to the poaching crisis. For one, it relies largely on tourism. "Tourism is often seen as a panacea, but most nature tourists to Africa go to a very few countries— particularly Kenya, South Africa, and Botswana—and, even there, tourism only meets all the costs of conservation in a few places," said Rosie Cooney, chair of the International Union for Conservation of Nature's Sustainable Use and Livelihoods Specialist Group. "In much of the rest of Africa it is currently completely unrealistic for tourism to finance conservation outside of a small number of attractive places."

As a result most protected areas fail to even cover their own operational costs, pointed out Vanda Felbab-Brown in *The Extinction Market*. Unlike beautiful and dynamic Kenya, vast areas of northern Botswana, for example, feature flat, monotonous mopane woodland that would never work as a tourist draw. Other destinations may be plenty attractive but are too logistically challenged to appeal to all but the toughest sport hunters or die-hard birders. The majority of tourists require high-quality accommodation, easy wildlife viewing options, clean water, tasty meals, trained staff and guides, and reasonable transportation options, Cooney said—all of which requires a level of capacity and infrastructure lacking in many parts of rural Africa.

Even in well-established hubs like Kenya, though, the tourism industry can be fickle. After the Gulf War broke out in 1990, for example, visitors dropped by 80 percent as geographically illiterate Westerners mistook East Africa for the Middle East. Likewise, Kenya is thousands of miles from West Africa, yet in the months following the 2014 Ebola outbreak, tourism dropped by 15–20 percent. More localized incidents can also cause immediate damage to the industry: many travelers cancelled their trips following Nairobi's Westgate mall attack in 2013, for example. If tourism dwindles for long enough, then conservation will be impacted in places that depend on it for revenue. As Watson said, "Communities are not protecting wildlife because they like the look of it but because it is an asset, a resource that they're generating benefits from."

Lewa and other places like it enjoy certain advantages that contribute to their success. Wildlife tourism is found all over Kenya, but many of the wealthiest visitors beeline for private conservancies. Prince William, for example, has long favored Lewa: he spent time there as teenager, dated Craig's daughter (and later attended her wedding on the property), and proposed to Kate Middleton while vacationing there in 2010. As Tim Wittig, a conservation scientist and illicit trade expert at the University of Groningen, put it, "Lewa is certainly one of the most effective examples of counter-poaching in Kenya and all of Africa, but it should be seen as an anomaly with probably very limited relevance as a template for other protected areas, given that virtually nowhere else has the same amount of resources, celebrity attention, top-level buy-in, and other advantages that they are fortunate enough to enjoy."

Elite visitors, Wittig added, help attract others like them, some of whom become generous and dependable donors. In 2015, donors contributed about 70 percent of Lewa's $4.5 million earnings. To put it into context, Lewa's 2015 earnings break down to about $47,300 per square mile, compared to the Kenya Wildlife Service's (KWS) earnings of about $3,900 per square mile in 2014. Yet the KWS is charged not only with the taking care of around 10,000 square miles of national parkland but also with managing the entirety of Kenya's wildlife—all of which belongs to the state, regardless of whether it's in a private conservancy, national park, or farmer's field. Combine that with KWS's large, budget-gobbling headquarters, and the figure available for field operations quickly drops. (Lewa, however, also invests in more than just conservation: it spends nearly 40 percent of its revenue on development projects in neighboring communities.)

Although Lewa and the KWS frequently collaborate and share a close, productive relationship, jealousies do exist. "If you're going for holiday, Lewa Downs is a very nice place, and they do good conservation work," said Clark, the honorary KWS warden. "But keep in mind: it's a nonprofit business. Generally, Lewa and some other conservancies do a relatively good job because their budgets are proportionally much better than the KWS. One reason for this is because the conservancies are rather good at attracting journalists, who provide the publicity that facilitates fund-raising and contributes to inappropriate allocation of resources. Wealth also attracts more wealth, and when wealthy donors decide to give a pile of money, they usually also say, 'I want to go visit my project and I want to stay in good lodges while I'm there.' Some of the conservancies charge hundreds of dollars per night and serve dinner on china plates and crystal glasses, while the national parks are running on old tires. Yet the KWS rangers are the ones who carry the largest burden of protecting elephants, and they're the ones who have absorbed the biggest sacrifices. Donors are not looking where the problems are." Others, however, don't see it this way. As one conservationist flatly told me, "Why should Lewa be punished for doing a good job?"

Questions of fairness aside, for a variety of reasons, Lewa and certain other stellar examples of conservation will likely remain exceptions to the rule. That doesn't make them any less inspirational: they prove that success can be achieved. As Timothy Tear, executive director of the Wildlife Conservation Society's Africa program, summarized, "That places like Lewa are succeeding in spite of seemingly insurmountable pressures is where hope is found."

MY TIME AT LEWA QUICKLY PASSED IN A WHIRL OF CAMOUFLAGE-CLAD RANGERS, photogenic wildlife, and memorable personalities. I was soon back in Nairobi, heading to O. R. Tambo International Airport in the back of a cab. I'd been chatting on and off with the driver, Frida, a petite mother of two, and as we passed a dark expanse to the right—the edge of Nairobi National Park—she spoke up once again. "This is the place where a lion recently broke out of the park. The lion tackled a guy on a motorcycle on his way home from work. So the press started making jokes, saying that all the men in Nairobi will now be using lions as an excuse: 'I swear, honey, it was a lion! That's why I'm late!'" She laughed, shaking her head. "So, what brings you to Kenya?"

As I explained that I came to learn more about the wildlife and poaching situation here, her eyes, reflected in the rearview mirror, grew serious. "It negatively affects me when people kill animals, because I drive people who come to see them," she said, her previously bubbly voice now low and stern. "I ask myself if the people who do poaching are not educated, or maybe their leader is rich and wants to be richer. Either way, it's just for them. Maybe you benefit in the short term by killing an animal, but you're negatively impacting all of us for the future. It's just so unfair—the animals affect our country so positively. God has made it that they're here in Kenya, and we should take care of them. Why do some people have to disturb them, then?"

"Do you like wildlife yourself?" I asked.

"Yes, I like animals! It's amazing to see them. And I love watching the tourists when they see the animals. They are so happy!"

Hearing this woman—just an average citizen—speak so passionately about her natural heritage reminded me of something Richard Leakey had written years ago about his hope for his country, a hope that "all Kenyans, even the poorest villager, would come to see the animals and the parks as belonging to them." This, he believed, would be "the best means for building a future."

PART III
THE SAVING GAME

"We can judge the heart of a man by his treatment of animals."

—Immanuel Kant, *Lectures on Ethics,* 1775–1780

The elephant herd at Zakouma National Park in Chad.

A rhino undergoes a dehorning procedure at John Hume's in South Africa.

A tiger farm in Laos's Golden Triangle Special Economic Zone.

A bear rescued from the bile industry relaxes at the Animals Asia sanctuary in Vietnam.

A pangolin rehabilitated by Save Vietnam's Wildlife awaits release.

Ten

A PARK REBORN

T<small>RY</small> telling your friends and family that you're planning a trip to Chad, and you'll likely get a variety of reactions, starting with, "*Chad?* What's in Chad?"

I couldn't blame anyone for their ignorance or paranoia. Chad is one of the least visited countries in the world, and in the few-and-far-between instances that it makes the news in the West, it's usually for some new insurgency or suicide bomber attack. But although it's easy to fixate on the negative, there is more to the place than rebels and extremists—including some incredible conservation accomplishments.

I, too, had to clarify Chad's location on a map when it first came up in conversation. That Central African country, I learned, is in the Sahel—an east-west belt between the Sahara and savanna—an expanse that's not quite desert but not quite grassland, either. Nearly twice the size of Texas, Chad is the fifth-largest country in Africa but is inhabited by a mere 13 million people.

The French claimed Chad as a colony in 1913 and promptly separated the country into "useful Chad," the wetter south, and "useless Chad" in the more arid north. The rulers divvied up resources and investments accordingly, and in the process exacerbated tensions among the two-hundred-plus distinct ethnic groups living there. France's legacy can still be felt today not only in the Francophone country's baguette-filled cafés, but also in the persistent ethnic divisions that continue to stymie nation building.

Like many African countries, Chad fell into civil war and authoritarian and military rule following independence in 1960. Several decades later, Idriss

Déby Itno led a rebellion against the government and took control. Though not exactly a dictator, he's been president ever since—in spite of several attempted coups. Anti-corruption posters line the capital's streets, but cronyism and government misuse of funds have worsened in recent years, especially since oil drilling started in the early aughts. Chad, according to Transparency International, ranks 159th out of 176 nations for corruption.

Security in some parts of the country is indeed also wobbly. The US State Department's travel warning points out that suicide attacks carried out by the Nigerian Islamist terrorist group Boko Haram took place in the capital as recently as 2015. Kidnappings for ransom, unexpected eruptions of violence, and encounters with landmines near the Sudanese border are all possibilities if you visit Chad, the warning continues.

Although there is a real threat of violence, especially along some border areas, State Department alerts tend to be a bit overblown. And it's not as though Chad is unique in its potential for danger. As a source there later put it, "Do I not go to Paris because I might be machine gunned in a night club? Or to the US because I read about a different gun massacre every other week?" I agreed with those sentiments. And, like others who dare to venture to Chad, I was rewarded with a firsthand look at one of the most unlikely and spectacular conservation successes in Africa, at a place called Zakouma National Park.

In 2002, Zakouma was home to some 4,000 elephants, but by 2010 that figure had plummeted to a mere 450 or so—a breathtaking 90 percent decline. Everyone said the park's elephants would be gone within two or three years, poached to extinction. Yet that did not happen—quite the opposite, in fact. Poachers were purged from the park, and, for the first time in more than a decade, the elephant population began to grow. Foreign and Chadian tourists alike have returned, and plans are in the works to form a new national park in the region, expanding the elephants' protected range. Zakouma, in other words, has been transformed from bloodbath to bastion of hope.

I first heard about Zakouma's phenomenal success in Kenya when I chatted with Lorna and Rian Labuschagne, the South African couple with whom I shared a bus at the Giants Club summit. They took over Zakouma's management in 2011, and on the bus they spoke to me of Sudanese militants on horseback, of full-on gun battles with AK-47s and rocket launchers, of legions of elephants mowed down in a matter of days—of Kenya's poaching problem being child's play compared to what Chad contends with.

The stories stuck with me, and, as the months passed, I found myself wondering how they did it. How do you pivot from impending extinction to almost zero poaching in just a few short years? In a field often consumed by bad news, this was a conservation success story that I wanted to tell. Doing so, though, would require me to travel to Chad to visit Lorna and Rian in the field—which is precisely how I found myself cruising at 30,000 feet above North Africa, bound for N'Djamena.

ON THE FLIGHT TO SOUTH AFRICA A FEW MONTHS EARLIER, I REMEMBER STANDING in line for the toilet, laughing with a fellow passenger about a group of Americans—Texans, specifically—sitting nearby. For the eleven-hour duration of the trip from London to Johannesburg, all four wore surgical masks and plastic gloves. I had assumed they had some sort of tragic autoimmune disease, but no. They'd told the guy in line with me that, in fact—bless their hearts—they were taking precautions against contracting Ebola.

The flight from Paris to N'Djamena, however, was a completely different rodeo: this was no amateur hour. Around half the passengers appeared to be from Chad or to be visiting family that lived in Chad—from a tween kid wearing an Old West–style black cowboy hat and boots to a group of women with dark lips and striking hand tattoos. Besides the Chadians, most passengers were male, with a military look. Topping the group off were several Chinese, of the business rather than tourist variety, and one Caucasian nun.

Loitering near the gate was also Patrick Duboscq, a retired French SWAT officer who I had been told would meet me at the airport. Rather than spend his retirement relishing in the comforts of country life, Patrick opts to work seasonally at Zakouma, where he trains rangers. He didn't exactly fit my mental image of what an elite chief ranger trainer should look like. He was quite short, a little soft in the belly, and wore glasses. He spoke English with a French accent so thick that it might have been a parody.

Also true to stereotypes, he quickly brought up the subject of food—specifically, his love of it. "I'm a Frenchman, of course!" he declared, with no hint of sarcasm. He admitted that he has shopaholic tendencies at his town's weekly produce market and added that he and his wife take gastronomic tours of France and sometimes make border runs to Spain just to buy ham.

Rivaling Patrick's passion for food, though, is his compassion for wildlife.

"My family loves animals, we always have," he said. When his son traveled to a park in Ethiopia a few years back, it dawned on him such places could benefit from his dad's expertise. Patrick thought this was a great idea. His mother tongue made him a particular asset in Francophone countries like Chad, which is how he wound up at Zakouma. He takes the job there very seriously. "This is my last fight," he said. "I'm sixty-two." In addition to training the park's sixty or so rangers, he also serves as a sort of surrogate father for the men, playing football (a.k.a. soccer) with the guys, having dinner with their families, and always making himself available via Skype when he's not in Chad. "I trust my guys completely," he said. "I believe we have one of the best park defenses in Africa."

Our conversation was interrupted as boarding began and Patrick took his seat on the other side of the galley. I drifted in and out of sleep as we headed south and the sky gradually turned from blue to golden to star studded. When we began our descent into the N'Djamena International Airport five hours later, I looked out the window to see a collection of fuzzy blue and orange lights glowing in the distance. Aside from that faint beacon, there was nothing to break the blackness. Had I not known otherwise, I would have guessed we were flying over a dark, shipless sea.

I waited for Patrick on the tarmac, where the night air smelled of smoke and it was cooler than I expected. Many of those on our flight—including Patrick—had obviously done this before: they practically sprinted up the airport steps, competing to be first in line at customs. "The line moves pretty quickly these days," Patrick said when I finally caught up. "It used to take hours and hours."

Anti–ivory trafficking signs in English, French, Arabic, and Chinese lined a wall to our left, and Patrick followed my gaze. "Those signs are useful, because a lot of Chinese people come here for business and oil," he said. "I heard from a friend working in China that some Chinese people thought ivory grew on trees. They had to put a pamphlet out to educate them otherwise." I raised an eyebrow. "It's true! Look it up."

The line moved slowly, and at last it was my turn to speak with the border agent, a tough-looking guy in army greens. He asked what I was doing here, and in my feeble French, I stammered that I was visiting Zakouma National Park.

"Rachelle Love . . . ," he replied, looking at my passport. His serious demeanor melted into a look of amusement. "Votre nom est Rachelle *Love?* Oh là là!"

"Euh, oui, c'est moi!" I replied indulgently (this happens quite often at customs checks).

Still giggling, he waved me through. Chad, I realized, was already defying expectations. I handed my yellow fever vaccination card—mandatory for getting into the country—to a guy wearing a grubby white lab coat, who glanced at it briefly before allowing me to pass. Patrick and I sat around for forty minutes more waiting for his bags—he checked two massive suitcases, which he told me were full of foie gras—and then another thirty minutes in a chaotic line for use of the airport's one and only bag-scanning machine—a requirement for exiting. By the time we emerged, it was 10 p.m.

We passed just a couple of other cars on our drive into town. Scant street-lights barely lit sidewalks that were half-submerged in orange sand and cast shadows on a few shuttered shops. Dark roundabouts orbited weatherworn patriotic monuments—a bunch of cow heads; a rusted figure on horseback, raising a spear overhead. A few guys leaning on beat-up motorcycles loitered on corners, but, other than that, the city and my hotel seemed deserted. (As I'd learn that Saturday night, however, if you know where to look, it is possible to party in N'Djamena until 4 a.m.—but that's another book!)

THE THREAT TO CHAD'S ELEPHANTS BEGAN CENTURIES AGO, WHEN ARAB-speaking nomads developed a culture of elephant hunting. Spears have since been replaced with guns, but the practice persists today.

La Chasse Oubliée (The Forgotten Hunt), a beautifully—and sometimes graphically—illustrated book by former park warden Jean-Luc Temporal, is perhaps the best resource for learning about the nomads' ancient and destructive art. Temporal himself became acquainted with the hunts firsthand while working in the Central African Republic in the 1970s and 1980s. Small parties of men on horseback journey from as far as Sudan to reach the elephant-rich savannas and forests of Central Africa. "They are called *les cavaliers*," Temporal wrote, "or 'knights.'"

Descended from various Muslim despots, another term for these men is Janjaweed, or "armed horsemen." Their centuries-long résumé of raiding and trade includes slaves, livestock, weapons, drugs, and ivory, and they also rent out their services to various militaries, including the Sudanese army. The Janjaweed are not a specific national or insurgent group but opportunistic mercenaries and outlaws—nomadic pastoralists who take up arms to supplement their income.

Temporal's book focused solely on their elephant dealings. When embarking on hunts, the men, he learned, always traveled light, carrying a single long spear with a spade-shaped point, plus a bit of tea and dried food to subsist on. Upon finding an elephant herd, they circled it like velociraptors until they managed to separate one animal from the others. Once the hunters settled on a victim, "the animal is doomed," Temporal wrote. They pursued the isolated elephant, wearing it down and putting more distance between it and its family. Eventually, one man would pull out in front, distracting the elephant and giving his comrades a chance to strike. They thrust their spears into the animal's anus and rolled them around, either severing the sciatic nerve to cause paralysis or simply letting the internal damage take its toll. "In this world of the bush, where death is always discreet, fast and habitual, on such a day it takes a tragic turn," Temporal wrote. "Slowly, the noble beast sinks, and the tension breaks."

The hunters, "impassive and mute," would then dismount from their horses to claim their prize. For them, death was a triumph, "the final moment that culminates after days and days of research and long rides," Temporal wrote. Sometimes they hacked out the ivory on the spot—starting by cutting off the elephant's limp trunk—but, alternatively, they may let the carcass rot for a few days, allowing them to yank the tusks free from the slick gore. The animal's meat, however, they never touched; according to Temporal, the ivory was "the one and only objective." Once they gathered enough of it, they loaded up their horses and headed home.

Some Westerners may admire the *cavaliers* for their boldness and courage, Temporal wrote, or celebrate the men's technique as a continuation of a cultural art passed down from generation to generation. But such people, he continued, are ignorant of the full story. They do not realize "the scope of the massacres for which [the *cavaliers*] are responsible." They have decimated and continue to decimate Africa's wildlife, he pointed out, driving the disappearance of rhinoceros throughout Central Africa and now aiding in "the annihilation of countless elephants."

When Temporal recorded these observations in 1989, he also speculated that modernity might cause the *cavaliers'* murderous traditions to gradually fade away. It has not. If anything, modernity has grown the market for ivory and increased the Janjaweed's destructive potential. Poaching in Chad and the surrounding countries is still carried out by the same small, focused teams of Arab-speaking men on horseback, but now they carry assault rifles instead of spears.

What was once a handful of animals killed at a time has mushroomed into entire herds mowed down in minutes, threatening the very existence of the region's elephants. In the 1970s, around 300,000 elephants lived in the Sahel, but, by the mid-aughts, fewer than 10,000 remained. When researchers surveyed twelve western Sahel countries in 2011, they found that half of the twenty-three elephant populations they spotted were composed of fewer than two hundred animals—a sign that they would almost certainly soon be gone, given that "historically, most populations numbering less than 200 individuals in the region were extirpated within a few decades."

For years, though, Zakouma stood out as one of the Sahel's few elephant strongholds, with nearly half of the region's entire population—more than 4,000 animals—found there in 2000. Created in 1963 as a safe haven for animals, Chad's first national park seemed to be living up to its original purpose. But it soon became apparent that even Zakouma was not immune.

Dolmia Malachie, coordinator of Chad's National Elephant Action Plan, was one of the first to sound the alarm. Starting in 2000, he spent months at a time in Zakouma, where he was conducting elephant research for his PhD. Poachers, by then, had nearly wiped out elephants in neighboring countries, and Chad, Dolmia discovered, now seemed to be the target of their guns and greed. During his first rainy season in the park, Dolmia almost lost his life when a group of poachers shot at him. A ranger as well as a student, he returned fire and escaped. "After that, I told myself never again in the rainy season will I come here," he said.

There's a reason, Dolmia found, that poachers tended to strike in the rainy season, which lasts from the end of May to early November. For those five months, foreign conservationists return to Europe, and rangers take a holiday as well, leaving the park abandoned and defenseless. Janjaweed poachers did not care about getting wet: if the water was too deep to ford on foot or horseback, they simply used large dried bottle gourds as floatees. They'd set up camp in a dry area and then get to work with killing.

Once they collected a certain quota of ivory, they'd call in camel trains to take their booty back to Sudan. Although Chad itself doesn't have a significant ivory market, its eastern neighbor does. Sudan is one of the few places where the ivory market has expanded rather than shrunk since the 1990s, and it takes just ten days by horseback to travel from Darfur to Zakouma. Success drives success, and the more poachers who returned home with big ivory paydays, the more who decided to get in on the take. "Poachers who came, they kill, kill, kill many elephants for one or two weeks, and then they go," Dolmia said. "That is the process." He could see that Zakouma's elephants would soon be gone.

Zakouma, at the time, was partly managed and primarily funded by the European Union, which donated nearly $1 million annually. From 2001 to 2007, Spanish conservationist Luis Arranz was the EU's man on the ground. "The weakness that caused this crisis was primarily the lack of anti-poaching reaction from the government," Dolmia said. "But it was also Luis. When I first saw the elephant carcasses, I said 'We have to inform the government.' But he said, 'No, no, don't inform them!'" (Arranz contested this version of events. He said that elephant numbers were increasing until 2005, and that he never denied or hid the problem.)

Whatever the case, things only got worse from there. Rebellions within Chad and clashes with Sudan rocked the country from 2005 until 2010, creating a veil of chaos that made wildlife crime all the easier to get away with, including Zakouma, which was quickly losing its elephants. In 2006, conservationist and *National Geographic* explorer J. Michael Fay visited the park for the second year in a row to conduct aerial surveys and was dismayed to find nine hundred fewer elephants than in the previous year. But rather than assume that Zakouma may have a poaching problem, Arranz and Fay wondered whether the elephants had moved somewhere else, or whether Fay had missed a herd or double-counted some animals the year before. "Luis denied that elephant poaching was such a problem, right up to the point that people realized this thing is almost gone," said Rian, who took over management in 2011.

Indeed, it soon became increasingly difficult to overlook the source of the problem. In a second 2006 survey—which Arranz said he proposed—Fay discovered the rotting bodies of a hundred elephants just outside of the park's boundaries. Their corpses were riddled with bullets, their tusks hacked off. "Seeing the inert, dismembered bodies of elephants is every bit as disturbing to me as seeing the bodies of humans killed in war," Fay later wrote in *National Geographic*. He saw the perpetrators, too: poachers fleeing the scene shot at Fay's plane as he took photos of them.

"[Management] must have seen the problem before, but they wouldn't admit it," Rian said. "They tried to put it under the carpet, probably because it was embarrassing to find fifty elephants massacred. But the red lights came on when Mike Fay was here and showed that there is massive, massive poaching, especially in the wet season."

Arranz, however, said that he personally informed President Déby that poaching was on the rise during a 2007 visit to the park, and that he asked the government send extra guns and ammunition. The president delivered on that request, but Arranz—who had grown unpopular among Environment Ministry officials—departed later that year. "In my time in Zakouma, I lost seven rangers killed by poachers and we twice received the visit of the rebels," he said. "I can understand that people think that things could have worked better—I respect their opinion, even if talk from an office in N'Djamena is easy—but to lie telling that I tried to hide the poaching is not honest. We worked really hard."

What, then, allowed the situation to deteriorate to that point? Rian sees the failure as multifold. Money, he believes, was being misallocated toward monitoring and research rather than supporting rangers or protecting wildlife. Funds were also distributed on set five-year schedules that were tied to projects with predefined beginnings and endings. This caused the park to constantly go through cycles of destruction and rebirth, rather than strive toward a long-term management vision. "With all due respect, I saw their strategy, and they didn't have any idea what to do here," Rian said. "I don't think they had the experience to know what it takes."

Finding someone to get the situation under control proved challenging, however. After Arranz moved on, a couple of other managers came and went, including an American who lasted just two months. As the situation became increasingly dire, the EU ambassador to Chad proposed a radical fix: call in African Parks, a South Africa–based nonprofit organization that specializes in rehabilitating failing protected areas. African Parks takes on cases that no one else will, oftentimes in difficult-to-work places that are mired in turmoil, political instability, or other hardships. Zakouma, in other words, was a perfect fit.

For Chad, however, handing Zakouma over to African Parks would mean surrendering all managerial control. This was something Dolmia—whose trust of foreigners running his country's parks had crumbled ten years earlier—especially feared. "I'm not enthusiastic about your African Parks thing, especially this model of taking the responsibility from the government," he protested. He became one of the proposal's most outspoken opponents, and he convinced all his friends in the ministry to speak out against African Parks' involvement, too.

The plan would have failed right there, except for one hitch: President Déby—whose word is final—didn't agree with his ministers. "The president just said, 'This is the way we're going to do it,'" Rian recalled. In 2010, Déby signed a twenty-year agreement with the nonprofit group, and that was that. Zakouma's fate was now in African Parks' hands.

I AWOKE AFTER AN ALL-TOO-SHORT NIGHT OF SLEEP, BUT EAGER TO SEE WHAT THE day held. The driver showed up ten minutes ahead of our scheduled 6:30 a.m. pickup, with Patrick already in the car, which we shared with a swarm of buzzing mosquitoes. *Glad I got that yellow fever vaccination,* I thought.

We swung by Chez Wou, a hotel that caters primarily to Chinese clientele but happens to be the Labuschagnes' accommodation of choice when in the capital. Rian emerged in his typical uniform of green shorts and sandals—a striking figure at six feet two. His deep-lined features, slightly reminisent of Picasso, seemed permanently set in a brooding scowl. As in Kenya, he struck me as both authentic and capable.

"Rachel, hello," he said, shaking my hand briskly.

"Rian, I brought you and Lorna foie gras that my father made himself!" Patrick cut in delightedly.

"Oh, so you're one of those people who enjoys torturing animals," Rian replied in a deadpan tone. Patrick seemed not to hear.

Joining us was also Chris Thouless, a visiting scientist from Kenya. I asked whether he'd ever been in Chad before. "No, but I was across the river in Cameroon twenty years ago, and there was fighting going on here—it was a bit mad and dangerous," he replied in a polished British accent. "So I've seen N'Djamena, but I've never been here before."

Chris spent the past twenty-five years in Africa, mostly Kenya, but in his youth he bounced around various university towns in the UK and United States, reflecting his physicist father's career trajectory. Just weeks before I met him, he had undertaken the last of such journeys, this time to Stockholm, where his father accepted the Nobel Prize in physics. Chris seemed to have inherited his dad's keen intelligence and focus: over the three days I spent with him, he hardly ever strayed from the topic of wildlife, even over drinks or breakfast. Like me, he was here to learn the secrets behind Zakouma's success—lessons he hoped to disseminate elsewhere in Africa through his job at Save the Elephants, a nonprofit founded by famed elephant expert Iain Douglas-Hamilton. The group conducts research and supports conservation projects, including those in need of emergency funds or that no one else will support.

With Rian and Chris now collected, we made the short drive back to the airport. But rather than going through security at the main building, we took a bumpy, unpaved back road that brought us directly onto the tarmac. We passed an Ethiopian Airlines jet and several UN Humanitarian Air Service planes before stopping at Rian's tiny Cessna 180, parked in some grass. It was painted green and white—African Parks' team colors—with the name "Minnie" printed on its side, in homage to a major Zakouma donor's wife. After a few inspections, the four of us squeezed in.

Rian pulled the plane out and radioed our intent to depart; there was no outbound traffic, and we were immediately cleared for the three-hour flight to Zakouma. "On hot days, there are mirages on this runway," he said just before advancing to full throttle. He earned his casual confidence in the cockpit, I later learned, through years of practice. Once, he even flew all the way from Chad to Tanzania without a break—an eleven-hour journey. When I asked how this was biologically possible, he replied, "I don't go to the bathroom. Others must use a bottle."

We lifted gently off the ground, and I pressed my face to the window, eager to get a view of N'Djamena. Glowing in the dusty morning haze and cradled by the Chari River's lazy loop, the city's few multistory hotels stood out against an otherwise flat landscape of squat buildings and bushy green trees. The streets were laid out on a neat grid, but within each of those orderly blocks was a scrambled mess of metal roofs, assembled willy-nilly like a pile of dominoes on the floor. Soon, any semblance of order disintegrated, replaced by haphazardly placed basic concrete buildings, which in turn gave way to brown, empty desert. Every now and then a small village appeared, the Hershey's Kiss–like thatched roofs of its residents' homes arranged in a circle. But mostly the land lacked all signs of human intrusion: no roads, no fields, no buildings.

"It's a remarkably empty country," Chris commented into his mic.

"Everyone is up north," Rian said. "But you won't find much wildlife outside of the national parks. Bushmeat isn't a big thing here, but in the dry season water runs out and the animals concentrate at the few remaining wet places. That's when people will shoot them, so they don't compete with the cattle. Everyone here has arms."

When we finally crossed into Zakouma's airspace, the landscape again changed, growing thicker with brush, most of it brown in the dry season. Here and there, a splash of football-field green surrounded thin puddles of muddy water tenaciously resisting the draw of the African sun. The grasslands were peppered with birds and beasts: ostrich, tiang, giraffe, roan antelope, hartebeest, and more. We flew over an 850-strong herd of buffalo, dust trailing in its wake like smoke, and stirred up a flock of several hundred of pink pelicans that looked like snow against the land.

"If everyone's stomachs are up to it, we can go see the elephants," Rian said.

"I'm up to it," Chris immediately replied.

I gave the thumbs up sign. Patrick was still snoozing.

"Okay, we're up to it. Patrick has no say," Rian said. "*Ou se trouve la position des elephants çe matin?*" he asked Zakouma's radio operator, making zero effort to make his French sound remotely French. A garbled answer came back. "They're about twenty kilometers from here," Rian said. He turned the plane in a southerly direction, gliding above a thin river and sending dozens of lounging crocodiles slithering into the latte-colored water.

Ten minutes later, the elephants came into view. My mouth fell open slightly at the sight: there were hundreds of them. Many were loitering around the muddy water, some with their trunks stuck out like straws, others just hanging out with friends and family. Babies slipped between adults' legs and imitated their elders with their tiny trunks, and adolescents wrestled, pitting mini-tusks against each other.

Rian turned the plane in a tight, tilted ellipse and circled the herd like a vulture. I felt the first hints of air sickness as the world sped by beneath us at an unnatural angle. We flew over the forest, brimming with yet more elephants on their way to the river. They marched in follow-the-leader lines of five or six, flowing through the trees like water on a windshield. We circled back around to the group in the river, and Rian dipped the plane low enough to send a jolt of eye-widening adrenaline through my body. *Dying in a fiery crash while observing one of the largest surviving herds of elephants in Central Africa wouldn't be the worst way to go,* I thought.

Rian performs overhead surveys like this one almost every morning to check on the animals and get a general lay of the land: "In an hour's time, I know exactly what's happening in the park. This stands in contrast to the pre–African Parks way of doing things," he said, which, at one point, didn't even include a plane. "I cannot imagine how you would manage the park without flying," Rian said. "You'd know what's happening fifty yards around you, but nowhere else."

Though the scene was dazzling, I was glad when we headed back to the base—the loop-the-loop ride had started to make me wonder whether the Cessna came stocked with barf bags. Zakouma's headquarters was marked by a small assembly of scattered buildings and a short airstrip. Rian's landing was so smooth as to be almost imperceptible.

We taxied down the dirt airstrip to a wide, open garage, and Rian cut the engine. Patrick, now awake, burst from the back with the exuberance of an eight-year-old making an entrance at his birthday party, wildly embracing a group of men who had gathered around the plane. They wore fitted camouflage pants, matching tight shirts, and big lace-up boots, and a couple sported black or camo-printed scarves draped around their heads and necks like Audrey Hepburn. Most were tall and young, and all were in very good shape.

I happily jumped into a round of introductions, shaking hands with the men. One asked me whether it was my first time in Zakouma, and I said, actually, it was my first time in Chad. "*Votre première fois au Tchad!? Ah, bienvenue!*" he exclaimed. Chris, meanwhile, wasted no time breaking out what I came to understand was his most precious possession, a pair of high-quality binoculars that support his voracious birding habit. He was peering intently at a tree where he'd already spotted a bee-eater with a snazzy emerald breast and ridiculously long tail feathers. For someone like Chris, Zakouma is nothing short of paradise: 389 species of bird are known to live here, with more added to the list each year.

Lorna joined us now, too, her slender frame petite next to Rian. She was all smiles and warmth—the perfect foil to his sternness.

"Shall we drop by the house for a coffee?" Lorna asked.

"That would be lovely," Chris said. I emphatically agreed.

THE LABUSCHAGNES LIVED IN A SQUAT CEMENT HOUSE PAINTED THE COLOR OF turmeric and surrounded by tall yellow grass and weedy brush. A punching bag hung outside in the sun (Rian's favorite outlet for releasing stress) and a rusty old Chinese machine gun—discovered half-buried in the garden when they first moved in—propped open the kitchen door. Despite the heat, inside it was cool as a cave, and the treasures found there reflected a lifetime of adventure, travel, and conservation: handwoven carpets and brightly stained leather poufs; walls decorated with masks, paintings, and prints of African places, people, and animals; and bookshelves brimming with dusty, cobweb-covered curios. The couple's bathroom reading, I amusedly noted, included riveting titles such as *Cessna Pilot* and *The Color Encyclopedia of Incredible Aeroplanes*.

The best part of the house, though, was the back porch. It overlooked a water hole, just steps away, where animals ranging from roan antelope and warthogs to eagles and finches stopped by daily for a dry-season drink. Of them all, the Labuschagnes' favorite visitor was an elephant bull named Hap Oor ("a bite out of the ear" in Afrikaans) for a large hole in his left ear. Sometimes, Lorna told me, Rian took out the hose and sprayed water directly into Hap Oor's grinning mouth.

Today, though, it wasn't Hap Oor but wealthy foreign funders who were visiting the Labuschagnes' porch, escorted by Josh Iremonger, a guide from Botswana with a Jesus-style haircut and goatee, and a camera lens as long as my arm. His clients, two older couples, had flown down from Europe to enjoy Zakouma's wildlife, which they directly support through donations from the major charities they run, the Dutch and Swedish Postcode Lotteries. Normally Rian and Lorna don't go out on safari with tourists, but they were making an exception for these generous VIPs.

Some people scoff at the idea of privileged Western visitors breezing through Africa on comfortable safaris. When I later posted a photo on Facebook of the Dutch and Swedish group having a candlelit dinner under the stars, for example, a friend snarked in the comments, "Are these all rich tourists getting an 'authentic' experience?" Although, yes, that is technically true, it's also true that the park couldn't exist without them. Chad certainly isn't going to cough up the $2 million-plus annually that it takes to run Zakouma, and African Parks secures its funds purely through donations. For the people who make that possible, a nice visit once in a while (which they also pay for) doesn't seem that outrageous an ask. That's not to say that the model isn't broken elsewhere, but, in the case of Zakouma, foreign visitors are a significant and genuine boon.

The funders had already been in Zakouma for nearly a week, and they had seen giraffe, buffalo, antelope, lions, birds galore, and even a leopard. But they had yet to see any of the park's famed elephants.

We all piled into a Toyota Land Cruiser, a former rebel vehicle that President Déby had donated to the park. When Rian first got it, it still had a machine gun mounted on top, but he transformed it into a bespoke tourist shuttle. He tricked it out with a roof made from a handwoven mat of the sort usually used by nomads for sleeping and installed seven cushy luxury 4 × 4 seats, which he had dug up on a trip to Dubai and had reupholstered in sumptuous local camel and cow leather.

"In Tanzania, you can just order a safari car," he said. "Here, you have to make it from scratch."

The jet lag and five-hour night of sleep were beginning to bite, and, as we set off down a bumpy dirt road, I couldn't help but promptly pass out into a shirt that Chris politely offered as a pillow. When the car came to a stop forty-five minutes later, I blearily looked up just in time to see an elephant sprint across the road and disappear into the thick bramble. We waited in tense silence for more elephants, but, when nothing happened, began inching slowly forward. The brush completely obscured the first elephant from sight, but we could hear it, and it seemed to be alone. Where, then, were all the others from Zakouma's five-hundred-strong herd?

We parked and walked down a steep hill toward a muddy river bank—the same one that all those crocodiles had been slithering into earlier, I uneasily realized. Piles of fresh dung, frisbee-sized footprints, and saplings snapped like twigs confirmed that the elephants had recently been by, and, as we got closer to the river, trumpeting and deep, growl-like noises revealed their current where-abouts, on the other side of the muddy water. Shining and still, the river stood between us like an uncrossable chasm.

"It's okay," one of the Dutch visitors said, not quite managing to conceal the disappointment in his voice. "It's never guaranteed to see them. They are wild animals." The group seemed resigned to give up.

Without a word, though, Rian took off his sandals and eased into the knee-deep water. He crossed over, put his shoes back on and disappeared up the bank, not looking back. We all stood there, staring. Time passed, and the group began to grow restless. Josh took a few photos with his phallic lens, Chris raised his binoculars to look for birds, and the tourists chatted among themselves and kicked at the dirt. I was just beginning to consider getting back into the car to go to sleep when Rian emerged from the forest and calmly crossed back over. "The elephants are over there," he stated matter-of-factly. "It's not deep, if you'd like to go see them. But it's up to you."

The Dutch couple immediately said they were in; the Swedish lady hesitated, but her husband firmly stated his intention to go. "Fine," she said. "Peer pressure."

I unlaced my shoes, took off my socks and stepped into the water. It was pleasantly warm and the slick mud—composed of a fair share of elephant poop—squished between my toes. I stumbled a couple of times, tripping on underwater pockmarks left by so many elephant feet, but managed to slowly waddle my way across.

We scrambled up the bank and quietly fell in line behind Rian, who navigated through the tall grass and thin trees with ease. We had walked about two hundred meters when Rian put up a hand in a "Halt!" motion and pointed. The elephants! We had caught them at lunch. Using their dexterous trunks, around fifty adults were stripping branches from trees and shoving the bushy end into their mouths like broccoli. A few babies moved around them, trunks flopping and charming in their awkwardness.

Suddenly, a large bull stepped out from behind a bush, maybe thirty feet from us. I took an instinctive step back. "Shhhh," said Rian under his breath. "Do not speak. Stand still." As if obeying that command, the bull—ears flared, head cocked at a haughty angle, and tusks gleaming in the afternoon sun—also froze. Clearly, he was considering what to do with us. I was suddenly thankful for the ranger who stood nearby with the gun strapped across his chest. Some of the tourists wildly snapped photos, though I could manage only a few, even as the moment stretched on for what seemed like minutes. Instead, I simply stood there, gawking. Finally—apparently deciding we weren't worth troubling with—the bull turned and lumbered back to his family.

Adrenaline-fueled elation coursed through us once we safely recrossed the river and returned to the car. "I've been a guide for fourteen years, and that was one of the most incredible elephant walking experiences I've ever had," Josh earnestly declared. "The hairs on my arms are still standing up."

"The crocodiles and the mud were pushing it with me," the Swedish lady said wryly.

"Not the big bull that could have charged us?" the Dutch guy replied, grinning at her. They all laughed.

Even Rian, who was sitting quietly in the front, looked pleased.

JUST A FEW YEARS AGO, THE CHANCE TO HAVE SUCH AN ENCOUNTER WITH ZAKOUma's elephants would have struck many as impossible: impossible that an increasing number of tourists are traveling to this remote corner of Central Africa, and impossible that the elephants there—traumatized by years of slaughter—would allow humans to approach so close. That the elephants still exist at all, however, would have seemed the biggest impossibility.

Their unexpected recovery was a mix of luck, trial and error, and expertise. The biggest factor, though, was Rian and Lorna's unparalleled devotion to saving the herd. On my second day in Zakouma, I joined the couple at dusk at Tinga Camp, where most of Zakouma's tourists stay, including Chris and me. We pulled up chairs outside of the elevated mess hall pavilion, next to a steep embankment that led down to a dry riverbed. Baboons wrestled and shrieked below, adding to the chirps, tweets, and trills of Zakouma's many birds that filled the calm air. This evening I was to hear just how they pulled off the success.

"It has more to do with experience than actual paper qualifications," Lorna began with a smile. "You'd think after thirty years of work, you wouldn't need more experience. But Zakouma has taught us a lot."

Five years ago, they were "living in paradise," as Rian put it, hunkered down in a little camp on a Tanzanian beach. They were working for Paul Tudor Jones II, a wealthy American businessman whose philanthropic projects include conservation in Africa. Though they loved their boss, as time passed they began to believe that they could be making a more significant difference elsewhere, at a site more desperately in need of help.

They'd scarcely put out word that they were in the market for a new job when a call came from a friend who worked at African Parks. A position had just opened in Chad, he said, and the two of them seemed a perfect fit. It wouldn't be easy, though; the place was being overrun by poachers, and the elephants seemed almost certainly doomed. But should Lorna and Rian succeed in turning the situation around, that victory would be entirely theirs and their team's. It sounded like exactly the challenge the Labuschagnes had hoped to find.

They knew nothing about Chad, however, and their first impression was not positive. "I didn't like it at all," Rian recalled of their initial visit to Zakouma. "It was so flat—there was nothing to climb." That Chadians speak French was also daunting, as neither of them spoke a word. Even more problematically they found themselves questioning the very premise of trying to implement conservation in a region gripped by so much turmoil. Flying over the park, they could see the white bones of elephants scattered all around. "There's no hope for it, nothing," Rian thought.

Yet, in the end, they decided to take the position. For one, their daughters—both of whom are even more hard core than their parents, having taken jobs in the Democratic Republic of the Congo and the Republic of the Congo—thought it was a great idea. It also helped that, just before they started at Zakouma, the family took a trip to Mali, where they attended a desert music festival in storied Timbuktu and journeyed by boat for three days along the Niger River. The trip was an eye-opener: they delighted in the Sahelian nomads' easy friendliness and warmed to the sprawling, flat landscapes. Perhaps they could grow to love Zakouma, after all.

Vacation time was over, though, when they arrived at their new post in early 2011. Immediately, they launched into action, starting with major changes to the work schedule. From now on, they announced, everyone stays at the park year-round, regardless of the rain. Not surprisingly, there was much grumbling, to the point of a near-revolt; the staff's months-long holiday, after all, was being taken away. But Rian and Lorna dug in their heels and insisted this was the way forward. They created an all-weather airstrip and hunkered down for their first rainy season.

Getting to know the animals they were tasked to protect was also a priority. They soon realized that no one really knew exactly where the elephants were at any given time. "Everyone had a different answer," Rian said. "They had no idea." So they put radio tracking collars on ten elephants and began monitoring their movements.

Once the elephants were found, rangers were needed to watch over them. Chadians have a strong horseback riding culture, and the Zakouma patrols had previously used horses. But their animals had all died before the Labuschagnes arrived, forcing the rangers to travel by foot. So African Parks brought in more horses, which the Labuschagnes realized are better suited to the challenging Zakouma landscape than bikes, boats, trucks, or motorcycles.

Communication was next on the list. Previously, the park had just a single satellite phone, which the Zakouma staff would fight over to use for personal conversations. Rian and Lorna brought in proper radios and installed a two-hundred-foot tall antenna whose coverage radius stretched nearly forty-five miles. They also gave radios to village elders outside of the park. Chad's agricultural communities and indigenous nomads do not usually engage in elephant poaching themselves, but for years they have borne the burden of poachers seeking free food on their way in and out of the park. "Chadians are a traveling people, and it's in their nature to offer help to people passing through," Rian said. "It's also difficult for poor villagers to say no, especially if the guys are armed." The Labuschagnes promised heightened security in the region and encouraged the elders to phone in suspicious activities.

Almost immediately, the villages began opening up. Some unscrupulous rangers, they learned, were using their position of power to extort money. Rian worked with Chad's ministry to dismiss those men and urged the elders to call them if any wise guys from Zakouma ever approached them again. That was only one facet of the corruption at play in the park, however. An internal investigation also revealed numerous "bad apple" rangers who were involved in the elephant killings themselves. Some sold information to poachers about where the elephants would be while others ensured criminals would not be caught by sending patrols in the opposite direction. Those men were obviously dismissed, as was the head of anti-poaching, who they discovered had been turned as well. By then, the Labuschagnes reputation in the region as powerful and omniscient had been solidified. "There were rumors that we knew everything that's going on," Rian said. "That was actually bullshit—we were walking in the dark—but the incident with the head of anti-poaching gave the impression that we're completely on top of it and we'd clean up anyone involved in it."

With the park finally free from corruption, it was time to whip the sixty remaining straight-arrow rangers into shape. Weapons skills is a necessary part of a Zakouma guard's job, but it became apparent that the men faced a steep learning curve. Most hailed from villages surrounding the park and were docile, good citizens with little or no experience handling guns, let alone dealing with potentially deadly criminals. The Sudanese men coming into Zakouma, in contrast, had "years and years of shooting and killing experience," Rian said. "They're like the Somalis. If we have a conflict with them, we know we just have to shoot it out."

Weapons themselves weren't a problem; the park had too many, Rian said, the result of President Déby, "in a sort of panic," sending two trucks loaded with ammunition when the poaching crisis was reaching its crescendo. Conflict engagement, however, was an issue. The rangers approached altercations as though they were Rambo, wildly spraying the area with bullets. "It was, shoot everything you have, and then go in and see if there's anything left," Rian said. "The more noise the better." Ask them to hit a simple target, however, and they struggled.

To transform them, Rian recruited Patrick, who started with the most basic of basics: paintball guns. From there, he followed the same steps he would had he been training the Paris SWAT force, including pistol, sniper, and combat shooting. The newly proficient rangers could now engage in gunfights using fewer bullets while landing more accurate shots. Just as important as the technical training, however, was the mental conditioning. Local lore has it that the Sudanese enjoy some sort of magical protection—that they have great power and cannot be harmed. "We had to build up the men's confidence and trust in themselves," Rian said. "We had to convince them, if you have an AK-47, you have a hell of a lot of power. You can do something."

By 2012, THEIR EFFORTS HAD PAID OFF: THINGS WERE LOOKING UP AT ZAKOUMA. The Labuschagnes knew of only seven elephants that had been killed the year before, and they felt ready to expand operations. Transmissions from the ten elephants' radio tracking collars indicated that, when the rains come, Zakouma's mighty herd splits, with two-hundred-odd members heading sixty miles north, to a water-logged marsh called Heban. Although the Heban site sits well beyond Zakouma's border, Rian considered it necessary to build an airstrip and a base there (it's too wet to drive in the rainy season). This allowed him to send rotating teams on two-week missions to keep an eye on the demi-herd, once it moved north that year.

In August, a group of six men nicknamed Team Buffalo spotted the tracks of three horses and one person. Ibet Idriss, Buffalo's leader, suspected that whoever left the tracks was up to no good, and he radioed in the information. Sure enough, the next afternoon the rangers heard around fifty gunshots. The weather was too poor for anyone to fly up from Zakouma, however, and team Buffalo didn't manage to locate the site of the shooting on foot. When the plane reached them the following day, the pilot spotted the poacher's camp from the air and discovered the poached remains of a collared elephant known as Z6, her tusks still attached.

Team Buffalo organized a raid of the poacher's camp, but, when they arrived, they found only one very surprised man there. He opened fire and they returned shots, but he bolted and managed to escape. Looking around them, the rangers realized they had stumbled on a formidable elephant-killing operation. They confiscated over a thousand rounds of ammunition plus solar panels, satellite and cell phones, tools, horse medicine from Sudan, and a large stash of powdered and dried food.

They also found evidence pointing to the men's involvement with the Sudanese army, including military uniforms and a faded, handwritten note issued by a Sudanese military commander giving leave to his soldiers, whom he identified by ID number and name. The military link was later confirmed by C4ADS, a nonprofit organization that analyzes global conflict and transnational security issues; by the Enough Project, another nonprofit, dedicated to combatting genocide; and by Interpol. "Sudan is under sanctions, and with the dry-up of oil, it is currently unable to pay its Darfur militias and paramilitaries except in allowing them to loot, raid, or—in this case—kill elephants," one expert told Lorna and Rian. (That the Sudanese government is involved in illegal ivory trade is not breaking news. As far back as 1997, Esmond Bradley Martin found evidence that soldiers and other government officials were the main supplier of tusks in Sudan.)

With their camp destroyed and horses and possessions confiscated, the soldiers-cum-poachers were now stranded in the middle of nowhere with zero logistical support. Everyone at Zakouma assumed the threat had been neutralized, that the criminals would have no choice but to slink back to Sudan, tails between their legs.

That's not what happened, though. Nearly a month after the raid, early the morning of September 3, the poachers crept into the rangers' camp. Crouching behind the sleeping men's tents, they silently waited in the dark until the sky began to lighten and the Zakouma guards emerged from their tents. As they knelt for their morning prayer, the poachers opened fire. Five of the rangers sustained multiple gunshot wounds and fell to the ground, dead. A sixth, Hassan Djibrine, ran.

Djimet Seid, the camp manager and cook, was also shot but managed to hide in some bushes. Bleeding and trembling, he watched the poachers load up four of the rangers' horses with firearms and ammunition, and then flee the scene. Even after they'd gone, Djimet remained frozen for several hours. He finally summoned the courage to limp back to camp, where he moved two of the bodies into a hut and—too exhausted to do more—covered the other three with tarps. Somehow, he then managed to walk and swim twelve miles to the nearest village to get help.

When word got back to Zakouma, shock spread through the staff. Rian had not seen this coming—no one had. In hindsight, however, the event made sense: the poachers, in a way, had no choice but to attack the rangers' camp. "They couldn't just go back to Sudan empty-handed and say, 'This is what happened, sorry,'" Rian said. "They'd probably be shot." With the Zakouma horses and weapons in tow, however, they could return victorious and proud for having retaliated. (Notably, however, their loot did not include ivory from the elephants they had killed.)

The Labuschagnes obviously wanted to launch into immediate action. The poachers were on the loose, and Hassan, the ranger who had fled, was still out there. But local Chadian officials would not let Rian or his men go to Heban, claiming it was too dangerous. "We couldn't even put anyone on their tracks, because the government was worried about everyone's safety," Rian said. In the meantime, the culprits had ample time to escape.

An excruciating five days after the incident, they were finally allowed to fly north. The camp was a horror show. The place had been completely ransacked, and in the heat and damp, the men's bodies had begun to decompose, as had the bloated remains of one of the horses lying nearby. Rian had brought a doctor and a spiritual leader along to confirm the manner of death, and to perform a short ceremony. The bodies were impossible to move, so the team—joined by villagers who had made the long walk to offer help—dug graves right where the men had fallen. They left the spots unmarked, as is often the custom in Chad, but "we made sure it was done in a good way," Rian said. Later, he installed a small brass memorial plaque, though the last time he was there, he found that children had vandalized it.

As for Hassan, the ranger who disappeared, no one ever heard from him again, but he is presumed dead. The area he fled into is a solid wilderness of thick vegetation submerged in deep water. The other rangers at Zakouma believed that Hassan could swim, but, even so, drowning is a possibility, and he could have also been shot; Djimet, the cook, wasn't sure. Although the Labuschagnes put together a ten-man search party after they secured permission to fly north, at the last minute, Hassan's family called it off. "It's the will of God," they told Lorna and Rian.

Understandably, morale at Zakouma hit an all-time low following the incident. Rian and Babakar Matar Breme, the assistant park manager, had to go house to house, informing the deceased rangers' families that their husbands and fathers would not be coming home. Many of them had multiple wives, fifteen children or more, and had been the sole breadwinners. "It was very, very difficult," Rian said. Meanwhile, many of the remaining rangers went on strike for two weeks, and some used the incident to demand higher pay. African Parks—and Rian and

Lorna personally—faced accusations and grilling from the government: Why did they send so few people so far outside of Zakouma's boundary, and why didn't they react when villagers spotted strangers still in the area? How could they have let this happen? They could only apologize and answer honestly, knowing all the while that even as they sat in long meetings, answering the same questions over and over again, they were losing more precious time that could have been spent pursuing the poachers before they crossed back into Sudan.

It was tempting to call it quits right there, but Rian and Lorna did the opposite. The Heban incident made them all the more determined to forge ahead and ensure that their men had not died in vain. More than anything, they wanted to catch the killers. Intelligence gathering was the first step: they extracted more than 150 numbers from the poachers' cell and satellite phones—all contacts in Sudan and Chad—and handed the evidence over to the police. They also had the phones' text messages translated, which—though peppered with military acronyms—proved disappointing. The majority were ads and hypocritical Koranic verses, considering the phones' owners:

> Smiling in the face of the morally corrupt is a charitable work, and frowning is a declaration of war on others. Meet your brother with a smiling face.
>
> He who sows goodness reaps tranquility and he who sows evil will reap thunderstorms. You should choose what you want to sow.
>
> The mansions of paradise draw near by prayer. And if you do not pray, then you stop the angels from building your mansion. Remember Allah and He will remember you.

Photos on the phones proved more interesting. One showed three people standing in front of a bushy green tree: a man in a clean white shirt with soft, gently smiling features (he was later identified as leader of the poaching group); a preteen boy in a button-down baby blue shirt, his hand affectionately placed on the man's shoulder; and a woman in a long red head scarf and a black dress, caught mid-blink. They just looked like a normal family. Other images showed several women—beautiful and young—with ornate tattoos on the bits of their bodies not concealed by scarves and long, bright dresses.

The Labuschagnes made fliers featuring these photos and offered a reward for information. They also distributed images of the unique horse saddles the poachers had stolen (Lorna has them custom made in South Africa to fit Chad's horses, which tend to be on the small side). Despite the efforts, nothing came back. No calls, no intel—nothing.

Unbeknownst to the Labuschagnes, though, one of the murdered rangers' family members was also pursuing the case. A traveling trader whose work often took him to Sudan, months later he caught word that one of the poachers, a man named Soumaine Abdoualye Issa, was hiding out in a village near the Chadian boarder. The trader spoke with his guard buddies on either side of the border, and they agreed to help him arrest and extricate the poacher. They succeeded. On the way to prison, the authorities stopped by Zakouma to allow Rian and several others to question him.

Soumaine was a small man, standing at just five foot six and wearing no shoes. Though physically unremarkable, he left a chilling impression. "He had absolutely no fear," Rian recalled. "No fear of dying." Speaking Chadian Arabic through a translator, Soumaine straightforwardly told his story. He was born in 1985 in Chad and is primarily a nomadic herder. He often takes his animals into Sudan. Recently, he was passing through Kutum—a dingy desert town in north Darfur, plagued by unrest and lawlessness—when he heard talk that several men were preparing for an elephant poaching mission to Chad. It sounded like a pretty good gig to Soumaine, so he contacted them.

The men—two of whom were brothers—told him they'd done this before but that they could use some additional help. Mohammed al-Tijani Hamdan—the sweet-looking guy from the family photo—was the leader; he was not rich, but he was perceptive. "He has an ability to recognize a person who is scared," Soumaine said. "He looks in your eyes and he can see if you are a warrior or not, [a man] who is brave and who will follow him. He is a known poacher on that side of Sudan." Like any scrupulous employer, though, Mohammed—who Soumaine said has a military background—was looking for someone with relevant experience. "Why should I hire you?" he asked.

Soumaine proudly described his involvement in the 2007 Mahamat Nouri rebellion: "I can use a firearm and I am not afraid."

He got the job.

Before the mission, the men played a traditional card game meant to reveal their fate and determine whether they should proceed. Soumaine's card, to his dismay, was black. "I knew that I would be arrested during this mission," he said. "I could feel it." But he wanted the money, so he shrugged it off and reassured his partners that he was still in.

The four set out for Chad with three horses, four guns, and 4,500 rounds of ammunition. As Soumaine pointed out, "You can buy firearms everywhere in Sudan." The journey went fairly smoothly; they sold around five hundred rounds of ammunition in a market along the way, and although they exchanged some bullets with border guards, they managed to skirt capture by fording a river at night. "We were not afraid of anybody," Soumaine said. "We openly walked with firearms."

All told, it took them fourteen days to reach Heban. "We knew that elephants would be in this area because everybody knows that during the rainy season the elephants leave the park and come to the Heban area," Soumaine said matter-of-factly. He and his colleagues also knew that Zakouma had brought in a new aircraft, and that the rangers there were starting to make poaching more difficult. "You have to prepare better if you're attacking the Zakouma elephants, and pay more attention," Soumaine said. "We'd rather take a chance when the elephants are outside the park, in the rainy season."

It was Soumaine's first time in the area, but the others "knew it very well," he said. They sought out the location of the elephants from a local they met— Soumaine recalled only that the man had a limp—who pointed them in the right direction. They knew he had told them the truth when they heard trumpeting and bellowing at night.

The four men established a system: the military guys would go off to poach, and Soumaine would stay behind to keep an eye on the camp and make tea (perhaps he wasn't quite as skilled with weapons as he had claimed). The poachers hunted at midday, usually shooting the animals behind the front legs to cripple them. They killed nine elephants in four days—a pace they intended to keep up for some time. They didn't know who they'd sell the ivory to when they returned to Sudan, but they were confident that they would easily find a buyer. "The prices are growing," Soumaine said. He was looking forward to celebrating.

Things were going so well, in fact, that even as they ramped up operations in Heban, they discussed future trips to collect more ivory, weighing the pros and cons of various hunting grounds. Chad's elephants were the closest, Mohammed mused, but Cameroon and the Central African Republic's wildlife defenses are so shoddy that all you really have to do is show up. Indeed, eight months before Soumaine set off for Heban, a safari lodge operator in Cameroon's Bouba N'Djida National Park—about four hundred miles from Zakouma—had sent word to the Cameroonian government that poaching was on the rise. No response came, and the Janjaweed poachers continued to pour into the protected area, bringing with them AK-47s, RPG-7 rocket-propelled grenade launchers, and M80 explosives. "Don't worry," they told the spooked villagers living nearby. "We'll be here for three months, and in that time we plan to kill as many elephants as possible. Then we'll leave." True to their word, they soon left, leaving behind the bodies of at least three hundred elephants. The government never showed.

In Chad, however, things did not go so smoothly for the poachers. On August 12, the Zakouma rangers burst into the men's camp, sending Soumaine fleeing. "We lost everything," he said. He and the other three poachers survived on guinea hens and a gazelle they shot, and they also secured some flour from a local village, but the situation was becoming dire. "It was not enough food," he said. "We decided to attack the guards."

Soumaine claimed he was not involved in the assassination mission itself. He waited behind. When his partners returned, they came with horses, arms, and food. There was no ivory, but at least they had something. When they finally reached Sudan nine days later, however, an argument broke out about how to divide the Zakouma camp booty, and Soumaine got ditched. No doubt disappointed, he sold his assault rifle—all he had to show for his involvement in the expedition.

With that, he concluded the story: "I admit guilt in elephant poaching and the death of Zakouma scouts."

Everyone in the room believed that Soumaine was telling the truth, and, indeed, much of what he said corroborated what the team already knew happened, or suspected had happened. "The only gray area is whether he was actually there with the shooting of the scouts," Rian said. The authorities took Soumaine to a military camp jail. After a month, though, there was a mysterious prison break. Many people escaped, including Soumaine. There were rumors of bribes sent from his family, and of government involvement.

"It's very difficult for an outsider to understand," Rian said. "We may say the government is useless and corrupt for letting all these people get out of prison, but we don't understand how families and people sort these things out among themselves. You have to be born here to understand how that works, and you shouldn't apply a Western legal system way of thinking about how things are done. The legal system here exists on paper, but down on the ground, it doesn't function. Things are judged in a different way."

No further leads ever surfaced on Soumaine's whereabouts, and the government soon dropped the case. "Very quickly, things here are forgotten," Rian said.

As for the other three men involved in the crime, they also escaped justice: "They disappeared into the Sudan, and there was nothing more."

HEBAN WAS A TRAGEDY LIKE NO OTHER IN THE PARK'S HISTORY. YET SOME PROG-ress came of the incident. For one, it raised Zakouma's international profile. The *New York Times, National Geographic,* CNN, and other major media outlets all ran stories about the park's struggle and loss. Donations came pouring in, which the Labuschagnes used to purchase a second aircraft along with better communication equipment, firearms, and ammunition.

They also decided to create an elite group of specially trained rangers, called the Mambas. Patrick handpicked top performers and instructed them in the science of evidence gathering, in effective combat shooting, and in rapid deployment. Unlike the men at Heban, some of whom were in their fifties—"good ol' eco-guards," as Rian described—all of the Mambas are young and super fit.

Issa Idriss, twenty-one, works as a Zakouma ranger and driver for the Mambas, and he hopes to someday earn a coveted spot on the team. Soft spoken and shy in my presence, he fidgeted and hunched in his tough army greens when I met him briefly at headquarters. But despite his introversion and baby face, he already has an adult's outlook on life: His father was one of the men gunned down at Heban.

Upon hearing the terrible news, his first reaction was worry for his twenty-one siblings who were now stranded without a breadwinner. "My father taught me to be a good man," he said. "We used to sit around the fire, and he'd tell me about life. He wanted me to work hard so I could look after my brothers and sisters."

To Issa's relief, African Parks provided money to support the family, including a new house and education for the children (the Chadian government provided no additional support). Within a year, Issa secured a job at Zakouma. Rather than feel resentful toward the park for costing his father his life, he felt proud and thankful for the opportunity. "My father died because he was looking after the reserve," Issa said. "He died for the elephants. He knew it was dangerous work, but he wanted to keep it safe. He didn't want everyone coming in and killing everything. He liked this job very much, and he liked the reserve. I now work here, as my father would have wanted, and someday I want my sons and daughters to work here, too. That would make me happy."

Heban changed not only the rangers' behavior but also the elephants'. Immediately after the shooting, something seemed to click in their minds: all two hundred of them headed straight back to the park. They've remained there ever since, no longer undertaking their long rainy season journey north. In that way, they have aided in their own recovery by making the job of protecting them that much easier.

Since 2012, the news out of Zakouma has been predominately positive. When I visited in January 2017, it had been a year since the park had lost any elephants that they knew of ("It's unbelievable how quickly a carcass disappears," Rian pointed out), and, despite the twenty-five elephants killed on the Labuschagnes' watch, very little ivory has left the park since 2011. All the naysayers in the government, including Dolmia, have also come around. It took a couple of years, but even he had to admit that African Parks was doing a good job. "It was a really slow process for me," he said. "But I finally realized that they did have the capacity and the skill and knowledge to manage the park. Rian has done a fantastic job. I don't know of any other park manager who did as great of a job as he was able to do."

Perhaps the strongest marker success, though, is the fact that the elephants have begun to behave again like proper elephants. For the first two years that Lorna and Rian lived at Zakouma, they saw just one new calf—a chillingly abnormal situation, like *Children of Men* but for pachyderms. Lorna and Rian believe the elephants were simply too stressed to reproduce. By 2013, though, it seemed that they were finally beginning to relax enough to get down to business. Twenty-one tiny calves appeared, followed by another fifty over the next two years and seventy in 2016. The herd—one of the largest in Africa—is growing: from around four hundred elephants in 2012, the count now exceeds five hundred. Rian expects the park will break a thousand in seven or eight years.

"One part of it is we just came in at the right time," Rian said, explaining his and Lorna's success. "If it would have been a thousand elephants broken into four groups, then we probably would have had a harder time. I think the biggest thing we did is, every time something happened, we learned and over-strengthened the system. You shouldn't just say it's normal to have an elephant killed. Nothing is normal in an elephant being killed. You have to absolutely overreact."

As he and Lorna spoke to me of these things in the fading light at Camp Tinga, one of those very elephants decided to come say hello. For much of our chat, a bull had been munching on trees a comfortable distance away, but now he seemed singularly focused on our group. His towering bulk was headed straight toward us.

"Oh, this is the elephant with the sore ear," Rian said calmly, rising to his feet. So, this was the famous Hap Oor.

"He's fine, though," Rian continued. "I've watched him eat and he's fine."

Is he fine? I wondered incredulously. The elephant was gargantuan—at least ten feet tall—and his tusks stuck out from either side of his trunk like giant skewers for human shish kabobs.

"Awww," Lorna cooed. "Well he's obviously happy to be here. I think he likes to be around people."

Rian hastily moved up to the elevated mess hall pavilion, which put him at eye level with Hap Oor. He'd procured a teapot and was slowly pouring a thin stream of water from its spout onto the ground, apparently as an enticement. "Hap Oor, come!" he called affectionately but sternly, as though speaking to a mischievous mutt. "Come and say hello!"

The elephant didn't even look over. Instead, his gaze continued to fixate on Lorna and me. I began to feel uneasy.

"Come, Hap Oor! Come!"

The elephant took another step toward us.

I stopped typing and smiled nervously at Lorna. "Is this okay?" I asked, quietly but urgently.

Her face now registered a degree of worry. "Be very still," she said softly. "Don't make a sound." When a woman who has spent thirty years living among elephants seems concerned about an elephant standing ten feet away, well . . . let me just say the effect is like a pilot coming over the loudspeaker and saying, "Brace for impact."

Oh, God.

In addition to Lorna's unease, my panic also stemmed from a story Chris had told me earlier that day, in which he had swiftly annihilated my blissful ignorance concerning the nature of elephants and the degree of danger those lovable animals pose to people. It started innocently enough, with a lunchtime discussion of the previous afternoon's extraordinary elephant encounter.

"So is it not at all dangerous, getting so close to the elephants as we did yesterday?" I had obliviously asked him, remembering a talk I'd heard in Kenya about sometimes lethal human-elephant conflicts.

He gave me a long look.

"I was probably the most nervous person in the group yesterday," he said at last, "because I've seen firsthand what elephants can do. Though I was comforted by the thought that some of the others in that group were probably slower sprinters than me." He chuckled wryly.

I waited for him to elaborate, but he seemed disinclined. Curiosity would not allow me to let this go, though.

"Have you had many close calls?"

"Yes."

Another long pause.

"For example . . . ?"

"I once saw someone get run through with a tusk."

Oh sweet Lord.

"After you see that, it changes you. I got a medal from the queen for saving that person, actually, who happened to have just been appointed to be my boss. The elephant ran its tusk through her leg, then picked her up with its trunk and broke a bone in her neck. It had just thrown her to the ground and was kneeling—it had short tusks so it couldn't use them effectively from a standing position—and it was about to deliver the coup de grâce when I came at it. I didn't think, I just reacted. I ran up and bashed it in the head with my hand."

"Wow . . . she must have been a very good boss!" I mustered weakly, unable to think of an appropriate response to a story like that.

"Well, not quite that—I didn't want my project to end if she got killed. I was quite enjoying the job!"

We both laughed.

"Did you consider switching to a different research focus after that?" I asked. "I don't know that I'd be able to work with elephants ever again if that had happened to me."

"Oh yes. After the incident, it took me a long time to get back to the point that I'd be close to elephants on foot in thick bush. Anything can set them off, especially the bulls. It could be that they lost a fight earlier that day and they're in a bad mood, or that they're just put out with life in general and they decide to take it out on you. My principle now is always run if they come for you with intent. No matter how calm they are, you have to remember that they're capable of taking you apart in a moment."

Taking you apart. Back at Camp Tinga, that was the precise phrase that came to mind as Hap Oor continued to take step after step toward Lorna and me. Should he decide to charge, there was nowhere for us to go. The steep riverbank was to our backs and a curtain of thick brush boxed us in to the right. Unlike during the encounter yesterday, I was well aware that there were no armed rangers around to intervene in case things went south, while valiant, medal-winning

Chris couldn't save us, either, as he was out on an evening safari. I felt utterly vulnerable, my fate completely in the hands (or trunk) of this wild animal.

Rian, though, wasn't going to just stand by. Yet if he feared for his wife and this rando journalist guest, he did not show it. Confidently and calmly he descended the pavilion steps, all the while still holding the teapot out in front of him.

"Hap Oor! Hap Oor, come!" he commanded. To my utter relief, the bull froze. He still faced Lorna and me, but he seemed distracted now. Lorna's eyes were fixed attentively on the elephant, but her features were now a mask—impossible to tell whether she was reciting the Lord's Prayer or this was just another day at the park for her.

Hap Oor, at last, turned toward Rian. I let out my breath, which I realized I'd been holding. My hands, I noticed, were shaking.

Lorna allowed herself a small smile. "Rian, that's enough," she called, softly but forcefully. Rian led the elephant around the campfire pit and toward the brush, walking backwards so as not to avert his eyes from the bull. Hap Oor, either finally taking the hint that he was imposing or maybe just bored with us, shouldered his way into the bushes, where he began placidly eating again.

Rian coolly retook his seat. "He's dominant—he won't take shit from you— but I believe that he will not come and smash and charge you," he said. "Unless, that is, he's in musk."

That was hardly a reassurance, but I'd take it. Trying to conceal my trembling hands, I opened my computer back up and cleared my throat.

"So! Um . . . we were talking about what else has led to Zakouma's success?"

Rian resumed the conversation as though nothing had happened. "You can always say you'll bring in an expat or another consultant to prop up the thing, but if you get the people living around that park to take ownership, then you have the best chance of survival," he said. "Local schoolchildren from around the region are the future of this place."

Given that simple fact, each day in the dry season the Labuschagnes bus in 40 people from surrounding villages, many of them kids. The numbers quickly add up: more than 5,000 people made the journey last year. The Labuschagnes meet with them on their porch (sometimes introducing them to Hap Oor) and tell them about the park, why they're here, and what they hope to accomplish. The guests take a game drive, enjoy a meal, and everyone leaves with a T-shirt that says, "I visited Zakouma."

"They've been living close to the park but have never seen a giraffe or an elephant or a roan antelope," Lorna said. She added that Chadians pay no entrance fee at Zakouma, and they can stay here for free (their costs are largely subsidized by foreign visitors). "The mistake most parks make is they don't allow the local population to come in for nothing or for a very small amount," Lorna said. "We felt it was more important to get people here than to get a park fee out of them."

In conservation, of course, you can never fully breathe a sigh of relief. A protected place, a group of animals—they always face the possibility of destruction. No matter how well things are going, the situation could change.

Indeed, in some ways, Zakouma's success is the biggest threat to its future. As the elephants start feeling safer, they will probably break into smaller groups and begin straying outside of the park's borders once again, making the task of protecting them more difficult. According to Chris, "That's something African Parks will likely have to face up to over the next few years."

There is a strong chance, though, that the elephants will soon have a second safe haven to go to, should their population outgrow Zakouma. In October 2017 President Déby gave African Parks managerial control of a nearby 1-million-acre reserve called Siniaka-Minia. Although the place has been protected on paper for years, on the ground it is not. Allowing African Parks to take the reserve under its wing will bring funding and rangers and create a possible future migration site for Zakouma's growing elephant population.

Rian and Lorna, however, will not be around to see those goals realized. They recently decided to move on; their last day at Zakouma was just a few short weeks after my visit. When they told Patrick this news over dinner the first night, his eyes widened: "No! It is a disaster!" But they don't see it that way. They are happy with the work they've done at the park, but they feel it's time to allow someone with different ideas and strengths to make Zakouma even better.

Regardless of who takes up the managerial post, though, they have the utmost confidence in the team they've built. Zakouma's employees—from the men taking care of the horses to the rangers out in the field—want the park to work. They're proud of it, and they're also enterprising. Should something change, Rian has faith that they would be able to adapt. As he said, "If you leave, if there's political turmoil—whatever happens—so long as you have the support of the people on the ground, that team goes forward."

MY THREE DAYS AT ZAKOUMA PASSED ALL TOO QUICKLY, AND I FOUND MYSELF
wishing I'd booked more time there. The evening before my departure, we took
a drive. Hoary buffalo with birds perched comically on their horned heads glow-
ered at us from the side of the road, and giraffe ran across the grassy savanna so
gracefully it was as though they were moving in slow motion. We passed hartebeest with crazily stretched out faces (I called them weirdos, and Chris noted,
seemingly only half in jest, "It's possible that they think we look funny") as well
as taiga antelope, reedbuck, and waterbuck. An Egyptian mongoose shot into the
brush, and we stopped to let a four-foot-long constrictor cross the road. All we'd
missed was a pangolin, though as Chris jokingly told me, "You don't deserve a
pangolin! You have to put in twenty years of effort first." (He'd recently had his
very first pangolin sighting, recalling, "The sound of a pangolin is like wind rus-
tling through dry leaves.")

Above all else, though, there were the birds. Every few moments we stopped
so Chris and Lorna could grab their binoculars and get a close-up look at the
latest feathered specimen.

"Chris, what's that one?" I asked, pointing to a tomato-red bird with a tur-
quoise head and downwardly curved beak.

"Carmine bee-eater, like the color."

"How about those?"

"Those would be—what are those—ah yes, saddle-billed storks."

"And that one?"

"That's a ground hornbill."

"But he's in a tree!"

"Ahem, the name does not change just because the bird is in a tree!"

We stopped the car as the sun was touching down on the horizon, igniting
the sky pastel pink, yellow, and orange. Beers miraculously appeared, as they
tend to do at sundown in Africa, and Rian, ever the badass, popped them open
with a knife. Lorna chatted amicably with a couple of other guests who had
stopped by, and Rian gazed at the picture-book scene in front of us, scowling
in deep thought. Hundreds of pink pelicans, all settling in for the evening, were
chatting up a storm mere feet in front of us.

"Hey Chris," I said, grinning, "what are the pelicans saying?"

He paused, then puckered his lips like a beak, permitting himself to play
along: "Oh, chaps! There are people! The sun is about to go down! We must talk
about it!"

It was a great last night.

The next morning, Chris and I climbed into Zakouma's second Cessna, the one purchased after the Heban incident. This one was named Nikolai, after a donor's dog. Jérôme, a French veterinarian-cum-pilot who recently joined the team, would be flying us back to N'Djamena. ("The job's not as romantic as it sounds, but you can still find romantic moments," he told me whimsically.)

As we gently lifted off, I looked down to see Rian and Lorna. They'd driven to the edge of the runway in their former rebel vehicle, ensuring, to the very end, that we were taken care of. Both were smiling and waving, their arms held high as if in jubilation.

Chris would later tell me that Zakouma's recovery is extraordinary, that the Labuschagnes played a phenomenal role in saving the park's elephants, which otherwise would almost certainly be confined solely to memory today. What's more, he continued, Zakouma serves as an inspiration to other parks across Africa, proof that—no matter how desperate the situation may seem—there is still a chance of turning things around, so long as the leadership is strong and the team is devoted and steadfast.

Seeing Rian and Lorna together there on the runway, waving in unison in the golden Chad dawn, I had no doubt that it was their fierce commitment—not only to wildlife, but also to each other—from which they drew the strength to give Zakouma's elephants a future.

Eleven

IF RHINOS COULD CHOOSE

Squinting in the morning light, I awoke as the car turned onto a bright orange dirt road crossing a flat expanse of stunted gray shrubs and pale dry grass. I'd flown into Johannesburg hours earlier from the United States and was headed southwest, toward a town called Klerksdorp where I had an unusual appointment: a visit to the world's largest rhino ranch. While there, I'd interview the owner and witness dehornings, a veterinary procedure that involves sawing off a sedated rhino's horns. Unlike elephant tusks, which are teeth, rhino horns, being more akin to fingernails or hair, grow back when cut. Over the course of a thirty-five- to forty-year life, a rhino on an eighteen-month trimming schedule will produce about 130 pounds of horn.

Noticing I was awake, my driver, Gerhard Oosthuizen, greeted me. "This is very much the heartland of South Africa," he said in a thick Dutch Afrikaans accent. Turning onto an even narrower dirt road, we stopped at a white gate adorned with two signs. One warned, "Dangerous Animals"; the other depicted a rhino with a red *X* over it and "Anti Poaching Unit Armed Patrol" written beneath.

"It's been thirty or forty years since I opened a farm gate," Gerhard said. Jumping out of the car, he asked me to take a photo of him, to show his kids.

Rhinos—bovine-like and placidly grazing—appeared here and there on either side of the road. Rather than dagger-like points, their horns were flattened tree stumps—the result of regular dehornings. We passed a farmhouse with a bright green lawn filled with geese and chickens, and trees just beginning to put out yellow-green spring leaves. Funny little rodents that looked like crosses

between a squirrel, chipmunk, and prairie dog—South African ground squirrels,
I later learned—popped up out of the weeds to check us out.

Beyond the farmhouse, more rhinos came into view. "This gang's got rhinos
like others have cattle!" Gerhard noted with enthusiasm. "It's just sickening what
the poachers are doing to our country's assets. That the government can't stop
it—well, it makes me wonder if they're in on the take."

"In on the take?"

"That they're involved! I must say, though, it's awful nice to get someone
from New York writing about our rhino problem."

That South Africa has a rhino problem is well known. The country is home
to around 70 percent of the world's 30,000 remaining rhinos, but since 2013
poachers have killed more than one thousand rhinos annually in South Africa
alone. Not all were government property. South Africa allows for private ownership of wildlife, and over 30 percent of the country's 20,000-odd rhino fall into
this category. Of the 6,000 or so poached there since 2008, 1,200 were killed on
private land. Some rhino owners and their staff have been stabbed, raped, and
attacked by poachers, and around seventy individuals have called it quits as a
result. They simply could no longer handle the economic or emotional trauma of
keeping rhinos.

Many South Africans fervently believe that the killing can be significantly
curbed with a simple solution: making the sale of rhino horns legal. Of the country's 330 private owners, 85 percent are in favor of this scheme. This includes
John Hume, the owner of the ranch I was visiting today. Hume owns more rhinos
than anyone else in the world—1,400 and counting—and his stockpiled horn collection is likewise the largest possessed by an individual. He and another private
rhino owner named Pelham Jones are among the most outspoken proponents of
the legal trade. (Jones, however, is more demure than Hume when it comes to
revealing his rhino number: "It's like asking how much money you have in the
bank," he said.)

Jones got involved in 2008, after learning that two rhinos had been poached
at a private ranch near his home. The news rattled him, and he suspected it was
a harbinger of things to come. "You just had to look north over our border, to
Zimbabwe and beyond, to clearly see what was happening," he said. Sure enough,
South Africa's long-standing record as a safe haven for rhinos was soon undone.
"All of a sudden, it came in very aggressively," he said. "You didn't have to be
a rocket scientist to work out that the criminal poaching syndicates had finally

realized that we weren't as tough as we portrayed ourselves to be—that we were actually a vulnerable target. They've exploited us ever since."

When Jones learned that despite the increasing danger posed to rhinos and their owners there was no official representative body looking out for people in his position, he founded a nonprofit organization called the Private Rhino Owners Association. Although Jones may at first seem like an unlikely crusader—his grey mustache, glasses, and receding hairline reminded me of my freshman biology professor—he has been tirelessly advocating on behalf of his members ever since. As one source told me, "Pelham doesn't stop talking. I went to a meeting last year where he and another guy got into a fight and Pelham got punched—and he still didn't stop talking!"

Legalization of rhino horn trade is high on the group's agenda. "If legal trade is allowed, it would give us revenue back to pay for the cost of security and conservation," Jones said. "The rhino will overnight become the most valuable—and accordingly—most protected animal on the African continent."

To be clear, no one thinks that legalizing trade in rhino horn is the silver bullet to end the killings. Doing that will require a multipronged attack that includes, among other things, strengthening law enforcement and reducing demand for rhino horn. But legalized sales could earn funds for more rhino protection. As Michael 't Sas-Rolfes, a conservation economist and mid-career doctoral candidate at the University of Oxford, explained, "You sell the product to get money to invest in more protection, more rangers, more sophisticated surveillance equipment— whatever it takes to make it more expensive and difficult for poachers."

The proceeds from horn sales could indeed pay for a considerable amount of heightened protection: Hume alone has around five tons in storage, worth some $45 million.

EIGHT RHINOS HAD ALREADY BEEN DEHORNED THAT DAY BY THE TIME GERHARD and I arrived at Hume's sprawling property, and a handful more were on the roster for the morning. Two white Toyota pickups, both adorned with rhino emblems, met us near the farmhouse. Their beds were crowded with men in bright blue Dickies-like work suits. "Hop in the back, and hold on," commanded the ranch manager, Johnny, who was driving one of the vehicles.

Careful not to flash the men as I climbed up in my dress, I'd barely taken a seat atop a precariously balanced box when the truck zoomed forward. We sped across the property, passing rhino after rhino and squinting in the gritty wind. "Mind your lens," said Rory Turbitt, a gruff but friendly guy with pointed features, a mess of dark hair, and skin reddened by the sun. "The dust recently got into another journalist's camera and broke it."

Shouting above the roar of the wind, Rory explained that he was a former PH, or professional hunter, who now did security for Hume. Testifying to this fact, his left arm bore a rhino tattoo with "APU" (anti-poaching unit) written under its trotting feet. I was surprised to find that I wasn't the only one who had spent the night in the air; Rory had been in a helicopter, surveying the ranch's 20,000-acres until daybreak, he told me.

The team manager radioed in a location—he'd just spotted an animal whose dehorning time had come—and the truck veered right. By now I'd completely lost my sense of direction; everything was flatness, rhinos, and dust. Moments later, we abruptly came to a stop. A dart gun's shiny muzzle emerged from the rolled-down passenger's window with a woman's silver-ringed finger positioned on the trigger. She aimed at a female rhino with a calf.

Bang!

Rhinos scattered all around, but Michelle Otto, a burly wildlife veterinarian with a Lara Croft—like thick braid, had hit her mark. We trailed the irritated mother, who ran a short distance and then slowed. She began to stumble left, then right, then left again—a rhino wino, woozy from the tranquilizer. The trucks came to a quick stop, and the men leapt out; a dozen of them surrounded the female, arms outstretched to ease her fall. There was a *thunk!* as two tons of wrinkly gray flesh hit earth. The rhino was out cold.

The team began working in efficient unison, with the rapid ease of people who have carried out the same tasks many times. They shoved the rhino into a sitting position and daintily folded her front legs under her massive body like a geisha. One man slipped a baby blue rhino eye mask—complete with a horn hole—over her face while another popped in massive rhino-sized ear plugs. "620, 290, 238, 480," called out a guy with a tape measurer, taking the dimensions of her horn, while another jotted them into a record book.

Finally, out came an electric reciprocating saw with a long, narrow blade. Johnny fired it up and pressed it against a magic marker line that someone had drawn around the base of the rhino's front horn. *Zzzzzzzz!* The blade bit into the material, sending white chips flying like sawdust. He moved the saw to and fro like a lumberjack, working his way toward the horn's center while another teammate continuously sprayed the cut with a water spritzer, cooling the blade. Within minutes, the horn popped neatly off, revealing a beautiful, almost quartz-like pattern of soft pink, creamy white, and a teardrop-shaped black center. Wasting no time, Johnny moved on to the rhino's second, smaller horn.

"This is what makes rhinos worth more dead than alive," said Stefran Broekman, a security guard who caught the horn as it popped off. "It feels like a big rock when you saw it off."

He handed me the horn, which was indeed quite heavy for something about the size and shape of a British Christmas pudding. Staring down at it, I felt both stunned and curious. It was incredible to think that so many animals and people had died for this material. I took a sniff, but—unlike the fungus-ridden nub of horn that Hoài had brought to the restaurant in Vietnam (in Chapter 3)—this fresh one had no discernible odor. I touched my finger to the cut side, allowing some of the sprinkle-sized white shavings to stick to it, and then gingerly placed them on the tip of my tongue. I tasted nothing—only hard grit that broke apart into smaller bits of grit between my teeth.

"It's like tough fingernails," I told Stefran.

"Yeah, that's horn. Just like your fingernails," he shrugged. Taking it back from me, he labeled its underside with a magic marker—"STUD 10 30"—for record keeping. Later that day, this horn and others just harvested would be taken by an armed escort to a fortified safe at a secret location. Before being locked in insect-proof boxes, each horn would be microchipped; DNA samples would be collected; and, later, a report would be sent back to the government.

With both horns now removed, Michelle injected the sedated rhino with an antidote to wake her up. I scrambled back just as the rhino began to come to. She shook her head and then stumbled to her feet. Her calf—which had all the while been orbiting the scene like a hyperactive sheepdog, panting and squealing—ran up to its mother. With that, the two trotted off.

I joined the team for two more dehornings, both of which went just as smoothly as the first, before the wind put the kibosh on any further work that day (the darts, which cost $70 each, could fly away). Indeed, my body and face were now a Donald Trump shade of orange from what had quickly turned into a mini-sandstorm. As Michelle joked, "You'll get home like, 'Oh I've got this beautiful tan!' Nope—just the dust."

Dirty, disheveled, and increasingly delirious from lack of sleep, I was now due to meet John Hume, the rhino king himself. I was unsure of what to expect, and a bit nervous. In interviews and stories I had read, Hume seemed gruff, radical, and in your face about his strong beliefs. As a source who knows Hume told me, "John's a real stereotype: he has the mentality of a swashbuckling entrepreneur and a Rhodesian (not a Zimbabwean), and he's not used to people saying no to him. He's never had to answer to anyone other than himself."

He also does not mind doing business with unscrupulous individuals such as Dawie Groenewald, a wealthy safari operator and fellow rhino ranch owner who faces more than 1,800 counts in a South African indictment, including for allegedly killing at least thirty-nine of his own rhinos for their horns. After Groenewald allegedly tricked nine American hunters into illegally shooting eleven rhinos on his property so he could sell their horns on the black market, the United States also issued an eighteen-count indictment and extradition request on grounds of conspiracy, money laundering, and wildlife crime.

Hume does not subscribe to the "wheeling and dealing" business style that Groenewald is notorious for, but he has bought more than one hundred rhinos from the alleged criminal, and by his own admission has no qualms doing business with scumbags. As he told journalist Julian Rademeyer, "I will buy rhinos from the devil himself, especially if I think I may be saving the rhino's life. Bring me any fucking crook, murderer. . . . If he's offering to sell me a rhino and it suits me, I'll buy it anyway."

Hume himself has never been accused of any crime, and guilt by association, of course, does not a criminal make. But, from a distance, his comments and ties to Groenewald do give a certain impression—one that made me wonder about what kind of man I'd be dealing with. As I mulled all of this over, Gerhard pulled up at a brick house situated behind a stone wall. "Okay, this must be the place," he said. "This ginormous thing standing here."

I wouldn't have described it as ginormous. A cactus garden stood out front with a little rhino statue in it, and Jack Russell terriers swarmed the car as I stepped out. Although the house was nice, it was not spectacular—more like a decent home you'd find in a middle-class US suburb. Had I passed it there, I'd never have guessed that its owner was a wildly successful businessman who ran a multi-million-dollar rhino operation.

Hume's secretary, a slightly frazzled middle-aged woman, greeted me at the door and offered me coffee and cookies. Hume, she told me, was still engaged in another meeting. I took a seat across from her in a rather spartan room with stone floors and a few African wildlife–themed paintings on the wall and began scratching the ears of an orange cat named Chancellor who came over to say hello. Ten minutes or so later, two well-known rhino experts—Esmond Bradley Martin and Lucy Vigne—unexpectedly emerged from the office. Now, it was my turn.

As I entered, Hume rose from behind an imposing desk to give me a firm handshake. He was tall, with a bushy white beard and a massive belly precariously contained by a khaki button-down shirt. We took a seat at a wooden table spanning the length of the room, upon which his secretary immediately placed a tray containing more coffee and cookies. He peered at me from behind frameless rectangular glasses, his expression stern.

"I was just getting to know your cat," I began, to break the ice. "Are you a cat or dog person?"

"I'm neither—I'm an animal person!" he declared in a strong, deep voice. "I've got four dogs and nine bloody cats. I've always been an animal lover—very, very much so." Already, I was relaxing: this big, belligerent old man and I did have something in common, after all.

Hume, who was seventy-four when I interviewed him, quickly walked me through his life story. He grew up on a farm in what was then Rhodesia, a "typical hunten and shooten and fishen boy" (in Rhodesian parlance). He always wanted more, though—not because he didn't like farming but because he thought "there must be an easier way of making money." He dropped out of school at fourteen, and by eighteen, he owned his first piece of property. He expanded from there to hotels, gold mines, a supermarket, a taxi company, and timeshares. By 1993, with millions in the bank, he was ready to semi-retire. He'd always imagined spending his golden years on a farm, perhaps breeding cattle—but times had changed. Wild game ranches, not livestock ones, were now all the rage. So Hume began researching exotic animals, especially rhinos. The more he learned about those big, docile beasts, the harder he fell.

"At that point, I'd never met a rhino," he said. "If you asked me what my favorite animal was then, it would have been an eland or sable. But after meeting my first rhino in 1993, over the next few years I became aware not only of what wonderful-natured animals they are, but that they're facing extinction. I became aware of what was happening, and what had happened, with tens of thousands of these wonderful animals slaughtered in Africa. I wanted to make a difference, and I thought the best way to do that is to breed rhinos. Slowly but surely, I've become more and more a fan of rhinos—stupidly, I think. But then we do a lot of stupid things in our lives, and I've enjoyed doing this one."

Hume bought his first white rhinos in 1993 and his first black rhinos a few years after that. Perhaps the world's wealthiest pet hoarder, he's steadily accrued more since then. He welcomed his thousandth calf on December 28, 2016, a male that Hume's wife named Spartacus. He speaks of his rhinos as if they are old friends whose personalities he knows inside and out. "White and black rhinos have got very different natures, but both are wonderful natures," he said affectionately. White rhinos, he explained, are passive and "user friendly." Even when darted, a white rhino "wants to make it work"; it will only charge when backed into a corner. Black rhinos, however, are full of bluster, snorts, and mock charges. Unlike a buffalo, though, a black rhino, Hume said, is "not really a killer—he's just showing off."

When rhino poaching rose like a plague around 2008, Hume's operations were spared for several years. Then, in 2013, "all hell broke loose," he said. In quick succession, four of his rhinos were killed. He hired a few security guards, but they made no difference; he lost another ten in 2014. The only way to stop the killings, he realized, was to transform his security into a militaristic, highly sophisticated operation. Eventually, he was forced "to build a village"—a helicopter hangar, arms storage facilities, and barracks for security guards and their families. (Although Hume has turned over "vast amounts" of evidence to the police following poaching incidents and incursions, no arrests have ever been made. When I asked why not, he looked at me for a long moment and then laughed. "Do you know Africa? Go into a police station sometime and see how it looks—then talk to me about the chances of catching poachers.")

Hume and the other private rhino owners' similarly high security investments seem to be working somewhat—especially compared to the government's efforts. In 2013, private individuals owned a quarter of the nation's rhinos and suffered a quarter of the total poaching losses, while in 2016 they owned a third but losses hovered around 15 percent. Indeed, when I met him, Hume proudly told me he had just celebrated nine months without losing a rhino. Sustaining that victory comes at a steep cost, however: He spends $175,000 per month on security alone. He makes money by breeding buffalo and sable, but those sales cover only six to eight weeks of his annual costs. Funds for the remaining ten months come straight out of his savings account. "The world has no clue of the difficult task of keeping rhinos from extinction," he said.

Jones estimates that, between 2008 and 2016, private rhino owners collectively spent $145 million protecting their animals. Even as security costs have risen, profits have fallen. Sales of living rhinos (as opposed to horn) are at an all-time low: fifteen years ago, owners could expect to get $12,000 to $60,000 (inflation adjusted) for a rhino, but now the same animals go for $8,800 to $44,000. Mostly, though, rhinos just aren't selling. Everyone knows those animals are living targets, and no one wants to sacrifice his or her bank account or even life owning and protecting them.

No one, that is, except Hume and a few other holdouts. "I've gotten myself into what seems like one hell of a corner," he said. "Now I have a two-legged operation: breeding and protecting rhinos. It's my business, my life. It's what I want to do. But I only have enough money to keep doing what I'm doing for two to three more years. I hope to someday recoup my investment—but will I? If I run out of money, thereafter do I stop my security operations and try to find buyers? No one wants rhinos, except for a few idiots like myself. I backed the underdog because I thought it deserved a chance, but who the hell needs friends with enemies like that?"

FOR MANY NORTH AMERICANS, THE IDEA OF SELLING PRODUCTS FROM THREATened species triggers a knee-jerk reaction: not acceptable. South Africans, however, tend to feel the opposite. As with Namibia and several other Southern African countries, South Africa has a long history of sustainable use, a term popularized in the 1980s. Though still controversial, it holds that if wildlife can be exploited for commercial interests, protecting and setting land aside for it is justified. "If it pays, it stays," as some Southern Africans like to say. Such payments take the form of hunting; culling for meat, tusks, horns, or pelts; ecotourism; and more. Pretty much anything goes, so long as those activities fall within the law and don't impact overall wildlife populations.

So ingrained are these concepts that South Africa's constitution stipulates its citizens' rights to sustainable use of wildlife, including the right to own game and to exploit that game through legal sales or hunts. Many believe these provisions are a boon to the country's economy and conservation achievements. Indeed, up to 20 million wild animals live on nearly 9,000 private ranches, the area of which adds up to be nearly three times the collective size of South Africa's government-run parks. In 2014, revenue from hunts and meat sales of some of those animals totaled nearly $200 million, while the ranching industry provided jobs to 65,000 people.

The groundwork for these operations was laid in the 1960s, when a growing number of conservationists in Southern Africa began to champion private game ownership and use. One of them was Ian Player, a South African warden and conservationist who is credited with saving southern white rhinos from extinction. In the 1950s, fewer than five hundred survived, and all were confined to a single reserve in South Africa. The reserve had reached carrying capacity for the rhinos, and conservationists felt stuck. Player realized that the species' numbers could be further expanded if animals were translocated to other reserves and zoos, enlarging their range. Although this idea had first been put forth by an American naturalist in 1925, the feat was—until Player came along—considered impossible, as doing so required safely capturing and moving animals that weighed up to 4,000 pounds. That changed in 1960, when Player teamed up with Toni Harthoorn, a Kenya-based veterinarian who was developing rhino-friendly sedatives delivered in a dart-syringe. "Immobilization," Harthoorn told Player, "is going to change the whole picture of game conservation."

He was right. After much experimentation, a year later Player and his colleagues transported their first rhino, a female named Amber, from the Umfolozi Game Reserve to Mkuze Game Reserve a hundred miles away. The latter habitat hadn't seen rhinos in more than a century. Amber, unfortunately, didn't survive long after arrival, but failure soon yielded to success. By 1970, the project, dubbed Operation Rhino, had transferred 400 rhinos back into former habitats and 150 more to zoos around the world. "We could look back with justifiable pride . . . and say to the world, we have saved the white rhino for you," Player wrote of his legacy. "We have made our contribution to the next generation."

Player's expansion strategy also included the introduction of rhinos onto privately owned land, a development that eventually led to private ownership rights. The crux of private ownership, he believed, was allowing people to make money off their animals not only through tourism but also hunting. In 1968, with the white rhino population now up to 1,800 animals, South Africa reopened rhino sport hunting. By the early 1970s, rhino owners were enjoying returns many times over their initial investment. Fees for American and European hunters climbed exponentially through the 1980s, with some rhino owners charging up to $25,000 to bag a single animal by the end of the decade. They often reinvested the profits in buying more land and more rhinos.

South Africa's success was the exception to the rule, however. As the country's rhino population steadily grew, those in other African countries fell—mostly to poachers' bullets and machetes. As discussed in Chapter 3, from 1970 to 1980 alone, the continent's rhino population was halved. Yet South Africa's rhino numbers increased—growing by 130 percent between 1997 and 2007—which many took as proof that hunting and other forms of sustainable use had saved the animals from extinction. As Player, shortly before his death in 2014, told Rademeyer, "The great irony is that rhino were nearly wiped out in the nineteenth century by hunters. But it is through hunting in the twentieth century that rhino populations have exploded."

The truth is probably a bit more nuanced, however; hunting has contributed to conservation in South Africa and elsewhere, but conversation has ultimately succeeded due to diversification. As 't Sas-Rolfes explained, "Trophy hunts and the sale of game for meat provide a safer, more pragmatic business model than one that relies solely on aid or on tourism, which can go up in smoke if you have a terrorist attack, for example. That's why South Africa has been so successful: it's found different ways to generate money out of wildlife, beyond just tourism."

For years, that success included legal sale of rhino horn within the country's borders. In 2006, Hume, for example, sold 185 pounds of horn at $455 per pound to a man named Adriaan. Adriaan was so enthusiastic about the horn that he took not only whole specimens but also the small, cut-up bits left over from making dagger handles. Although none of the material Adriaan bought could legally leave South Africa, almost certainly all of it did. As Hume recalled telling his manager at the time, "I bet you any money you like that that horn is on its way to the Far East in days."

By 2008, the price of rhino horn had shot up to nearly $2,000 a pound on South Africa's legal market, and, officially, 220 pounds sold that year. The true amount, though, was probably much more. Mandatory horn registration databases fell 3,900 pounds short of what the government predicted they should show. Amid skyrocketing prices and demand for rhino horn in Asia, it was pretty obvious what had happened to that missing material—and, most likely, to much of the legally sold horn as well. As the government wrote in a 2014 report, "It is suspected that many of these horns were subsequently exported illegally out of the country."

Fed up with the abuse of its legal sale system—or, as Jones put it, "in the stupid belief it would stop the leakage of horns out of the country"—in 2009, the government put a moratorium on the domestic trade of rhino horn. Registered trophies from legal hunts were still permitted, but, otherwise, any sale of rhino horn was prohibited. Many rhino owners felt they were being punished for the government's inability to get a handle on wildlife crime. As Jones explained, "If Toyotas are being stolen in South Africa and being taken into Mozambique, do not put a moratorium on Toyota. Look at your border crossings and law enforcement."

In any case, the moratorium clearly did not end the leakage of rhino horn out of South Africa. Jones also blames the 2009 ban for causing greater poaching, by making horn artificially scarce: in 2008, 83 rhinos were killed for their horns, while, in 2010, 333 were. Over 1,000 rhinos have been killed there each year since 2013, and most of their horns are presumed to leave the country.

Tom Milliken, who runs TRAFFIC's program for elephants and rhinos, takes issue with this interpretation of the numbers, however. "We know poaching was going up before they stopped pseudo-hunting and issued the moratorium," he said. "It was those illegal sales coming out of the private sector that got the Vietnamese interested in the first place." Regardless of the cause, the figures have remained disastrously high in recent years, to the point that, since 2014, some experts believe that rhinos have hit the tipping point at which the number of deaths exceeds the number of births.

Jones and others see this as a classic example of how prohibition alone typically fails to end demand for a banned product and instead simply moves its commerce underground—as in the failure of prohibition of alcohol in the United States in the 1920s or the current "war on drugs." Following this thinking, pro-traders tend to paint rhino horn as the marijuana of banned wildlife products—something controversial but something that they hope society will come to terms with legalizing.

"The early war on drugs was 'Just say no: all drugs are bad and banned,'" explained 't Sas-Rolfes. "But now we realize all drugs are not the same: marijuana is not as bad as heroin, and LSD is very different than cocaine. With marijuana, we're now taking a more sophisticated, nuanced, and harm-reduction-based approach, which has so far been hugely successful. Likewise, with rhino horn, at the moment we're saying it's all bad and needs to be banned and we need to educate those silly Asian people. But you can't just tell people what to do like that. It's a crude, blunt tool, and I think it's going to fail." (Others, however, say this is a mischaracterization. "Organizations like WildAid go out of their way to avoid telling people what to do, particularly in Asia," said conservationist and lawyer Ronald Orenstein. "Trying to convince someone to do something isn't telling them to do it.")

The private rhino owners, however, can't do much about the ban on international trade of rhino horn: it went into effect in 1977, and changing it would require a two-thirds majority vote in favor of a CITES pro-trade proposal, such as the one Swaziland put forth (and lost) in Johannesburg, days after I visited Hume's ranch. When it comes to South Africa's moratorium on domestic trade, however, the private owners have significantly more leverage. For one, the law seems to be on their side. The moratorium, they assert, violates their constitutional right to sustainable utilization of wildlife. "In simplistic terms," Jones said, "it would be like I'm a sheep farmer and I'm told by the government that I may not sell wool." Additionally, the government did not follow due process of notifying the public before the ban went into effect.

In 2015, Hume and another private rhino owner—a man named Johan Kruger, whom Groenewald, the safari operator accused of all the rhino crimes, has said he is bankrolling—took the matter to court, challenging South Africa's Department of Environmental Affairs. Hume was absolutely determined to win. As a source told me, "John thinks he's come up with a solution to a problem. But now he's encountered all this resistance, and he's never had anyone say no to him before. So bloody hell, he's going to do what he has to do to prove he's right." Indeed, he and Kruger won their case, and judges ruled in their favor in three appeals. In April 2017, South Africa finally set aside the moratorium and reopened the market to domestic trade of rhino horn.

When I interviewed Hume in September 2016, however, this was all still up in the air. He told me that—immediately following what he saw as his inevitable success in getting the moratorium taken down—he planned to organize a rhino horn auction, starting with one hundred sets of horns of all shapes and sizes and probably selling them for $4,500 per pound. "I want to go have an auction in the Chinese community, in the casino or mall," he said. In the end, though, he opted instead to hold an online auction first, with a website available in English, Chinese, and Vietnamese. In August 2017, Hume opened bids for seventy-six individual sets of horns to buyers who paid a $7,600 registration fee. The auction yielded fewer sales than expected, but Hume still considered it a success.

The Private Rhino Owners Association hasn't moved as quickly, but it is in the process of setting up a Central Selling Organization and Central Storage Facility that provides a straightforward platform for rhino owners to market their horn lawfully, for a 10 percent commission (some of the proceeds will be invested in community conservation projects). As Jones wrote in an internal memo, the system is meant to ensure that illegal "blood horns" from poached rhinos do not get laundered into the legal trade, and to minimize risk to sellers and buyers by ensuring all transactions are compliant with domestic and international legislation.

What will become of the horns that are sold? Hume has received calls from South Africa–based Chinese businessmen interested in setting up a medical facility that caters to Asian tourists and residents, and there's also talk of developing a domestic rhino horn carving industry. It's likely, however, that the very criminals who are now trafficking in horn from poached animals may get involved in the legal horn trade and may mix their illegal spoils with legitimately acquired horn. This is not a deal breaker, however. As Jones said, "Morally, it is of huge concern to work with those individuals, but if we have to do business with the devil to achieve a particular outcome and ensure species survival, then so be it."

Hume agreed: "I think we have to swallow that very bitter pill. If we don't work with these kingpins, then they'll just go poach more rhino. I think we have to say 'Come, let's be friends now.' Plus, with the way they're going, in six years' time they will be out of business because the rhinos will be gone. If they come deal with us, then they'll be in business forever."

He also doesn't worry that some or all of the horn he sells legally in South Africa may find its way illegally to Vietnam or China—in fact, he believes that would be a boon. "It doesn't bother me at all, because that's what we need to do. We need to throw six to eight tons a year at them, to satisfy their demand, which we can!" he said, his voice rising to a boom. "Every rhino horn that is stopped from going to the East is a nail in my rhinos' coffins."

Hume's lawyer, Izak du Toit, went so far as to characterize the smuggling of horn out of South Africa and into Asia as a heroic and justified form of civil disobedience. "I've compared it to apartheid," he told *National Geographic* reporter Bryan Christy in 2016. "Black people had to transgress the very law they objected to in order to show it was illegal."

TO SAY THAT MANY CONSERVATIONISTS AND ACTIVISTS DO NOT SUPPORT LEGAL trade of rhino horn is putting it lightly. Opposition ranges from practical to emotional. For starters, rhino owners are often accused of being more concerned with profit from their animals' horns than with the animals themselves. "It's just human greed," said Dex Kotze, a South African businessman, conservation strategist, and founder of the nonprofit group Youth 4 African Wildlife. "John Hume is poised to make a lot of money."

Jones, however, takes issue with this accusation. "None of us bought rhino because we wanted to get into the rhino trade; we bought rhino because we're conservationists," he said. He and other private rhino owners receive no assistance, subsidies, tax breaks, or incentives from the government, he pointed out, and yet they continue to keep rhino, even though it costs them, in some cases, millions of dollars. "Animal rights organizations cast us as being this despicable group of money makers, but if it's through profitability that we can sustain a species, then that is to be applauded," he said. (He noted, too, that it's not a crime to wish to make money from your assets: "We do not live in a socialist state. We live in a capitalist state, like America. There's nothing wrong with making profit.")

Although those are fair points, many conservationists believe that the legal trade is simply too risky. As Crawford Allan, senior director of TRAFFIC at WWF, said, "We can't experiment with rhinos because there are too few of them left." To this, Hume countered, South Africa already ran its own "disastrous" experiment on rhinos: the 2009 moratorium, which "escalated our poaching by thousands of percent." The sooner trade opens up, the better for rhinos, he said. He added that he cannot wait around until the demand reduction campaigns of TRAFFIC and others catch on. "The demand reduction people keep on telling us how their demand reduction is working—so why are my rhinos still dying?" he said. "The current program—without me selling my rhino horn—will definitely lead to my rhinos' deaths. Do you want to sanction that? Poaching's already rampant now—I say, let the genie out of the bottle!"

WWF has come out clearly against the trade. "We don't take our positioning lightly on this, and we don't take a negative position for the sake of it because it seems like the right thing to do publicly," Allan said. "Right now, it would be a disaster to legalize rhino horn trade." Even if prices drop, desperate poachers will continue to poach, he said, and black-market products will inevitably be laundered into the legal trade.

The arguments for and against legalizing trade in rhino horn rage on, seemingly endlessly. To support their position that the trade is sustainable and controllable, many private rhino owners point to the case of the vicuña. In the 1960s, those South American camelids—whose wool is some of the most expensive in the world—were hunted to the brink of extinction; just 10,000 or so animals, or 1 percent of their former numbers, remained. By the 1990s and 2000s, however, the tide had turned, thanks to organized community-led efforts to sustainably ranch vicuña and harvest their wool. Populations hover around 450,000 today. "I promise, like the vicuñas of Africa, rhinos will bounce back like you can't believe," Hume said. South Americans, he added, coined the phrase "Shear a vicuña to save a vicuña"; South Africa's equivalent, he said, should be "Save the rhino, not the horn." (What rhino ranchers often do not mention, however, is that it took more than a decade for the vicuña market to stabilize and that trade of those endangered species was strictly banned until populations rebounded. Vicuña poaching is also on the rise, with more than 5,000 animals found dead from 2010 to 2015—likely a significant underestimate.)

Another primary fear of trade opponents is that there are not enough rhinos left to satiate the market and, moreover, that legalization could actually stimulate demand, leading to a vicious cycle of even more poaching. Proponents, however, calculate that there *are* enough rhinos left to satisfy demand, a quantity they define based on the number of animals currently being poached: 1,200 to 1,500 sets of horns per year.

There are some roundabout indications that they may be right—that Vietnam and China have reached their rhino horn equilibrium and that what you see now is what you've got in terms of total consumer demand. This idea comes from Martin and Vigne's latest price data: in 2014, the wholesale price in China and Vietnam for a pound of rhino horn hovered around $29,500, but, by the end of 2015, the price had halved, to about $14,700 per pound. Rhino horn traders told Martin and Vigne that the drop stemmed from the fact that there is just too much rhino horn floating around in the market now. "They say the demand for the horn just isn't there," Martin said. "We've also talked to various conservationists about this, and they say that's all that can make sense." Assuming this is correct, then taking into account the thirty tons of horn already stockpiled by the government and the six tons held by private rhino owners, Hume calculated that the country already has enough rhino horn to satiate fifteen to thirty years' worth of demand. Private owners also claim that ten tons of fresh horn can be added to the pile each year.

Others call bullshit on much of this. For starters, a 2014 South African governmental report estimated that, in 2017, the country could, in total, produce only about 3.3 to 5 tons of rhino horn—not the 10 tons the private breeders claim. Moreover, whether it's 3 or 10 tons, Kotze doesn't think it would be enough. Just look at the numbers, he said. According to his calculations, if just 1 percent of the population in China, Hong Kong, Taiwan, Vietnam, and Thailand (1.5 billion people total) use just one gram of rhino horn per year (a minuscule amount), that's nearly 15 tons annually; if 5 percent uses five grams per year, that's a whopping 375 tons. Those figures only increase from there, as both populations and wealth grow. "You can have four John Humes running around and you're not going to have enough to supply them," Kotze said.

Lynn Johnson, founder of the nonprofit organization Breaking the Brand, also pointed out that it's erroneous to assume that demand is in the region of 1,500 horns per year. The level of demand, she wrote, cannot be deduced from how many horns have been poached, because we're dealing with a supply-restricted market. In other words, the level of supply is not an indication of actual demand. This is why, she continued, up to 90 percent of what is labeled "rhino horn" in Vietnam is actually fake: demand is much higher than supply.

Indeed, a serious concern, as discussed in Chapter 3, is that legal trade might expand demand for rhino horn, creating what experts refer to as a "reverse stigma effect." According to this logic, some people today aren't using rhino horn because it's illegal and they don't want to break the law. If that stigma were suddenly lifted, however, it may give those people the nudge they need to try it out. "If you make it legal, then the people who were not buying rhino horn because of a sense of right and wrong will then think it's acceptable," Allan said. "You'll grow this part of society."

Some research backs this hypothesis. In 2014, the National Resources Defense Council teamed up with a market research firm in China to survey more than 2,000 people in five Chinese cities about rhino horn. Once the data were in, they used a sophisticated statistical model to account for gaps and extrapolate their findings. Surprisingly, no one had conducted this type of research since the 1980s, so the team had no idea what it would find.

The results, it turned out, were not encouraging for legal trade advocates. Of those surveyed, 1.4 percent had likely bought rhino horn in the last year, and just over 8 percent probably bought it in the past ten years. Even more worryingly, though, the researchers calculated that latent demand for rhino horn in China is five times greater than what could be produced legally. Confirming fears about a possible reverse stigma effect, some people said they do not buy rhino horn right now only because it's illegal or because they are concerned about wildlife conservation. "Demand is already big in China, and demand would be bigger if rhino horn were legalized," said study author Alexandra Kennaugh. "I'm not opposed to trade at all—and there may be some conditions in the future where the trade would be good—but that's certainly not now. Policy makers and conservationists have to think about 'do no harm' first."

In 2016, Yufang Gao, a doctoral student in anthropology and conservation at Yale University, published further evidence in support of Kennaugh's findings. An increasing number of rhino horns, he found, have turned up for sale at Chinese auction houses—from just 26 in 2000 to 2,700 in 2011. China banned rhino horn from auctions in 2012, but, nevertheless, Gao wrote, "the threat that the art market poses to rhino conservation is not yet fully curbed." For now, he believes that rhino horn is *you jia wu shi,* as the Chinese say: the price remains high, but there is no turnover. Instead, collectors and investors are holding onto their stock, waiting for sales to reopen so they can sell their goods at an acceptably high price.

Legalized international trade of rhino horn remains a pipe dream for private rhino owners and other advocates, and both Vietnam's and China's domestic laws continue to strictly forbid its sale. Yet South Africa's legal domestic trade has the potential to contribute, illegally, to those markets (for some private rhino owners hoping to satiate demand, however, this seems to be precisely the goal). "South Africa is one of the most developed countries in Africa, and with all the resources they have—all the expertise and security—they cannot protect 1,200 rhinos a year," Allan warned. "It would be madness for anyone to open up the trade because the systems are not in place to secure the sales or the supply." He added that the cost of poaching will always be far cheaper than that of legal rhino horn, so, even if trade should be legalized globally, the killing would continue.

But even this argument is questioned; 't Sas-Rolfes calls it highly misleading. To compare legally harvested horns with trafficked ones, he explained, all production and supply costs must be taken into account, including the cost of transporting a hot horn from rural Africa to Vietnam. Although the actual act of poaching may be relatively cheap, the fees for everyone working in the network and the bribes paid along the way quickly add up. This is why rhino poaching declined in the 1990s, 't Sas-Rolfes said—not because demand went away but because costs became too high after China and other countries cracked down. This is also why the new wave of rhino horn criminals in South Africa at first chose to exploit a legal loophole and undertake pseudo-hunting, rather than engage in straight-up poaching and trafficking. Even the convoluted pseudo-hunting scheme was cheaper and easier than dealing with the hassle and expense of smuggling.

But 't Sas-Rolfes did agree with Allan insofar as the crux of the situation comes down to governance—"with good governance, the flow of supply can be controlled; without it, it can't"—but he countered that South Africa can and does protect some 18,000 rhinos per year that are not poached. That number will likely go up, he said, once the proceeds from legal horn sales are reinvested in security, as planned. "The debate is really about whether creating an appropriately structured legal trade regime can help to improve governance, or whether it will undermine it," he said. "Many believe that the trade ban has actually undermined good governance by penalizing responsible rhino managers and providing an opportunity for criminals."

This long debate over methods of rhino conservation and governance aside, there are also, finally, moral arguments pro and con legalization. Philosophical questions over how humans harvest animal parts are too broad to explore here, but Peter Knights, executive director of the nonprofit organization WildAid, raised one interesting ethical issue at a panel on legal trade at the CITES meeting, asking the audience, "If people are using rhino horn for cancer, how do you feel about that? What are the ethics of giving someone a placebo for cancer?" Likewise, in *The UN's Lone Ranger,* John Sellar wrote, "There seems something almost immoral in legalizing the trade," as it provides "victims of one of the world's most debilitating and fatal diseases" with "a treatment that would do them no good whatsoever."

Nor is rhino horn always harmless. As detailed in Chapter 3, Nguyễn Hữu Trường, an immunologist at Hanoi's Bạch Mai Hospital, regularly sees patients complaining of rashes, stomachaches, and diarrhea after taking rhino or buffalo horn. That may be fine for some middle-aged guy who took too many shots of rhino horn while out drinking and then came down with a nasty case of the squirts the next day. But for someone who is seriously ill, rhino horn's side effects could, literally, be grave.

In Hume's opinion, though, any health risks attached to rhino horn are insignificant in the grand scheme of things. We do things all the time that aren't good for us, he pointed out, and indeed, he readily admitted that he himself is no stranger to the world's delicious vices. "Unfortunately, as you can see from my build, I have a problem," he said. "I like Kentucky Fried Chicken. I like hamburgers and booze. Yet we attack rhino horn—why? What about cigarettes, McDonald's, and Coca-Cola?"

BACK IN HUME'S OFFICE, I FLEXED MY CRAMPING FINGERS AND CLOSED MY LAPtop. I'd exhausted my list of questions. As I thanked him and prepared to say goodbye, he surprised me with an unexpected offer: "Would you like to go see the rhinos having lunch?"

By this point I was yearning for the sweet oblivion of the back seat of Gerhard's car, but this opportunity sounded like it was worth delaying a nap. Hume lumbered to his feet, and we headed outside, where his wife, an outspoken Ukrainian, waved to him from the porch and dogs shot around like overexcited electrons. Three managed to jump into the cabin of Hume's truck before he shut the door. The five of us headed out, not through the front gate but through his backyard, which opened onto his expansive property.

The rhinos' lunch, it turned out, was held in a sprawling field, made barren and dusty from so many hungry animals' multiton footsteps. They gather here once a day to scarf down two trailer loads of food—a mix of alfalfa, mass-produced feed, and agricultural leftovers—doled out in widely scattered circular concrete containers. Rhinos—too many of them to count—stood with their noses to the containers. A few buffalo and sable had also snuck in for an easy treat, while shy eland lingered on the sidelines, waiting for the crowd to clear.

"This is the one place you'll see over a hundred rhinos in one spot," Hume said. "But I get people sending photos of this area around, as if it's my entire operation. They say, 'This is Hume's farm, where rhinos are kept like pigs in a sty.'" Indeed, *National Geographic* had published a photo of this very feed lot weeks before my visit and that image had painted a somewhat deceptive picture in my mind. I'd expected to find rhinos crammed together in an industrial feedlot, when in fact Hume's rhinos live at a density of about one per 7.5 acres.

Hume slowly circled the truck around the field, passing a water hole and a couple of giraffes. A few men in blue uniforms drove by, and Hume waved to them out of his open window, jostling his terriers for space. We took a turn, heading down a bumpy road into thicker bush punctuated by scraggly trees. "Let's see if we can find a black rhino," he said. He owns only seventeen of those critically endangered animals live, he explained, mostly because they're a bit difficult to keep. Unlike white rhino, they are picky eaters, and there aren't many trees in this part of the country to supply the leaves they need. The bulls also have an inconvenient tendency to kill each other.

Just then, Hume spotted a black rhino mom and a calf up ahead, nibbling on some branches. To be honest, I couldn't tell the physical difference between these two black rhinos and the many white rhinos I'd seen that day. Temperament-wise, however, the contrast was immediately clear. Hearing our truck, the mother stiffened and reared around toward us, ears pricked and head held at a haughty angle. "Come now, darling, I don't want to hassle you," Hume said to her in an imploring voice. "You can eat your lunch."

The rhino was not having it. She began to approach the truck, head still thrown high and eyes wide like a spooked horse. Hume slowly reversed, and—seemingly satisfied—the rhino turned and headed into the bush, her baby trotting behind her. "You've gotta be careful with these guys. Or else you'll have a horn up your bum," Hume said, smiling. "You can see straight away she's got a different attitude."

To my surprise, rather than call a truce, he put the truck back into gear and began creeping up on the rhinos from behind. That was it for the mom. She swung her massive body around and began trotting—and then running—toward the vehicle. A rush of adrenaline swept through me and I braced myself. *She's going to ram us!*

Hume threw the truck into a bumpy reverse, and we accelerated backward. "I'll be good, I'll be good!" he yelled giddily. The mother slowed, snorted, and then came to a halt right in front of us. She and Hume had been through this before, apparently. "She usually stops just short of the vehicle—though sometimes she'll give it a few butts," he explained, chuckling. "I just got this vehicle back from being fixed because of that, actually."

Rhino sightings accomplished, we started looping around toward his house. "So, how do you feel about your rhinos?" I asked—though I already suspected the answer. "Are they like cats and dogs to you, or more commodities?"

"They're more like my cats and dogs, unfortunately," he replied, his tone earnest. "And very unfortunately, I become emotional. It's very wrong—it does not help my rhino."

He sniffed, and, to my utter disbelief, I saw that, behind his glasses, his blue-grey eyes were gleaming. He was tearing up! Nothing I'd read or heard about Hume had prepared me for this.

"It's not easy to see one—dead," he added, his voice catching on the last word.

The moment passed, and we rumbled along in silence. "Do you ever regret going down this road with the rhinos?" I finally asked.

"Of course, I regret it, I've often regretted it," he replied without hesitation. "But if you have ten kids, you don't say that you don't love all ten of your kids because you should have only had five."

Back at the house, I thanked him and patted the dogs good-bye.

"I am telling you, I am not wrong," Hume said as I shook his hand. "Rhinos would be very happy if they could answer you. They would say, 'We will let you take our horn once every couple years to save our species.' Knowing rhinos, I am absolutely convinced they would be very happy to make this very small sacrifice."

Now that a real-world experiment is under way to test that contentious hypothesis, for better or for worse for the rhino, we will all likely soon find out.

Twelve

MY TIGER WINE IS CORKED

Tᵧ dropped a dollar on the bar and swiveled his chair toward me. "So, what's your Eastern European hooker name gonna be?"

"Melania, duh! And you should be Dmitry, my pimp-slash-brother."

"I love it!" Ty said, taking a swig of his sixth Pabst Blue Ribbon. "But what about Paul?"

"Paul gets to be my john! He can just use his normal name."

"Oh my God, YES! I'm gonna have to buy some pimp clothes!"

"We'll have to gamble and drink a lot, to make sure we don't raise suspicions. Think we can handle it?"

"We can start all of that on the flight over!" Ty threw his arms up in a hooray motion, spilling a bit of his beer. "Should we do accents? We should do accents!"

"Of course ve do accent, my brother!" I replied, channeling Beck Bennett's *Saturday Night Live* Vladimir Putin. "Ve do thees thing right!"

Perhaps I should back up, starting with the circumstances that led Ty (remember him from Chapter 1?) and me to a dive bar in Brooklyn, strategizing our descent into sex work. It all began when I caught a whiff of an enigmatic place called the Golden Triangle Special Economic Zone. From what I read, this bizarre Chinese casino development in northwestern Laos offered a playground of illicit delights ranging from drugs and prostitution to illegal ivory and rhino horn. Restaurants, meanwhile, were said to be supplied by an onsite "zoo" that could be more accurately described as a live meat market for endangered species. Like a supermarket tank of lobsters, the zoo reportedly allowed customers to choose the tiger, bear, or pangolin they want to dine on.

As horrific as it sounds, the Special Economic Zone zoo from hell isn't some exceptional one-off: it's typical of so-called wildlife farming, a loose label for the thousands of places throughout China and Southeast Asia that claim to engage in commercial breeding of wild animals. The label spans a diverse array of facilities, from a family in suburban Hanoi who keeps a few bears in their backyard and illegally sells the animals' bile, to a sprawling operation in China that breeds hundreds of tigers and peddles their parts out the back door.

Wildlife farming is often touted as a possible conservation solution, with proponents arguing that simply domesticating and raising the animals that people want—even endangered ones, like tigers—will satiate demand and stem poaching of wild populations. It sounds like a reasonable idea at first, but a closer look at the evidence shows it's naively optimistic and its proponents are usually, if not always, motivated solely by profit. In reality, wildlife farms often launder illegally captured wild animals into the global market as pets, or—as in the Special Economic Zone—they breed protected species only to sell them as meat, medicine, and trophies, fueling appetites for these products.

The Golden Triangle Special Economic Zone's story began in 2007, when a Hong Kong–registered company called the Kings Romans Group signed a lease with the Lao government for a nearly forty-square-mile backwater plot in Bokeo Province, just across the Mekong River from Thailand. Not much is known about the company's shady owner, a businessman from Harbin named Zhao Wei. He seems to have gotten involved in the casino business in Macao in the 1990s and later expanded operations to Mong La, a notorious rebel-run border town in Myanmar. There, he reportedly buddied up with local militias and rebel leaders, from the United Wa State Army, including major methamphetamine producers. Money from the booming Burmese narcotics trade allegedly propped up his Mong La enterprises, according to Thai officials and the US government.

Zhao denied his involvement with the drug trade in an interview with *Al Jazeera* in 2011, but, in 2018, the US Department of the Treasury issued sanctions against the Zhao Wei Transnational Criminal Organization for "horrendous illicit activities," according to Sigal Mandelker, treasury undersecretary for terrorism and financial intelligence. As described in the memo, this includes "engaging in drug trafficking, human trafficking, money laundering, bribery and wildlife trafficking, much of which is facilitated through the Kings Romans Casino." The casino itself "facilitates the storage and distribution of heroin, methamphetamine and other narcotics for illicit networks, including the United Wa State Army."

Lao police make regular confiscations of illegal narcotics on the premises—including a stash of methamphetamines valued at $1.6 million in 2012—and officials believe that traffickers use the casino as a front for legitimizing drug money. "Money laundering and facilitating movement of large amounts of cash is what concerns us most," said Jeremey Douglas, regional representative for Southeast Asia and the Pacific at the UN Office on Drugs and Crime. "Thai officials at the highest levels have told us that they are aware of large amounts of cash being taken in to legitimize it."

Laos, however, has been nothing but welcoming. Officials extended a personal invitation for Zhao to invest, and he recently extended his lease from fifty to ninety-nine years. Of the total concession Zhao was awarded, around twelve square miles were roped off for the duty-free Kings Romans casino area, complete with hotels, restaurants, and shopping centers catering to an elite Chinese clientele. Although technically in Laos, it's China in everything but geography: Kings Romans runs on Beijing time, has Chinese cell phone coverage, quotes prices in Chinese yuan (and does not accept Lao kip), is patrolled by Chinese security guards, and is primarily staffed by Chinese workers who speak only Chinese.

Not unlike Pinocchio's Pleasure Island excursion, there is also nearly limitless opportunity to engage in illegal delights not as easily attainable back home. That the Golden Triangle Special Economic Zone is a hotbed for not only drugs, child prostitution, and human trafficking but also for wildlife crime first came to international attention in 2015, when two nonprofit organizations, the London-based Environmental Investigation Agency (EIA) and Education for Nature–Vietnam, released a report titled *Sin City*. The document detailed "blatant illegal wildlife trade by Chinese companies," including open sale of a host of endangered species, live and dead—tigers, leopards, elephants, rhinos, pangolins, bears, and more. The entire place is "a national embarrassment," the investigators concluded, but apparently it enjoys high-level political support. The former Lao prime minister and president both made well-publicized visits, and former Lao officials—including one who was responsible for upholding wildlife conservation laws—serve as chairs on Special Economic Zone committees.

As Debbie Banks, EIA's campaign leader for tigers and wildlife crime, summarized, "Laos is a basket case"—which is why she and her colleagues decided to go public with their findings, rather than quietly approach the government. "Various NGOs working in Laos told us the government will do nothing if we just give them the results of our investigations—that they won't even bother to react," she said. By making their report freely available online, they hoped "to create a bit of a shitstorm" that would shame authorities into action.

The shitstorm, however, turned out to be more of a light shitshower. Though Banks and her coauthors urged the international community "to stop fawning over lip-service commitments to combating organized wildlife crime," lip service was exactly what the Lao government dished out when the media spotlight was briefly turned on it. Fighting bad publicity with good publicity, it broadcast footage of a raid of four Special Economic Zone restaurants on Lao National Television's *English News Program*. Viewers saw officials order the restaurants closed and then light a pile of tiger skins and some boxes labeled "tiger wine" on fire in a parking lot.

After that, though, they opted for an "alternative facts" approach and shrugged off further allegations. "This news item about the uncontrolled sale of protected species is untrue," Chanthajon Vagfaxeng, vice chair of the Golden Triangle Special Economic Zone, said on camera. "Our checks didn't reveal as many illegal items for sale as the NGO claimed." The news piece cheerily concluded with praise of Kings Romans' dedicated efforts to protect the environment. No arrests or prosecutions ever resulted from the raid, and the government never released an inventory of products they seized or burned. "It was a purely cosmetic enforcement effort," Banks said. And possibly free publicity for Kings Romans, too.

The Chinese government, meanwhile, had also been content to turn a blind eye to the Golden Triangle Special Economic Zone and other similarly lawless border towns in Laos and Myanmar, writing such places off as other countries' problems, despite being run and patronized by Chinese. Two years after the *Sin City* report came out, it's still business as usual in the Ciudad Juarez of Laos.

I was interested in seeing such flamboyant disregard for the law firsthand, especially the zoo-cum–wildlife farm. That I'm not Chinese, however, was a problem. Pretty much everyone who visits Kings Romans is either Chinese or, to a lesser extent, Thai, and people are wiser now to foreigners who turn up, associating them with pesky journalists and tree-hugging activists who inevitably bring trouble. To deflect attention, Banks advised that I adopt one of two possible guises: a backpacker or a Russian prostitute. "They're the only kinds of foreigners regularly seen there," she said.

For me, the decision was a no-brainer: I'd go as a prostitute, obviously. I basically already had the clothes for the job, and, at my age, posing as a backpacker seemed a bit off. If I were really going to do this undercover thing right, though, I needed a hidden camera, so I ventured into Manhattan to visit subtly named shop called Spy Store. I settled on a hidden camera watch, already conveniently designed to look like something an eastern European hooker might wear: pink faux alligator-skin straps with a matching pink watch face blinged out with layers of bright pink rhinestones.

Ty and my husband, Paul, were easy enough to recruit for the roles of pimp and john, but, to make the most of this trip, I also needed to find a translator— someone who spoke not only Lao but also Chinese. Finding a person with these particular linguistic skills to join us was a challenge, to say the least. For one, people really didn't want to go to Kings Romans. As a Laos-based journalist told me, "I know many people, but the element of risk is very high, and I have to say that I am unwilling to commit anyone to [the job] if they don't have local support." She added that I should be very careful, for "all is not what it seems"— prompting me to wonder whether my life was turning into a low-budget thriller.

Luckily, I did eventually find someone to come along, a local tourist guide / undercover operative whom I'll call Pong. I found Pong through Karl Ammann, the Kenya-based photojournalist known for his controversial tactics—he often buys wildlife contraband to get criminals to let their guard down—and for his outspokenness, including his knack for getting in peoples' faces with his camera. "Karl Ammann is kind of one of the early cowboys in Africa," a source told me. "He's done things no one else would, he's fearless. You have to be worried when standing next to him about who might see you, though."

Karl himself is well aware of this. "I'm considered a radical extremist," he said. "I don't rely on donor money, so I can say what I want to say." When I first contacted him by e-mail, he went out of his way to emphasize how important candidness is to him:

> I would be happy to talk to you about my experiences. However, after watching
> developments on the ground in Africa for more than forty years and then also
> in SE Asia for the last twenty-five years, I am no longer one of the people who
> believe any of these battles are being won. I know tons of people making a
> pretty good living presenting such beliefs to a wide segment of the public and
> donor community, but most of this I would classify as feel good tales or selling

Band-Aids to be put on a patient dying of terminal cancer. So I have this caveat
that I do not want my input in any project or book interpreted as part of any
feel-good message. The only objective I have left in this business is to be able to
look into the mirror in the morning.

I guess that's what a lifetime spent working in conservation will do to a guy, I
thought. I assured him that I wouldn't make him sound overly optimistic, and we
scheduled a call.

Karl was one of the first to expose the illicit tiger farm business in Southeast
Asia, and it was his work that Banks and her colleagues built upon for their *Sin
City* investigation. As he discovered through several years of investigations, tiger
zoos and farms across the region are run like a mafia, with managers swapping
tigers between facilities and across borders, monopolizing the trade by owning
stakes in multiple businesses, and flouting various nations' laws with impunity.
Bosses also have operatives working at all levels of the supply chain. One woman
in Laos, for example, was formerly an associate of Vixay Keosavang, the notorious kingpin behind the South African rhino pseudo-hunts, but now works as
a smuggler for the tiger farmers. She told Karl she could get anything across an
international border for a fixed price per wholesale pound.

"If there is a demand, there will be a supply," Karl said, speaking with a
thick Swiss-German accent in a world-weary tone. "And the demand is not going
down. In fact, I believe it is going up."

A small slice of these unsavory operations hit Western headlines in 2016,
when the Tiger Temple—a popular Thai tourist site where monks "lived in harmony" with 150 tigers and visitors paid to interact with them—was busted for
alleged illegal activities, including animal cruelty and wildlife trafficking. A government raid turned up around seventy dead cubs in the freezer and stuffed into
jars, along with tiger skins, bone products, and other evidence that the temple
had been trafficking both wild and captive-bred animals into the trade. As Karl
pointed out, "Just because they were monks didn't mean they weren't interested
in profit."

In most media takes, however, the Tiger Temple story read like an isolated
occurrence that was now taken care of. The temple was shuttered, the animals
were rescued, case closed. Unfortunately, the truth isn't quite as "feel good," as
Karl would say. The Thai government did seize 137 tigers from the temple, but,
less than a year later, a new offshoot facility was already under construction next

door, large enough to house five hundred tigers. The Tiger Temple crackdown "probably drove some players to be more careful with their trading activities," Karl said—but not so careful as to get out of the business. "Maybe it's arrogant, but I feel sometimes like the wise man in the village of idiots," he continued. "I see things that no one else seems to see and I try to put films together that illustrate that, but it seems like a lot of people just don't want to see these realities."

Meanwhile, other facilities throughout Thailand continue to operate just as the Tiger Temple did—only sans monks and on a much larger scale. In *The Tiger Mafia,* Karl's documentary about the farms, a mustachioed and oftentimes excessively sweaty Karl takes viewers to a few such places, including the Sriracha Zoo, located outside of Bangkok, and the Tiger Kingdom in Chiang Mai. Like the Tiger Temple, those facilities specialize in churning out tiger cubs—to the point that pigs are used as surrogate mothers to feed them all (cubs are immediately taken from their moms because breeders want females to go back into heat). Tourists pay steep prices for the privilege of playing with the babies and taking selfies with adolescent tigers under three years old, generating thousands of dollars each day for the zoo. Profits don't end there, however. Once the tigers hit sexual maturity, they become too aggressive and unpredictable to handle. They disappear, sold to the highest bidder.

"The question none of these visitors ever asks is what happens to these tigers at the end of the day," Karl said. "None of these people have any idea that they're financing this kind of operation. That, in three years, the guy they're petting today will be a piece of meat on a plate at Kings Romans Casino."

According to evidence Karl and others have gathered, some tigers are sold directly to customers who buy them for their parts. Others are shipped—legally or illegally—to different farms, including in Laos, Thailand, Myanmar, and China. Some may be sold for $50,000 to Chinese buyers, who tend to select male tigers—they want the penis—or to Vietnamese buyers, who don't care about the animal's sex. Overwhelmingly, the operations get away with such sales. When the Vietnamese owner of one such farm in Thakhek, Thailand, recently got into some legal trouble with the police and local government over his tiger dealings, he told one of Karl's operatives that he paid a bribe of $1 million to keep the facility going.

Although international trade of tigers remains firmly banned by CITES, the legality of domestic trade is murkier and varies from country to country. Thailand and Vietnam do not allow trade of tigers or their parts, and Laos likewise prohibits trade of wild tigers. But—with government permission—Laos does permit sale of wildlife parts from second-generation exotic animals bred on farms, tigers included. At least two major tiger farms in Laos have been granted governmental permission to sell animals, although conservationists have yet to find evidence that the Golden Triangle Special Economic Zone facility is also on that list. Laos recently announced that it intends to phase out tiger farms, however, so it could be optimistically assumed that all permissions have been revoked; for now, the situation is unclear.

China, on the other hand, prohibits trade of tiger bones yet issues government permits for trade of tiger skins from captive-bred animals. Illegal international smuggling of captive-bred tiger parts—including bones—is rampant, however, and evidence exists that wild tigers are illegally laundered into the legal skin trade as well. Conservationists believe that the farming business plays an increasingly significant role in the decline of tigers in the wild, by keeping demand alive and by providing a means of laundering.

I couldn't retrace Karl's meticulous steps, but I wanted at least to see a tiger farm for myself. In the days leading up to the trip to Laos, however, it was difficult to keep my anxiety at bay. I'd heard so many warnings about Kings Romans that I began to worry I might be leading us into some sort of serious trouble or danger. I had a nightmare in which I was eaten by a tiger, and another in which I was kidnapped and molested by a drug lord. As if reading my mind, even my editor at the New York Times, who had commissioned a story about tiger farming, called me for a safety pep talk: "If you feel like you might be in danger, I want you to leave. I don't want to give the impression that we're sending freelancers to places where their lives might be at risk."

I assured him that I would heed that warning. On that note, I packed up my hidden camera watch and whore clothes, took a deep breath, and headed to the airport.

Laos is a bit of a cultural and economic outlier in Southeast Asia. The French, who gained control of the Portugal-sized country in 1893, coined a handy phrase for summarizing the lifestyle differences between the landlocked nation and its neighbors: "The Vietnamese plant the rice, the Cambodians tend to it, and the Lao listen to it grow."

The slower pace of life in Laos, a country of about 6.5 million, remains evident today, from the ever-present hammocks that accommodate impromptu naps, to the country's affectionate, informal slogan, "Laos: Please don't rush." Another of the most frequently used phrases you'll likely hear in Laos is *bor pen yang*—"no problem." Tracing its roots to the Buddhist concept of accepting life's circumstances, it's a classic reaction to everything from a friend's apology for arriving a few minutes late to a bus breaking down in a torrential rain on a mountain road with no cell service, miles from the nearest village.

The undeniable charm of Laos, however, is hampered by its undeniable poverty. It may share a border with busybodies Vietnam, Thailand, and China, but it's a world apart from those economic dragons. Nearly 25 percent of the population lives below the poverty line. The country remains heavily dependent on foreign aid, thanks to the compounding legacies of colonialism, clashes with Thailand, tumult among ethnic minorities (including guerrilla warfare), and the Vietnam War (Laos was hit with more than 2 million tons of American ordnance, making it the most heavily bombed country per capita in history).

Corruption also plays a key role in the one-party socialist republic's persisting problems. Transparency International ranks Laos as 123rd of 176 countries for corruption, tied with a handful of others, including Sierra Leone, Moldova, and Honduras. Those who dare speak out against the system do so at their own peril. Privileged foreign visitors to Lao gilded temples and relaxed riverside retreats tend to see few of these problems, however.

We started our journey in Vientiane, perhaps the world's sleepiest capital. In 2006, I spent two months in Laos conducting aquaculture research with a team of French scientists, and, for me, Vientiane will always conjure memories of hazy orange dirt roads, weathered colonial architecture, and ramshackle catch-of-the-day cafés lining the sandy banks of the Mekong. While still laid back, I was saddened to find the city transformed, and not for the better: tacky, slapstick bars choked formerly charming fountain plazas; merchants aggressively hawked cheap sandals, T-shirts, and bags; and cars and motorcycles blasted horns and exhaust on congested roads.

Thankfully, I didn't have to dwell on the cruelty of time's forward-marching arrow for long. We'd scheduled to fly out early the next morning for Huay Xai, gateway town to the Golden Triangle and the closest airport to Kings Romans. The hour-long flight took us over steep forested hills that melted into undulating rice paddies and quiet little villages. Like a faithful companion, the mighty Mekong's brown vein followed us north.

Pong quickly found us at the airport, which was no more than a concrete shack in the middle of a field. He was trim and short, with neatly combed black hair and classically handsome features. He spoke English with casual coolness, and his eyes were intelligent and alert. He explained that he met Karl six or seven years ago, through a Thai tourism company. The two have frequently worked together since then on missions throughout Laos, to the point that Pong jokingly calls Karl his father.

We piled into an oversized van driven by a skinny kid—the son of a friend of Pong's—who looked like he'd be up to some sort of minor delinquency were he not chauffeuring foreigners around. Most roads in this part of Laos are treacherous, pockmarked affairs, but the one we pulled onto was smooth concrete. It was constructed by Kings Romans and leads straight to the casino, Pong explained. I noticed, though, that it was conspicuously bereft of any ads for the casino. "There used to be signs, but they were only written in Chinese," Pong explained. "The local government protested and said the first words should be in Lao, then in Chinese, so they had to take the signs down."

Along with neighboring Thailand and Myanmar, this corner of Laos is the world's number two opium producer, second only to Afghanistan. Pong himself drinks opium tea at home, and he likes to throw a little marijuana into a nice bouillon. "It's good for relaxing," he noted. It's easy to get those sort of things here; some of his friends keep poppy fields, though one was recently on the receiving end of a police raid and had to pay a steep fine. Indeed, the government isn't completely turning a blind eye. Just a couple of months ago, Pong said, five people were arrested in a nearby "drug village," with seizures including heroin and methamphetamine as well as thirty-six fancy cars, hotels, and land. Car showrooms, he added, are favorite fronts for drug dealers and other traffickers, because it makes the task of laundering easy: "You just say, 'Oh, I'm getting a new car.'"

Casinos and drugs go well together. Gambling is illegal in Laos except in designated Special Economic Zones, but even there Lao people are not supposed to partake; a sign at the Kings Romans casino reads "No Lao People Allowed." Even so, plenty of locals manage to finagle their way in, where they inevitably accumulate debt and get into other forms of trouble. "Anywhere you have a casino, you have problems with gambling, PTT—that's what we call prostitutes—and drugs," Pong said. "People have lost their homes and their families to the casino and drugs. If you finish your money, you get a loan off your car or something. But for one day the lenders charge 10 percent interest—per day, not per month!"

"So if I was a Chinese tourist, would it be possible to get high tonight?" I asked Pong.

"Sure! The initial investment that built Kings Romans was all drug money. The big boss is trying to convert dirty money to clean money."

Officials don't seem to mind, he added: Laos itself reportedly owns a 20 percent stake in the place, and much of these proceeds no doubt go into pockets rather than toward bettering the country. "With the new government, though, we hope to change a lot of things," he said, referring to Thongloun Sisoulith, prime minister as of 2016, who claims to be bent on reining in corruption in Laos.

We were nearing our destination. Pong decided to take us the back way into Kings Romans, driving past small palm shacks—a "PTT village," he said—and by modest concrete buildings with Beer Lao signs out front, a not-so-secret signal, he said, that those businesses have prostitutes. Most of the girls, he added, come from the central part of the country, recruited by friends who already work here and lured in by the promise of high prices paid by Chinese clients. Depending on how pretty the girl is, an hour or two with a Kings Romans prostitute costs as much as $85, while an entire night runs up to $145.

We stopped the van to allow a herd of water buffalo to cross, tails swinging casually in the sun, and then continued on our way. A few moments later the casino's golden dome and giant crown-shaped roof appeared over the treetops—a completely surreal sight amid the rice paddies, livestock, and fish ponds that otherwise characterized the area.

Pong pointed to a building on the right—the Special Economic Zone's jail, where people who "have problems with Kings Romans" wind up. He told us he stopped by the prison once to meet a friend and the men he saw locked up there were "hanging on the bars like monkeys." Just behind the jail was the big boss Zhao's house, not visible from the road. "It's guarded by dogs and guns," Pong said. "Karl wanted to go there but I told him, 'No, if you go, you go alone.'"

Zhao and his wife, Guiqin Su, a source later confirmed, are indeed said to reside there, but they keep a low profile. According to a source—whose tip came from the Kings Romans zookeeper—"Mr. Zhao travels with two bodyguards and frequents the Pleasure Palace in town. He's said to have a cold relationship with his wife. They have three grown children, and his wife has a small farm near their residence where she keeps about ten tiger cubs. They will be used for restaurant meat when they are bigger."

Around 9,000 people supposedly live at Kings Romans, 6,000 of whom are Burmese workers and their families—both documented and undocumented. Pong wanted to show us where they live. The Burmese worker camp, as it's called, would be better described as the Burmese ghetto. Dilapidated shacks competed for space with heaping piles of garbage animated by copious swarms of flies and pecking chickens. Barefoot kids in threadbare clothes ran down dusty dirt lanes, past ditches full of rancid, trash-choked, black water. Yet, against this backdrop of overwhelming squalor, some of the lopsided shanties showed clear signs of care—a bed of well-tended geraniums here, a tidy little shrine there. I was struck by the heartbreaking futility of these small markers of pride.

We took a turn and passed into the Chinese workers' village. Though the Burmese workers' camp was located just four hundred meters down the road, this was an entirely different world. Neat concrete homes were lined up in rows behind a cheery, arched sign marking the entryway. The streets were paved, and each house seemed to have a motorbike or car parked next to a fat satellite dish. Across the street was a well-tended commercial center selling everything from oranges to hammers to television sets.

We then passed an overgrown field—supposedly the future site of horse races—and a large billboard advertising a "Battle of the Boxers" event that had taken place several weeks earlier. I wouldn't have guessed it, but this was apparently the main drag leading to Kings Romans casino. The street was painted in faded yellow and red, and grass sprouted through cracks on the road. An empty area marked a site used for cock and water buffalo fights, across from a derelict, half-constructed building that Pong said was supposed to become a shopping mall but looked as if it had been abandoned years ago. The Kapok Garden Hotel—our base for the evening—stood next door. Painted baby blue and adorned half-heartedly with some neon red garnishes around Romanesque pillars, the Kapok Garden looked like the love child of a Motel 6 and a decrepit Southern plantation.

We pulled around several nonfunctional, half-empty concrete fountains full of brown slime, into a parking lot full of white Toyota Mark IIs, the vehicle of choice for the Kings Romans Group. We were joined there by Ear (pronounced "Air"), a member of the Phunoi group, a Lao ethnic minority hill tribe. Having grown up near the Chinese border, Ear spoke some Chinese and would be our interpreter for the trip (he did not, however, speak any English). He previously used his language skills to land a job at Kings Romans, where he worked for three years before getting fed up with how things were run. "There were too many bosses," he said.

As the guys gathered their luggage, I quietly pulled Pong aside. I was currently wearing a nice summer dress, of the sort one might don for a family picnic, but I planned to change into my prostitute gear after we checked in. This seemed to warrant some kind of warning.

"Just so you know," I began in a hushed, conspiratorial voice, "I'm going to dress like a prostitute."

Pong nodded slowly, processing what I was saying.

"For disguise," I clarified.

"Oh, yes!" His nodding picked up pace.

"So don't judge."

He promised he wouldn't and asked whether I'd brought a hidden camera. I told him I had.

"Good," he said simply, and we headed inside.

As we entered the hotel, I felt let down. I knew we were journeying into a seething bed of crime, but, at the same time, I expected Kings Romans to be luxurious, in a tacky, over-the-top sort of way—the Trump Tower of Laos, if you will. After all, wasn't this place supposed to cater to the wildly wealthy? Nothing I'd seen thus far gave the impression that anyone with money would ever come here. These feelings were further reinforced by the hotel's reception area, which was decidedly not nice. In fact, it was downright shabby, with stained faux leather couches, cigarette-ash-covered coffee tables, and a few cluttered check-in desks. Behind the desks hung four clocks with city names printed beneath them; Beijing was the only one I recognized. It and another clock were set to the exact same time, while the other two clocks were also set to the same time, but an hour ahead of the first two.

Ear filled out our Chinese paperwork for us and got our keys. I asked Pong if it's true that Karl's hotel room was bugged—something Karl had warned me about in advance, which had made me wonder whether he was just being paranoid. But Pong said he thought Karl's room probably was bugged, and ours might be, too. "By the way," he added helpfully, "don't use the condoms in your room because they charge three dollars for one condom. We had a problem with an American cameraman who didn't want to pay."

"There might be worse consequences than the three-dollar charge . . . " Ty wryly noted.

Though the ground floor seemed virtually deserted—all the room doors were open, revealing untouched, made-up beds—the staff had split us into what seemed like oddly deliberate room choices. Paul and I were A102, while Ty was A124, down opposite ends of the first-floor hallway—as far from each other as possible. Karl later confirmed to me that these are indeed the very rooms the staff always place him and his camera crew in, and Banks experienced the same during her visit.

The room, like everything we'd seen so far, sucked. Cheap art hung askew over the bed, and the purple comforter was marred by a cigarette burn and a cloudy white stain whose origins I strongly did not want to know. The off-white walls bore large cracks and grey skid marks from shoes and furniture scrapes, plus a few gray-brown blotches that marked the remains of long-smooshed mosquitos. The bathroom, meanwhile, was little more than a concrete square, with no separation between toilet, sink, and grimy, naked showerhead. The space was perfumed by an incessant stench of sewage, leading Paul to guess that we were situated directly above the hotel's cesspool.

I pawed through a hardback brochure on the desk (a sticker on the front read "NOT [A] PRESENT" in English). Inside were color photographs of a tiger skeleton submerged in wine and of packaged tiger wine bottles, and ads in Chinese next to the photos stated that tiger penis wine and leopard penis wine were available here at Kings Romans, to "teach travelers about Chinese wine culture." Charming. I took some photos of the brochure (given that it wasn't a present) and then got to work examining all the shelves, light fixtures, and electronics for hidden cameras or mics. Although nothing looked fishy, I decided to operate under the assumption that we were being watched. Paul and I had joked about "putting on a show" for the Chinese spies, but now I felt uncomfortably exposed. I decided to change clothes in the bathroom.

My outfit for the day was a pair of teensy white Daisy Dukes, a white tank top two sizes too small that my friend Julio had given me to promote his bar, lace-up sandals, lots of eyeliner and pink lip gloss, and braided pigtails. Plus, of course, the bulky, bejeweled spy watch. A Chinese policeman raised an eyebrow as I strode into the reception area, while Ear's expression registered as dumbstruck glee. As I chatted with Paul and Ty, Ear surreptitiously took out his phone and snapped a photo. Cool-as-a-cucumber Pong, on the contrary, didn't bat an eye.

Not to be left out, Ty and Paul had also changed into costume. Ty's Dmitry consisted of faux-torn jeans, a black shirt unbuttoned to sleazily low depths, a gold chain nestled around wisps of ginger chest hair, and Eurotrash sunglasses. Paul had slicked his dark hair back and was wearing jeans with an oversized, island-themed wifebeater that revealed his brilliantly white, sun-starved arms. He likewise tied his outfit together with a gold chain, courtesy Ty.

We'd planned to spend just one night in Kings Romans, and it was already past noon, so we had no time to waste checking out the town. Wildlife shopping was the first order of business. A five-minute walk from the hotel revealed a formidable, several-stories-tall gate marked "Chinatown" in Lao, Chinese, and English. Its intricate woodwork was painted in bright blues, greens, and reds, and swirling gold dragons grinned at us from two square panels.

The gate opened onto a gray cobbled pedestrian street with two matching rows of quaint but cheaply made buildings featuring wooden doors, gray shingled pagoda-style roofs, and sun-bleached red lanterns. The town came with its own soundtrack; currently, something that reminded me of a Chinese instrumental cover of Whitney Houston's "When You Believe." Despite the friendly facade, many of the shops were locked up, seemingly for good. Their grimy windows revealed barren shelves and floors littered with dust, cigarette butts, and beer cans. Shoppers were scant as well; the few other people who passed us by appeared to be workers rather than tourists. Ear, speaking through Pong, explained that the derelict shops are indicative of the "crazy Chinese" proclivity to "build lots of buildings, but they're all empty."

"It feels like a ghost town," I agreed. It all seemed rather eerie and strange.

Adam Dean, a photographer who shot images in the Special Economic Zone for a *New York Times* story I wrote about wildlife farming, later pointed out to me, though, that Kings Romans isn't really that odd of a place. "Down to the fittings in the hotel, the street furniture, and the half-complete construction, I just felt that I was in a third-tier Chinese city that's not finished," he said. "The wildlife side of it didn't feel like China, but, other than that, I wasn't that weirded out by it."

We ducked into a shop called Yi Pin Tang, passing through thick, clear plastic drapes of the sort used in a professional kitchen. Four long glass cases stood in front of us, and I immediately spotted the stark white of ivory, the muddled brown-black-gold of rhino horn, and the glint of so many bottles of tiger bone wine. Bingo. The staff were sitting on a wooden couch, drinking tea. Pong and

Ear engaged them while Paul, Ty, and I looked around. I crossed my arms, trying to be as casual as possible as I filmed with my watch; when no one seemed to notice, I got a bit bolder, contorting my arm for better angles.

The shop's inventory was formidable: dozens of ivory chopsticks, bracelets, and necklaces; around fifteen large ivory statues; several intricately crafted full elephant tusks; ten or so daggerlike tiger teeth; ornate rhino horn goblets, bowls, bracelets, and Buddha statues; gallon-sized bags of rhino horn shavings; cartons of tiger bone wine bottles; and tiger bone bracelets that looked like something Wilma Flintstone would wear. All of it was almost definitely illegal. Through Ear, Pong asked to take a photo of the tiger wine, and one of the women shook her head no. When I tried to engage her about prices, she instructed us to come back later, when the owner would be there (later, however, they were closed).

We moved on to a nicely decorated place next door, where a plump middle-aged woman in a blue shirt, loose pony tail, and beaded ivory necklace welcomed us. A vat of golden liquid stood on a shelf with a long, curled object inside. "Hey, Love, I think that's a tiger penis," I whispered to Paul. Her glass cases revealed dried elephant skin, porcupine quills, ivory galore, tiger teeth, a bag of powdered rhino horn, and tiger claws with some flesh still attached that she'd placed in a shallow bowl of water, giving them the look of succulent stone crab claws. She also had a small swatch of tiger skin, perhaps a tip-off that a full skin could be procured.

The shopkeeper was unusually friendly and came over to offer assistance. "Where from?" she asked me in stilted English. I considered saying Romania, sticking to our eastern European guise, but went with New York instead—a lucky move, because she used that information to switch a translator app on her phone to English.

I inquired about a necklace with red beads and what looked like a circular black stone hanging from the bottom. The shopkeeper fiddled with her phone, then pushed a button. "Rhinoceros horn," a robotic female voice announced, making the shopkeeper grin. The asking price, she said, was over $2,000. A clunky bracelet next to the necklace—also rhino horn, which the woman's phone informed us was "for man"—cost even more, about $2,300.

The woman pointed to the black part of the necklace again—the part actually composed of rhino horn. "Drug," the woman's phone stated, as she mimed shooting herself up with a needle. She seemed quite amused now.

"Jesus, it's so expensive," Paul said, as we thanked the shopkeeper and left.

"Well, it's magical drugs," I muttered sarcastically.

We left the main drag, and Pong pointed out an imitation imperial hall, complete with a tiger skin spread out on a large wooden throne. Ancient Chinese fancied that the stripes on a tiger's head formed the character for "king," so warlords used to sit atop tiger skins to show their power. At Kings Romans, tourists can pay to do so, too. Like the rest of the town, though, the hall looked derelict and cheap.

"I really expected this place to be nicer—to cater to a clientele that's actually discerning," Paul said. "But there's a complete inattention to detail, and everything is totally run down and sad. If products from the illegal wildlife trade are signs of wealth and status, well, I'd like to know where wealthy people are getting those things, because I really don't think it's Kings Romans."

Ty, overhearing him, nodded emphatically.

The tour was concluding, and we headed down a sunny side street toward the entrance gate. "From here on, these shops are for PTT," Pong said, gesturing at a row of massage parlors. "Take a name card and you can call the girls tonight! Ten minutes later there will be a knock on the hotel door." Pong was obviously joking with us, but I noticed that both Ear and the driver pocketed a card as we walked by.

As we climbed into the van, I asked Pong what he thought of all of this. "I once told Karl that we need to help our own species first, and after that, the animals," he began after a thoughtful pause. "He said, 'Pong, imagine this world with no animals, only humans! We should make everything balanced.' I thought about it, and now I think it's bad to kill lots of animals, just for this. We don't use them for these kinds of things, but the Chinese do."

TIGERS HAVE FACTORED INTO TRADITIONAL CHINESE MEDICINE FOR UP TO THREE millennia, and over the centuries practitioners have adopted a true nose-to-tail approach. Though none of the big cats' parts have been shown to have any medical value (placebo effect excluded), pretty much everything has been assigned a use. Whiskers quell toothaches, meat cures malaria, fat stops vomiting, blood strengthens willpower, noses sooth children's epilepsy, teeth purge sores from a man's penis, eyeballs and bile prevent convulsions, and penises banish impotence and promote longevity. Of all the tiger's parts, though, its bones are the most

sought after. In Li Shih-chen's 1597 *Materia Medica,* they are said to remove evil
and calm fright; cure ulcers, dysentery, and sores from rat bites; soothe joint and
muscle pain; prevent infection, devil possession, and scabies in newborn children; help with burns and toenail problems; and more.

These days, bones tend to be consumed in the form of tiger bone wine. Tra-
ditionalists consider it a cure-all tonic for traumatic injuries, aging, osteoporo-
sis, and fatigue, and more recently it has also evolved into a supposed virility
booster. Brewers soak a handful of bones or even an entire skeleton for months
in rice wine, oftentimes along with additional ingredients like ginseng and other
wildlife products. The flavor, according to a 2005 production feasibility study
published by the Hunan Sanhong Pharmaceutical Company Limited, is quite
lovely: "A refined taste shall be soft and tender to the mouth, gentle to the throat,
unstimulating to the head and subtle to the taste of herbs, with a seamless merge
of alcoholic and herbal fragrances," the company claimed. (Michele Penna, a
Beijing-based journalist who visited Kings Romans and sampled tiger wine there,
described it a bit differently to me, however: "It tasted like crap.")

Besides wine, tiger bone paste—the stinky, caramel-like substance I was
shown in Chapter 2 by Mr. M in Hanoi—also remains popular among Vietnamese and Chinese users. At a party I recently threw in my Brooklyn apartment, a
Chinese American friend even casually mentioned that her parents had brought
some of this stuff back for her on their latest trip home. "Grandma used to put it
on my knee when I fell down and hurt myself," she giggled. She added that it's
still plenty popular and that I shouldn't have much trouble finding it if I asked
around in Beijing.

Poaching is the biggest threat to tigers today, although that wasn't always
the case. From the eighteenth to twentieth centuries, sport hunters in India and
Southeast Asia killed the big cats by the thousands, along with prey species that
the predators depended on for survival. Even as this practice subsided, habitat
loss and revenge killings for tiger attacks on livestock continued to hammer
populations.

China's tigers were by and large spared, however. In the mid-twentieth century, around 4,000 of the big cats lived throughout the country, most of which
were South China tigers, an endemic subspecies. That abruptly changed in the
mid-1950s, when Mao Zedong decided that tigers were a nuisance that needed to
be eradicated. The government issued a tiger bounty, and citizens enthusiastically

responded, turning in thousands of skins from animals they killed. The bounty also likely helped to fill China's "bone bank," a hoard of tiger bone—no one knows how much—used to supply pharmacies across the country.

In 1977, with just four hundred South China tigers remaining, the government suddenly realized that its big cats might be something worth keeping around. Officials did a 360, canceling the bounty, banning tiger hunting, and listing the animals as protected species. Living as they did in the epicenter of demand, though, China's tigers continued to decline despite the hunting ban, especially as the country's tiger bone bank dried up in the late 1980s.

By that time, fur was no longer the most valuable part of a tiger. India— which currently holds about half of the world's remaining tigers—began intercepting hundreds of pounds of tiger bones being smuggled to China; and South Korea, Taiwan, and Singapore likewise raked in tiger bones by the tons in the 1990s. China also continued to export tiger-based products abroad, including 27 million pills, balms, powders, and ointments from 1990 to 1992. To manufacture all those goods and more, Tongrentang, the country's oldest and largest traditional medicine company, was burning through almost 7,000 pounds of bones per year—equivalent to three-hundred-plus tigers.

It all proved too much for the South China tiger. In the early 1990s, surveys conducted in a few mountainous reserves revealed the last tracks of the subspecies ever recorded in the wild. Captive populations derived from six founders are all that remain today.

China's native tiger was gone, but that didn't stem the country's demand for tiger parts. Farming, the government decided, could prop up the trade permanently and sustainably. With support from the State Forestry Administration, in 1986 China established its first commercial tiger farm, and several years later the country passed a wildlife law that encouraged breeding, domestication, and use of endangered species. As Lishu Li, program manager of wildlife trade at the Wildlife Conservation Society's China office, said, "We have such a long history of agriculture in China that we believe we can cultivate and control everything."

China, however, had overlooked one serious obstacle impeding its farming plan: global public relations. The world had recently taken notice that tigers seemed bound for extinction. In 1987, CITES elevated tigers to its highest tier of protection, banning all commercial international trade in their parts. That seemed to have little impact in China, though, so in 1993—responding to pressure by conservation organizations—US president Bill Clinton threatened to impose sanctions on China and Taiwan unless they addressed their roles in the illegal trade of tiger and rhinoceros parts. To the relief and delight of many, China's State Council swiftly reacted, issuing a domestic ban on rhino horn and tiger bone that very year.

Typical of such brief victories, China's decisions looked good mostly on paper. By 1994 it was clear that reality wasn't matching up. The country had been caught exporting more than a ton of tiger bones to South Korea and seemed to have "misplaced" more than three tons of rhino horn. Also, at this critical moment, the United States dropped the ball. Rather than take the advice of thirty-nine congresspersons who were pushing for formal sanctions against China for its broken promises, Clinton instead announced that China had progressed in "key areas," so sanctions were not warranted.

Demand in China for traditional medicine made from tigers has not gone away, and tiger products have also begun evolving beyond their historic uses, morphing into luxury goods meant to show off one's status and refinement. Like serving bottles of Krug during Prohibition in the States, the illegality surrounding tiger wine is actually an enticement: it demonstrates that you're powerful enough to flout the law. Around 2009, jewelry made from tiger bones, teeth, and claws also started coming into vogue—a practice that "is absolutely not a traditional use," according to Li. Some of that is likely driven by the "cultural collectors" that I described in Chapter 5, while some seems to be inspired by pop culture, including two Indiana Jones–style book series—Notebook for Stealing a Tomb and The Ghost Blows the Light Off—and a Mongolia-themed series (and movie adaptation) called Wolf Totem. All are heavy on mystique, adventure, and wildlife, and all are extremely popular in China.

It's difficult to be optimistic. From 100,000 tigers in the nineteenth century, fewer than 4,000 remain in the wild today—a 96 percent drop. They continue to be poached—the remains of 1,755 tigers were seized in the illegal trade from 2000 to 2015. Of the eight subspecies, three are already extinct, and one is extinct in the wild. Vietnam, Laos, and Cambodia have virtually no tigers left, and China, with just 7–50 wild tigers, will likely join that list soon.

Tigers in captivity, on the contrary, are flourishing, with tiger farms springing up across Asia like poisonous mushrooms. Farmed animals kept in captivity now far outnumber wild populations: in Laos, there are more than 700; Thailand,

1,450; Vietnam, 200; and China, 5,000–6,000. Still more are holed up in other Southeast Asian countries.

Though these numbers might suggest that breeding preserves tigers, it has been well documented that farms serve as a flimsy front for illegal trade, especially at China's notorious facilities. In January 2011, I popped into the Siberian Tiger Park, one of the country's largest farms, located in Harbin, in the frigid Manchurian north. Originally supported by government subsidies, the Harbin farm was set up in the late 1980s to breed tigers for their bones, but now it presents itself as a safari-style family adventure destination. When I visited, the Japanese friend I was traveling with and I were the only foreigners on a packed bus of enthusiastic Chinese patrons. We rumbled through a tacky gate shaped like a tiger's open mouth and into a barren swath of frozen land surrounded by a high fence. Tigers were everywhere in the snowy enclosure, lounging on wooden platforms, napping under naked trees, and pacing along the fence line. A couple of small, separate outdoor cages also contained huddles of emaciated lions and panthers that appeared even more ill suited to the subzero weather than I was.

At one point on the tour we stopped at a metal staircase that led up to a fenced-in overlook. A sign in Chinese and English listed "Price for Live Animals," including pheasant ($14.50), sheep ($87), duck ($14.50), and even cattle ($290). A woman in our group purchased a live chicken ($7.25), which she dangled over the cats' enclosure. Clucking hysterically, the bird peered down at its doom—a writhing orange and black mass of hungry felines. A couple of the cats made desperate lunges at the chicken, grasping at the air like drunk coeds at a Mardi Gras parade. The crowd shrieked in delight, while my friend mumbled, "Oh, God . . . oh, God . . . " At last, the woman dropped the bird, sparking a frenzied tug of war and a flurry of brown feathers. As we got back onto the bus, I looked back to see a smear of bright red blood in the snow—the only evidence that remained of the cruel spectacle.

What I didn't see on my visit to the Harbin Tiger Park, however—but what I likely could have seen had I been Chinese and asked the right questions—were the freezers full of tiger carcasses and the tiger bone wine made and sold onsite, according to several sources. In 2012 and 2013, Banks and her colleagues at EIA catalogued these illegalities at the Siberian Tiger Park and other major tiger farms in China, and tiger bone wine was again filmed for sale in Harbin in 2016 by an undercover ITV News crew. A gift shop worker readily told the undercover

ITV reporters that the wine made there is both legitimate and available; a media representative subsequently denied the claim by phone but did not answer the reporters' follow-up questions.

The government is likely well aware of this. A 2005 investigation conducted by the International Fund for Animal Welfare of five major tiger farms revealed that all maintained factories for making tiger bone wine, and that their products were given "special permission" for sale by two governmental bodies. The key for circumventing the law seemed to be simply taking the bones out before bottling up the wine—the equivalent of arguing there are no grapes in a bottle of Bordeaux because they can't be seen floating around in it. The bottles sell for $300 to $1,600, investigators found, mostly to government officials and businessmen. One of the companies even sends them as gifts to ministry officials in Beijing for holidays.

Although tiger bone is banned by Chinese domestic law, tiger skin is not. A legal loophole still allows sale of skins from farmed animals that die naturally. According to an internal statement issued by China's State Forestry Administration in 2007, this practice is in line with "the current international trend of protecting wildlife"—a claim that is clearly not true. The EIA investigation revealed that government-authorized fur trade spurs laundering of poached wild tiger skins into the trade, while others have found that the law also encourages some farmers to starve their cats to induce a "natural" death.

All of this—the wine, the skins, the endangered animals bred like livestock— flies in the face of a 2007 CITES agreement that countries with "intensive operations breeding tigers on a commercial scale" should do so only with the aim of supporting wild tiger conservation, and that captive tigers "should not be bred for trade in their parts and derivatives." Contrary to most CITES decisions, this one pertained to both domestic and international trade. China, however, has ignored it.

When I had a Chinese assistant reach out to China's CITES representatives to request an interview about wildlife farming for the *New York Times* and for this book, Meng Xianlin, executive director general, brusquely declined. But Michael 't Sas-Rolfes, the conservation economist at the University of Oxford, has spoken with a range of relevant Chinese representatives, including from the government and private sector, about this subject. In 2007, he accepted a state invitation to visit the country as part of a group fact-checking mission to examine the possibility of reestablishing a legal domestic trade of farm-supplied tiger parts. Based on what he learned then and in the years since, he does not believe China's tiger farms will be shuttering any time soon. Several key players indicated that they remained committed to maintaining or reviving use of animal-based traditional medicines—including ones from endangered species—and that their proposed blanket solution was farming. Diminishing wildlife populations concerned them insofar as those trends impacted important commercial products, much less so in terms of conservation. They also felt shunned by the Western NGO community, who they claimed had refused to engage with them. "They seemed to be of the view that either in situ conservation would succeed without their input, or in situ conservation would fail, in which case they would be left with the last remaining stocks," 't Sas-Rolfes said. "They therefore had nothing to lose by maintaining their captive populations."

Many experts believe, however, that tigers themselves have everything to lose. Scott Roberton, director of counter–wildlife trafficking at the Wildlife Conservation Society's Asia Program, pointed out that the problems with maintaining a legal market for tiger parts are the same ones that have plagued the ivory industry for years. "Legal trade stimulates demand, confuses law enforcement efforts, and opens a huge opportunity for laundering in illegal products—which is why ivory markets are now being closed globally," he said. "There just isn't the capacity within these countries to manage a legal trade in a watertight way."

Indeed, in a 2008 Wildlife Conservation Society study of seventy-eight Vietnamese exotic animal farms, researchers found that 42 percent of owners admitted to regularly laundering animals from the wild; some also sold animals to traders to smuggle across the Chinese border, while others regularly bribed local officials. A 2016 Education for Nature–Vietnam study of twenty-five exotic farms likewise found that all engaged in some form of illegal activity, ranging from forging papers to supplementing farmed stock with wild-caught animals.

Even if all such operations were run by honest individuals, however, farms would not relieve all pressure on wild populations. As I witnessed in Chapters 1–3, many people in Vietnam, China, and elsewhere in Asia overwhelmingly prefer products from wild animals, not farmed ones. Mr. M, the traditional medicine user in Hanoi, said it best: "Outsiders like you cannot go to Vietnam's bear and tiger farms, but I have been, and I have seen the poor health of the animals there. So I prefer animals from the wild."

WITH THE CHINATOWN TOUR WRAPPED UP, OUR STRANGE POSSE OF TRASHILY DRESSED foreigners and linguistically talented Lao men headed to the nearby Kings Romans zoo-cum-farm. Unlike many such facilities in the region, this one was open to the public and didn't even charge admission. In fact, when we visited the litter-strewn, baseball-field-sized lot, there wasn't a single staff member around.

We entered from the back, down an overgrown path that led to the tigers. Their enclosure consisted of two long, perpendicular rows of wire, fence, and bars that were divided into smaller cells, not unlike a prison. Their cages were about twenty feet by ten feet—hardly sufficient for eight- to thirteen-foot-long animals that occupy territories of up to four hundred square miles in the wild—and each cage held one to three tigers.

Though all had presumably spent their lives behind bars, their intelligent eyes glinted with an intense, coiled energy that captivity could no doubt never stamp out. Some paced back and forth in graceful frustration; others lay inert on the grimy concrete floor, napping. Seeing those animals up close—even separated by several layers of rusted metal bars—clearly brought into focus just how massive tigers are, and how powerful. Despite their size, though, in their wholly feline antics, it was impossible not to see in them my own cat, Kit, and feel immediate empathy. Even in a New York City apartment, she has far more real estate than any of these cats—twenty times her size—will ever enjoy. Kit also, of course, will never be slaughtered and turned into a bottle of booze.

Pong broke the silence with some tiger farming factoids. He counted twenty-four tigers now, down from twenty-seven a few months ago when he last visited with Karl. "I think they killed and ate a few, maybe for Chinese New Year," he said. "Live animals are about $40,000 to $50,000."

"You can buy a *live* tiger?" Paul asked incredulously.

"Yeah, a lot of people want to pretend they shot it in the forest. So the owners give it a sleeping pill and release it, then you shoot it and take pictures. You can also take the skin and bones home."

"Jesus . . . " Ty said, the color seeming to drain from his already pale face.

We proceeded on, passing a cage of raucous macaques and another holding deer resting on a concrete floor covered in urine and feces. I spotted a lone porcupine lounging in a kennel-sized cage and a terrified civet in a cat-carrier-sized box; they were no doubt trapped days before in the nearby forest and were now awaiting the pot or the pan. A separate line of cages was filled with bears, many of which displayed clear signs of captivity-induced mania: frenzied pacing and relentless head banging. Unlike the tigers, the bears, apparently, had already been broken mentally.

"Do you think people actually come here to look at these sad animals?" Paul asked.

"They come here to look at the animals they want to eat," I sighed.

No one wanted to linger at the zoo, so we headed back to the Kapok Garden to get ready for dinner. Sticking with the lady of the night theme, I changed into a slinky red dress with black mesh cutouts, plus blood-red lipstick and black heels. We regrouped with Pong at the God of Wealth, supposedly Kings Romans' nicest and priciest restaurant. It was one of the places raided in 2015 for selling wild-meat, but it had reportedly gone right back to business as usual after the publicity stunt.

Tiger and other exotic delicacies wouldn't be on offer to us, though. As soon as Pong walked into the florescent-lit dining hall, the overweight owner recognized him from his work with Karl. "You can eat here," she shot, eyes narrowing, "but don't ask for the special menu again!" Dean, the *New York Times* photographer, ran into no such issues when he ate at the God of Wealth, however. He speaks Chinese and was accompanied by a Chinese colleague, and they were able to order a plate of tiger meat for $45. "The taste, if you are interested, was strong, musky, gamey," he told me. The restaurant next door, New Tender Fish, also confirmed to him that they serve tiger meat and even showed him two live pangolins in cages next to the kitchen, priced at nearly $600 each.

The God of Wealth staff wasn't exactly careful in front of us either, though. Moments after forbidding us from seeing the wildlife menu, a server confirmed to Ear that a large vat of brown liquid with some slimy-looking debris inside was indeed home-brewed tiger bone wine, sold for $20 a shot. I got up and filmed it with my hidden camera watch, and, when no one seemed to notice or care, I took out my phone and took a couple of photos.

We skipped the tiger wine and ordered an assortment of dishes that looked appetizing in the picture menu but turned out to be tasteless and have a consistency like cardboard. Meanwhile, Ty, Paul, and I tried to procure what appeared to be the restaurant's token bottle of white wine, a dust-covered Jacob's Creek chardonnay priced around forty dollars. Though the same bottle would cost about eight dollars in the States, we were tired of beer and figured desperate circumstances justified the inflation. We had to ask the flummoxed waitress to chill the warm bottle, which she buried in an industrial-sized metal mixing bowl full of ice. "I think you're the first customer to ever ask for the wine," Pong said as this scene unfolded.

Our wine odyssey had only just begun, however. It still hadn't been served well into our abysmal meal, and, when we asked, the same waitress began struggling in vain to work the corkscrew. Giving up, she disappeared into the back, only to emerge minutes later with a glass pitcher full of liquid that looked like a kidney-failure patient's urine. "Um, that wine should not be that color," I said, even as she poured a bit of the cloudy brown-yellow fluid into my glass. But giving it the benefit of the doubt—and wishing desperately to make this work—I took a sip. *Mistake!* I immediately spat it back into the glass—it tasted like something unearthed from a five-hundred-year-old tomb. "We're not paying for that," I said. "It's gone bad."

Thus commenced a half-hour ordeal of arguing with the staff in our odd telephone game of English-to-Lao-to-Chinese-to-Lao-to-English. At some point, the manager got involved but would not come over to our table, causing the irked waitress to march back and forth between the boss and us, all the while sloshing the rancid wine on the restaurant floor. Ty tried to resolve the situation by pulling up an image of Jacob's Creek wine on his phone to show the staff the beverage's actual, intended color, and in response the waitress brought out the empty wine bottle itself, inadvertently revealing the cause of the problem: a rotten, disintegrating cork at the bottom of the bottle.

While everyone was arguing, I looked up in time to see another server emerge from the kitchen carrying a tray of what was obviously a giant bear paw covered in some kind of brown sauce. Displayed with the pads facing up, it looked disturbingly humanoid, as though the Yeti had had his foot cut off and cooked. The bear-toting waiter stopped by our table to take a look at the corked bottle, bringing the morbid plate inches from my face. Before I could snap a photo, though, he continued to a private room where boisterous laughter could be heard. I really wanted to see what else was behind that door, imagining whole smoked pangolins, sautéed tiger flanks, and white lines of powdered rhino horn.

Following my gaze, Pong noted that the crowd in that particular VIP room included many ladyboys.

"The ladyboy bear-eating convention—how did we not get an invite!?" Ty wondered.

"Maybe if I go and start gyrating in front of the window we'll get into the bear party," I suggested.

"Ty's definitely gyrated his way into bear parties before!" Paul cracked in a queeny voice, teasing our gay best friend. Ty smiled—guilty as charged.

As we wrapped up the excruciating meal, the staff finally acquiesced about the wine—but not before the seething waitress covered the tainted pitcher with Saran wrap and practically threw it into the fridge. Paul predicted that, out of spite, she planned to finish it herself after work.

"Oh, no," Ty countered. "That twenty-five-year-old bottle of corked Chardonnay is definitely going into the next batch of tiger wine!"

THE FUTURE OF CAPTIVE TIGERS IN LAOS IS UNCERTAIN, BUT THEY WERE GIVEN A recent glimmer of hope at the CITES meeting in 2016. CITES is often accused of pussyfooting around holding any of its members accountable, but, in a rare move, the Standing Committee threatened sanctions against Laos unless it started doing something—anything—to stop illegal wildlife trade within its borders. Someone suggested to the Lao CITES reps that they could, for example, shut down their tiger farms, to which the Lao officials reportedly responded, "We have tiger farms?" But it sounded like an easy enough task, so the Lao minister of natural resources and environment announced on the spot that his country was "looking for ways to phase out tiger farms." The news was met with much fanfare.

Progress on that issue has been slow, however, with basically nothing happening in the six months between the CITES conference and my visit to the country. As Banks told me back in a 2011 interview, "At these meetings, everyone pretends that if a country promises to do something, it's okay. It's almost like the word 'corruption' is left at the door."

Indeed, the odds do not seem high that Laos will follow through on its declaration. For one, like China, the Lao government has a history of involvement in tiger farming and the illegal trade. A confidential, leaked survey of wildlife farms conducted in March 2016 revealed that Lao authorities give annual permission to at least one business—Vinasakhone tiger farm in Khammouane Province—to kill and export animals to China and Vietnam, breaking Lao law and violating CITES rules.

As the report described, two-year-old tigers are sold—usually five at a time, at $30,000 a pop—to traders who come in person to make selections based on "whether the animal is pretty." The chosen ones are killed by electrocution; their intestines are removed; and then their skin, bones, and meat are wrapped in plastic for transport. The report added that the farm, which currently holds four hundred tigers, was founded on the premise of "scientific research." One of the owners also happens to be the godson of the former prime minister of Laos.

Vinasakhone isn't the only facility run by highly influential people, however. All the major tiger farm owners have clout. As of September 2017—a year since the CITES meeting—none of the farms had even allowed an audit of their animals. Most likely, it will take the prime minister himself getting involved before that happens, and his involvement is not certain. "Wildlife trade in Laos has been authorized at the highest levels for a long time, and many of the traders— particularly tiger farm owners—are well connected within government," a confidential source told me.

Indeed, a 2017 US State Department report identified Laos (along with Madagascar and the Democratic Republic of Congo) as a "Country of Concern" for illegal wildlife trade. The governments of those three nations are "actively engaged in or knowingly profited from the trafficking of endangered or threatened species," the report found, and "there are serious concerns that either high-level or systemic government involvement in wildlife trafficking has occurred."

If an audit should get done, what to do with all those tigers remains a challenge. The government initially assumed it could just release the animals into the wild, but conservationists quickly nixed that idea: Laos doesn't have enough large wild ungulates left to support a tiger population. Combine that with the captive-bred felines' lack of hunting skills and habituation to humans, and the country would be looking at unleashing seven hundred potential man-eaters. Keeping them probably won't work either. It costs thousands of dollars per year to feed a single tiger, and if well taken care of, they can live for up to twenty years, creating a serious financial burden. Euthanasia is also not a likely option, considering the heavily Buddhist outlook in Laos (not to mention the international headlines a mass tiger kill-off would generate).

The tiger farmers say that they are offering a solution. They want to turn their farms, which are currently off limits to the public, into Tiger Temple–like operations. Sakhone Keosouvan, one of the owners of Vinasakhone farm, has already started building a tourist resort and "zoo" about fifty miles from the Vietnamese border, where he intends to move his tigers. In January 2017, he and the other farm owners even paid for Lao officials to travel to Thailand on a "study tour" to see firsthand how the petting zoo model—a notorious cover for illegal trade—works. "Clearly, the tiger owners want the Lao officials to learn how to best play hide and seek, how to do window dressing and lip service, as the Thais seem to be very good at already," Karl said. "They'll study why the Tiger Temple closed down, how it managed to reopen, and how they can also do that under the eyes of the international community." Unfortunately, sources on the ground confirmed that the government does seem to be taking the bait and moving in this direction.

Conservationists, though, are doing what they can to encourage Laos to follow through on its promises. And at least the country is talking about ending tiger farming. Meanwhile, China is openly lobbying for the opposite. Representatives have been petitioning CITES to allow trade of farmed tiger parts since 1992, including at the most recent CITES conference. Although there's no sign of CITES permitting legal domestic trade of farmed tigers, China shows no sign of curtailing its breeding operations, either.

International pressure might be the best tool for persuading China to change its mind, but the situation is handicapped by an awkward fact: the United States is home to some 5,000 captive tigers, none of which serve any conservation purpose. Those animals are largely kept as pets in private zoos, backyards, basements, and even truck stops around the country, and their existence compromises the Americans' negotiation pull.

"When fingers are pointed at China about their tiger farms, they point the finger back at the United States and say, 'They have as many tigers as us, why are you not criticizing them?'" said Leigh Henry, a senior policy advisor at the World Wildlife Fund. "Definitely the majority of the focus needs to be on the farms in Asia, but the US would have a stronger voice in this matter if we'd already cleaned up the situation in our own backyard."

Should the United States work together with China and propose a mutual closure of domestic live tiger trade, China might be more keen to strike a deal, agreed Yannick Kuehl, former TRAFFIC's East and South Asia regional director. "One of the reasons the ivory ban was a success was because the US closed its market as well, so China didn't feel pushed against the wall and labeled the bad guy of the world," he said. "The same could be done for tiger farms."

BEFORE LEAVING KINGS ROMANS I DECIDED TO PAY THE TIGERS ONE LAST VISIT. The morning sun was warm and golden, and the red and yellow streets were empty, save for the occasional Burmese worker pedaling by on a rickety bicycle.

I could hear the tigers as I approached the zoo's back entrance. They were groaning in deep, drawn-out tones—what I'd describe as anguished or mournful, were I to anthropomorphize. It sounded like they were in pain. Stopping at the cages, a tiger directly in front of me turned and sprung up onto its hind feet, stretching its dinner-plate-sized paws up toward the ceiling and causing me to jump back at the unexpected movement. Towering over me, the tiger hung there for half a minute, reminiscent of the men Pong described seeing at the local prison.

Other cats were less energetic, though no less captivating. They lay in pools of sunshine, orange fur ablaze and crisscrossed with an extra set of stripes from the shadows of their cages' bars. Most of them looked up at me, holding my eyes in their unblinking yellow ones, almost defiant in their intensity. Even in captivity, they seemed fully in possession of this moment.

I suddenly noticed that I was not alone. A man had shown up, and he was smiling and snapping photos of the tigers with a tablet. Somehow I doubted he was taking pictures for the same reason I was. Instead, those images would likely be braggingly shown to the folks back home or—even worse—perhaps texted to family, friends, and colleagues to see whether there were any takers for remotely purchasing one of these animals. The moment broken, I turned to leave. As I walked, I could still hear the tigers groaning—a real-life Clarice Starling haunted by the cries of the lambs.

Ty, Paul, and I said our good-byes to Pong at Huay Xai. We then beelined to a bar on the main drag to debrief. I turned my phone's recorder on and asked whether they had any concluding thoughts on what just happened to us. "There's nothing to conclude except that it is a fucking disaster," Paul began, wasting no time. "Seriously: the size of the cages those animals were in were fucking shameful. Particularly because there's nothing but space around!"

I nudged the phone a bit closer to them.

"Wait, are you recording this!?" Ty demanded.

I laughed. "I thought you were too drunk to notice."

"Never!" he declared, then took a moment to sportingly clear his throat and put on a serious face. "For me, I feel like these couple days put fully in perspective the potential for humans to inflict misery—both on other people and on animals. Yes, I knew all these pieces before I came here—I've read news stories, I've seen Karl's tiger documentary. But seeing those people being horribly exploited in that Burmese shanty town and seeing those animals in that zoo, it just made me feel so naive. The full scale of suffering suddenly hit me. Honestly, I can't deal. Everything is so fucking awful that I don't even know how to think about it."

He looked down at my phone, bringing his mouth close to the speaker. "You get that recorded!?"

"Ha ha, yeah, I got it," I chuckled. "Anyway, it sounds like you're coming at this from an animal welfare perspective, though, whereas for me the even more important concern here is biodiversity—of the possibility of losing species forever, just because of this trade."

"From a gut level, yes, it's the welfare that's bothering me the most," Ty said. "That's what's hitting me emotionally."

"But either way, how do we get anyone to care?" Paul chimed in. "Fuck the longer view for tigers and elephants, what chance do other species have if humans don't even care about other humans?"

"What was it Karl said to you, again?" Ty asked. "'Do not say I am uplifting or positive'—wasn't that it? I get that now. Is it really hopeless?"

I didn't know what to tell him, so I just tried to answer honestly. "I think the road to ending this trade is going to be a long one. Species are going to go extinct along the way, and the process of reaching some sort of resolution will be full of suffering and needless death. But it all just depends on what people decide is most important at the end of the day. I really don't know what's going to happen."

Thirteen

RISING MOON BEARS

J ILL Robinson had no idea her life was about change one warm April morning in 1993 when she set out for a Chinese bear farm, located just across the border from Hong Kong. The thirty-five-year-old English expat had only just heard of this strange-sounding practice after a journalist friend had urged her to look into it. So she'd finagled her way into a tour group of around thirty other people, almost all from Taiwan and Japan.

The group pulled up to a nondescript gray village-style home—you'd never guess there were bears inside. The owners, a self-important man and his wife, ushered their guests inside to begin the tour. The purpose of bear farming, they explained, was to harvest bile, the digestion-aiding liquid produced by the liver of most animals—including humans—and stored in the gall bladder. Bear bile is special: it has multitudes of uses in traditional Chinese medicine. Selling it makes for a lucrative business.

As the couple proudly boasted about the potency of their bears' bile, Jill's attention was drawn to a staircase. Intrigued, she quietly broke away from the crowd and descended into the basement. The smell—an overwhelming stench of feces, urine, blood, infection, and death—hit her first, followed by the sound of strange clicking noises. The room was very dark, and, as her eyes finally began to adjust, "it was as if a horror story was unfolding itself, frame by frame."

Rows of wire cages stretched out before her, and each, she saw, held a bear. The cages were barely large enough to accommodate their miserable prisoners, all of whom were now fearfully gazing back at Jill. As she looked closer, she could see metal catheters protruding from puss-ridden holes in the bears' abdomens—permanent surgical implantations that made the job of bile extraction easier for the farmers.

Just then, Jill felt a tap on her shoulder. She swung around—to see not a person but a bear. The animal had reached her paw through the bars and touched Jill. Rather than recoil, however, "I did something so ridiculously stupid, but it seemed like the most normal thing into the world to do," she recalled. "I took her paw." Bears—especially stressed, scared bears—are unpredictable and aggressive; the animal could have mauled Jill's hand or worse. But all she did was gently squeeze her fingers.

Jill was an animal lover and an animal welfare activist, but prior to the tour she'd hardly ever given thought to bears. Cats and dogs were her specialty. Standing there in the dark, however, holding the bear's paw, she realized that she had found her life's calling. She would end bear farming. She never saw the bear from the basement again, but for Jill that brief encounter changed everything.

Jill Robinson's story has become the stuff of conservation legend, her activism propelling bear farming into the global spotlight and setting the wheels in motion for ending that cruel practice. Vietnam recently banned bear farming, and an increasing number of people in China are calling for an end to the practice as well.

Unlike the fate of the thousands of tigers kept on farms, for many captive bears, a happy ending does seem to be within reach. Damaged from a lifetime of trauma and lacking the skills needed to survive on their own, the bears can never return to the wild. But they can find solace at two rescue centers run by Animals Asia, the nonprofit Jill cofounded after her encounter at the bear farm. As farms continue to close, more and more bears are being given a chance at peace and happiness.

I MET JILL ON A GRAY SUNDAY AFTERNOON IN SAI KUNG, A BUSTLING FORMER fishing village in Hong Kong's New Territories famed for its fresh seafood, hiking trails, and beaches. It's also home to the Hong Kong Academy, a nonprofit international school where Jill was giving a keynote speech to around a hundred eleven- to fourteen-year-olds attending a global-issues-themed weekend camp, with topics ranging from human trafficking to urban sustainability.

I followed a cacophony of young voices to an auditorium. Jill stood at the front, setting up her laptop, while kids wearing name tags streamed in, chatting in groups and taking their seats. I overheard Jill ask one of the organizers whether it was okay if some of the photos in her presentation are "a bit gruesome." No problem, the woman replied, this audience could handle it.

Jill approached the microphone, and the kids piped down. Slender and athletic with shoulder-length wavy blonde hair and bangs, she has changed little since that first bear encounter in 1993. Her right arm was in a blue cast—the result of a recent tumble she took at an archery field in Scottsdale, Arizona. "You can see it's been a rough month for me," she began, gesturing at the cast. "It serves me right for wrestling bears to the ground." She paused. "That's a joke." The audience, catching on, giggled.

Jill began her talk with the story of the bear who took her hand and launched her life's mission. After cofounding the Hong Kong–based Animals Asia in 1998, she and her colleagues began tirelessly campaigning to convince the governments of China and Vietnam that "bear farming is simply wrong." Eventually they opened two sanctuaries, one in Chengdu and another outside of Hanoi, which have seen nearly six hundred rescued bears to date.

Of the world's eight species of bears, only the panda is spared the horrors of the bile trade. In North America and Russia, carcasses of wild black bears, grizzly bears, and polar bears have turned up missing nothing but their gall bladders, while in Ecuador, local hunters hired by Koreans poach Andean bears for the same purpose. Asia's native bears are the bile industry's most frequently exploited victims, however—not least because they live in the places where demand for their parts is most fervent. Two species in particular are favored for farming: the Asiatic black bear—also known as the moon bear, for the crescent white patch on its chest—and the Malayan sun bear, which has a comically long pink tongue and sometimes develops facial wrinkles that give the impression of an oversized pug or Shar-Pei.

In past centuries, bear meat, spinal cords, blood, bones, fat, and paws were used to treat everything from deafness to baldness, but today, it's predominantly the bile that people are after. Its use dates back to at least 659 CE, to China's first pharmacopoeia, and it's still prescribed in China, Vietnam, South Korea, Malaysia, Japan, and other countries for cirrhosis, ulcerative colitis, gallstones, pain, inflammation, fever, and more. Some of those countries ban bear bile; others do not.

However, unlike tiger bones, rhino horns, and many other products derived from endangered species, bear bile is no snake oil. It actually does work for treating some conditions. "It's easy to pooh-pooh certain holistic approaches to medicine, but when a culture has been using something for 3,000 years to treat maladies from A to Z, then you gotta start believing that maybe there's something to it," said Clifford J. Steer, director of the Molecular Gastroenterology Program at the University of Minnesota Medical School.

Ursodeoxycholic acid—bear bile's active ingredient—is found in all vertebrate animals, but bears (particularly black bears) have extremely high levels of it (*urso* means "bear" in Latin). In humans, for example, ursodeoxycholic acid composes just 1–3 percent of the total bile acid pool, whereas in bears it can be as high as 70 percent, depending on the species and time of year. Timing matters because ursodeoxycholic acid's job is to prevent apoptosis, or programmed cell death; bears seem to abound in it because of their hibernating lifestyles. "If we humans hibernated for six months, our bodies would fall apart, and we would not even be able to get out of bed," said Steer, whose team was the first to uncover the acid's anti-apoptotic abilities and to map the cellular mechanisms behind it.

Ursodeoxycholic acid's usefulness extends well beyond hibernation, however. In preclinical trials with animal models, Steer and his colleagues are exploring a myriad of other possible applications for the molecule, including slowing the progression of Huntington's, Parkinson's, Lou Gehrig's, and Alzheimer's diseases; treating kidney disease and diabetes; lessening the damage caused by strokes and heart attacks; and preventing retinitis pigmentosa, a genetic disease that causes blindness. Although ursodeoxycholic acid–based medicines for gallstones and a liver autoimmune disease are already approved by the US Food and Drug Administration (FDA), their potential for other conditions has failed to gain broader traction among pharmaceutical companies because the molecule is already available as a generic compound. The pharma business is generally interested only in profitable, patentable drugs. Because Steer and his colleagues are convinced that ursodeoxycholic acid holds "profound" promise, they are developing patentable molecular analogs that could potentially be approved by the FDA for treating a wide variety of diseases.

In Asia, however, there is no demand for molecular analogs; bear bile has always been the ursodeoxycholic acid delivery mechanism of choice. Prior to 1984, all bear products there came from wild bears, until North Koreans pioneered bear farming as means of attaining more bile with less effort. Advocates claimed that one caged bear produces the annual bile equivalent of forty poached wild bears. The practice quickly spread to South Korea, Vietnam, and China. Like tiger breeding, the idea was to mass-produce wildlife products to turn a profit. In Vietnam, for example, a farmer can earn $120 from a single one-hundred-milli-liter bile extraction (a little less than half a cup). It's such prices that have earned bear bile its nickname, "liquid gold." On Korean farms, farmers are also legally allowed to kill their animals at the age of ten for their whole gall bladders, which can go for as much as $15,000 per pound in Japan.

Conservation was never the goal of bear farming, even if it was claimed to be on paper. As far back as 1991, experts warned that bear farming does not pre-vent poaching and in fact promotes the commodification and destruction of bears by making bile cheaper and more available. The warning was ignored, and, sure enough, even as bear farms proliferated, wild Asian bear populations steadily declined. China won't say how many bears it keeps on its sixty-eight official farms—it's rumored to hover around 10,000—but the country likely has fewer Asiatic black bears left in the wild than on farms and possibly no sun bears left at all. South Korea, likewise, has more than 1,000 bears on farms but effectively none left in its forests. Hundreds of bears are also kept in facilities in Laos and Myanmar—virtually all of which are Vietnamese- or Chinese-owned—and sur-veys in those countries have confirmed the decline of wild bears.

Population declines are driven by an uncomfortable fact: almost all bears on farms come from the wild. Unlike farmed tigers, which breed quite well, bears are more finicky about reproduction, and they tend to have just a couple of cubs as opposed to a big litter. To get around this, hunters scour forests for bear fam-ilies, killing mothers and kidnapping the cubs. How do we know? In addition to surveys with local hunters who confirm as much, 35 percent of bears at Jill's rescue centers are missing limbs—a sure sign that they were trapped in snares. Experts who have visited bear farms in Southeast Asia have also found no breed-ing facilities there; bears cannot copulate in cages barely large enough to hold a single animal.

Those cages—what Jill refers to as "cages of shame"—are typically com-posed, top to bottom, of metal bars and are elevated off the ground for easier cleaning. The bears may never touch the ground throughout their thirty-year life, and, as a result, their paws develop contorted indentations from constant expo-sure to the cage bars. Even unluckier animals, however, are permanently kept in "crush" cages. Designed like coffins, those torture chambers aren't even large enough to allow the animal to sit up or turn around.

Jill made no effort to censor the excruciating details of the bears' lives for her young audience. Instead, she addressed the stunned crowd as though they were adults—although she occasionally braced them for what came next. "I need you to stay with me, with some of these pictures," she said, pausing between slides depicting sore-ridden bears crammed into rusted cages and close-ups of bears' deformed feet and rotten teeth. "I want you to leave this room understanding this issue and being committed to helping."

Judging from the open mouths and wide eyes around me, the audience did indeed seem to be with her. "I feel so bad for the bears!" a young voice behind me exclaimed in a whisper.

Farmers often pull out their bears' teeth or cut them down to the gum level, Jill continued, believing this will make their animals safer. But even bears left with teeth intact wind up shattering them anyway, by gnawing on their cage bars. Nutrition is also an issue: the animals are usually fed congee, a mix of rice and water—they frequently experience chronic eye problems and can go blind from lack of vitamin E—and, even in tropical heat, most are never given water apart from the congee mix, because many farmers don't think bears need water. As Jill pointed out, though, it's in a farmer's best interest to keep his bears in a state of near-starvation. Bile's natural purpose is to break down fat in food, and the liver produces more of it when an animal is hungry. Hungry bears, therefore, are profitable bears. (Unfortunately, dehydration first impacts kidney and cardiovascular system functioning rather than the liver, which is responsible for bile acid production, so a lack of water doesn't translate immediately into a lack of bile.)

Of all the horrors that befall captive bears, though, the bile milking process itself is likely the worst. In China, bears' gall bladders are surgically moved from where they naturally occur in the body, tucked beside the liver, to a position just under the animals' abdominal skin. Stitching the organ into place, the farmer then either implants a permanent metal catheter through the bear's skin into the gallbladder or else creates a crude permanent hole, or fistula, connecting the gallbladder to the outside.

Vietnamese farmers opt for a method that is less invasive but equally harmful in the long term. One person distracts the bear while another knocks it out with ketamine (a drug that's not only illegal but also tends to leave bears half conscious for the pain that follows). The farmer (or a vet they've hired) locates the bear's gall bladder with an ultrasound and then, using a long needle, attempts to stab through the liver to reach the gall bladder. Oftentimes, a dozen jabs are needed before the needle-wielder gets it right; some farmers even forego the ultrasound and just stab the bear blindly, testing the needle with their mouths to see whether they've hit their target (the bile has a telltale bitter flavor). Once they've found the gall bladder, they use a reverse pump to extract the bile.

The frothy yellow-brown liquid that results from the Vietnamese and Chinese extraction processes can be drunk or bottled on the spot, or else dried into crystals. The bile is then used to make not just medicines, teas, and wines but also new-fangled products like shampoos, face masks, and even toothpaste. Indeed, with so much excess bile available, companies have expanded the market beyond traditional uses. In China, probably only 20 percent of bear bile is used in medicinal products, according to Lixin Huang, vice president for China projects and executive director of the American College of Traditional Medicine at the California Institute of Integral Studies, told me. "The rest is used as components in nonmedical things like shampoo and drinks—things that are truly commercial products," she said.

Companies are eager to push extraneous bile products on people, but bear bile itself is also extraneous. There are both herbal and synthetic alternatives that work just as well. As far back as 1992, Chinese researchers attained positive results in clinical trials with synthetic ursodeoxycholic acid, but the State Food and Drug Administration ignored the findings and later denied it ever received the report before eventually admitting that it had. Outside of China, a handful of companies also produce synthetic ursodeoxycholic acid, including Prodotti Chemical and Food, a bulk pharmaceutical manufacturer in Italy. Scientists there acquire gall bladders from slaughtered beef cattle, then isolate certain bile acids from the bile and chemically transform it into ursodeoxycholic acid.

"The issue is how to convince the Chinese government to reduce their support of bear farming and the international sale of bear bile," said Steer at the University of Minnesota. On invited trips to China, he has shared the results of his peer-reviewed studies with experts there, including the finding that ursodeoxycholic acid produced by humans and bears is molecularly identical—bears just have more of it. "There are pundits in China who say, 'No, no, no, there's something magical about bear bile!'" Steer said. "But that's just not the case."

There may still be a work-around. Prodotti already does business with China in synthetic ursodeoxycholic acid, and other pharmaceutical companies are capable of putting Prodotti's product into an emulsion that looks and tastes like bear bile. "Even though it's not natural bear bile, patients will hopefully think that it is and still benefit from the same protective and healing effects as the hibernating black bear," Steer said. "I'm sure someone is going to become very rich off this, if they haven't already."

There is also a human health argument for promoting such alternatives. In Vietnam, doctors have reported patients sickened—some even fatally—after taking bear bile and developing septicemia or liver problems. This is because bile taken from abused, sick bears contains more than just bile: it's also ridden with pus, multidrug-resistant bacteria, urine, feces, and even cancer cells. Of the more than 250 ravaged gall bladders that Animals Asia veterinarians have removed from bile-extracted bears, 100 percent have been contaminated with such impurities (like humans, bears can survive without their gall bladder). Most of those organs also exhibited chronic inflammation, abnormal adhesions, inflammatory masses, or gallstones.

For years, however, Vietnam ignored these illnesses and poisoning, and actively promoted bear bile use, calling it "the people's medicine." Some doctors and government officials endorsed far-fetched claims about its efficacy for treating hangovers, impotence, and cancer (ironic, given that many of the bears themselves have cancer). By the early aughts, however, Vietnam's bears had almost disappeared from the wild, and bile poisoning cases were mounting. Following years of lobbying by Animals Asia, Education for Nature–Vietnam, and Free the Bears, in 2002, the government finally conceded, issuing a decision stating that farms may no longer collect bile from their bears. This was followed by a decree giving sun bears and Asiatic black bears the highest levels of national protection, meaning sale of their products—including bile—was now strictly illegal in Vietnam.

At the time these changes went into effect, Vietnam had 4,000 bears in captivity—up from just 400 in 1999. What to do with all those animals now that farming was illegal was a problem that the law tried to address with an ill-conceived provision: so long as bears were acquired before the ban and registered with a government-issued microchip, owners would be allowed to keep them. That didn't solve the cruelty issue, however, and it didn't provide a solution for bears whose owners were caught illegally harvesting bile. The easiest thing to do was just turn a blind eye. "Bears are big and they're dangerous," said Tuan Bendixsen, Animals Asia's Vietnam director. "Unless there's a place where the bear can go, a law enforcer will just give it back to the owner, even if they should be seizing it."

As a fix, in 2007 Animals Asia opened a rescue center near Hanoi. They currently have 161 bears, around 60 percent confiscated from farmers caught breaking the law and the rest voluntarily surrendered. Some bear owners are actually sad to see their bears go. One older couple in Hue had kept their bear for thirteen years, since it was a cub. Its cage was in their perpetually dark kitchen, and the bear's health was deplorable, to say the least. Nevertheless, the couple told Bendixsen they felt the bear was a part of their family. It wasn't the law that made them decide to surrender their animal, they added—they still regularly harvested and sold its bile—it was just that they were getting older and didn't have the strength to look after it anymore. "Usually, by the time people surrender their bear, they do it in a happy way," Bendixsen said. "We even had an owner later come to see their bear at the sanctuary. Instead of being kept in a cage, now it's outside, safe and happy. Their guilt has been removed."

Despite this option, many people hold on to their bears for an obvious reason: it's quite easy to get away with illegal bile harvesting. Of the 1,200-odd bears still living with their original owners today, Bendixsen estimates that the majority, if not all, are still being exploited for bile (the remaining 2,640 or so that are no longer with owners or rescued are suspected to either have died of their ill treatment on the farms, been illegally killed for their parts, or been sold to other bear farms in Asia). Neighbors of the farmers he visits confirm this, and the medical evidence does not lie. Using an ultrasound, Animals Asia vets can see fresh scratch marks and scarring on bears' livers.

To be found guilty of harvesting bile, however, Vietnamese law nonsensically stipulates that the culprit must be caught in the actual act of bile extraction by a law enforcement agent. It's as though a thief could only be arrested if a police officer sees him pocketing goods, or a murderer brought to court only if an official witnesses him pulling the trigger. Even so, bear owners who are foolish enough to get caught don't have to worry much. Despite the fact that extracting bile is an offense punishable by jail time of up to three years or fines over $2,000, to Bendixson's ire, they typically just receive a small fine and their bear might be taken away. "The authorities say, 'Tuan, you're happy now, you got the bear. Let it go,'" Bendixsen said. "It's true that we're most interested in the bear, but it's totally unfair. Until Vietnam enforces its legal deterrents, wildlife crime will continue and we're going to keep losing."

I wanted to see some of Vietnam's caged bears for myself, a task that likely would have been impossible were it not for Đỗ Doãn Hoàng, the investigative journalist who set up the rhino horn dinner in Chapter 3. I asked Hoàng whether he knew of a farm I could visit, and, to my delight, he offered to take me to one himself. The bear farmer was an acquaintance of Hoàng's family—his grandfather had been the farmer's teacher—but there was still no guarantee I'd get in. "Normally, it's impossible for any foreigners to visit," he warned me. "But let's go fishing, to see what we can get." Always the flirt, he added, giggling, that I should pose as his girlfriend.

On a Saturday morning in February, Hoàng; my translator, Mai Thị Hồng Tâm; and I met in a parking lot on Hanoi's outskirts and climbed into Hoàng's conspicuously large, tricked-out Ford SUV. Our destination was an hour northwest of the city, a town called Son Loc. When we arrived, I was surprised to find that the "farm" was not of the Old MacDonald variety but was instead a skinny blue and yellow building with shiny metal shutters—the sort of storefront you'd see in any Vietnamese city. Two signs, one above the door and the other on the sidewalk, read *Nhà Nuôi Gâu*—"House Where Bears Are." The sidewalk sign featured a black cartoon bear, the other a bucolic, sun-faded photo of a bear in the grass.

Obviously expecting us, the bear farmer emerged, smiling warmly. He was tall, with neatly combed black hair, gray slacks, and a button-down white shirt. He looked to be in his sixties. Hoàng had instructed me to stay in the car, but moments after embracing the farmer, he gestured for me to come out: "It's okay! No problem."

What had looked like a shop from the outside was in fact the man's home. We took a seat in the foyer at a wooden table, and the farmer fetched tea. On the wall hung a photograph of an elephant and a picture of the Clintons in their younger days, shaking hands with a man in a green military uniform—one of the farmer's friends, he told me proudly. The bear farmer himself had enjoyed an eclectic career, first studying to become a pilot (where he made friends with a Lao general, who Hoàng bragged could get him into one of the country's notoriously locked-down tiger farms) and was now working part time guarding Ho Chi Minh's mausoleum in Hanoi. We made relaxed small talk for a few minutes, until Hoàng told me that it's fine, I could ask the farmer anything. I started at the beginning: How did he get into bear farming?

"In 2000, the government encouraged citizens to raise bears so we can conserve them," the farmer said through Tâm's translation. "I got my bears when they were babies—I don't know where they came from. One bear at that time was worth two pieces of land, and I had thirty bears. When the government forbade us to take bile, I lost money. But I'm not bitter about how things turned out—it's okay. I made a lot of profit."

Hoàng had told me this farmer keeps only four bears, and I asked what happened to the others. "I released some into the forest, with help of the forestry department," he said. I cringed, realizing that those animals almost certainly starved to death. "The rest I donated to Tuan Bendixsen's center. And I keep four here at my home, for conservation purposes. They've been with me a long time— twenty years! They're my favorites."

I asked him whether they had names; they did not. And does he still take bile from them?

"No, I cannot take it because it's illegal," he replied automatically. "If the bear dies I can't even sell its fur or meat, I have to burn it. I don't use bile myself anymore, either. The signs outside aren't for advertising bile, they're just for students and people to come see, for conservation. From my heart, I just want to raise my bears until they die. Do you want to see them?"

I did. We passed through the kitchen, then down a couple of stairs into an enclosed back patio area with a metal roof. Even though the sun was out, it was very dark. Before I saw the bears—like Jill—the smell hit me: a warm reek of shit and rotten food, enough to make me want to gag. It emanated from four rusted, cobweb-covered cages lined up in a single row, each holding a large black bear. The cages were about as tall as the animals, were they to stand up on their hind legs, and just wide enough for them to roll over once if lying down. The bears were flabby and missing patches of fur on their faces and white crescent-mooned chests.

As I approached the cages, one bear sat up and stuck its nose to the bars, like a dog at the pound. I felt an urge to pet it but knew better. Its brown eyes were alert and imploring. Feeling a pang of guilt at my inability to help it or even interact with it, I moved on. Its neighbor in the next cage was lying splayed out on its back, feet propped up on the bars like a long-haul economy passenger futilely trying to find a comfortable position. The bear next to it was also on its back, and its rear end pressed against the bars to reveal a protruding, bright pink mass of cauliflower-like tumors. Both bears' feet were dry and cracked, and neither so much as look up as I passed by, walking slowly and deliberately so as not to slip in the slick layer of mud and waste puddled around their cages.

The final bear was also lying down, on its side rather than back. It stared at me from behind the bars, one paw outstretched, neither lifting its head nor breaking its gaze from mine even as the bear farmer's yippy dogs maniacally circled us. Something in its eyes reminded me of the culminating scene in *Full Metal Jacket,* when the wounded female sniper repeatedly beseeches, "Shoot me. . . . Shoot me. . . . " Death would surely be a preferable existence for this bear.

We left shortly after—though not before the bear farmer asked if he could get a photo with me—and in the car I asked Hoàng and Tâm what they thought of his story. Both insisted that the farmer was telling the truth about not harvesting bile anymore. If that was the case, I pointed out, then why was he so cagey about foreign visitors? It's because he's "really old and shy and not used to interacting with Westerners," Tâm assured me. I wasn't convinced. If he was no longer making money off the bears, then why go through the trouble and expense of keeping them, rather than just handing them over to the rescue center so they could have a good life? Surely the farmer could see that they were not thriving in those metal cages.

As it turned out, I was right to be suspicious. Bendixsen and his colleagues later looked into the farm and even paid the owner a friendly visit, hoping to convince him to sign over his bears to them. They learned, however, that the local government wants to reclaim the backyard land where the farmer keeps the bears, and he is using their presence as an excuse for not surrendering the real estate that their cages are squatting on by claiming that he has nowhere to move the bears. The local Forestry Protection Department, meanwhile, has allowed him to keep the animals despite not having properly registered to do so. "It's a mess," Bendixsen summarized of the case. When his Animals Asia colleagues dropped by, he added, the owner didn't even permit them to see the bears.

And the bile extraction denial? "I'd be very surprised if that farmer did not extract bile," Bendixsen said. "I've yet to come across people keeping bears and not extracting their bile illegally." I sighed. So much for good intentions and the owner's claim that he keeps the animals "from his heart."

Because bear farmers continue to harvest bile illegally from their animals, bile itself also continues to be illegally sold at pharmacies throughout Vietnam—even as opinions about bear bile have begun to change. In a 2010 survey of 152 traditional doctors in Vietnam, Animals Asia found that 93 percent were opposed to bear bile farming and that three-quarters had never prescribed bile.

Collaborating with Animals Asia, doctors from Vietnam's Traditional Medicine Association have also published a book describing thirty-two herbal substitutes for bear bile. Tran Van Ban, chair of the association, has even made ending bear bile use a personal crusade.

"It's not necessary to use such things from wild animals, because Vietnam has many similar medicines made from plants in the same group," he said. It's a message he has delivered on television, radio, and even at an elementary school alongside Prince William. Though Ban has noticed fewer and fewer patients asking for bear bile, some still hold fast to their beliefs—a problem he attributes to lack of knowledge and vanity. "People think only products from wild animals can help them," he said. "And some rich people want to use those products just because they have the money to do so. They want to be unique and special, to demonstrate that they are rich by showing off."

Ban believes that his and his colleagues' message is slowly taking hold, however—an assertion that a 2016 TRAFFIC study partially confirmed. In 2012, TRAFFIC researchers found that 56 percent of seventy-eight traditional medicine clinics surveyed in Vietnam sold bear bile, but by 2016 that proportion had fallen to 40 percent. Most sellers told the researchers that they acquired their bile from Vietnamese farms, but that bile from wild bears is still much preferred for its superior quality and premium price tag. Although the Animals Asia and TRAFFIC findings cannot be directly compared—they used different methodologies and took place in different cities—Bendixsen believes that both show that bear bile trade is declining but persisting.

Law enforcement has also gotten marginally better in recent years, but the fact that 40 percent of traditional medicine shops still sell bile means "we haven't gotten there yet," Bendixsen said. Many of his own relatives, he added, keep a small amount of bear bile at home for personal use. "Minor consumers, just ordinary people, use wildlife in very small amounts, but there must be millions of them, which adds up to a lot," Bendixsen said. "These are the people who are going to be really hard to target with law enforcement."

As such, education, especially of young people, may be the only hope of completely stamping bear bile out of Vietnamese culture. This is why Animals Asia puts outreach and education on the top of its priority list, just after saving bears. In 2016, nearly 5,000 people visited the nonprofit's bear sanctuary at Tam Đảo National Park, located an hour north of Hanoi, while more than 4,000 more attended off-site events.

After the experience at the farmer's house, I was eager for the cathartic experience of seeing bears at their very best, so I arranged to visit the rescue center one overcast afternoon. The air in the center's tree-covered mountain valley was wonderfully fresh compared to Hanoi's smoggy miasma and also cooler at this higher elevation. Notices on a gate out front read, "No Honking, Please," and "Save the Moon Bears," and bear-shaped garbage cans were stationed every few feet along the trail leading inside. Đỗ Thu Hằng, Animals Asia's education officer, met me for a tour. Wearing an Animals Asia T-shirt, Hằng knew her bear facts inside and out.

"Sun bears are the smallest bear species in the world, growing to 110–155 pounds, and they look like dogs. Moon bears, on the other hand, can grow up to 440 pounds," she said as she led me to a large, grassy enclosure with wooden climbing structures, like a children's jungle gym. "Our target is to rescue all the bears in Vietnam." Around five black bears were scattered throughout the space, and, sure enough, they did look a bit like oversized, wooly dogs. Spotting us, one trotted over to the fence, mouth hanging open in a grin, eyes bright and curious. He raised his nose, sniffing in our direction, and I responded by raising my camera. He began turning his head this way and that, as if deliberately posing for his close-ups.

All the bears have names—the curious one at the fence was Tao—and, once they settle in, each begins to reveal his or her highly individual personality. "Parly is very naughty, she climbs trees and breaks branches," Hằng said, pointing at a fat bear rooting around in the grass. "And that one—let me see his face—oh, that's Gus! Hello, Gus!" Gus—who was sitting upright on a large tire swing, serenely gazing forward as though in meditation—swiveled his head to look at us, as though annoyed by the interruption. Another bear, Faith, had made it to the top of a wooden structure in spite of her great girth and was batting at a blue hidden-food container extended on a rope. Playtime is integral for the rescued animals, Hằng said, not only to get them engaged psychologically but also to build up muscles and skills that they haven't used for years, if ever. When bears first arrive, sometimes they climb a tree or structure—a very natural act for a wild bear—only to struggle for hours figuring out how to get down.

At the bear hospital next door, Hằng handed me over to Mandala Hunter-Ishikawa, a senior veterinary surgeon. Originally from the United States, Mandala always knew she didn't want to spend her life working at a suburban clinic treating pampered pets. She decided to join the bear effort after seeing an article online about Animals Asia in 2013. We looked around the center's fully equipped lab and surgery room, and then Mandala asked whether I'd like to see three new arrivals, fresh off the truck yesterday from a rescue in central Vietnam.

They were being held in a nearby quarantine facility, where we donned full-body plastic suits and black boots, and stepped through a disinfectant foot drip. Rather than rescue a bear and then immediately toss it into its expansive new home, bears are slowly acclimated. They're first observed in quarantine for forty-five days, after which they enter a halfway house—a larger cage with toys and climbing gear but still not as potentially overwhelming as the final outdoor area, where lots of other animals are present. "We take them through gradual small steps to prepare them physically and mentally for going outside," Mandala said. "One bear may be totally easygoing and integrates well with the group, while another is very nervous. Some bears hide the past trauma well, others don't. And some just don't like other bears. We can accommodate all of that—we don't force them."

Held in red cages with bedding, banana leaves, toys, and a food and water trough, the new bears looked exhausted—and rightfully so. It had taken them nearly four days to get here. Two observers in blue scrubs sat in front of their cages, pen and paper in hand, and, as we approached, one of the bears made quiet clucking sounds—a sign of stress. Unlike the bears I saw outside, these animals were raggedy and skinny; one had a grapefruit-sized mass on its side—Mandala suspected a hernia—and another was missing all the toes on its paw. "This is probably the first time in a decade that these guys have had full stomachs and things to think about," Mandala said. "By next year, they'll be big, beautiful bears."

Many of the bears bounce back surprisingly well after years or even decades of abuse. Bears with no teeth develop hardened gums that allow them to eat, blind bears learn their way around outdoor enclosures, and stereotypic head-bobbing and other compulsive repetitive actions—also known as cage craziness—tend to lessen in intensity or even stop altogether. "We're never going to fix them 100 percent," Mandala said. "But we can give them the best life possible, to apologize for other humans who treated them so badly."

Sometimes, though, the bears' pasts catch up to them: around 35 percent of rescues die early from liver cancer. When a bear's time does come, he or she is buried in a tranquil wooded area called the Garden of Rest, along with favorite foods and toys. All the keepers turn out for a ceremony, which culminates in the reading of "Spirit of Hope," a poem written by a former bear manager named Tim Roberts: "You've left this world no longer a number, a letter or bear just the same, / For you will always be remembered as a bear with a name."

ALTHOUGH VIETNAM CONTINUES TO STRIVE TOWARD PUTTING AN END TO ALL BEAR farming, China has not expressed any interest at all in shutting it down. The China Association of Traditional Chinese Medicine, the country's largest traditional medicine group, remains aggressively pro–bear farming, likely because many of those promoting the practice are stakeholders in the profitable industry.

But there are some signs that change might be coming. KaiBao Pharmaceutical is China's largest bear bile merchant, purchasing half of the thirty-six tons of bile produced each year to make one of 243 state-approved medicines. In 2014, however, KaiBao announced that it was working on a product derived from slaughtered poultry bile that will replicate every component in bear bile—not just ursodeoxycholic acid. Jill suspects that the decision might be health driven; China has released no data on whether its citizens have suffered side effects from taking contaminated bear bile, as their neighbors in Vietnam have, but that doesn't mean it hasn't happened.

It could also be that China is beginning to take note of public opinion on bear farming. As far back as 1994, the Chinese Association of Medicine and Philosophy has insisted bear farming doesn't align with harmony in nature, and celebrities including Yao Ming, Karen Mok, Sun Li, and Zhang Yi have all condemned bear farming. Young people are also increasingly engaged in animal rights issues: Weibo, China's version of Twitter, is full of support for the bears. As Jill told me, "The best advice I ever got was from a Chinese governmental official who told me to start the debate in China. For sure, that's what's going to end this practice. It's not a bunch of Westerners coming in and saying you shouldn't be doing this—it's people in China."

Indeed, local activism is on the rise. In 2012, computer programmers crashed a pharmaceutical company's website when it proposed expanding its farmed bear population from 400 to 1,200. Protestors wearing bear costumes also showed up outside shops selling bear bile. In response, Shuting Fang, president of the pro-farming China Association of Traditional Chinese Medicine, issued a statement reassuring the public that "bile extraction is just as simple as turning on a water tap. Extracting bile is not painful and the bears are very comfortable."

Social media exploded, crucifying Fang for what they described as shame-
less dishonesty, and some news outlets published satirical cartoons of him. In
one, Fang is shown on all fours, his pants crumpled around his knees and grinning in pleasure as a bear shags his bare bottom from behind. A speech bubble
depicts his reaction: "Taking out a bear's semen is as easy as flushing the toilet!
It's natural and painless. Afterwards, the bear will happily go outside and play. I
don't feel anything different—it's even comfortable!"

Back in the Hong Kong auditorium, Jill kept her talk rated PG, wowing her
young audience with clips of adorable bear cubs running across a yard, of rescued bears—at first tentatively and then ecstatically—discovering the joys of a
bubble bath, and of bears climbing trees and splaying out on their stomachs in
carefree relaxation. Kids around me squealed.

Jill concluded with a plea for her audience to visit Animals Asia's social media pages and to do their part to end bear farming. "Thank you for helping these
bears, for giving them their days in the sun," she said, her voice earnest. "We're
never going to give up this endeavor, until bear farming ends—until the cruelty
ends."

After the presentation, several older girls approached the podium. One asked
Jill about volunteer opportunities, and another wanted to know whether she could
visit the rescue center next month, on a family trip to Chengdu.

"Of course, just e-mail me!" Jill replied enthusiastically. "If I'm on site, I'm
happy to host you. What are you doing in Chengdu?"

"Pandas were the original incentive . . . " the girl sheepishly admitted.

"Pandas!? You need to come see us."

I wandered into the hall outside, where some kids were still mingling after
the presentation. Two girls—one Asian, the other Caucasian—were chatting near
the door. Approaching them, I apologized for interrupting and explained that I
was curious to hear their thoughts about the bear talk.

"I thought it was really disgusting, how people are actually doing these
things to animals," the blond girl began, with hardly any hesitation. "I've done
a lot of projects on animals in school, and I think it's just really sad to see how
they're being treated. There's so many ways we could help them if we just work
together."

"I just hope that the presentation helps to inspire other people to at least help,
even if it's only a small change," her friend added.

I thanked them, and—as an afterthought—asked how old they were.

"Twelve," they replied in unison.

I was taken aback: I had assumed they were at least fourteen or fifteen. I left the school shaking my head in hopeful wonder at the precociousness of kids today. Sure, not every student gets to attend weekend workshops in Hong Kong on solving world problems, but those who do no doubt spread the message to their friends. If the two I met were any indication of their generation's values, well, I can't help but feel that it's only a matter of time before things change for the better not just for bears but for all wildlife. Whether many species can hold out that long, however, is the question.

Fourteen

ORDER AHEAD FOR PANGOLIN

About a year after my friend Thảo had called around to restaurants asking for pangolin, I heard from a couple of conservationists that it had become harder to find those strictly protected animals openly for sale in Ho Chi Minh City. Thiên Vương Tửu, the restaurant where Thảo, Ty, and I had seen the live cobra get its heart cut out, had even shuttered for good. As Thảo chipperly suggested, "Maybe it was your story that did it!"

I was curious to see for myself whether things had really changed, though. Thảo was busy this time, so I linked up with Tim Gerard Barker, an Aussie photographer with whom I'd exchanged a few Southeast Asia tips several years back. He had been living in Vietnam since then and was interested in wildlife trade issues; in one striking photo series, he documented the illegal bear bile industry. He was also the kind of guy who sportingly replies, "That would be great!" when you ask him whether he wants to go scouting the city's restaurants for pangolin.

Tim picked me up on his motorbike on a street corner near my hotel in District 1. Before we zipped off, he introduced me to Van Tran, an aspiring Danish Vietnamese photographer. Van had just moved to the city and offered to tag along to help with translations. Van wore his long black hair in a loose, low man bun, and the tattoo on his arm—fittingly for our mission—read, "Here today, gone tomorrow."

"Shall we just pick whichever place is closest?" Tim asked, referring to my list of pangolin-serving restaurants—the same one that had originally led me to Thiên Vương Tửu.

We wove through the revving traffic, with Tim jumping sidewalk corners and speeding down boulevards in a way that made me hold my breath. Our first destination was Hương Rừng, a two-story joint on a busy corner. The waiter seated us in a smoke-filled room next to a child's birthday party, and Van cut straight to the chase: "Do you have pangolin?"

"Not today," the waiter causally replied. "How about snake or turtle, instead? Or water monitor?"

We turned him down. Stop number two was Tràm Chim, a restaurant named after one of Vietnam's national parks. Its outdoor seating was fittingly decorated with lush potted plants and hanging vines. Lovely young women with sad eyes loitered in tight jeans and tank tops—Tim said they were probably available for hire—and waiters bustled from table to table, pouring beers. A large glass tank filled with an inch or two of dirty water held an assortment of writhing brown eels, fat frogs, and a dinner-plate-sized softshell turtle.

The plump manager came over to our table, and Van inquired about exotic options. "Just tell me what you want, and we can get it," the manager proudly replied, taking a worn, folded piece of paper out of his pocket. It was labeled "Today's specials" at the top, but it looked like it had been used for far longer than just today. Among its offerings were sturgeon, cobra, and civet, the latter advertised for sixty-three dollars per pound and served steamed or grilled, with stuffed intestines and a side salad. But no pangolin.

"We don't sell pangolin here, and I don't know where you can get it," the manager told us. "We have a turtle, though!" He picked up a long stick next to the tank and began poking the softshell turtle. It squished its already-tattered nose against the tank, vainly trying to escape as its feet slipped against the dirty glass.

It was getting late, so we decided to try just one more place, Việt Phố, a multisite operation that specializes in seafood. The location we visited was lively, large, and brightly lit, with tables inside and out. A tiered wall of aquamarine fish tanks held ten different kinds of mollusks; shrimp as long as my hand; and various large, defeated-looking fish.

As soon as Van asked about the jungle menu, the young waiter attending to our table went to fetch the manager, a thirtysomething guy in a pale green shirt. His belly overflowed onto tight black slacks, and his fingers sparkled with gold rings. "How may I help you?" he eagerly asked. Van explained that Tim and I were visiting from abroad and looking for something special.

"Well, we have snakes, turtles, fish, and shellfish," the manager said, pointing at the tanks. "And shark fin soup, too."

"We're looking for something a bit more different . . . " Van pushed. "Something like a pangolin."

"Oh, we have pangolin," the manager quickly confirmed. "We keep it off-site because we don't have the facilities here. They're all caught in the wild and kept fresh. We can have one here in thirty minutes if you'd like to place an order."

In an ill-conceived attempt to convince us, he took out his phone, Googled *con tê tê*—Vietnamese for "pangolin"—and then began scrolling through images of pangolins in trees, pangolins curled into balls, and tiny baby pangolins clinging to their mothers' backs. "Pangolin is very expensive because there's fewer and fewer of them left in Vietnam and they breed slowly," he said. He could sell us one for $120 per pound.

Perhaps sensing our hesitation, he typed in another search term—*chồn*—that brought up an image of an endearing, whisker-faced civet. "Civet is my favorite thing on the whole menu," he said. "It tastes like a sweeter pork, with less fat. We marinate it and then cook it in a hot pot, intestines and all. Pangolin, on the other hand, is tougher, because we drain out the blood to mix with liquor."

Unprompted, he told us to hold on a moment and then disappeared into the back. I asked Van what kind of impression he got from this guy. "He's totally open," he replied quietly. "Once I said we wanted to try weird food, he was keen to talk because it means we have a lot of money. I think he's accepting of the idea of foreigners thinking everything is strange."

Moments later, the manager returned alongside with a guy in a blue shirt and flip-flops carrying a yellow mesh bag in his left hand. Having seen such a bag before, I had a sinking feeling. Indeed, as they brought it closer, I could make out the shape of a struggling civet inside. This one seemed less beaten down than the animal I'd been shown months before with Thảo and Ty. It pressed its padded paws against the bag and sniffed the air with its button nose, curling its body this way and that in its search for a way out.

Living prop in hand, the manager picked up where he left off: "Civet is really good, I guarantee it. People order it every night. If you try it, you will love it immediately!"

"It's so cute," Van said. "Why not have them as pets instead?"

"They're too aggressive to keep as pets, so we eat them," the manager chuckled.

By this point, Tim had broken out his massive SLR and was snapping away, and I was doing the same on my iPhone. The manager seemed completely unfazed. Others on staff were not so laid back, however. A man in a white button-down shirt and black tie hustled over to our table.

"Hey, you shouldn't be showing this stuff off!" he hissed. The smile fell from the manager's face, and immediately the mood changed. Blue-shirt guy was shooed away, taking the civet with him, and the previously welcoming manager now seemed suspicious. He put his hands on the back of Tim's and Van's chairs and leaned over our table in an almost threatening manner.

"So, what was it you said you do, again?" he demanded.

"I'm studying here," Van replied, managing to maintain his cool. "These are my friends. They just came here on tour."

Seemingly satisfied—and obviously still desperate to make a sale—the manager nodded: "Okay, I see." He handed Van a business card. "Call me if you want to come back tomorrow to buy pangolin."

We ordered a plate of fried noodles to avoid raising further suspicion and ate in tense silence. With the image of the struggling civet still fresh in our minds, everyone looked a bit crestfallen. "You've just gotta look for this stuff to find it," Tim said as we all stared down at our plates. "It's not hard."

LUCKILY, THE STORY DOES NOT END THERE. HUMANS ARE THE GREATEST THREAT to pangolins' survival, but, as I was soon to witness, they are also their greatest hope. The day after the restaurant fiasco, I received a Facebook Messenger text from Nguyễn Văn Thái, executive director of Save Vietnam's Wildlife. Since founding the nonprofit in 2014, Thái has become one of Vietnam's leading voices for ending the illegal wildlife trade, not the least because he and his colleagues run the country's only rehabilitation facilities for confiscated pangolins. Unlike Animals Asia's rescued bear sanctuaries, however, release back into the wild is always the goal for creatures that find their way to Thái. He doesn't have the space to keep the thousands of pangolins that would eventually pile up, and they are notoriously difficult to keep alive in captivity. As opposed to the bears, they've also not spent decades behind bars, meaning their chances of quickly readjusting to life in the wild are high. As of mid-2017, more than four hundred rehabilitated pangolins had been given a second shot at life in the wild thanks to Thái and his colleagues' work.

In a couple of days, he texted me, he would be returning forty-six rescued animals to the forest—the largest pangolin release undertaken to date.

"I am not sure if you have time to join us?"

I told him I absolutely did. I cleared my schedule of meetings, cancelled a flight to Hanoi, and booked a ticket to central Vietnam.

THE ANIMALS THAT WIND UP IN THÁI'S CARE, IT MUST BE POINTED OUT, ARE THE equivalent of lottery winners. Thousands upon thousands of others seized from the trade are given no such second chance. CITES urges that confiscated creatures be dealt with humanely and in a way that maximizes their conservation value without contributing further to the illegal trade, but the treaty does not require countries to report how animals are disposed of. Unfortunately, what limited information is available about their fates is almost always discouraging. As Kelvin Alie, executive vice president of the International Fund for Animal Welfare, said, "The plight of live seized animals is almost like a forgotten issue in dealing with the illegal wildlife trade."

Although releasing animals back into the wild may sound like the best option, in fact, it frequently is not. For starters, it's often too expensive or logistically complicated to return them to their home country or habitat. If released into the wrong place, however, foreign species may establish themselves as invasives. Tam Đảo National Park in northern Vietnam, for example, is now home to alien southern and lowland snake species, while nonnative rhesus macaques released into Cát Tiên National Park have begun breeding with native long-tailed macaques, muddying the gene pool.

Even if appropriate habitat is available, simply dumping animals out of the box they were found in isn't ideal, either. Having spent extended amounts of time highly stressed out and usually in close quarters with other individuals of the same or different species, animals rescued from the trade may have picked up diseases that could infect their wild counterparts. Many are also discovered in states of extreme ill health; they have gone days without food or water, and they may suffer from infected wounds from snare traps or rough handling. Traders sometimes even force-feed pangolins a limestone slurry or inject water beneath their skin to increase their weight. Releasing them in such a state will only mean a slow, painful death.

More often than not, confiscated animals wind up back at police stations, held in the same nets, boxes, or crates that they were discovered in, or turned loose in a filthy, concrete-floored dark room, where they are left to slowly dehydrate, starve, or succumb to their injuries. The most unlucky ones of all may even wind up back in the trade, through both legal or illegal routes. Indonesia, for example, legally auctions off seized animals, as does Vietnam for many species (in 2013 Vietnam at least banned auctions of confiscated pangolins). China also sells seized wild animals—which the law prohibits euthanizing—into the pet trade or to restaurants or farms.

Little is known about quantities, but in 2016 a team of Oxford University researchers managed to get hold of rare customs records for confiscated wildlife rescues in Yunnan. As the researchers reported in *Science*, in that province alone, Chinese authorities seized 18,000 live animals from 2010 to 2015. Of those animals, 8,750 reptiles became pets, food, or sanctuary residents; forty-one slow lories were sold into the pet trade; and sixty-nine primates, forty bears, and nearly nine hundred exotic birds were kept in "appalling enclosures" in captivity until they died. The nearly three hundred pangolins that the Yunnan authorities transferred to sanctuaries were also all dead within weeks or months.

Proper rehabilitation facilities and permanent sanctuaries for wild animals require a level of expertise and funding beyond the ability of many countries to provide, but Thái and his colleagues at Save Vietnam's Wildlife are the real deal. The nonprofit's headquarters are situated within the misty, lush foothills of Cúc Phương National Park in northern Vietnam, not far from where Thái grew up. As a kid, he frequently saw pangolins near his home—but such sightings haven't occurred for years. "It's not only around here, but in many parts of Vietnam that pangolins have disappeared," he said. "It's really sad."

He and his colleagues are doing all they can to counteract the losses. From 2014 to mid-2017, they rescued nearly seven hundred pangolins and small carnivores, and they recently opened a second rehab center at Pù Mát National Park, located 160 miles south. Though pangolins are finicky and notoriously difficult to keep alive in captivity, their survival rate at the rehab center hovers around an impressive 70 percent. They also help small carnivores ranging from civets and spotted cats to hoary-looking binturongs, but the pangolins take up the bulk of their efforts.

New arrivals stay in quarantine blocks for thirty days and may eventually get moved into one of eight long-term enclosures. The "pangolarium," as the latter setup is fondly referred to, is a far cry from the bleak, cramped cages that other rescue centers tend to use. Leafy branches stretch from floor to ceiling and half-buried concrete tubes mimic natural burrows. Wire fencing forms the cage walls—perfect not only for climbing on but also for providing the pangolins with fresh air, appropriate temperatures and humidity, and even a view of the forest, located steps away.

Creating a suitable artificial habitat was only the first and easiest step, however. Pangolins are insectivorous, so feeding the animals requires caretakers to harvest ants in the forest, a task that always entails countless bites. A single pangolin eats more than half a pound of ants per day, so Thái and his colleagues sometimes spend hours searching for enough insects to provide all their animals with a proper meal. Diets are also supplemented with ground silkworm larvae and frozen farmed ants, but the latter are expensive, costing the small nonprofit up to $4,700 per month.

Thái and the rapid response team never know what the day will bring in terms of possible new arrivals and remote rescues. They might get a call from the police who have just found a truckload of three dozen pangolins in a province four hours away. Or it could be a Ho Chi Minh City businessman who received a pangolin as a gift but would rather see it returned to the forest than eaten. Sometimes, the staff is so overwhelmed that they must work through the night and well into morning. The quarantine center and pangolarium can accommodate 132 animals comfortably, and so far they have never been forced to turn down a rescue because of lack of capacity.

With poaching pressure in Vietnam so high, there's always a chance that the pangolins Save Vietnam's Wildlife helps will only be recaptured. Thái is aware of this: "If pangolins are just trapped again, then it doesn't mean anything if we rehabilitate and release them." He has tried to minimize this risk by using several carefully vetted release sites. All are difficult to access, all still have wild pangolin populations, and all have strong on-the-ground support from dedicated rangers and NGO personnel. "We know these places aren't 100 percent safe, but they're much better than many other parks in Vietnam," Thái said.

The pangolins are a full-time job unto themselves, but on top of that—and operating on a total budget of less than $100,000 annually—the nonprofit also trains park rangers, engages in community outreach, and conducts pangolin-related research. Its educational campaigns have reached more than 1,200 elementary students—many of whom had never visited the forest or interacted with animals before—and it recently opened a hands-on learning center at Cúc Phương.

Critically, all that work is conceived of and led by a predominantly Vietnamese team. "At Save Vietnam's Wildlife, Vietnamese staff are our key people, because we're the ones who need to be taking care of the environment," Thái said. "It's time for Vietnamese people to take action, before all our species disappear."

Until governments finally get around to full commitment to ending illegal wildlife trade, passionate, selflessly dedicated individuals like Thái and his colleagues likely represent our best hope for keeping the losses and extinctions somewhat at bay. As Natalie Kyriacou, founder and CEO of My Green World, wrote on Mongabay, "Although small and unassuming, these [grassroots] organizations are often able to score gains that large international agencies cannot. [They] can achieve what millions of misplaced dollars and brand promotion cannot: results."

Luckily, there are more and more people willing to get involved and pick up the slack for those who should be leading the fight against the illegal wildlife trade. The nonprofit group Education for Nature–Vietnam (ENV), for example, created a wildlife crime hotline that fields an average of three calls per day, ranging from a report of a caged bear spotted at a restaurant to an anonymous tip about a warehouse full of thousands of dead sea turtles. Since 2005, the hotline has logged 11,000 such cases, many of which are spotted by a volunteer network of 4,000 men and women across the country—90 percent of whom are under the age of twenty-five. They are the eyes and ears of the nonprofit's crime reduction efforts, monitoring businesses in their respective areas to ensure owners are in compliance with wildlife laws.

"Young people and college-age kids here come from an entirely different Vietnam than that of the people who are currently in power," said Doug Hendrie, director of wildlife crime and investigations at ENV. "Ten years ago, you could find hardly any sentiment about wildlife, but now there's homegrown animal welfare organizations popping up in cities across the county. Young people care about environmental and social issues, and they have a more global attitude in terms of their footprint on the planet. Volunteerism and activism is up, and it's changing Vietnam. In twenty years, they will make these values dominant in society."

WE'D BEEN DRIVING FOR A COUPLE OF HOURS WHEN KHOA—A TRUSTED CHAUFfeur who knew the secret location of the pangolin release site—slowed the car.

"Giờ ăn trưa," he said. *Lunchtime.*

Since leaving the airport, the scenery had become increasingly green and the roads increasingly steep. We stopped at the end of a long tunnel that terminated with a view of forest-covered mountains beyond, and Khoa didn't even bother pulling off to the side of the road. We hadn't passed another vehicle in half an hour.

We took a seat on the tunnel's ledge, beneath a graffiti tag that read "Fuck the State Love Nature" in English. From a small red cooler, Khoa laid out a feast of fruit, pork buns, and juice. The mountain air was clear and cool, and black butterflies drifted by lazily in the sunshine. All was silent save for a symphony of insects and a distant bird's call. "Maybe you only time come here in your life," Khoa said, adding to the poetry of the moment.

We continued on our way, making two brief stops at small shrines situated just off road. They looked like Smurf houses, complete with steeped red roofs and overhanging porches. Inside were offerings of cigarettes, cookies, and bottled tea. "You wait here, two minutes," Khoa said, taking some incense out of the glove compartment. When I reached for my camera, he shook his head emphatically. "No take photo! Here, people die." I watched silently as he lit the incense, placed it on the shrine, and bowed several times.

Finally, we pulled up at the ranger headquarters where we were meeting Thái. It was a simple yellow concrete building with a matching yellow concrete gate, all set against a backdrop of undulating green. The place was bustling with men in pine-colored uniforms, and Save Vietnam's Wildlife's bus stood out front. To reach this mountain station, "people and pangolins go together," as Thái had put it. More than fourteen hours earlier, the whole team—nine staff and forty-six pangolins—had loaded onto the bus. Now that they had finally arrived, they were busy unloading and organizing the animals. Covering the area around the bus was a clutter of pink, cream, and soap-green animal carriers and bespoke wooden crates decorated with Save Vietnam's Wildlife stickers. Some of the containers were silent, while scraping or jostling issued from others.

Thái stepped off the bus, carrying a cooler full of ants and larvae, wearing a characteristic expression best described as a mix of stress, worry, and determination. "Hey Rachel, how are you?" he asked, his voice weary. A little soft in the belly, he wore jeans and a dark blue shirt that would be the envy of any Brooklyn hipster. Above a kitschy photo of a pangolin it read, "Save Pangolins. Extra Special. Almost Extinct." I told him I loved the shirt and wanted it.

"I don't have any with me right now," he replied, taking me literally.

I've known Thái since he was a graduate student in the UK and Australia, and to say that he is serious about protecting his country's wildlife would be putting it lightly. He can also be quite outspoken when standing up for it. When I naively asked whether he would help me interview Tám Hổ, the pangolin hunter from Chapter 1, he quickly set me straight: "I do not want to see that. I would kill him or take his traps away when I am there." Likewise, when a media story I wrote about Save Vietnam's Wildlife was published with a title he did not agree with, I received an irate e-mail accusing me of disrespecting his and his colleagues' incredible efforts (I did not write the title in question—journalists hardly ever get to write their own headlines).

Although Thái should probably avoid a career in public relations, his fire and gall are precisely what make him an effective activist. Even if the odds are stacked against him, he does not back down from fighting for what he believes and standing up to those who disagree. Others in the conservation community have come to appreciate these qualities in him as well. "Once, after getting together with people to discuss all these high-level strategies for saving Vietnam's wildlife, Thái e-mailed the head of the United Nations Office on Drugs and Crime and cc'd all the important people, saying, 'Hey guys, I know you want to help Vietnam's animals. Well, there's twenty pangolins stuck in customs with no food, and they're going to die. We need money to feed them,'" a government contractor recalled to me, with a hint of awe in his voice at Thái's ballsiness. "That's why, when everyone else is trying to figure out who would be the best person to sit next to at meetings and conferences, I always beeline for the table with Thái. He is the greatest person alive." Thái, another colleague told me, "literally takes care of everything."

Indeed, at the ranger station, Thái was busy tending to the forty-six pangolins in his care, giving them one last meal from the cooler before the big event. He lifted a crate lid, revealing two scaly brown balls nestled in a bed of hay. Slowly, one of the balls unfurled and out poked a long, pointed face with bulging blueberry eyes; a wet, dog-like nose; and tiny, oddly human ears. The pangolin stuck its snout into the air, sniffing sleepily as Thái filled a small plastic tub with the insect mush from the cooler, which looked like a mixture of red and white quinoa. The pangolins—now both awake—loved it. They buried their pink faces in the bowls like happy puppies.

Thái and his staff continued their rounds, ensuring that each crate was taken care of. As I watched them, I realized that pangolins have very distinct personalities. Some were timid and quivering; others were bold and curious, rearing up on their hind legs to survey the world around them. A few even tried to instigate an escape. They all seemed gentle, however: none attempted to bite, and, when handled, they did not even struggle. If anything, they wrapped their strong, slinky-like bodies around the staff, clinging to them like a toddler in its father's arms.

The level of trust was shocking, considering what these pangolins had been put through by humans. Most of the animals being released today were discovered packed in boxes of ice in the back of a truck. Of the sixty-one confiscated by the police, twelve died from trauma and injuries, and several more are still recovering back at the pangolarium. The lucky forty-six would be divided into three groups, Thái explained, each of which would be taken to different parts of the forest so as to spread the pangolin love and ensure the solitary creatures had the best possible start.

Given that pangolins are nocturnal, the release would begin after sundown. As the shadows grew longer, the men at the ranger station began gearing up for the journey. They put on thick green socks that reached their knees and laced tightly over their pants—specially designed to keep leeches out—and, rather than boots, many wore plastic sandals. Each man took a carrier or crate, which he transformed into a pangolin backpack using an intricately tied green rope. From the cracks in one of those boxes emerged a quivering purple-grey nose and two pairs of long yellow claws—a pangolin finding its spot at the window like a pet settling in for a cross-country road trip.

I joined Thái's group, which included Bri Duff, a young, reserved volunteer from the Cleveland Metroparks Zoo. We were accompanied by half a dozen rangers. About a quarter of the rangers working here were reformed poachers, their manager told me. A ranger named Đoàn, for example, later explained that he originally turned to illegal logging and hunting after he lost his government job and could not find work. "It was necessary for my family," he said. "I had no choice." When he heard that a nonprofit was recruiting in the area, though, he immediately applied. "I love the forest very much," he said. "I wanted to become a protector, not a destroyer." Now, he's a forest guard team leader.

We headed down a fern-lined trail off the main road, which brought us to a thick wall of green. In we went. Beneath the canopy of tropical vines, Triassic-sized leaves, and dense branches, the light dimmed and the humidity grew heavier. I slipped on a headlamp that I'd bargained for in Ho Chi Minh City, knowing I'd soon need its guiding beam. The path was slick with mud and wet leaves and, to my disappointment, was also marred by quite a bit of trash. Unfortunately, as I learned during my days working with rangers in U Minh, the anti-litterbug zeitgeist has yet to take hold in Vietnam, even among those who serve to protect nature.

The rangers moved with quick, expert ease down the narrow trail. We scrambled beneath fallen logs and dodged sharp sticks and stumps. When I lost my balance, I made the mistake of grabbing a thorn-studded trunk for support. *Ten minutes in and I've already managed to injure myself,* I thought with embarrassment. I didn't have time to dwell on it, though; it was time for the first release. We stopped at a seemingly arbitrary spot on the path and made our way twenty feet or so into the thick surrounding forest. "Bri, do you want to release this animal?" Thái asked, removing the pet crate from his back.

Her voice quivered with a mix of surprise and delight: "Yeah!"

Thái sat a few feet away, angling his iPhone's camera at the crate's door as Bri gingerly opened it. A moment later, a nose appeared. The pangolin hesitated, then slipped out, marching directly over Thái's foot as it waddled its way into the forest. No fanfare marked the moment it disappeared into the brush. No one even said anything. But as we quietly made our way back to the path, I could see that Bri was glowing.

We ventured further into the wild, and night began to descend in earnest. The greens deepened to black, a breeze picked up, and the crickets' singing surged. All around us, spider eyes glittered, reflecting the light from our headlamps. The beam from mine was weaker than I had hoped but still strong enough to illuminate spaghetti-thin leeches that grasped at us from leafy perches. Paranoid about them falling on me, I compulsively rubbed my slick neck and swiped at my sweaty shoulders. By now I was completely soaked, but I didn't feel hot—just very wet.

We stopped for another release, and Thái asked whether I'd like to do the honors this time. He showed me how to turn the crate onto its side and to open the two wooden doors standing between the pangolin and freedom. From inside the now-open crate, the pangolin, wide eyed and unblinking, stared at us with a look that registered as "WTF?" We sat there and watched. The pangolin sat there and watched. No one moved. As the standoff continued, my squatting legs began to cramp. Thái swatted at mosquitoes and looked over his arms for leeches. Bri shifted on her feet. Still, the pangolin gave no signs of budging.

Eventually, Thái quietly inched closer and gently tapped the back of the crate. No dice. "They prefer to stay in the box instead of coming out into the open," he whispered. "In the wild, they spend a lot of time in their burrow."

Ten or fifteen minutes passed before Thái decided it was time for a serious intervention. As gently as possible, he wrenched out the pangolin, setting her onto the forest floor. She stood there, back arched like an angry cat, and then suddenly retracted into a ball. We were on a bit of a hill, and the now soccer ball-shaped animal rolled a few feet down before coming to a stop. More minutes passed and then finally—*finally*—out came her head, followed by one tentative foot, and then another, until—at last—she took a step. She was so hesitant, it was as though she was struggling to believe that her surroundings were real. Slowly and deliberately, she finally set off, slipping over a log with fluid ease before fading into the leaves.

We set off again. In the now pitch black, we fell more often. Bri slipped onto her butt; Thái tumbled onto his side. I had the feeling that I was groping through a dark, obstacle-studded dreamscape, never quite able to get my bearings. *This place belongs to the pangolins,* I thought, *not us soft humans.*

In quick succession, we set several animals free. Attesting to their varied personalities, some bolted from their cages without hesitation while others took a bit more patience and persuasion. A juvenile, maybe a foot long, headed straight for Thái's leg. He latched on cozily until Thái nudged the little guy onto a tree trunk, which he then climbed straight up, inchworm-style. "Look at him go!" Bri whispered. Another pangolin, a large one set free in one of the final releases, approached Thái and stood upright on its back feet, gazing at him for a moment before continuing on its way, as though to say thank you.

Two hours or so later, we emerged from the jungle, wet, muddy, bleeding, and bruised—but basking in the satisfaction of a job well done.

"That was awesome!" Bri gushed. "Definitely one of the coolest things I've ever done!"

I couldn't help but agree.

As we made our way back to the ranger station, I tried to imagine the unimaginable ordeal that these animals had gone through. So extreme was their experience that I could only conceive of it in the guise of horror or sci-fi. It must have been like getting abducted and tortured by hostile aliens; getting rescued by a group of benevolent but still terrifying aliens; and then, at last, being returned home.

It was impossible to say what fate awaited the newly freed pangolins out there in the dark. They might find themselves once again trapped in a hunter's snare, bound for one of the Ho Chi Minh City restaurants I had visited just days before. Or luck might remain on their side, and they would never see another human again. "If just one individual survives," Thái said, "it's a happy story." Yet, until people stop demanding their flesh and scales, their safety will never be guaranteed.

Back at the ranger station, the men had laid out a feast of sautéed pork, fish sauce–kissed eggs, and a hearty beef stew, all paired with plentiful bottles of warm beer. Faces grew red, and the mood was becoming increasingly raucous by the time I said goodbye to Thái and his smiling team. They had earned this celebration.

As Khoa and I pulled away, I glanced back one last time. The full moon was high in the sky, and the mountains' dark silhouettes stood out clearly in its light. Somewhere out there, in the now richer forest, beyond the warm glow of the ranger station, forty-six pangolins were scrambling up trees, lapping up ants, and lustily burrowing into the mud.

ACKNOWLEDGMENTS

THIS BOOK, IN MANY WAYS, IS THE CULMINATION OF A LIFETIME OF INTEREST IN the natural world. Innumerable people contributed, from my mother—who nurtured and supported a fondness for animals—to professors, teachers, and colleagues. Among them all, though, a few names stand out.

Dan Fagin's mentorship and encouragement played a major and ongoing role in *Poached*'s creation. Thanks are likewise due to Jane Dystel and Merloyd Lawrence for believing that the illegal wildlife trade was a subject worthy of a book, when so many others did not. Thanks also to Julie Ford and to Carrie Watterson for their skillful attentiveness to detail.

I am indebted to many others who donated their time and expertise to help me along the way. Steve Hall gave valuable feedback on early proposal drafts, while John Rennie provided pep talks at critical moments. Joey Power, Stephen Maxner, Bridie Andrews, and Steve Given all improved the text with insights from their respective fields, while Nguyễn Kim Thảo, Jason Lashbrook, and Jessica Peng kindly offered pro bono translations. Gratitude also goes to my dad, who proofread the manuscript from cover to cover in less than a week—just in time for my deadline.

I am thankful for the numerous sources who trusted me with their stories and patiently explained complex subjects. A special shout out goes to Ron Orenstein, who provided invaluable fact checking and feedback. Additionally—and in no particular order—Chris Shepherd, Vincent Nijman, Masayuki Sakamoto, Michael 't Sas-Rolfes, Rian and Lorna Labuschagne, Shaun Leavy, Nguyễn Văn Thái, Keith Roberts, Pete Newland, Debbie Banks, Otto Werdmuller Van Elgg, Dan Challender, Batian Craig, Nir Tenenbaum, Bill Clark, and Tim Tear all went above and beyond. Additionally, Brendan Rohr, Mary Dixon, and Stephen Sautner were exceptionally helpful with wrangling sources and information. A number of journalists were especially generous with sharing their time and insights, including Julian Rademeyer, Karl Ammann, Đỗ Doãn Hoàng, Tim Gerard Barker, and Michele Penna. Finally, I thank all the individuals who spoke with me confidentially, some of whom risked their jobs or safety to do so.

The year and a half I spent reporting and writing this book was taxing at times, including economically. I'd like to thank the magazine and newspaper editors—particularly Oliver Payne and Mike Mason—who helped me make ends meet (and spread the word about the illegal trade) by commissioning stories. The Pulitzer Center on Crisis Reporting awarded me a travel grant to cover several of those stories in South Africa and Malawi.

On a more personal note, I am indebted to my wonderful friends, who never failed to ask how the book was coming along (and when the launch party would be) and who kept peer pressure to a minimum when I had to hole up to write, even on summer beach days. In particular, I'd like to thank Danielle Venton for her delightful "Word Count Wednesdays," Amber Williams for selflessly listening to book-related venting, the Venerable Benkong Shi for good fortune, Merrick Zoubeiri for good company on the road, Chad Pugh for being "the man," Meghan Womack for generously offering her time, and Declan Kane for welcomingly distracting texts throughout the writing process. Kit was, as always, the perfect writing companion, and Ty Parker will forever be my pimp/brother/sidekick in reporting adventures.

Finally, and, most importantly, I must thank my husband, Paul Dix. He was a crucial sounding board and unwavering supporter. Without him, the scope of this book would have been much narrower, if it had been written at all. Thank you, love, I am forever grateful.

BIBLIOGRAPHY

ONE: THE HUNTER

Anon. (1999) 'Review of Significant Trade in Animal Species Included in CITES Appendix II: Detailed Reviews of 37 Species, *Manis javanica*', World Conservation Monitoring Center, IUCN Species Survival Commission and TRAFFIC Network Report to the CITES Animals Committee, Geneva, Switzerland.

Anon. (2016) 'The Status, Trade and Conservation of Pangolins (*Manis* Spp.)', IUCN SSC Pangolin Specialist Group CITES Document, Geneva, Switzerland.

Arsenyev, V. K. (2016) *Across the Ussuri Kray: Travels in the Sikhote-Alin Mountains,* J. C. Slaght, trans. (Bloomington: Indiana University Press).

Benitez-Lopez, A., et al. (2017) 'The Impacts of Hunting on Tropical Mammal and Bird Populations', *Science* 356: 180–183.

Boakye, M. K., et al. (2014) 'Ethnomedicinal Use of African Pangolins by Traditional Medical Practitioners in Sierra Leone', *Journal of Ethnobiology and Ethnomedicine* 10: 1–10.

Cheng, W., Xing, S., & Bonebrake, T. (2017) 'Recent Pangolin Seizures in China Reveal Priority Areas for Intervention', *Conservation Letters*: 1–8.

Connor, N. (2017) 'In Love with the Taste of Wildlife—Probe Launched After Officials Hold "Endangered Pangolin Feast" in China', *Telegraph,* bit.ly/2xMCEEd.

Cox, S. (2011) 'Is Vietnam the Next China?', *Economist,* Econ.st/2j1QRcT.

Ellis, R. (2005) *Tiger Bone and Rhino Horn: The Destruction of Wildlife for Traditional Chinese Medicine* (Washington, DC: Island Press).

Felbab-Brown, V. (2017) *The Extinction Market: Wildlife Trafficking and How to Stop It* (Oxford: Oxford University Press).

Heinrich, S., et al. (2017) 'The Global Trafficking of Pangolins', TRAFFIC Report, Selangor, Malaysia.

Kulkarni, C. G., & Adwait, D. (2011) 'Folk Therapies of *Katkaris* from Maharashtra', *Indian Journal of Traditional Knowledge* 10: 554–558.

Linder, A. (2017a) 'Guangxi Officials Investigated Over Claims That They Hosted Banquets Serving Pangolin Meat', *Shanghaiist,* bit.ly/2f17tgN.

Linder, A. (2017b) '"Pangolin Princess" Arrested in Shenzhen over Her Taste for Eating Endangered Animals', *Shanghaiist,* bit.ly/2eJ9v85.

Nguyen, X. D., Pham, T. A., & Le, H. T. (2001) 'New Information About the Hairy-Nosed Otter (*Lutra sumatrana*) in Vietnam', *IUCN Otter Specialist Group Bulletin* 18: 64–75.

Nuwer, R., & Bell, D. (2014) 'Identifying and Quantifying the Threats to Biodiversity in the U Minh Peat Swamp Forests of the Mekong Delta, Vietnam', *Oryx* 48: 88–94.

Pringle, J. (2004) 'Closing the Circle on Vietnam', *New York Times,* nyti.ms/2iYxlOs.

Redford, K. H. (1992) 'The Empty Forest', *BioScience* 42: 412–422.

Sanders, B. (2002) 'Fire Incident Assessment: U Minh Ha Forest and U Minh Thuong National Park', Integrated Fire Management Expert Group, bit.ly/2wDwWGa.

Saqalli, M., & Dosso, M. (2011) 'Draped Heterogeneity, Forced Uniformity: When Agro-environmental Policies Drive Family Development; The U Minh Thuong Forest Reserve (Mekong Delta, Vietnam)', *Journal of Field Actions* 5: 1–9.

Shibao, W. U., Liu, N., Zhang, Y., & Ma, G. (2003) 'Assessment of Threatened Status of Chinese Pangolin', *China Journal of Applied Environmental Biology* 10: 456–461.

Sodeinde, O., & Adedipe, S. (1994) 'Pangolins in South-West Nigeria—Current Status and Prognosis', *Oryx* 28: 43–50.

Sterling, E. J., Hurley, M. M., & Minh, L. D. (2006) *Vietnam: A Natural History* (New Haven: Yale University Press).

Sutter, J. D. (2014) 'The Most Trafficked Mammal You've Never Heard Of', CNN, cnn.it/2vJNj5g.

Vuong, Q. H. (2014) 'Vietnam's Political Economy in Transition (1986–2016)', Stratfor Worldview, bit.ly/2xMLPnY.

TWO: HER SISTER'S PANGOLIN SCALE GUY

Ammann, K., dir. (2017) *The Tiger Mafia*. Documentary film, not yet released.

Andrews, B. J. (1997) 'Tuberculosis and the Assimilation of Germ Theory in China, 1895–1937', *Journal of the History of Medicine* 52: 114–157.

Andrews, B. J., & Bullock, M. B., eds. (2014) *Medical Transitions in Twentieth-Century China* (Bloomington: Indiana University Press).

Anon. (2008) 'China Comes Down Hard on Pangolin Smugglers', Reuters, reut.rs/2w7aTEe.

Anon. (2016a) 'An Overview of Pangolin Data: When Will the Over-exploitation of the Pangolin End?', China Biodiversity Conservation and Green Development Foundation Report, Beijing, China.

Anon. (2016b) 'Time for Action: End the Criminality and Corruption Fueling Wildlife Crime', Environmental Investigation Agency Report, London, UK.

Anon. (2017) 'It's Not Just Pangolins, but How Many Other Endangered Birds and Animals Are Being Eaten into Extinction by Chinese People?', NetEase, Inc., bit.ly/2eIYcNv.

Chung, T. Y. R., et al. (2015) 'Survey on Pangolin Consumption Trends in Hong Kong', HKU Pop Site, bit.ly/2gEnOrx.

Ellis, R. (2005) *Tiger Bone and Rhino Horn: The Destruction of Wildlife for Traditional Chinese Medicine* (Washington, DC: Island Press).

Felbab-Brown, V. (2017) *The Extinction Market: Wildlife Trafficking and How to Stop It* (Oxford: Oxford University Press).

French, H. W. (2014) *China's Second Continent: How a Million Migrants Are Building a New Empire in Africa* (New York: Vintage Books).

Hu, X. M., Wen, C. P., & Xie, Z. J. (2012) 'History and Application of Pangolin Scales', *Chinese Archives of Traditional Chinese Medicine* 30: 590–592.

Levinovitz, A. (2013) 'Chairman Mao Invented Traditional Chinese Medicine', *Slate,* slate.me/2j1eYZs.

Li, J., et al. (2014) 'The Quality of Reports of Randomized Clinical Trials on Traditional Chinese Medicine Treatments: A Systematic Review of Articles Indexed in the China National Knowledge Infrastructure Database from 2005 to 2012', *BMC Complementary and Alternative Medicine* 14: 1–11.

Liebenberg, L., Kat, P., & Macsween, C. (2017) 'South Africa Moots an Annual Trade of 800 Lion Skeletons', LionAid, bit.ly/2j3BYHn.

Loh, T. L., Tewfik, A., Aylesworth, L., & Phoonsawat, R. (2016) 'Species in Wildlife Trade: Socio-economic Factors Influence Seahorse Relative Abundance in Thailand', *Biological Conservation* 201: 301–308.

Macsween, C. (2017) 'Irregular And also Likely Illegal—the Trade in Lion Products from South Africa to Laos, Vietnam and Thailand', LionAid, bit.ly/2wG6cos.

Shuang, L., Shanshan, G., Jianjun, P., & Jun, Z. (2016) 'Pangolins (*Manis*) Medical Efficacy and Clinical Application Research', *Forest Science and Technology* 7: 57–60.

Vickers, A., Goyal, N., Harland, R., & Rees, R. (1998) 'Do Certain Countries Produce Only Positive Results? A Systematic Review of Controlled Trials', *Controlled Clinical Trials* 19: 159–166.

Xu, B., & Ju, C. (2009) 'Farewell to Professor Zhang Gongyao's Ideals', *Australian Journal of Acupuncture and Chinese Medicine* 4: 28–29.

Xu, L., Guan, J., Lau, W., & Xiao, Y. (2016) 'An Overview of Pangolin Trade in China', TRAFFIC Briefing, Cambridge, UK.

Zastrow, M. (2017) 'Four in 10 Biomedical Papers out of China Are Tainted by Misconduct, Says New Survey', Retraction Watch, bit.ly/2zI7HoD.

Zhang, G. (2006) 'Farewell to Chinese Medicine', *Medicine and Philosophy* 27: 14–17.

Zhou, S. F. (2009) 'The Future of Traditional Chinese Medicine', *Australian Journal of Acupuncture and Chinese Medicine* 4: 23–24.

THREE: RHINO HORN IN THE COOKIE TIN

Anon. (2016a) 'Hanoi Statement on Illegal Wildlife Trade', Hanoi Conference on Illegal Wildlife Trade Report, Hanoi, Vietnam.

Anon. (2016b) 'South Africa Reports Small Decrease in Rhino Poaching, but Africa-Wide 2015 the Worst on Record', TRAFFIC, bit.ly/2eKIKQP.

Anon. (2017) 'Rhino Population Figures', Save the Rhino, bit.ly/2gKUa7N.

Barry, D. J. (1997) 'Termination of the Pelly Amendment Certification of Taiwan', Department of the Interior, *Federal Register* 62: 23479–23480.

Blee, A. (2017) 'Newly Approved Vietnamese Penal Code Should Enhance Efforts to Address Wildlife Trafficking', TRAFFIC, bit.ly/2xPb1u5.

Brait, E. (2016) 'Extinct 'Siberian Unicorn' May Have Lived Alongside Humans, Fossil Suggests', *Guardian*, bit.ly/2gLc2zc.

But, P. P. H., Lung, L. C., & Tam, Y. K. (1990) 'Ethnopharmacology of Rhinoceros Horn: Antipyretic Effects of Rhinoceros Horn and Other Animal Horns', *Journal of Ethnopharmacology* 30: 157–168.

Crosta, A., Sutherland, K., & Talerico, C. (2017) 'Grinding Rhino: An Undercover Investigation on Rhino Horn Trafficking in China and Vietnam', Elephant Action League Report, Los Angeles, US.

Ellis, R. (2005) *Tiger Bone and Rhino Horn: The Destruction of Wildlife for Traditional Chinese Medicine* (Washington, DC: Island Press).

Emslie, R., et al. (2015) 'African and Asian Rhinoceroses—Status, Conservation and Trade', IUCN Species Survival Commission (IUCN SSC) African and Asian Rhino Specialist Groups and TRAFFIC Report to the CITES Secretariat, Geneva, Switzerland.

Felbab-Brown, V. (2017) *The Extinction Market: Wildlife Trafficking and How to Stop It* (Oxford: Oxford University Press).

Gwin, P. (2012) 'Rhino Wars', *National Geographic,* bit.ly/2xbafus.

Johnson, L. (2015) 'Farmed Rhino Horn Not Seen as Substitute Product', Breaking the Brand, bit.ly/2j4lmPG.

Laburn, H., & Mitchell, D. (1997) 'Extracts of Rhinoceros Horn Are Not Antipyretic in Rabbits', *Journal of Basic and Clinical Physiology and Pharmacology* 8: 1–11.

MacMillan, D., et al. (2017) 'Demand in Viet Nam for Rhino Horn in Traditional Medicine', International Trade Center, Geneva, Switzerland.

Martin, E. B. (1982) 'The Conspicuous Consumption of Rhinos', *Animal Kingdom* 84: 20–26.

Martin, E. B., & Martin, C. (1982) *Run Rhino Run* (London: Chatto & Windus).

Martin, E. B., & Vigne, L. (2003) 'Trade in Rhino Horn from Eastern Africa to Yemen', *Pachyderm* 34: 75–87.

Milliken, T., & Shaw, J. (2012) 'The South Africa—Viet Nam Rhino Horn Trade Nexus', TRAFFIC Report, Johannesburg, South Africa.

Mills, J. A. (2015) *Blood of the Tiger: A Story of Conspiracy, Greed and the Battle to Save a Magnificent Species* (Boston: Beacon Press).

Nguyen, P. L., trans. (2011) 'Woman Poisoned by Rhino Horn', Education for Nature-Vietnam, bit.ly/2gMDOLZ.

Nowell, K. (2012) 'Assessment of Rhino Horn as a Traditional Medicine', TRAFFIC Report to the CITES Secretariat, Geneva, Switzerland.

Orenstein, R. (2013) *Ivory, Horn and Blood: Behind the Elephant and Rhinoceros Poaching Crisis* (Buffalo: Firefly Books).

Sellar, J. M. (2014) *The U.N.'s Lone Ranger: Combating International Wildlife Crime* (Dunbeath: Whittles).

Shabecoff, P. (1982) 'Rhinos Trapped in a Strange Web of Ritual and Economics', *New York Times*, nyti.ms/2gKVlUL.

Shepherd, C. R., Gray, T. N. E., & Nijman, V. (2017) 'Rhinoceros Horns in Trade on the Myanmar-China Border', *Oryx*: 1–3.

Thomas Parker, J. (2013) *The Mythic Chinese Unicorn* (Victoria: FriesenPress).

Vigne, L., & Martin, E. B. (2000) 'Price for Rhino Horn Increases in Yemen', *Pachyderm* 28: 91–100.

Vigne, L., & Martin, E. B. (2016) 'High Rhino Horn Prices Drive Poaching', *Swara,* July–September, 42–46.

Vu, H.N.D., & Nielsen, M.R. (2018) 'Understanding utilitarian and hedonic values determining the demand for rhino horn in Vietnam', Human Dimensions of Wildlife. Advanced online publication.

Zhang, G. (2011) 'How Did Rhinoceros Get Extinguished in China?', unpublished report, Hunan, China.

FOUR: THE HOLY GRAIL OF HERPETOLOGY

AFP (2015) 'Smuggler Caught in Indonesia with Rare Birds Jammed Inside Water Bottles', *Guardian,* bit.ly/2gHdZcf.

Anon. (2014) 'Seizures and Prosecutions: March 1997–October 2014', TRAFFIC Bulletin, Washington, DC.

Anon. (2015) 'This Odd World: Squeaking Crotch Foils Smuggling Attempt', *Jakarta Post,* bit.ly/2eLiTYX.

Anon. (2016) 'Report of the Attendance of the Seventeenth Meeting of the Conference of the Parties to the Convention on International Trade in Endangered Species of WildFauna and Flora (CoP XVII, CITES)' [in Indonesian], Ministry of the Environment and Forestry Report, Jakarta, Indonesia.

Auliya, M., et al. (2016) 'Trade in Live Reptiles, Its Impact on Wild Populations, and the Role of the European Market', *Biological Conservation* 204: 103–119.

Chng, S. C. L., et al. (2015) 'In the Market for Extinction: An Inventory of Jakarta's Bird Markets', TRAFFIC Report, Petaling Jaya, Malaysia.

Dell'Amore, C. (2009) 'Smuggler Caught with 14 Birds in Pants', *National Geographic,* bit.ly/2gHda3h.

Felbab-Brown, V. (2017) *The Extinction Market: Wildlife Trafficking and How to Stop It* (Oxford: Oxford University Press).

Lindenmayer, D., & Schleele, B. (2017) 'Do Not Publish', *Science* 356: 800–801.

Meihaard, E., & Nijman, V. (2014) 'Secrecy Considerations for Conserving Lazarus Species', *Biological Conservation* 175: 21–24.

Mills, J. A. (2015) *Blood of the Tiger: A Story of Conspiracy, Greed and the Battle to Save a Magnificent Species* (Boston: Beacon Press).

Nijman, V., & Stoner, S. (2014) 'Keeping an Ear to the Ground: Monitoring the Trade in Earless Monitor Lizards', TRAFFIC Report, Petaling Jaya, Malaysia.

Nuwer, R. (2014) 'The Black Market Trade for Endangered Animals Flourishes on the Web', *Newsweek,* bit.ly/1p6oEyV.

Shukman, D., & Piranty, S. (2017) 'The Secret Trade in Baby Chimps', BBC, bbc.in/2gH9cl4.

Smith, S. (2016) 'China Sentences International Ring of Radiated Tortoise Smugglers', WCS Newsroom, bit.ly/2w7x798.

Yaap, B., et al. (2012) 'First Record of the Borneo Earless Monitor *Lanthanotus
borneensis* (Steindachner, 1877) (Reptilla: Lanthanotidae) in West Kalimantan
(Indonesian Borneo)', *Journal of Threatened Taxa* 4: 3067–3074.

FIVE: WHITE GOLD

AFP (2015) 'Poachers Killed Half Mozambique's Elephants in Five Years', *Guardian,* bit.ly/2xbaDcb.

Andrews, B. J., & Bullock, M. B., eds. (2014) *Medical Transitions in Twentieth-
Century China* (Bloomington: Indiana University Press).

Anon. (1978) 'Economic Intelligence Weekly Review', Central Intelligence Agency
Report, Langley, US.

Anon. (2002) 'Back in Business: Elephant Poaching and the Ivory Black Markets of
Asia', Environmental Investigation Agency Report, Washington, DC, US.

Anon. (2012) 'Blood Ivory: Exposing the Myth of a Regulated Market', Environmental Investigation Agency Report, London, UK.

Anon. (2014) 'Vanishing Point: Criminality, Corruption and the Devastation of Tanzania's Elephants', Environmental Investigation Agency Report, London, UK.

Anon. (2016a) 'A Statement from the MIKE and ETIS Technical Advisory Group on
Recent Claims That the CITES-Approved Ivory Sales in 2008 Caused a Spike
in Poaching Levels', MIKE and ETIS Technical Advisory Group Document,
Geneva, Switzerland.

Broad, S., ed. (2007) 'TRAFFIC Bulletin Volume 21', TRAFFIC Bulletin, Washington, DC, US.

Burn, R. W., Underwood, F. M., & Blanc, J. (2011) 'Global Trends and Factors Associated with the Illegal Killing of Elephants: A Hierarchical Bayesian Analysis of
Carcass Encounter Data', *PLOS ONE* 6: e24165.

Chase, M. J., et al. (2016) 'Continent-Wide Survey Reveals Massive Decline in African Savannah Elephants', *PeerJ* 4: e2354.

Chokshi, N., & Gettleman, J. (2016) 'African Elephant Population Dropped 30 Percent in 7 Years', *New York Times,* nyti.ms/2wlCxtg.

Crosta, A., Sutherland, K., & Beckner, M. 'Blending Ivory: China's Old Loopholes,
New Hopes', Elephant Action League Report, Los Angeles, US.

Do, Q. T., Levchenko, A., & Ma, L. (2016a) 'Errors Do Not Drive Conclusions in
Our Original Post: Response to Hsiang and Sekar's Response', alevchenko.com,
bit.ly/2vMJaxa.

Do, Q. T., Levchenko, A., & Ma, L. (2016b) 'To Trade or Not to Trade Elephant Ivory?
That's Going to Be the Question', Development Impact, bit.ly/2eGA5LD.

Douglas-Hamilton, I., & Douglas-Hamilton, O. (1992) *Battle for the Elephants* (New
York: Viking).

Editorial Board (2016) 'The Scourge of the Ivory Trade', *New York Times,* nyti.
ms/2xPwC5T.

Ellis, R. (2005) *Tiger Bone and Rhino Horn: The Destruction of Wildlife for Traditional Chinese Medicine* (Washington, DC: Island Press).

Farand, Chloe. (2017) 'Ivory Stained with Tea to Make It Look Older and Bypass the Law Sold in UK, WWF Says', *Independent,* ind.pn/2gI14qu.

Felbab-Brown, V. (2017) *The Extinction Market: Wildlife Trafficking and How to Stop It* (Oxford: Oxford University Press).

Gabriel, G. G. (2013) 'Impact Evaluation on Ivory Trade in China IFAW PSA: "Mom, I Have Teeth"', International Fund for Animal Welfare Rapid Asia Flash Report, Beijing, China.

Gabriel, G. G., Hua, N., & Wang, J. (2011) 'Making a Killing: A 2011 Survey of Ivory Markets in China', International Fund for Animal Welfare Report, Yarmouth Port, US.

Gao, Y. (2014) 'Elephant Ivory Trade in China: Comparing Different Perspectives', *Tropical Resources* 32–33: 101–107.

Gao, Y., & Chun, Y. (2013) 'China Refutes Ivory Protection Accusations', *People's Daily Online,* bit.ly/2w8bsO4.

Gao, Y., & Clark, S. (2014) 'Elephant Ivory Trade in China: Trends and Drivers', *Biological Conservation* 180: 23–30.

Hernandez, J. C. (2017) 'In Banning Ivory Trade, China Saw Benefits for Itself, Too', *New York Times,* nyti.ms/2wJJVEO.

Hsiang, S., & Sekar, N. (2016a) 'Applying Econometrics to Elephant Poaching: Our Response to Underwood and Burn', G-FEED, bit.ly/2w83h4u.

Hsiang, S., & Sekar, N. (2016b) 'Does Legalization Reduce Black Market Activity? Evidence from a Global Ivory Experiment and Elephant Poaching Data', NBER Working Paper Series 22314.

Hsiang, S., & Sekar, N. (2016c) 'Errors Drive Conclusion in World Bank Post on Ivory Trade and Elephant Poaching: Response to Do, Levchenko & Ma', G-FEED, bit.ly/2gHUyQS.

Hsiang, S., & Sekar, N. (2016d) 'Normality, Aggregation & Weighting: Response to Underwood's Second Critique of our Elephant Poaching Analysis', G-FEED, bit.ly/2xPAkMR.

Larson, E. (2013) 'The History of the Ivory Trade', *National Geographic,* bit.ly/2eGrvMZ.

Leakey, R., & Morell, V. (2001) *Wildlife Wars: My Fight to Save Africa's Natural Treasures* (New York: St. Martin's Griffin).

Levin, D. (2013) 'From Elephants' Mouths, an Illicit Trail to China', *New York Times,* nyti.ms/2vLT1n4.

Levin, D. (2014) 'Chinese President's Delegation Tied to Illegal Ivory Purchases During Africa Visit', *New York Times,* nyti.ms/2eLS7zH.

Lusseau, D., & Lee, P. C. (2016) 'Can We Sustainably Harvest Ivory?', *Current Biology* 26: 2951–2956.

Maisels, F. (2013) 'Devastating Decline of Forest Elephants in Central Africa', *PLOS ONE* 8: e59469.

Mathieson, K., & Larsson, N. (2016) 'China to Set Date to Close Ivory Factories', *Guardian,* bit.ly/2gN6zrX.

Meijer, W., et al. (2017) 'Demand Under the Ban—China Ivory Consumption Research', TRAFFIC and WWF Report, Beijing, China.

Messer, K. (2000) 'The Poacher's Dilemma: The Economics of Poaching and En-forcement', *Endangered Species Update* 17: 50–56.

Myers, S. L. (2017) 'Weaning Itself from Elephant Ivory, China Turns to Mammoths', *New York Times,* nyti.ms/2eL8BIn.

Newman, J. (2014) 'Ivory Responses: Full of Sound and Fury, Signifying Nothing', Environmental Investigation Agency, bit.ly/2m14TL4.

Orenstein, R. (2013) *Ivory, Horn and Blood: Behind the Elephant and Rhinoceros Poaching Crisis* (Buffalo: Firefly Books).

Perez, J. (1990) 'Ivory Trading Ban Said to Force Factories to Shut', *New York Times,* nyti.ms/2w81ln7.

Reeve, R., & Ellis, S. (1995) 'An Insider's Account of the South African Security Forces' Role in the Ivory Trade', *Journal of Contemporary African Studies* 13: 226–243.

Russo, C. (2014) 'Report Alleges Governments' Complicity in Tanzanian Elephant Poaching', *National Geographic,* bit.ly/2wH1qan.

Sellar, J. M. (2014) *The U.N.'s Lone Ranger: Combating International Wildlife Crime* (Dunbeath, UK: Whittles).

Somerville, K. (2016) *Ivory: Power and Poaching in Africa* (London: Hurst).

Thornton, A. (2007) 'Made in China: How China's Illegal Ivory Trade Is Causing a 21st Century African Elephant Disaster', Environmental Investigation Agency Report, Washington, DC, US.

Thornton, A., & Currey, D. (1991) *To Save an Elephant* (Toronto: Bantam Books).

Thouless, C. R., et al. (2016) 'African Elephant Status Report 2016: An Update from the African Elephant Database', Occasional Paper of the IUCN Species Survival Commission 60, Gland, Switzerland.

Underwood, F. (2016a) 'Critique of Hsiang and Sekar Paper Linking Legal Ivory Sale to an Increase in Illegal Killing of Elephants', fmunderwood.com, bit.ly/2w7EwFE.

Underwood, F. (2016b) 'Understanding Hsiang and Sekar's Analysis', fmunderwood. com, bit.ly/2xPPwJM.

Vigne, L., & Martin, E. B. (2014) 'China Faces a Conservation Challenge: The Ex-panding Elephant and Mammoth Ivory Trade in Beijing and Shanghai', Save the Elephants & the Aspinall Foundation Report, Nairobi, Kenya.

SIX: THE $50,000,000 BONFIRE

Anon. (2015) 'Wildlife Offenses in Kenya—"Points to Prove": A Guide for Prose-cutors and Investigators Including Standard Operating Procedures and Sample Charges', Kenya Wildlife Services, Office of the Director of Public Prosecutions and National Police Service Report, Nairobi, Kenya.

Anon. (2016a) 'Ivory Stockpiles: Proposed Revision of Resolution Conf. 10.10 (Rev. CoP16) on Trade in Elephant Specimens', CITES Document Submitted by Benin, Burkina Faso, Chad, Kenya, Niger, Nigeria, and Senegal, Geneva, Switzerland.

Anon. (2016b) 'Stopping the Money Flow: The War on Terror Finance, Testimony of William Woody', US Department of the Interior, Office of Congressional and Legislative Affairs, Washington, DC, US.

Anon. (2017) 'Operation Crash', US Fish and Wildlife Service Office of Law En-
    forcement Fact Sheet, bit.ly/2wKmWLu.

Beagle, P. S. (1968) *The Last Unicorn* (New York: Penguin Random House).

Biggs, D. (2016) 'Elephant Poaching: Track the Impact of Kenya's Ivory Burn', *Na-
    ture* 534: 179.

Braczkowski, A., et al. (2018) 'Reach and Messages of the World's Largest Ivory
    Burn', *Conservation Biology,* bit.ly/2GHcha8.

Christy, B. (2012) 'Blood Ivory', *National Geographic,* bit.ly/2xQpqW4.

Comer, C., & Dixon, J. (2004) 'Joint Undercover Operation Links International Black
    Market to Virginia Mountains', National Park Service, bit.ly/2eJKfv2.

Douglas-Hamilton, I., & Douglas-Hamilton, O. (1992) *Battle for the Elephants* (New
    York: Viking).

Felbab-Brown, V. (2017) *The Extinction Market: Wildlife Trafficking and How to
    Stop It* (Oxford: Oxford University Press).

Gitari, E., et al., eds. (2016) 'Outcome of Court Trials in the First Two Years of Im-
    plementation of the Wildlife Conservation & Management Act, 2013', Wildlife-
    Direct Report, Nairobi, Kenya.

Joyce, C. (2016) 'Chinese Taste for Fish Bladder Threatens Rare Porpoise in Mexico',
    NPR, n.pr/2ePr1HP.

Kahumbu, P. (2016) 'Kenya Jails Ivory Kingpin for 20 Years', *Guardian,* bit.
    ly/2wN3yLS.

Kahumbu, P., Byamukama, L., Mbuthia, J., & Drori, O. (2014) 'Scoping Study on the
    Prosecution of Wildlife Related Crimes in Kenya Courts: January 2008 to June
    2013', WildlifeDirect Report, Nairobi, Kenya.

Leakey, R., & Morell, V. (2001) *Wildlife Wars: My Fight to Save Africa's Natural
    Treasures* (New York: St. Martin's Griffin).

Ledger, J. (2016) 'Burning Ivory: The Lunacy Continues', *African Hunting Gazette,*
    bit.ly/2f851E0.

Mattox, H. E. (2013) *A Conversation with Ambassador Richard T. McCormack*
    (Bloomington, Indiana: Xlibris).

Morrison, S. (2014) 'Dr. Paula Kahumbu Interview: Africans Must Be Equal Partners
    in a War on Elephant Poachers', *Independent,* ind.pn/2wLGFLC.

Nuwer, R. (2016) 'Kenya Sets Ablaze 105 Tons of Ivory', *National Geographic,*
    bit.ly/1SVZS2O.

Orenstein, R. (2013) *Ivory, Horn and Blood: Behind the Elephant and Rhinoceros
    Poaching Crisis* (Buffalo: Firefly Books).

Patidar, K. A., Parwani, R., & Wanjari, S. (2010) 'Effects of High Temperature on
    Different Restorations in Forensic Identification: Dental Samples and Mandible',
    Journal of Forensic Dental Sciences 2: 37–43.

Rademeyer, J. (2012) *Killing for Profit: Exposing the Illegal Rhino Horn Trade* (Cape
    Town: Zebra Press).

Rademeyer, J. (2016a) 'Beyond Borders: Crime, Conservation and Criminal Net-
    works in the Illicit Rhino Horn Trade', Global Initiative Against Transnational
    Organized Crime Report, Geneva, Switzerland.

Rademeyer, J. (2016b) 'Tipping Point: Transnational Organized Crime and the "War" on Poaching', Global Initiative Against Transnational Organized Crime Report, Geneva, Switzerland.

Rotich, N., et al. (2014) 'Lifting the Siege: Securing Kenya's Wildlife', Task Force on Wildlife Security Report for the Ministry of Environment, Water and Natural Resources, Nairobi, Kenya.

Samper, C. (2016) 'WCS Praises Kenya for Massive Elephant Ivory and Rhino Horn Burn Scheduled for Saturday, April 30', *National Geographic,* bit.ly/2eKuPql.

Somerville, K. (2016) *Ivory: Power and Poaching in Africa* (London: Hurst).

Steyn, P. (2015) 'Life-Size Ivory Elephant Sculpture Unveiled in Botswana', *National Geographic,* bit.ly/2ePeiFl.

Telma Jemio, M. (2016) 'Wildlife for Sale: Jaguars Are the New Trafficking Victims in Bolivia', Mongabay, bit.ly/2vQTzIh.

Thornton, A., & Currey, D. (1991) *To Save an Elephant* (Toronto: Bantam Books).

Weru, S. (2016) 'Wildlife Protection and Trafficking Assessment in Kenya', TRAF-FIC Report, Cambridge, UK.

SEVEN: THE CITES CIRCUS

Actman, J., & Bale, R. (2016) 'Mid-century Nuclear Weapons Tests Can Help Fight Elephant Poaching', *National Geographic,* bit.ly/2wLOD6w.

AFP (2017) 'Record Haul of Pangolin Scales Seized in Malaysia', Phys.org, bit.ly/2xeKpG7.

Anon. (2016a) 'An Overview of Pangolin Data: When Will the Over-exploitation of the Pangolin End?' China Biodiversity Conservation and Green Development Foundation Report, Beijing, China.

Anon. (2016b) 'Report on the Elephant Trade Information System (ETIS)', CITES Document 57.6, Geneva, Switzerland.

Anon. (2016) 'The Status, Trade and Conservation of Pangolins (*Manis* Spp.)', IUCN SSC Pangolin Specialist Group CITES Document, Geneva, Switzerland.

Anon. (2017) 'What Is CITES?', Convention on the International Trade in Endangered Species of Wild Fauna and Flora, bit.ly/2gMaBge.

Challender, D. W. S., Harrop, S. R., & MacMillan, D. C. (2015) 'Understanding Markets to Conserve Trade-Threatened Species in CITES', *Biological Conservation* 187: 249–259.

Cohen, A. (2017) 'Protecting Pangolins on World Pangolin Day', International Fund for Animal Welfare Press Release, Washington, DC, US.

Christy, B. (2016) 'A Bombshell in the World of Rhinos', *National Geographic,* bit.ly/2gOAmQO.

Cruise, A. (2016a) 'Trade Sanctions for Three Countries over Illegal Ivory', *National Geographic,* bit.ly/2gPjOs0.

Cruise, A. (2016b) 'Why Some Countries Don't Want to Do More to Protect Elephants', *National Geographic,* bit.ly/2vK1H9i.

Heinrich, S., et al. (2017) 'The Global Trafficking of Pangolins', TRAFFIC Report, Selangor, Malaysia.

Krishnasamy, K., Milliken, T., & Savini, C. (2016) 'In Transition: Bangkok's Ivory Market', TRAFFIC Report, Petaling Jaya, Malaysia.

Mills, J. A. (2015) *Blood of the Tiger: A Story of Conspiracy, Greed and the Battle to Save a Magnificent Species* (Boston: Beacon Press).

Orenstein, R. (2013) *Ivory, Horn and Blood: Behind the Elephant and Rhinoceros Poaching Crisis* (Buffalo: Firefly Books).

Outhwaite, W., & Brown, L. (2018) 'Eastward Bound: Analysis of CITES-listed Flora and Fauna Exports from Africa to East and Southeast Asia', TRAFFIC Report, Cambridge, UK.

Rademeyer, J. (2016a) 'Beyond Borders: Crime, Conservation and Criminal Networks in the Illicit Rhino Horn Trade', Global Initiative Against Transnational Organized Crime Report, Geneva, Switzerland.

Sellar, J. M. (2014) *The U.N.'s Lone Ranger: Combating International Wildlife Crime* (Dunbeath, UK: Whittles).

Zhang, S. Y. (2016) 'Proposal for Experimental Research on Captive Breeding of Pangolins in Uganda (CBPU),' Asia-Africa Pangolin Breeding Research Center Limited Report, Kampala, Uganda.

EIGHT: OF PROSTITUTES, POACHERS, AND POLITICIANS

Anon. (2014) 'Case No: 849/2013', Supreme Court of Appeal of South Africa Judgement, Johannesburg, South Africa.

Anon. (2015) 'Nearly 500 Mozambican Poachers Killed in S. Africa's Kruger Since 2010—Former Leader', Reuters, reut.rs/2wP35ca.

AP (2015) 'Bodies of Dozens of Elephants Found Poisoned in Zimbabwe', *Guardian*, bit.ly/2gSsduZ.

Christy, B. (2016) 'Inside the Deadly Rhino Horn Trade', *National Geographic*, on.natgeo.com/2vKPfpT.

Crosta, A., Sutherland, K., & Beckner, M. (2015) 'Blending Ivory: China's Old Loopholes, New Hopes', Elephant Action League Report, Los Angeles, US.

Davidson, K., & Ladkani, R., dirs. (2016) *The Ivory Game*, Vulcan Productions.

Davies, C. (2016) 'The Tangled Routes of Global Elephant Ivory Trafficking', Environmental Investigation Agency, London, UK.

Davies, N., & Holmes, O. (2016a) 'The Crime Family at the Center of Asia's Animal Trafficking Network', *Guardian*, bit.ly/2eKJzFE.

Davies, N., & Holmes, O. (2016b) 'Revealed: How Senior Laos Officials Cut Deals with Animal Traffickers', *Guardian*, bit.ly/2eKvSX2.

De Lange, I. (2015) 'Rhinos Were "Surplus", Court Told', *Citizen*, bit.ly/2xf770v.

Douglas-Hamilton, I., & Douglas-Hamilton, O. (1992) *Battle for the Elephants* (New York: Viking).

Felbab-Brown, V. (2017) *The Extinction Market: Wildlife Trafficking and How to Stop It* (Oxford: Oxford University Press).

French, H. W. (2014) *China's Second Continent: How a Million Migrants Are Building a New Empire in Africa* (New York: Vintage Books).

Fuller, T. (2013a) 'In Trafficking of Wildlife, Out of Reach of the Law', *New York Times*, nyti.ms/2wMyvT9.

Fuller, T. (2013b) 'U.S. Offers Reward in Wildlife-Trade Fight', *New York Times*, nyti.ms/2wOKSeU.

Fuller, T. (2015) 'Laos, Destination in Illegal Ivory Trade, So Far Eludes Global Crackdown', *New York Times,* nyti.ms/2weGIln.

Hubschle, A. M. (2016) 'A Game of Horns: Transnational Flows of Rhino Horn', International Max Planck Research School on the Social and Political Constitution of the Economy Dissertation Series, Cologne, Germany.

Hume, J. (2013) 'Saving Rhino from Extinction', AfricaHunting.com, bit.ly /2xieIM6.

Kaiman, J. (2014) 'China-Africa Relations Hurt by Bad Chinese Behavior, Says Ambassador', *Guardian,* bit.ly/2xbnB9l.

Leakey, R., & Morell, V. (2001) *Wildlife Wars: My Fight to Save Africa's Natural Treasures* (New York: St. Martin's Griffin).

Milliken, T., & Shaw, J. (2012) 'The South Africa—Viet Nam Rhino Horn Trade Nexus', TRAFFIC Report, Johannesburg, South Africa.

Mills, J. A. (2015) *Blood of the Tiger: A Story of Conspiracy, Greed and the Battle to Save a Magnificent Species* (Boston: Beacon Press).

Nixon, R. (2015) 'U.S. Pours Millions into Fighting Poachers in South Africa', *New York Times,* nyti.ms/2gOEsoo.

Orenstein, R. (2013) *Ivory, Horn and Blood: Behind the Elephant and Rhinoceros Poaching Crisis* (Buffalo: Firefly Books).

Rademeyer, J. (2012) *Killing for Profit: Exposing the Illegal Rhino Horn Trade* (Cape Town: Zebra Press).

Rademeyer, J. (2013) 'Marnus Steyl Update', Vimeo, bit.ly/2f7VAFN.

Rademeyer, J. (2016a) 'Beyond Borders: Crime, Conservation and Criminal Networks in the Illicit Rhino Horn Trade', Global Initiative Against Transnational Organized Crime Report, Geneva, Switzerland.

Rademeyer, J. (2016b) 'Tipping Point: Transnational Organized Crime and the "War" on Poaching', Global Initiative Against Transnational Organized Crime Report, Geneva, Switzerland.

Sellar, J. M. (2014) *The U.N.'s Lone Ranger: Combating International Wildlife Crime* (Dunbeath, UK: Whittles).

Somerville, K. (2016) *Ivory: Power and Poaching in Africa* (London: Hurst).

Taylor, A., et al. (2014) 'The Viability of Legalizing Trade in Rhino Horn in South Africa', Department of Environmental Affairs Report, Pretoria, South Africa.

Verwoerd, M. (2016) 'Rhino Statistics: The Devil Is in the Details', traveller24, bit.ly/2wd844x.

Wasser, S. K., et al. (2015) 'Genetic Assignment of Large Seizures of Elephant Ivory Reveals Africa's Major Poaching Hotspots', *Science* 349: 84–87.

Wittig, T. (2016) 'Poaching, Wildlife Trafficking and Organized Crime', *Whitehall Papers* 86: 77–101.

Young, J., sr. prod. (2016) *The Poacher's Pipeline, Al Jazeera* documentary, bit.ly/2nposgF.

NINE: THE FRONT LINE

Anon. (2015) 'Annual Report 2014', Kenya Wildlife Service Report, Nairobi, Kenya.

Anon. (2016) 'Annual Report 2015', Lewa Wildlife Conservancy Report, Isiolo, Kenya.

Douglas-Hamilton, I., & Douglas-Hamilton, O. (1992) *Battle for the Elephants* (New York: Viking).

Felbab-Brown, V. (2017) *The Extinction Market: Wildlife Trafficking and How to Stop It* (Oxford: Oxford University Press).

Leakey, R., & Morell, V. (2001) *Wildlife Wars: My Fight to Save Africa's Natural Treasures* (New York: St. Martin's Griffin).

Sellar, J. M. (2014) *The U.N.'s Lone Ranger: Combating International Wildlife Crime* (Dunbeath, UK: Whittles).

Singh, R. (2016a) 'Ranger Insurance Report', WWF and Ranger Federation of Asia Report, Washington, DC.

Singh, R. (2016b) 'Ranger Perceptions: Africa', WWF and TRAFFIC Report, Washington, DC.

Singh, R. (2016c) 'Ranger Perceptions: Asia', WWF and Ranger Federation of Asia Report, Washington, DC.

Smith, D. (2013) 'Fighting the Poachers on Africa's Thin Green Line', *Guardian*, bit .ly/2xTPAYZ.

Somerville, K. (2016) *Ivory: Power and Poaching in Africa* (London: Hurst).

Wall, J., Wittemyer, G., Klinkenberg, B., & Douglas-Hamilton, I. (2014) 'Novel Opportunities for Wildlife Conservation and Research with Real-Time Monitoring', *Ecological Applications* 24: 593–601.

Walters, A. (2014) 'Kenya Is Thousands of Miles Away from the Ebola Outbreak, but Tourists Are Still Staying Away', PRI, bit.ly/2weGLXt.

TEN: A PARK REBORN

Aworawo, F. (2015) 'The Legacy of French Colonial Policy on the National Building Process in Chad, 1900–1975', *Lagos Historical Review* 15: 111–122.

Bouche, P., et al. (2011) 'Will Elephants Soon Disappear from West African Savannahs?', *PLOS ONE* 6: e20619.

Chene, M. (2014) 'Overview of Corruption and Anti-corruption in Chad', Transparency International Anti-corruption Helpdesk, Berlin, Germany.

Douglas-Hamilton, I., & Douglas-Hamilton, O. (1992) *Battle for the Elephants* (New York: Viking).

Fay, M. (2007) 'Ivory Wars: Last Stand in Zakouma', *National Geographic*, bit .ly/2f9QatK.

Martin, E. B. (2005) 'Northern Sudan Ivory Market Flourishes', *Pachyderm* 39: 67–76.

Orenstein, R. (2013) *Ivory, Horn and Blood: Behind the Elephant and Rhinoceros Poaching Crisis* (Buffalo: Firefly Books).

Somerville, K. (2016) *Ivory: Power and Poaching in Africa* (London: Hurst).

Temporal, J.-L. (1989) *La chasse oubliée* (Paris: Gerfaut Club).

ELEVEN: IF RHINOS COULD CHOOSE

Anon. (2016) 'Frequently Asked Questions About the Rhino Trade', Private Rhino Owners Association, bit.ly/2vL1zXh.

Christy, B. (2016) 'South Africa Just Lifted Its Ban on the Rhino Horn Trade', *National Geographic*, bit.ly/2gPytQp.

Felbab-Brown, V. (2017) *The Extinction Market: Wildlife Trafficking and How to Stop It* (Oxford: Oxford University Press).

Gao, Y., Stoner, K. J., Lee, A. T. L., & Clark, S. G. (2016) 'Rhino Horn Trade in China: An Analysis of the Art and Antiques Market', *Biological Conservation* 201: 343–347.

Hume, J. (2013) 'Hume Letter', VivaAfrika, bit.ly/2vLfH2Y.

Johnson, L. (2016) 'Smart Trade—NO, Foolish Assumptions—YES', Breaking the Brand, bit.ly/2xSksbm.

Kennaugh, A. (2016) 'Rhino Rage: What Is Driving Illegal Consumer Demand for Rhino Horn', Natural Resources Defense Council Survey, New York City, US.

Martin, E. B., & Martin, C. (1982) *Run Rhino Run* (London: Chatto & Windus).

Milliken, T., & Shaw, J. (2012) 'The South Africa—Viet Nam Rhino Horn Trade Nexus', TRAFFIC Report, Johannesburg, South Africa.

Neme, L. (2014) 'U.S. Indictment Accuses South African Brothers of Trafficking Rhino Horns', *National Geographic,* bit.ly/2wfESK5.

Nuwer, R. (2015) 'Poaching Upsurge Threatens South America's Iconic Vicuna', Mongabay, bit.ly/2gPK0Pv.

Nuwer, R. (2016) 'Legal Trade in Rhinoceros Horns Could Save the Species from Extinction—or Hasten Their Demise', *Newsweek,* bit.ly/2gemaLB.

Orenstein, R. (2013) *Ivory, Horn and Blood: Behind the Elephant and Rhinoceros Poaching Crisis* (Buffalo: Firefly Books).

Orenstein, R. (2015) 'Does Trade in Vicuna Wool Provide an Example for Rhinoceros Conservation?', Report for Born Free, unpublished.

Player, I. (1972) *The White Rhino Saga* (New York: Stein and Day).

Rademeyer, J. (2012) *Killing for Profit: Exposing the Illegal Rhino Horn Trade* (Cape Town: Zebra Press).

Sellar, J. M. (2014) *The U.N.'s Lone Ranger: Combating International Wildlife Crime* (Dunbeath, UK: Whittles).

Taylor, A., et al. (2014) 'The Viability of Legalizing Trade in Rhino Horn in South Africa', Department of Environmental Affairs Report, Pretoria, South Africa.

't Sas-Rolfes, M. (1990) 'Privatizing the Rhino Industry', Free Market Foundation Paper, Saxonwold, South Africa.

't Sas-Rolfes, M. (1997) 'Elephants, Rhinos and the Economics of the Illegal Trade', *Pachyderm* 24: 23–29.

Vigne, L., & Martin, E. B. (2016) 'High Rhino Horn Prices Drive Poaching', *Swara,* July–September.

TWELVE: MY TIGER WINE IS CORKED

Anon. (1994) 'Pelly Amendment to the Fishermen's Protective Act; Request for Certification of the People's Republic of China and Taiwan; Conservation of Endangered Species Subject to Illegal International Trade', Office of the Federal Register, *Federal Register* 59.

Anon. (2005) 'Hunan Sanhong Pharmaceutical Company Limited "True Tiger Wine" Project: Feasibility Studies Report', Environmental Investigation Agency Translated Document, London, UK.

Anon. (2007) 'Made in China: Farming Tigers to Extinction', International Fund for Animal Welfare Report, Beijing, China.

Anon. (2008a) 'Commercial Wildlife Farms in Vietnam: A Problem or Solution for Conservation?', Wildlife Conservation Society Report, Hanoi, Vietnam.

Anon. (2008b) '*Panthera tigris* ssp. *Amoyensis* (South China Tiger)', International Union for Conservation of Nature Red List of Threatened Species, Cambridge, UK.

Anon. (2013a) 'Hidden in Plain Sight: China's Clandestine Tiger Trade', Environmental Investigation Agency Report, London, UK.

Anon. (2013b) 'Tiger Farming Timeline', Environmental Investigation Agency Document, London, U.K.

Anon. (2015a) 'Authorities in the Golden Triangle Special Economic Zone of Bokeo Province Close Four Restaurants After Selling Protected Wildlife', Lao National Television-English News Program, bit.ly/2wQLqB5.

Anon. (2015b) 'Bokeo Bans New Banana Farms After Chemical Scares', *Vientiane Times*, bit.ly/2xVVfOg.

Anon. (2015c) 'Dok Ngiew Kham Group Pays US$6.3m in Taxes', *Vientiane Times*, bit.ly/2vTW3pm.

Anon. (2015d) 'Laos: UPR Submission', Human Rights Watch Report, New York City, US.

Anon. (2015e) 'Sin City: Illegal Wildlife Trade in Laos' Golden Triangle Special Economic Zone', Environmental Investigation Agency Report, London, UK.

Anon. (2016a) 'Application of Article XIII in the Lao People's Democratic Republic', CITES Document 12.1, Geneva, Switzerland.

Anon. (2016b) 'Basic 2016 Statistics: Economic Research and Regional Cooperation Department', Asia Development Bank Document, Mandaluyong, Philippines.

Anon. (2016c) 'Captive Tigers in the U.S.', WWF Article, Washington, DC.

Anon. (2016d) 'Decisions of the Conference of the Parties to CITES in Effect After Its 17th Meeting', CITES Document, Geneva, Switzerland.

Anon. (2016e) 'Wildlife Crime: Education for Nature-Vietnam', ENV Bulletin, Hanoi, Vietnam.

Anon. (2017a) 'Report to Congress on Eliminate, Neutralize, and Disrupt Wildlife Trafficking Act of 2016 PL 1114-231, Sec. 201', US Department of State, Washington, DC.

Anon. (2017b) 'The State of the Tiger', Panthera, New York City, US.

Anon. (2018) 'Treasury Sanctions the Zhao Wei Transnational Criminal Organization', US Department of the Treasury press release, bit.ly/2E3OMXu.

Charnovitz, S. (1994) 'Environmental Trade Sanctions and the GATT: An Analysis of the Pelly Amendment on Foreign Environmental Practices', *American University International Law Review* 9: 751–807.

Edward, D. (2016) 'Tiger Bone Wine "Fueling Illegal Wildlife Trade"', ITV News Investigation Finds', ITV News, bit.ly/2wOYyJb.

Ellis, R. (2005) *Tiger Bone and Rhino Horn: The Destruction of Wildlife for Traditional Chinese Medicine* (Washington, DC: Island Press).

Fa, L. H. (2007) 'State Forestry Administration Notice no. 206', Environmental Investigation Agency Translated Document, London, UK.

Guynup, S. (2016) 'Tiger Temple Accused of Supplying Black Market', *National Geographic,* bit.ly/2gSELyq.

Guynup, S. (2017) 'Months After Raid on Infamous Tiger Temple, Plans for Offshoot Zoo Forge Ahead', *National Geographic,* bit.ly/2eU41aM.

Hay, W. (2011) 'Laos Casino Under Suspicion over Drugs Trade', *Al Jazeera,* bit.ly/2ChsgG4.

Holland, H. (2014) 'China's Expanding Middle Class Fuels Poaching, Decadence in Myanmar', *National Geographic,* bit.ly/2gSFVOk.

Liu, Z., et al. (2016) 'Perception, Price and Preference: Consumption and Protection of Wild Animals Used in Traditional Medicine', *PLOS ONE* 11: e0145901.

Mills, J. A. (2015) *Blood of the Tiger: A Story of Conspiracy, Greed and the Battle to Save a Magnificent Species* (Boston: Beacon Press).

Ray, N., Bloom, G., & Waters, R. (2014) *Laos* (Melbourne: Lonely Planet).

Souksavanh, O. (2016) 'Chinese Banana Plantations Lose Their Appeal in Laos as Pollution Concerns Grow', Radio Free Asia, bit.ly/2xTczCx.

Stoner, S., & Krishnasamy, K. (2016) 'Reduced to Skin and Bones Re-examined: An Analysis of Tiger Seizures from 13 Range Countries from 2000–2015', TRAFFIC Report, Petaling Jaya, Malaysia.

Strangio, S. (2016) 'The Rise, Fall and Possible Renewal of a Town in Laos on China's Border', *New York Times,* nyti.ms/2eUS2Kh.

THIRTEEN: RISING MOON BEARS

Anon. (2010) 'Herbalists Decry Bear Bile Use', *Viet Nam News,* bit.ly/2wOSOz3.

Anon. (2012) 'Bear Bile and Traditional Chinese Medicine (TCM)', Animals Asia Document, Hong Kong, China.

Anon. (2014) 'Synthetic Bile Plan Could End Demand for Bear Bile', Animals Asia Article, Hong Kong, China.

Ellis, R. (2005) *Tiger Bone and Rhino Horn: The Destruction of Wildlife for Traditional Chinese Medicine* (Washington, DC: Island Press).

Li, S., et al. (2016) 'Substitutes for Bear Bile for the Treatment of Liver Diseases: Research Progress and Future Perspective', *Evidence-Based Complementary and Alternative Medicine* 2016: 1–10.

Livingstone, E., & Shepherd, C. R. (2016) 'Bear Farms in Lao PDR Expand Illegally and Fail to Conserve Wild Bears', *Oryx* 50: 176–184.

Vang, S., Longley, K., Steer, C. J., & Low, W. C. (2014) 'The Unexpected Uses of Urso- and Tauroursodeoxycholic Acid in the Treatment of Non-liver Diseases', *Global Advances in Health and Medicine* 3: 58–69.

FOURTEEN: ORDER AHEAD FOR PANGOLIN

D'Cruze, N., & Macdonald, D. W. (2016) 'A Review of Global Trends in CITES Live Wildlife Confiscations', *Nature Conservation* 15: 47–63.

Kyriacou, N. (2016) 'Are Grassroots Organizations Our Best Hope for Combating the Illegal Wildlife Trade?', Mongabay, bit.ly/2vMswdg.

Macdonald, D. (2016) 'Out of the Frying Pan and into the Fire?' Wildlife Conservation Research Unit News, bit.ly/2eUBfqE.

Nuwer, R. (2016) 'Pangolins Released into Wild May Be Recaptured and Eaten', *National Geographic,* bit.ly/2g76fQT.

Sterling, E. J., Hurley, M. M., & Minh, L. D. (2006) *Vietnam: A Natural History* (New Haven: Yale University Press).

Zhou, Z. M., et al. (2016) 'Rescued Wildlife in China Remains at Risk', *Science* 353: 999.

INDEX